THE WESTMINSTER CONFESSION OF FAITH
With study notes by JJ Lim

Explanatory notes © 2013, 2018 by JJ Lim

This edition published in 2018 by
Pilgrim Covenant Church
Singapore

All Scripture quotations are from The Holy Bible: King James Version

Dedicated

to

Michael Sing
(16 Jan 1956 – 3 Sep 2018)

and

Raymond Lee
(10 Feb 1963 – 28 Nov 2017)

Amongst the first to make use of these notes;

Amongst the first to attain to glory in Christ.

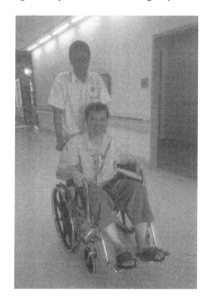

Brothers-in-arms now reunited.
Isaiah 57:1

Content

Foreword

The Westminster Confession of Faith (WCF) is often seen as a church standard, and so it is. The theologians of the day, called the divines, who assembled at Westminster, produced this confession of faith for the lords assembled in parliament. However, you might be interested to know that this Confession had a message to the general reader. It was a kind of foreword that was written to you the "Christian reader" and addressed especially to the heads of families.

It would thus be remiss of me to write this foreword without pointing to that of the original 1658 document, for there are important words of gravity, and these words spoke severely to me.

"It is an uncomely sight to behold men in years babes in knowledge; and how unmeet are they to instruct others, who need themselves to be taught which be the first principles of the oracles of God, Heb. 5:12. Knowledge is an accomplishment so desirable, that the devils themselves knew not a more taking bait by which to tempt our first parents, than by the fruit of the tree of knowledge; So shall you be as gods, knowing good and evil."

Fathers, we have a duty to lead the family in the faith. This duty involves knowing the faith, being a living witness of the faith, and stirring up the next generation to live and die for the faith. For this I am most grateful that the Westminster divines have produced such a robust confession of the faith, that we in the spirit of the Berean Christians should receive with all readiness of mind, and check daily in the scriptures whether those things are so.

This commentary of the WCF comes as another blessing to assist us in these duties. Pastor JJ has a particular gift of distilling an issue to its essence and communicating it most logically and succinctly. A devourer of good books and with a memory to match his appetite, he has combed the literature and presents these with the clearest premise, one that will greatly help the student of the word rightly divide the word of truth and come to a position he needs not to be ashamed.

May I encourage all readers, but especially the fathers, to use this commentary to strengthen your faith and that of your household. And may I encourage all that desire the goodly office of an elder to go the extra step of attempting the worksheets that will challenge and consolidate your understanding.

Men of God, we have much work to do. "Watch ye, stand fast in the faith, quit you like men, be strong" (1 Cor 16:13).

Tim Law
Tasmania 2018

Preface

On 13th May 1643, an ordinance for the calling of an ecclesiastic assembly was introduced in the House of Common in London. The final form of this ordinance, which was approved by both houses of Parliament on 12th June 1643, is printed with most copies of the original *Westminster Confession of Faith*. But the initial and fuller statement proposes that the assembly be called "for settling the government and liturgy of the Church of England, and for vindicating and clearing of the doctrine of the said church from false aspersions and interpretations as should be found most agreeable to the Word of God, and most apt to procure and preserve the peace of the church at home, and nearer agreement with the Church of Scotland and other Reformed Churches abroad."[1]

The assembly convened on 1st July 1643 at the Westminster Abbey and is thus called the *Westminster Assembly*. The Assembly set out, at first, to revise the *Thirty-Nine Articles* of the Church of England. But by 12th October 1643, in the wake of the signing of the *Solemn League and Covenant* between Scotland and England two months earlier, the Assembly was instructed to cease work on the Thirty-Nine Articles and to begin to work on a new confession of faith.

Under this mandate, the Assembly would meet until 22nd February, 1649 in over 1,163 recorded sessions. In all, about 120 English divines, 10 Scottish commissioners and 40 lay assessors participated in the Assembly. Through vigorous debates, consensus and majority rules, the Assembly produced a Confession of Faith, a Larger Catechism, a Shorter Catechism, a Directory of Worship, the Presbyterian Form of Church Government and even a Psalter for singing by the churches, among other documents.

The Westminster Confession of Faith was completed and presented to the Parliament on 4th December 1646. But Parliament required the Assembly to furnished proof-texts from Scripture, and it was completed on 26 August, 1647. The Confession was duly approved the next day, 27th August, 1647, by the Assembly of the Church of Scotland, and adopted as part of the subordinate standards of the church. Due to the unstable political situation in England, it was however, never fully adopted by the Church of England. Nevertheless, it was modified and adopted by Congregationalists in England, in the form of the *Savoy Declaration* of 1658; and subsequently the Baptists of England modified the Savoy Declaration to produce the Second London Baptist Confession of 1689.

---

[1] Cited in Alexander F. Mitchell, *The Westminster Assembly: Its History and Standards being the Baird Lecture for 1882* (reprinted by Still Waters Revival Books, 1992), 111-2.

Apart from the Presbyterian Church in Scotland, the *Westminster Confession of Faith* was adopted by the Presbyterian Church in the United States of America in 1789, with several revisions. Further amendments were made in 1887 and 1903, etc. Pilgrim Covenant Church (PCC) in Singapore was constituted in 1999 with the original 1646 version of the Confession, together with its Catechisms, as the subordinate standards of the church. However, in view of the political-social situation in Singapore, the Confession was adopted with a declaratory preface which includes the following words:

> In view of the fact, however, that Singapore continues at present to be a multi-religious society, it is deemed that the modifications, —pertaining to the role of the civil government in chapters 23 and 31, —as adopted by the First General Assembly of the American Presbyterian Church in 1789 would be open to less dispute and abuse. These modifications are included in the footnote and deemed to be applicable until such time the Lord may be pleased to transform Singapore into a Christian nation. The original statements, —which envisaged a national church endowed by the state in line with the provisions of the Solemn League and Covenant subscribed in 1643, is nevertheless retained with an understanding: firstly, that the ideals hoped for by the divines are not impossible, —all things being possible with God (Lk 18:27); secondly, that the power of the civil magistrate, —to take order in the Church and call synods, —referred to in paragraph 23.3 and 31.2 are only applicable where the civil magistrate is constituted on true Christian principles; and thirdly, that kingship and authority of Christ over our nation is no way diminished even if the civil magistrate may be openly antagonistic towards Him (Dan 7:14). Such being the case, the original statements are not, in fact, erroneous, though less rigorous when applied to a multi-religious society such as Singapore.

The present commentary is based on the *Westminster Confession of Faith* so adopted. It was originally produced as Sabbath class notes for the founding members of PCC, and came with a set of exercises which all elders of the church were required to complete. In my humble opinion, it can at best supplement the excellent commentaries of AA Hodge, Robert Shaw, GI Williamson and even RC Sproul. Nevertheless, a number of brethren in PCC and elsewhere have found the notes useful as an introduction to the Confession and have urged its publication for a number of years. It is my prayer therefore that the Lord will bless this feeble effort for his own glory.

—JJ Lim, July 2018

The Place & Necessity of Creeds & Confessions in the Modern Church

Adapted from *PCC Bulletin*, vol. 8, no. 17, dated 29 Oct 2006

On October 31st, 1517, a Roman Catholic Monk by the name of Martin Luther, a professor in theology, nailed a Latin pamphlet which he had written onto the door of the castle church of Wittenberg, Germany. In this document, today known as the 95 Thesis, Luther exposed a number of gross errors of the Roman Catholic Church, and called for any academician who would be inclined to do so to prove him wrong in a public debate.

No one took up the challenge. Instead, someone took down the pamphlet, translated it into German, and made multiple copies it. So in a very short while, the document went viral all over Germany and beyond. It was the start of a great religious revolution known as the Protestant Reformation.

Half a millennial has passed. Many of the things that Luther and his successors taught have become strange in the ears of contemporary Christians. Many do not even know the difference between Roman Catholicism and Protestantism apart from the perception that Rome prays to the Virgin Mary while Protestants do not. Many Protestant know Martin Luther King, jr., the American civil rights activist, but know not his name sake.

What shall we do to arrest this sad state of affair in the church? I believe that apart from teaching church history and promoting the reading of church history books, it is necessary for the church to be brought back to a proper understanding of the place and necessity of creeds and confessions. History has shown that apart from churches which maintain a firm and honest emphasis on creeds and confessions, most others have drifted away from the moorings of the 16th Century Reformation and the biblical Christianity taught by the Magisterial Reformers such as Ulrich Zwingli, John Calvin, John Knox, etc.

But is there a biblical basis for creeds and confessions? What are the uses of creed and confessions in the Church? To what extent should creeds or confessions be binding to members?

1. Biblical Basis

Many modern evangelical Christians are quick to say that they believe in no creed but the Bible. But this statement is in itself a creedal statement, and therefore makes it self-contradictory.

You see, the English word 'creed' really comes from the Latin word "credo" which means "I believe." A biblical creed, then, is really expression or statement of belief concerning what the Bible teaches. When a church adopts a "creed," she is essentially confessing her faith or belief corporately. For this reason, creeds are also known as confessions of faith, an example being the *Westminster Confession of Faith*.

Numerous passages in the Scripture instruct us to confess our faith. The Lord Jesus says, "Whosoever… shall confess me before men, him will I confess also before my Father which is in heaven" (Mt 10:32). The word translated "confess" is the Greek *homologeô* (ὁμολογέω). It is a compound word that has two parts, "*homo*," which means "same" and "*logeô*," which means "say." Thus, *homologeô*, refers to saying the same thing, or rather speaking in agreement with something already affirmed. To confess Christ before men is to openly acknowledge who He claims himself to be.

Likewise, the apostle Paul says in Romans 10:9-10, "If thou shalt confess with thy mouth the Lord Jesus, and shalt believe in thine heart that God hath raised him from the dead, thou shalt be saved. [10] For with the heart man believeth unto righteousness; and with the mouth confession is made unto salvation."

Obviously, Paul could not be saying that we are saved by faith *plus* the act of public profession of our faith. What he is saying, rather, is essentially that one may know he is saved if he believes with his heart, and that what he believes is consistent with his confession of the faith once delivered unto the saints. That is, one can only be saved if the content of his faith is in agreement with what the church has down the ages understood to be the truth.

Likewise, when the apostle beseeched the Corinthian church "by the name of our Lord Jesus Christ, that [they] all speak the same thing" (1 Cor 1:10), he is in fact, telling them to confess the same faith. How might they do so except they have a statement of faith or a confession of faith, however primitive or simple it might have been?

Herein is the first biblical basis for using a confession of faith, namely that the scripture calls us to confess our faith and to confess it together.

But secondly, the apostle Paul instructs Timothy: "Hold fast the form of sound words, which thou hast heard of me, in faith and love which is in Christ Jesus" (2 Tim 1:13). The word translated 'form' (ὑποτύπωσις, hupotupōsis) means 'schema' or 'system.' Strictly speaking, the Bible does not present such a form that we can retain in our memory. A form or system requires some form of organization of the biblical data mined from everywhere in the Scripture. Only with an adopted Confession with its associated catechisms can we effectively hold fast a form of sound doctrine in our minds.

And thirdly, when we use creeds or confessions, we are simply affirming our belief in the illuminating work of the Holy Spirit (Jn 16:13). We agree with those who refuse to hold creeds in high regards that the Holy Spirit illumines our minds individually so that we can all understand the Scripture. But unlike them, we recognize that God's gift is given in different measure to different individuals (Eph 4:7). And we believe that our Confession of Faith and other Reformed Confessions were written by learned and godly men who were richly endowed with the Holy Spirit and enabled to interpret and expound the Scripture with uncommon clarity and accuracy, and consensus when more than one author is involved. And their spiritual wisdom and faithfulness to the truth have been confirmed not only by their peers but by the church searching the Scriptures to see if the things they taught are in accordance with the Scripture.

This being the case, when we adopt a Confession as a church, we are, in effect, acknowledging that the church does not begin with us and the Holy Spirit is not our sole possession. The Holy Spirit did not only inspire the Scripture, He illumines that God's children might understand it. Written Confessions represent the Spirit's work in the history of the Church. We should therefore regard the approved confessions highly and use them to guide our own interpretation of the Scripture.

In this regard, we agree with the eloquent statement of Dr G.I. Williamson:

The Bible contains a great wealth of information. It isn't easy to master it all - in fact, no one has ever mastered it completely. It would therefore be foolish for us to try to do it on our own, starting from scratch. We would be ignoring all the study of the Word of God that other people have done down through the centuries. That is exactly why we have creeds. They are the product of many centuries of Bible study by a great company of believers. They are a kind of spiritual "road map" of the teaching of the Bible, already worked out and proved by others before us. And, after all, isn't this exactly what Jesus promised? When he was about to finish his work on earth, he made this promise to his disciples: "*When He, the Spirit of truth, is come, He will guide you into all truth*" (Jn 16:13). And Christ kept his promise. When the Day of Pentecost came, he sent his Spirit to dwell in his people. The Holy Spirit was poured out - not on individuals, each by himself, but on the whole body of Christian believers together (Acts 2). And from that time until this, he has been giving his church an understanding of the Scriptures. It is no wonder that the church expressed itself from very early times through creeds... And right here we see one of the most important things about a creed that is true to the Bible - it remains true down through the ages. It does not need to be changed again and again, with each generation, because it deals with things that are unchanging. Thus, an accurate creed binds the generations together. It reminds us that the church of Jesus Christ is not confined to one age, just as it is not confined to any one place. In other words, there is a unity in what Christians have believed, right down through the ages. Just think of it: when we confess our faith together ... we join with all those believers who have gone before us. Does not this demonstrate that there is indeed just one Lord and one true faith?[2]

So then, the use of confessions has a strong biblical basis, because firstly we are commanded in the Word of God to confess our faith together; secondly, we are taught to retain in our minds a system of doctrine; and thirdly, we are convinced from the Scripture that the Holy Spirit is not only given to us, but, in fact, given in greater measure to our godly and learned fathers in the faith,

---

[2] G.I. Williamson, *The Heidelberg Catechism: A Study Guide* (Phillipburg: P&R Publishing, 1993), 2-3.

some of whom were used by the Lord to pen and to hand down their exposition and creedal systematization of the Word of God.

But what are the uses of confessions of faith?

2. Uses

Dr A.A. Hodge has outlined the uses of confessions very succinctly:

> They have been found in all ages of the church useful for the following purposes: (1) To mark, preserve and disseminate the attainments made in the knowledge of Christian truth by any branch of the church in any grand crisis of its development. (2) To discriminate the truth from the glosses of false teachers, and accurately to define it in its integrity and due proportions. (3) To act as the bond of ecclesiastical fellowship among those so nearly agreed as to be able to labor together in harmony. (4) To be used as instruments in the great work of popular instruction.[3]

Developing on this outline, we may think of three inter-related uses for confessions in the church.

Firstly, there is a *Unifying Use* as already alluded by the fact that part of the biblical basis for the use of confessions is so that the church may confess the same truth.

The apostle Paul speaks of the church as having "One Lord, one faith, one baptism" (Eph 4:5). But unless the church interprets the Scripture in the same way on major issues, there can be no true unity of faith. So Paul also speaks of how the gifts of the Holy Spirit pertaining to the conveyance of knowledge are given to various individuals in the church "for the perfecting of the saints, for the work of the ministry, for the edifying of the body of Christ: [13] Till we all come in the unity of the faith, and of the knowledge of the Son of God, unto a perfect man, unto the measure of the stature of the fulness of Christ..." (Eph 4:12-13).

A confession of faith which is produced through the collective exercise of the gift of the Spirit is therefore an indispensable tool to maintain the unity of the church.

---

[3] AA Hodge, *Outlines of Theology* (Edinburgh: Banner of Truth Trust, 1991 [1860]), 114.

In this regard it is important to note that in a Reformed church, the 'official' or constitutional doctrinal position of the church should not be the pastor's position (as in the case independent non-creedal churches). Rather, it should be the doctrine spelt out in the church's adopted confession. Where the confession is silent on any matters, then members should be allowed to differ. A church should never be allowed to split over issues that are extra-confessional. On the other hand, if an officer of the church differs from the confessional position on a point of doctrine and seeks to promote his view, then he could be censured for having a divisive spirit.

Secondly, Confessions have a *Didactic Use*. That is: they and especially their associated catechisms may be profitably used for the systematic instruction of children and adults alike.

In additional to that, statements in the Confessions and Catechisms may be quoted authoritatively in sermons to clarify or state a doctrine without having to prove its veracity again.

Thirdly, a Confession of Faith has a *Corrective Use*. That is: Since a confession of faith contains the accepted or adopted doctrinal position of the church, anyone who promotes a different doctrine can be lawfully adjured to refrain. And if he continues to promote his opinions contrary to the confession, he may be dealt with disciplinarily by the church. Thus, if a minister of a church which upholds the historic *Westminster Confession of Faith* were to become a Dispensational Premillennialist, it would be proper for him to resign from the pastorate, or be dealt with disciplinary by the courts of the church.

3. Extent of Authority

A church that solemnly adopts a confession for the afore said reasons must decide the extent to which the creed should be given power to bind the conscience.

In this regard, two errors must be avoided.

First, we must avoid the error of making the Confession a powerless symbol in the church. Sadly, this has become the case in many modern Presbyterian churches where the stated confession of the church is the *Westminster Confession of Faith*, whereas the ministers and elders teach and defend

Arminianism and Dispensationalism; and where the worship is contemporary to the exclusion of Psalms.

But secondly, we should avoid the error of making every member in the church subscribe to the confession of faith. The church belongs to Christ, and so we have no right to make the doorway to the church narrower than it already is.

Thus, we agree with the judgment of Dr A.A. Hodge:

> The matter of all these Creeds and Confessions binds the consciences of men only so far as it is purely scriptural, and because it is so. The form in which that matter is stated, on the other hand, binds only those who have voluntarily subscribed the Confession and because of that subscription.

> In all churches a distinction is made between the terms upon which private members are admitted to membership and the terms upon which office–bearers are admitted to their sacred trusts of teaching and ruling. A church has no right to make anything a condition of membership which Christ has not made a condition of salvation. The church is Christ's fold. The Sacraments are the seals of his covenant. All have a right to claim admittance who make a credible profession of the true religion, that is, who are presumptively the people of Christ. This credible profession of course involves a competent knowledge of the fundamental doctrines of Christianity, a declaration of personal faith in Christ and of devotion to his service, and a temper of mind and a habit of life consistent therewith. On the other hand, no man can be inducted into any office in any church who does not profess to believe in the truth and wisdom of the constitution and laws it will be his duty to conserve and administer. Otherwise all harmony of sentiment and all efficient co–operation in action would be impossible.[4]

In other words, officers of the church, especially elders should subscribe fully to the Confession of Faith and be able to defend it without equivocation. On the other hand, ordinary members of the church need only to have a credible profession of faith. Of course, since two cannot walk together except they be agreed (cf. Amos 3:3), the elders of the church should, when admitting anyone who is known to differ from the doctrine of the confession, admonish

---

[4] AA Hodge, *Outlines*, 114

him not to promote his own peculiar doctrine and require him to submit to the teaching of the church which is in accordance with the Confession of Faith.

Conclusion

The Lord himself says:

> "Stand ye in the ways, and see, and ask for the old paths, where is the good way, and walk therein, and ye shall find rest for your souls" (Jer 6:16).

Not everyone will agree with everything in the *Westminster Confession of Faith*. But it is my firm conviction that it is the most succinct, accurate and biblically balanced confessional document ever produced by the Church of the Lord Jesus Christ since the days of the apostles. It paints for us, I believe, a precise and reliable picture of what the Old Paths which the Lord speaks about should look like to us in these last days. It is the faith once delivered unto the faith, even a faith which we should earnestly contend for (Jude 3). It is therefore my prayer and hope that in these days of theological and ecclesiastical declension and divisions, more will discover this Old Path and seek to walk in it to find the rest that the Lord speaks about and to glorify Him, our King, our Maker and Redeemer before the watching world. Amen.

The Remarkable Providence Leading
to the Westminster Assembly

1517   31st October. Martin Luther nails his famous 95 Theses.

1526   William Tyndale's English New Testament (completed 1 year earlier) reaches England.

1536   Henry VIII and the English Parliament separate the Church of England from Rome because the Pope would not sanction his proposal to divorce Queen Katherine.

1538   Henry VIII changes his position again, and authorises 6 articles which essentially brought many of the Roman Catholic doctrine and practices back into the Church of England. Many who are persuaded of the truth of the Protestant faith (eg, John Hooper, Miles Coverdale) leave for the continent, and come under the influence of the Continental Reformers like Zwingli and Calvin.

1547   Edward VI becomes king. The Protestant Reformation in England advances dramatically. Key players are Thomas Cranmer (Archbishop of Canterbury), Nicholas Ridley (scholar) and Hugh Latimer (preacher).

           John Knox becomes preacher at St. Andrews Castle (Scotland), but when it falls to the French, he is captured and made a French gallery slave for 19 months. Upon his release in 1549, he comes to England and pastors a congregation for the next 5 years.

1553   Mary Tudor, Roman Catholic, becomes queen in England. 300 English Protestants were martyred (including Latimer, Ridley, Cranmer), and 800 flees to the Continent, where they imbibe the doctrinal tenets of the Continental Reformers.

1554-59   John Knox flees. While in exile in Geneva, he studies under John Calvin: "the most perfect school of Christ that ever was in the earth since the days of the apostles."

1558   Queen Elizabeth I ascents to the throne and establishes the Elizabethan Compromise, which is insufficiently Reformed to satisfy those who would soon be known as Puritans. Many of these Puritans are strict Calvinists who are religious refugees returning from Switzerland.

1559   The English Puritans who had returned from Geneva had become parish ministers. But the Archbishop Matthew Parker who had not been in exile, carries out a policy of conformity to the Anglican church. Under his advice, the Queen issues the Act of Uniformity which authorises the

Anglican Prayer Book for public worship and lays down penalties for those who refuse to use it or who speak against it.

Thus, the English returnees could not implement their Presbyterian ideals. Instead they formed "classes" (from Latin *classis* or division) for mutual study and the encouragement of preaching. These advocates the Presbyterian system. Two men's views are particularly influential: Walter Travers (1548-1635) and Thomas Cartwright (1535-1603), professor at Cambridge University; both friends of Theodore Beza. Their views would later influence the Westminster Divines.

In Scotland, Knox arrives in May. Shortly after, he and others writes the Reformed Scottish Confession and establishes the first truly Presbyterian Church based on the teachings he had received at Geneva. The church is to be governed by a plurality of elders.

1561 Belgic (or Netherlands) Confession is composed largely by Guido de Bres, one of several itinerant preachers during those days of persecution.

1563 The Heidelberg Catechism is written by Zacharias Ursinus, professor at Heidelberg University and Caspar Olevianus, court preacher of Heidelberg; and published on the behest of Elector Frederick III. The Thirty-Nine Articles of Religion of the Church of England is also established this year under the direction of Matthew Parker, the then Archbishop of Canterbury.

1583 John Whitgift becomes Archbishop of Canterbury and enforces conformity to the ceremonies of the Anglican Church, leading to oppression of Puritan nonconformists. Presbyterian classes are driven underground, but their influence persists. Many of the Puritans favoured the Presbyterian form of church Government.

1603 James VI of Scotland becomes James I of England. The Puritans initially have hopes that their situation will improve since James I is a Scottish Calvinist much influenced by John Knox. They present the king with the Millenary Petition.

In 1604 they met with the new king at the Hampton Court Conference to present their requests. The bishops and the puritans debated. The king presided as chairman. One of the Puritans accidentally used the term 'synod'. The king immediately felt threatened: "If you aim at a Scottish Presbytery, it agrees as well with a monarchy as God with the devil! no bishop, no king."

The king threatens to "harry them out of the land, or else do worse." James had heartily embraced the Anglican system. Although he approved of a new translation of the English Bible (KJV), after the conference, 300 Puritan clergymen are deprived of their livings. Large numbers emigrate, many to Holland where they would later sail the Mayflower to America.

1611   The KJV is published.

1618   The Book of Sports is first published, encouraging sports on Sunday afternoons in direct contradiction of Puritan Sabbatarianism. This is cited by the seventeenth-century British church historian Thomas Fuller as one of the leading causes of the English civil war.

1618-19   Synod of Dordrecht (Netherlands) meets concerning the five points of the Remonstrance.

1620   Puritan Separatists (led by John Robinson) leave Holland and found the Pilgrim colony at Plymouth, Massachusetts in America. These are either congregational or Presbyterian.

1625   Charles I, unsympathetic to the Puritans, becomes king.

1628   William Laud (1573-1645) becomes Bishop of London and undertakes stringent measures to stamp nonconformity out of the Anglican Church. Laudian oppression is a leading contributor to Puritan migrations to America such as the large group led by John Winthrop in 1630.

    The notorious William Laud, is however to become a very important figure in Presbyterian history. "Surely the wrath of man shall praise thee: the remainder of wrath shalt thou restrain" (Ps 76:10). An Arminian, he appears to be using Arminianism as an instrument to bring the Church of England back to the Roman fold.

1629   Members of parliament speak openly against Arminianism and Catholicism amongst other issues. This angers king Charles I, who then decides to rule without Parliament for the next 11 years.

1633   King Charles appoints William Laud as Archbishop of Canterbury.

1637   William Laud extends his influence, and decrees that the Anglican Prayer Book should be read also in Scottish churches. There is great opposition, and soon the people rise in revolt. They will not be ruled by bishops. The people flock to sign the National Covenant upholding Presbyterianism.

1639	The First Bishops War breaks out in Scotland. The Scottish Army would march into England in 1640.
1640	The king finds it near impossible to force the Scots into submission. He runs out of money and ability to raise troops for his military campaigns. Soon he is compelled to recall the Parliament. Only Parliament could raise taxes.
	Parliament meets twice, and in the second, known as the Long Parliament, it decides to curtail the power of the king. The rift between parliament and king widens.
1642	The First English Civil War (1642-46) breaks out. This time, it is between Parliament's New Model Army led by Oliver Cromwell and the king's army.
	Immediately, John Pym, parliamentary leader and a Puritan, appeals to Scotland for help. Scotland agrees. But as part of the agreement, the English parliament would be required to undertake positive steps for the reformation of religion in doctrine, worship, discipline and government of the church, according to the Word of God. The English parliament agreeing to these terms decides to convene an assembly of English and Scottish ministers to bring about the necessary changes.
1643	Jun 12: Ordinance passed by Parliament to convene an assembly of divines.
	Jul 1: The assembly convenes at the Westminster Abbey and is thus called the Westminster Assembly. It would meet until Feb 22, 1649. In 1,163 sessions, about 120 English divines, 6 Scottish commissions and 40 lay assessors would meet. They begin as an attempt to revise the Anglican Thirty-Nine Articles, but ends with a whole new Standard which includes the Westminster Confession, a Larger Catechism, a Shorter Catechism, a Directory of Worship, the Presbyterian Form of Church Government and a Psalter for singing by the churches among other documents.
1646	May 5: Charles I surrenders to the Scots, signalling the defeat of his army by the New Model Army and ending the First English Civil War.
	Dec 4: *The Westminster Confession of Faith* is presented to Parliament. Parliament requires the Assembly to furnish proof-text.
1647	Apr 26: Proof-texts for *Confession* is furnished to Parliament.
	Aug 27: *The Confession of Faith* is approved by Church of Scotland.

Oct 15: *The Larger Catechism* is completed.

Nov 25: *The Shorter Catechism* is presented to Parliament.

1648   Apr 14: The Catechisms are presented in final form.

Apr 30: The Second English Civil War breaks out between the Scots, Presbyterians and supporters of the Charles I on the one hand, and supporters of Oliver Cromwell and independency on the other hand.

1649   Jan 30: Execution of Charles I.

Feb 22: Last numbered Plenary Session of Assembly

1652   Mar 25: End of Assembly's work of examination for ministerial candidates.

1653   Cromwell is sworn in as Lord Protector.

1658   Death of Oliver Cromwell

1660   Restoration of Charles II

1662   Act of Conformity excludes Nonconformists from Church of England

WCF 01: OF THE HOLY SCRIPTURES

The Westminster Confession of Faith was written as a unifying creed for the use of the church. It was intended as an authoritative document. However, it was never intended to supersede the Holy Scriptures as the primary standard of the Church. The church's primary standard must remain the Scripture, while the Confession and her catechisms are to be regarded as Subordinate Standards. They are Subordinate Standards because they are derived from the Scripture in a process of exegesis and systematisation. They are authoritative in churches which subscribe to them because we believe that they are faithfully biblical, representing the teachings of the Scriptures in a systematic and unambiguous way, not contradicting it in any way, and not adding to it. That this is the intended place of the *Westminster Confession of Faith* in the Church is clearly indicated by the opening chapter of the Confession. The Scriptures must remain the foundational standard of the Church, even as the Confessional Standard of the church is built upon it.

Purpose and Means of Special Revelation

1.1 Although the light of nature, and the works of creation and providence do so far manifest the goodness, wisdom, and power of God, as to leave men inexcusable;[1] yet they are not sufficient to give that knowledge of God, and of His will, which is necessary unto salvation.[2] Therefore it pleased the Lord, at sundry times, and in divers manners, to reveal Himself, and to declare that [i.e. that which is] His will unto His Church;[3] and afterwards, for the better preserving and propagating of the truth, and for the more sure establishment and comfort of the Church against the corruption of the flesh, and the malice of Satan and of the world, to commit the same wholly unto writing:[4] which maketh the Holy Scripture to be most necessary;[5] those former ways of God's revealing His will unto His people being now ceased.[6]

[1] Rom 2:14–15; 1:19–20; Ps 19:1–3; Rom 1:32; 2:1; [2] 1 Cor 1:21; 2:13–14; [3] Heb 1:1; [4] Prov 22:19–21; Lk 1:3–4; Rom 15:4; Mt 4:4, 7, 10; Isa 8:19–20; [5] 2 Tim 3:15; 2 Pet 1:19; [6] Heb 1:1–2.

- Scripture leads us to understand that God has revealed himself in two ways. Theologians speak of these two ways as 'General Revelation' (cf. Ps 19:1-6) and 'Special Revelation' (cf. Ps 19:7-14).

- Nature and the works of providence are part of God's general revelation. They not only demonstrate the existence of a God, but that He is the Living and True God by manifesting His goodness, wisdom and power (see Ps 19:1, 3; Rom 1:20). Man is therefore inexcusable, who denies His existence or refuses to seek Him. This is especially so as man is created in the image of God (Gen 1:26), and has eternity set in his heart (Ecc 3:11). There are no authentic atheists. The only way that a man can speak as if he does not believe in the existence of God is to hold down the truth in unrighteousness (Rom 1:18).

- But nature does not reveal God completely nor does it reveal God's redemptive plan for man. This is especially since spiritual things are spiritual discerned (1 Cor 1:21; 2:13-14).

- God therefore reveals Himself specially in many ways, such as in visions and prophesies in time past (Heb 1:1). But if these were not recorded down they would be lost through the ravages of time, human weaknesses, the malice of Satan, and the influences of the world.

- Therefore, to ensure that the truth is preserved and propagated, God had His words committed to writing (Prov 22:19–21; Rom 15:4; Isa 8:19–20). By the time the Holy Scripture was completed, the former ways of God's revelation to man ceased (2 Pet 1:19).

- God still speak to man by nature and providence, but no more by special revelation. This biblical assertion is corroborated by God's providence in which many so-called "anointed Charismatic preachers" have shown themselves to be false prophets because their 'prophecies' did not "come to pass" (see Dt 18:20-22).

- We should learn to read the book of providence, but it must always be interpreted with the Scriptures rather than with superstitious fancy.

The Composition and Use of the Scripture

1.2 Under the name of Holy Scripture, or the Word of God written, are now contained all the books of the Old and New Testament, which are these: [See formatted table below] All which are given by inspiration of God to be the rule of faith and life.[1]

[1] *Lk 16:29, 31; Eph 2:20; Rev 22:18–19; 2 Tim 3:16.*

Of the Old Testament:

	Nomic / Historic	Poetic	Prophetic	
Pentateuch	Genesis	Job	Isaiah	Major Prophets
	Exodus	Psalms	Jeremiah	
	Leviticus	Proverbs	Lamentations	
	Numbers	Ecclesiastes	Ezekiel	
	Deuteronomy	Song of Songs	Daniel	
Pre-Monarchy	Joshua		Hosea	
	Judges		Joel	
	Ruth		Amos	
Monarchy	1 Samuel		Obadiah	Minor Prophets, Pre-Exilic
	2 Samuel		Jonah	
	1 Kings		Micah	
	2 Kings		Nahum	
	1 Chronicles		Habakkuk	
	2 Chronicles		Zephaniah	
Post-Exilic	Ezra		Haggai	Minor Prophets, Post-Exilic
	Nehemiah		Zechariah	
	Esther		Malachi	

Of the New Testament:

Historical	Didactic		Apocalyptic
	Pauline Epistles	General Epistles	
Matthew	Romans	Hebrews	Revelation
Mark	1 Corinthians	James	
Luke	2 Corinthians	1 Peter	
John	Galatians	2 Peter	
Acts	Ephesians	1 John	
	Philippians	2 John	
	Colossians	3 John	
	1 Thessalonians	Jude	
	2 Thessalonians		
	1 Timothy		
	2 Timothy		
	Titus		
	Philemon		

- These books alone are the authoritative and sufficient rule of conduct and faith for the Christian (see Eph 2:20, 31; 2 Tim 3:16–17; Lk 16:29).

- *WSC 2:* What rule hath God given to direct us how we may glorify and enjoy Him? *A.* The Word of God, which is contained in the Scriptures of the Old and New Testaments, is the only rule to direct us how we may glorify and enjoy Him.

1.3   The books commonly called Apocrypha, not being of divine inspiration, are no part of the canon of the Scripture, and therefore are of no authority in the Church of God, nor to be any otherwise approved, or made use of, than other human writings.[1]

[1]*Lk 24:27, 44; Rom 3:2; 2 Pet 1:21.*

- Only 66 books (39 in the Old Testament, and 27 in the New Testament) were inspired by God, and therefore, these alone have authoritative use in the Church of Christ.

- The Roman Catholic Church and the Orthodox Church have added other books known as Apocrypha to their Old Testament. But only 39 books in the Old Testaments were inspired by God. These 39 books appeared in the Hebrew Canon which many believe was drawn up, or should we say affirmed, by the council led by Ezra the Scribe at about 300 B.C.

- Our Lord's use, and therefore, endorsement of this Canon can be seen in His speaking of the Old Testament as the "the Law of Moses, prophets and the psalms" (Lk 24:44). These three terms correspond to the three division of the Hebrew Old Testament, namely: (1) *Torah* (Law—Pentateuch); (2) *Nebi'im* (Prophets—Joshua, Judges, Samuel, Kings & all the prophetic books except Lamentation and Daniel); and (3) *Kethubhim* (Writings—the rest of the books, including the poetic books, of which the book of Psalm is the largest; and Chronicles, which is the last book in the Hebrew canon).

- This canon excludes the apocrypha, which is a collection of fifteen late Jewish books, written during the period 170 B.C. to A.D. 70, some of which were included in the Septuagint (Greek translation of the Old Testament commonly in used in the days of our Lord and His apostles). These books are: 1 & 2 Maccabees, Baruch, Tobit, Judith, The Wisdom of Solomon, Sirach (Ecclesiasticus), additions to Esther, Susanna, Bel & the Dragon, 1 and 2 Esdras, Prayer of Manasseh, Psalm 151 and 3 Maccabees. The Roman Catholic Bible includes the first 10 of these books; while the Greek Orthodox Bible includes all 15 books.

- Our Lord makes no reference to these books, and therefore certainly did not countenance their use at all. They, moreover, contain theological contradictions as well as accounts that are quite clearly fictional, or at least embellished versions of historical accounts.

- Accordingly, these books are *"of no authority in the true Church of God."* And neither should we approve of them, nor give higher regard to them than any other human writings. We, as such, agree with Article 6 of the *Belgic Confession*: "All of which the Church may read and take instruction from, so far as they agree with the canonical books; but they are far from having such power and efficacy that we may from their testimony confirm any point of faith or of the Christian religion; much less may they be used to detract from the authority of the other, that is, the sacred books." We must, however, clarify that these books should never be used in such a way as to give the impression that they are Scripture, whether in public worship or in any devotional exercises.

- The canon of Scripture, we must insist with BB Warfield, is a collection of inspired books rather than an inspired collection of books.[5]

1.4   The authority of the Holy Scripture, for which it ought to be believed, and obeyed, dependeth not upon the testimony of any man,

---

[5] To illustrate his point Warfield spoke of how a Roman Catholic scholar insisted that had his church told him that Aesop's Fables were inspired, he would have believed it is inspired. See John H. Gerstner, 'Warfield's Case For Biblical Inerrancy', in *God's Inerrant Word: An International Symposium On The Trustworthiness Of Scripture*, ed., John Warwick Montgomery (Minneapolis: Bethany Fellowship, 1974): 115-42, at 134-5.

or church; but wholly upon God (who is truth itself) the author thereof; and therefore it is to be received, because it is the Word of God.[1]

[1] 2 Pet 1:19, 21; 2 Tim 3:16; 1 Jn 5:9; 1 Th 2:13.

- The Bible is not just an ancient book. It is the inspired Word of God. It contains nothing but truth, for God is *"truth itself"* for the ultimate determiner of what is truth is God himself. And the Bible contains the whole truth which God has determined that man should know.

- The Bible, being the Word of God, is ultimately and absolutely authoritative and so demands our absolute belief and obedience. Every believer can, and must, rest on its teachings, trust it utterly and depend on it fully and sufficiently for all that we need to know concerning how we may live our Christian lives (2 Tim 3:16–17, 2 Pet 1:3)

- The Bible is authoritative because God is the author, therefore no one, not even the Church, may vest it with any amount of authority. Neither should logic, archaeology and other apologetic methods be used to vest it with authority, even in an evangelistic situation.

Evidences Testifying that the Bible is the Word of God

1.5 We may be moved and induced by the testimony of the Church to an high and reverend esteem of the Holy Scripture,[1] and the heavenliness of the matter, the efficacy of the doctrine, the majesty of the style, the consent of all the parts, the scope of the whole (which is, to give all glory to God), the full discovery it makes of the only way of man's salvation, the many other incomparable excellencies, and the entire perfection thereof, are arguments whereby it doth abundantly evidence itself to be the Word of God; yet notwithstanding our full persuasion and assurance of the infallible truth, and divine authority thereof, is from the inward work of the Holy Spirit, bearing witness by and with the Word in our hearts.[2]

[1] 1 Tim 3:15. [2] 1 Jn 2:20, 27; Jn 16:13–14; 1 Cor 2:10–12; Isa 59:21.

- Although there is no question that the Bible is the inspired Word of God, it is helpful for us to see that there are internal and external evidences that confirm this fact to be so.

- The external evidences are secondary to the internal evidences but important:

   (1) *The testimony of the Church.* The Church has through all ages, held the Scripture with high and reverential esteem, and regarded it as the Word of God. This cannot be the primary evidence since the Church can and often does err. But the fact that the Church continues to hold it as the Word of God even in her darkest days speaks of something special about it.

   (2) *The Bible has been subject to God's special care so that it has been preserved as no other writings on earth.* For example, no other ancient writings have so many extent manuscripts as the NT: 24,633 in total.

   (3) *The efficacy of the doctrine contained in it.* More lives have been transformed by the reading of the Bible than by any other book.

   (4) *Confirmation of archaeology and science.*

- Internal Evidences

   (1) *The heavenliness of the matter.* No book, religious or otherwise, is so heavenly-minded as is the Bible. Nowhere else will one find the equivalent of the parables of Christ or the Psalms.

   (2) *The wonderful discovery of the salvation plan.* God's wisdom is seen throughout, and in every minute detail. Why does Christ have to be fully God and fully man, and be born of a virgin?

   (3) *The consent of all the parts.* The fact that the Bible does not contradict itself at any point surely points to the Divine author. Although many have claimed contradictions in the Bible, no one has yet proven a single error or contradiction.

   (4) *The Bible claims itself to be the Word of God* (OT—2 Sam 23:2; Acts 4:24–25, NT—2 Pet 3:16);

(5) *The many predictions from both the OT and NT that have been fulfilled* (e.g., Ps 22:16–18; Mk 13:2).

- Despite these evidences, or if you like, proofs, we must affirm that "*full persuasion and assurance of the infallible truth, and divine authority [of the Scriptures], is from the inward work of the Holy Spirit, bearing witness by and with the Word in our hearts.*" The Holy Spirit, in other words, works in our hearts to testify that the Bible is the infallible Word of God (1 Jn 2:20, 27; Jn 14:26; 1 Cor 2:10–12; Isa 59:21). This is the experience of all born-again believers who are walking in obedience.

Sufficiency of the Scripture

1.6a The whole counsel of God concerning all things necessary for His own glory, man's salvation, faith, and life, is either expressly set down in Scripture, or by good and necessary consequence may be deduced from Scripture: unto which nothing at any time is to be added, whether by new revelations of the Spirit, or traditions of men.[1]...

[1] *2 Tim 3:15–17; Gal 1:8–9; 2 Th 2:2.*

- All things pertaining to man's salvation, faith and life, and the glory of God is either expressly set down in Scripture or may be deduced from what is revealed (Jn 15:15; 2 Pet 1:3). Therefore, nothing is to be added to the Scripture. There are no new revelations; and traditions of men must never be seen as being on par with, and be added to the Word of God (Gal 1:8–9; Rev 22:18; Dt 4:2; Prov 30:5–6).

- Roman Catholics; cults such as Mormons, Jehovah's Witnesses; and Charismatics have erred in this respect.

1.6b ...Nevertheless, we acknowledge the inward illumination of the Spirit of God to be necessary for the saving understanding of such things as are revealed in the Word;[2]...

[2] *Jn 6:45; 1 Cor 2:9–12.*

- Although God's revelation is complete, the work of the Holy Spirit is not done. We need Him to illumine His revealed Word to us so that we may understand and apply it into our lives (1 Cor 2:9–12). The Holy Spirit illumines not only by enabling us to connect logically the things that we are hearing or reading, but also by bringing to remembrance the truths that we already know (Jn 14:13, 26).

1.6c …and that there are some circumstances concerning the worship of God, and government of the Church, common to human actions and societies, which are to be ordered by the light of nature, and Christian prudence, according to the general rules of the Word, which are always to be observed.[3]

[3] *1 Cor 11:13–14; 14:26, 40.*

- The Word of God has very specific instructions to regulate the manner in which we should worship God (cf. *WCF* 21.1 on the Regulative Principle of Worship) and how the church should be governed. But that does not mean that the instructions are exhaustive. The fact is: there are certain aspects of worship and church government which are left to common sense, for example: how the worship hall is to be arranged, what time the church should worship on the Lord's Day, how frequently should the elders meet to deliberate on matters, whether the deacons should meet together with the elders, etc. In such cases, we must exercise Christian prudence, making sure that the general rules of Scripture be not violated (e.g., 1 Cor 14:40).

- There are many aspects of our life that the Scripture does not give explicit instructions, such as the choice of recreation we may engage in, and how we should organise a business entity, etc. In such cases, the principles that are found in the Scripture must be used as the basis of our decisions, together with common sense and Christian prudence. For example, in deciding whether we should engage in a particular recreation, we may ask in addition to whether it is safe and enjoyable to us: (1) Does it glorify God? (2) Is it profitable? (3) Does it edify or build up others? and (4) Is it enslaving? (1 Cor 10:31; 1 Cor 10:23-24; 1 Cor 6:12b).

Perspicuity of Scripture

1.7   All things in Scripture are not alike plain in themselves, nor alike clear unto all;[1] yet those things which are necessary to be known, believed, and observed, for salvation, are so clearly propounded and opened in some place of Scripture or other, that not only the learned, but the unlearned, in a due use of the ordinary means, may attain unto a sufficient understanding of them.[2]

[1]2 Pet 3:16; [2]Ps 119:105, 130.

- Not every part of the Scripture is easily understood by all. This is especially so in the Old Testament, where many find entire books, such as the minor prophets difficult to understand. But the same is true even in the New Testament. The apostle Peter found some of what the apostle Paul wrote "hard to be understood" and that "they that are unlearned and unstable wrest, as they do also the other scriptures, unto their own destruction" (2 Pet 3:16).

- These difficult passages allow room for believers to grow in their knowledge of Scripture over their entire lifetime.

- That said, however, it is a matter for thanksgiving that those things which are necessary to be known, believed, and observed, for salvation and the Christian life are clearly expressed in one part of Scripture or another, so that these verities may be sufficiently understood by all (Ps 119:105, 130).

- Even the unlearned (who knows how to read), can have sufficient understanding of God's will pertaining to these essential verities, simply by reading through the Scriptures. "The entrance of thy words giveth light; it giveth understanding unto the simple" (Ps 119:130) says the Psalmist.

- This does not, of course, deny the use of commentaries or seeking the counsel of more learned and matured believers such as ministers and elders.

The Inspiration of the Scripture

1.8a The Old Testament in Hebrew (which was the native language of the people of God of old), and the New Testament in Greek (which, at the time of the writing of it, was most generally known to the nations), being immediately inspired by God, and, by His singular care and providence, kept pure in all ages, are therefore authentical;[1]...

[1] Mt 5:18.

- The *autographa* or the original manuscripts of the Scripture in Hebrew (and Aramaic) and Greek, were verbally and plenarily inspired by God; and are, therefore, inerrant, infallible and authoritative.

- It is verbally inspired in that every sentence, every word, and in fact every jot and tittle in the original language is inspired by God (Mt 5:18). The process of inspiration is through the sovereign superintendence of His Spirit so that while the humanness, character and style of the inspired authors are not in any way diminished, the outcome of the result is the holy, infallible Word of God.

- It is plenarily inspired in that it is wholly, not partially, inspired of God. Neither is one part of the Scripture more inspired than another part (see 2 Tim 3:16).

- But how do we know that the Scripture is authentic since the original manuscripts no longer exist? God, through His special providential care, has preserved thousands of hand-copied manuscripts of the biblical text. Although some of these inadvertently have transcription errors, yet not all of them err at the same positions, and so the 'errors' can be easily detected and corrected.

- For this reason, though many versions of the Bible are available today, the differences between the versions are really not as significant as some may make them out to be when we consider the overwhelming material agreement between them. We may liken, for example, the Authorised Version which we use to a meter ruler which we can buy off the shelf. These rulers may not be as minutely precise as the International Prototype Metre, platinum-iridium alloy bar that is kept at zero degrees in the International Bureau of Weights and Measures located in Sèvres, France. But for all intends and purpose they may be used and regarded as '*authentical*.'

1.8b ...so as, in all controversies of religion, the Church is finally to appeal unto them.[2] ...

[2] Isa 8:20; Acts 15:15; Jn 5:39, 46.

- Since the Scripture (in the original language) is not only inspired by God, but preserved through the ages by God's providential care, it must be the final standard of appeal whenever there is any controversy regarding the Christian faith and practice (Isa 8:20; Acts 15:15; Jn 5:39, 46).

1.8c ...But, because these original tongues are not known to all the people of God, who have right unto, and interest in the Scriptures, and are commanded, in the fear of God, to read and search them,[3] therefore they are to be translated into the vulgar language of every nation unto which they come,[4] that, the Word of God dwelling plentifully in all, they may worship Him in an acceptable manner;[5] and, through patience and comfort of the Scriptures, may have hope.[6]

[3] Jn 5:39; [4] 1 Cor 14:6, 9, 11–12, 24, 27–28; [5] Col 3:16; [6] Rom 15:4.

- But not everyone understands the original languages, so how can they know what it contains and do as they are commanded to, unless a translation to the vernacular language is given to them?

- Only with the Bible translated to the common language of the people, may Christians everywhere search and study the Scriptures as did the Berean Christians (Acts 17:11).

The Infallible Rule of Interpretation

1.9 The infallible rule of interpretation of Scripture is the Scripture itself; and therefore, when there is a question about the true and full sense of any Scripture (which is not manifold, but one), it must be searched and known by other places that speak more clearly.[1]

[1]*2 Pet 1:20–21; Acts 15:15–16.*

- The Bible is inerrant in that there is absolutely no error, mistake or contradiction in it at all. This stems from the fact that God Himself is the Divine Author, and for this reason, the infallible rule of interpretation of Scripture is the Scripture itself. This is known as the rule of the analogy of faith. If, therefore, the Scripture gives an interpretation to a particular text, then we must not seek any other interpretation. Thus, we must agree that the prophet Isaiah was prophesying about the virgin birth of Christ in Isaiah 7:14 because this is the inspired interpretation given in Matthew 1:23.

- Note also the parenthetical remark that there is only one true and full sense in any Scripture text. This general rule applies to almost all parts of Scripture and must be observed when we study the Scripture. There are a few places where Scripture itself suggests that there are different levels of interpretation, particularly in the area of prophecy. An example would be Matthew's reference to Hosea 11:1 as being fulfilled by the return of the Lord from Egypt whereunto his earthly parents had brought him to flee from the persecution of Herod. The *prima facie* meaning of Hosea 11:1 as seen in the context in the book of Hosea is about the redemption of Israel out of Egypt. But the apparently manifold meaning of these passages can easily be resolved when we understand that much of the Old Testament has a typical fulfilment in the person and work of Christ in the New Testament. That being the case, we must not only interpret each passage according to its historical, grammatical meaning; but be prepared to see the typical meaning, especially when the New Testament makes it clear that such a type is intended by the Holy Spirit. Where a type is intended, the *"true and full sense"* of the text must include a reference to the antitype just as the "true and full" description a ray of light should include a reference to the source of the light and the objects on which the ray of light falls on. But this apparent exception is generally applicable only to Old Testament passages. When interpreting the New Testament, there is no need to search for typical fulfilments.

The Authority of Scripture

1.10 The supreme Judge, by which all controversies of religion are to be determined, and all decrees of councils, opinions of ancient writers, doctrines of men, and private spirits, are to be examined, and in whose sentence we are to rest, can be no other but the Holy Spirit speaking in the Scripture.[1]

[1]Mt 22:29, 31; Eph 2:20; Acts 28:25.

- The Holy Spirit inspired the Scripture; and He enables us to understand the Scripture by bringing to mind related Scripture (which we have heard or read) and enabling us to make logical connection between the passages. It is in this way of inspiration and illumination the Holy Spirit speaks to us in and through the Scripture.

- It is by way of the Scripture, that the Holy Spirit exercises His role as the Supreme or Ultimate Judge to settle "*all controversies of religion*"; to determine the soundness of the "*opinions of ancient writers, doctrines of men, and private spirits* [i.e. individual believers expressing the opinions that they have arrived at on particular passage or verse of scripture]."

- We must rest upon His sentence as final. Therefore, the Scripture is our final authority and appeal in all areas of doctrine and Christian life. Our Lord, who Himself is the Living Word of God, in His controversies with Satan and the Jews, appealed to Scripture (Mt 4:4, 7, 10; 22:29, 31).

- Human authorities, whether Church Fathers, Popes, bishops or pastors; and human experiences must be judged against the Scriptures. Creeds and Confessions are authoritative only in so far as they are loyal to the Scripture.

- We therefore speak of our Confession of Faith and Catechisms as the Subordinate Standards of the Church. The Scripture is the

Standard. We hold our Subordinate Standards in high regard only because we are persuaded that it is a faithful interpretation and exposition of the Scripture, which was put together by the collective wisdom of our fathers of the faith under the providential guidance and illuminating work of the Holy Spirit. For this reason, when our private interpretation of a passage or verse of Scripture, differs from the Confessional interpretation, we must never assume that the Confession is wrong. Unless we are fully persuaded that our interpretation is correct after careful and exhaustive study with the corroboration of other learned and pious believers, we must give precedence to interpretation of the Confession as the voice of "the *Holy Spirit speaking in the Scripture.*"

- And since Creeds and Confessions are subordinate standards, we should appeal to the Scripture rather than to our Creeds and Confessions when disputing with those who do not subscribe to the same Confession, who may differ from us on particular doctrines.

WCF 02: OF GOD, AND OF THE HOLY TRINITY

The Westminster Confession of Faith is a doctrinal statement of faith that summaries what we are to believe concerning God and what duties He requires of us. Why then does it begin with a doctrine of the Scripture rather than a doctrine of God? The answer is really very simple: namely that God has chosen to reveal Himself to us largely through the Scriptures. Nature reveals something about God to us too, but it is too general for us to know Him sufficiently to enjoy a relationship of mutual love with Him. Thus, it is essential for us to know God's Word before we know God. By His Word, we learn that the God we worship differs so drastically from the gods of man's imagination, or the gods of men who refuse to believe the Scripture, that we cannot agree with those who say that all religions point to the same God. The God of the Bible is not the same as the god of Islam or modern Judaism. Both of these refuse to accept the New Testament as the Word of God. Neither is He the same as the gods of polytheistic religions such as Hinduism or even Mormonism. Neither is He the god of Liberals or Unitarians who reject the doctrine of the Trinity. The God of the Bible is the alone Living and True God. He is personal, triune, transcendent, sovereign and loving. This is the God we worship and confess. This is the God who is introduced and affirmed in this chapter of our Confession of Faith.

The Nature of God

2.1 There is but one only[1] living, and true God,[2] who is infinite in being and perfection,[3] a most pure Spirit,[4] invisible,[5] without body, parts,[6] or passions;[7] immutable,[8] immense,[9] eternal,[10] incomprehensible,[11] almighty,[12] most wise,[13] most holy,[14] most free,[15] most absolute;[16] working all things according to the counsel of His own immutable and most righteous will,[17] for His own glory;[18] most loving,[19] gracious, merciful, long-suffering, abundant in goodness and truth, forgiving iniquity, transgression, and sin;[20] the rewarder of them that diligently seek Him;[21] and withal most just, and terrible in His judgments;[22] hating all sin,[23] and who will by no means clear the guilty.[24]

[1] Dt 6:4; 1 Cor 8:4, 6; [2] 1 Th 1:9; Jer 10:10; [3] Job 11:7–9; 26:14; [4] Jn 4:24; [5] 1 Tim 1:17; [6] Dt 4:15–16; Jn 4:24; Lk 24:39; [7] Acts 14:11, 15; [8] Jas 1:17; Mal 3:6; [9] 1 Kgs 8:27; Jer 23:23–24; [10] Ps 90:2; 1 Tim 1:17; [11] Ps 145:3; [12] Gen 17:1; Rev 4:8; [13] Rom 16:27; [14] Isa 6:3; Rev 4:8; [15] Ps 115:3; [16] Ex 3:14; [17] Eph 1:11; [18] Prov 16:4; Rom 11:36; [19] 1 Jn 4:8, 16; [20] Ex 34:6–7; [21] Heb 11:6; [22] Neh 9:32–33; [23] Ps 5:5–6; [24] Neh 1:2–3; Ex 34:7.

- ***There is but one only, living, and true God.***

  (a) There is only one God. The Scripture affirms monotheism, not polytheism, tritheism, pantheism, panenthism or atheism.

  (b) He is the only Living God. Idols of wood and stone are dead (Ps 115:4–7).

  (c) He is the only True God. All gods of human (and satanic) invention are false (1 Cor 10:20; Jer 10:10–15).

- **God is *a most pure spirit, invisible, without body, parts, or passions*:**

  (a) God is not like man having a body. He is, therefore, invisible and immaterial. When fingers, eyes, ears, etc., are ascribed to God in Scripture, they must be taken *anthropomorphically*.

  (b) God is one. He is without parts unlike man which is constituted of soul and body, which body is divisible into parts. Cut off the hands and feet of a man, and he will still be recognised as him. He changes his mind totally about a decision he made, and he is still him. Take away his mental capacity, and he will still be him. But God is indivisibly one: take off any of His perfections, and He ceases to be. Take away His holiness, and He would not be. Take away His goodness, and He would not be. Take away His justice, and He would not be. The same is true of every of His perfections. The same is true in regard to His will and purpose. If He changes His mind about anything, He would not be (cf. Mal 3:6; Num 23:19). Thus, there can be no inconsistency of purpose or will within the Godhead.

  (c) God is without passions or human emotions. More specifically, God does not have motions or perturbation in His being relative to perceived good or evil. God is love; He does not experience love as man does. God is merciful; He does not need external stimuli to evoke a sense of mercy. When God is said to grieve, to be full of fury and revenge, or to be jealous, or even delighted, these are *anthropopathic* expressions to describe the purposeful works or actions of God in such a way as to communicate to man a sense of responsibility towards His revealed will. We may indeed speak of God being grieved, but we must not imagine that He is grieved because He made a mistake or that He was not in sovereign control or that He had not foreseen what was going to happen. Neither should we speak of God desiring the salvation of the reprobate because He has decreed their reprobation.

- **Communicable & Incommunicable Attributes.**

  God may be apprehended by examining His Incommunicable and Communicable attributes.

  (a) *Incommunicable* attributes are:
  - i. His Infinity;
  - ii. His Eternality, self-existence or aseity;
  - iii. His Unchangeableness or Immutability;

  (b) His *communicable* attributes are the attributes that man created in His image are granted possession of to a degree, such as wisdom, power, holiness, justice, goodness and truth.

  > WSC 4 What is God?
  >
  > A. God is a spirit,
  >
  > infinite, eternal and unchangeable   ⇦ Incommunicable attributes
  >
  > in His being, wisdom, power, holiness,   ⇦ Communicable attributes
  > justice, goodness and truth.

- **God is *infinite in being and perfection***: He is infinite in His being (or essence or existence). He is infinite in His perfection (or moral, communicable attributes).

- **He is *infinite in being*.** This means He is unbounded and unlimited in His being or essence, which means He is:

  (a) *Immense*—God is so great that the universe cannot contain Him, i.e., He is not bounded by space: He is transcendent (cf. 1 Kgs 8:27).

  (b) *Eternal*—God is not bounded by time: He has no beginning and no end (cf. Ps 90:2; 9:7; 2 Pet 3:8).

  (c) *Incomprehensible*—finite beings cannot fully comprehend Him apart from what He has chosen to reveal of Himself (cf. Job 11:7).

  (d) **Omnipresent**—God is in all of space, i.e. everywhere present: He is immanent (Not as the pantheist who says God is space and space is God).

- **God is *immutable*:** He does not change in His being or purpose (Num 23:19; Ps 33:11; Mal 3:6). He introduced Himself as "I AM THAT I AM" (Ex 3:14), which also mean "I will be that I will be." Neither does God increase or decrease in glory or blessedness.

- **God is *almighty*:** He is infinitely powerful or omnipotent. "With God all things are possible" (Mt 19:26). He is not only the Creator but Sustainer of the world. "The LORD hath made all things for himself: yea, even the wicked for the day of evil" (Prov 16:4).

- **God is *most wise*:** God's wisdom is infinite. Thus, He directs all things which He created to their proper end, namely His own glory. "O LORD, how manifold are thy works! in wisdom hast thou made them all: the earth is full of thy riches" (Ps 104:24).

- **God is *most holy*:** He is infinitely holy. He is transcendently holy (see Isa 6:3; Hab 1:13). So God hates sin and is angry with the wicked every day.

- **God is *most free*:** He does whatever He pleases after His own counsel (Ps 115:3; Eph 1:11). He is not affected by anything external to Him. Thus, He works *"all things according to the counsel of His own immutable and most righteous will, for His own* *glory."* Though He hears and answers prayers, prayers do not change His mind.

- **God is *most absolute***: As the "I AM" (Ex 3:14), He is the perfect Being. He is not only immutable, but perfect in every sense of the word. Or as James E. Dolezal puts it:

"This means that no principle or power stands back of or alongside God by which he instantiates or understands his existence and essence. He alone is the sufficient reason for his own existence, essence, and other attributes. He does not possess his perfections by relation to anything or anyone other than himself."[6]

- **God is infinitely good**: He is "*most loving, gracious, merciful, long-suffering, abundant in goodness and truth, forgiving iniquity, transgression, and sin.*" His goodness can be seen *absolutely*—i.e., as it is in Himself; or relatively, —as it is exercised towards His creatures.

Seen *absolutely*, God's goodness is an intrinsic perfection that is immutable and impervious to human assessment, for it is the standard that determines what goodness is. God is always good. "There is none good but one, that is, God" (Mt 19:17).

Relatively, His goodness may also be considered as *general* or *special*. If viewed as *general*, then the recipients of His goodness are all His creatures (cf. Ps 36:6–7; 145:9; Mt 5:45). Though commonly known as "common grace," it is better designated temporal-benevolence because whatever good that a reprobate receives in this life will add to his damnation at the judgment. If viewed as *special*, then the recipients of God's goodness are the elect in Christ (Ps 73:1; Eph 1:5–6). There is forgiveness only in Christ.

- **God is *most just***: So He will punish sin. He is "*the rewarder of them that diligently seek Him; and withal, most just, and terrible in His*

---

[6] James E. Dolezal, *God without Parts: Divine Simplicity and the Metaphysics of God's Absoluteness* (Oregon: Pickwick Publications, 2011), 1.

judgments; hating all sin, and who will by no means clear the guilty."

The Nature of God Elaborated

2.2   God hath all life,[1] glory,[2] goodness,[3] blessedness,[4] in and of Himself; and is alone in and unto Himself all-sufficient, not standing in need of any creatures which He hath made,[5] nor deriving any glory from them,[6] but only manifesting His own glory in, by, unto, and upon them: He is the alone fountain of all being, of whom, through whom, and to whom are all things;[7] and hath most sovereign dominion over them, to do by them, for them, or upon them, whatsoever Himself pleaseth.[8] In His sight all things are open and manifest,[9] His knowledge is infinite, infallible, and independent upon the creature,[10] so as nothing is to Him contingent, or uncertain.[11] He is most holy in all His counsels, in all His works, and in all His commands.[12] To Him is due from angels and men, and every other creature, whatsoever worship, service, or obedience He is pleased to require of them.[13]

[1] Jn 5:26; [2] Acts 7:2; [3] Ps 119:68; [4] 1 Tim 6:15; Rom 9:5; [5] Acts 17:24–25; [6] Job 22:2–3; [7] Rom 11:36; [8] Rev 4:11; 1 Tim 6:15; Dan 4:25, 35; [9] Heb 4:13; [10] Rom 11:33–34; Ps 147:5; [11] Acts 15:18; Ezk 11:5; [12] Ps 145:17; Rom 7:12; [13] Rev 5:12–14.

- **God is wholly self-sufficient**. He *"hath all life, glory, goodness, blessedness, in and of Himself; and is alone in and unto Himself all-sufficient, not standing in need of any creatures which He hath made, nor deriving any glory from them, but only manifesting His own glory in, by, unto, and upon them."* He has no need for any created thing. He has life in and of Himself unlike man who is totally dependent on God for his being and life. He is infinitely and perfectly glorious and no one can add to His glory. When man is said to glorify him it is but to show forth his glory. He is good in and of himself, and His goodness is not dependant on perception or judgement of the objects of His benevolence. And He is altogether blessed in and of himself, nothing and no one can add to His blessedness. He did not create to make himself happier or to fulfil a need.

- **God is the *alone fountain of all being***: He is the source of all existence and life, for "in him we live, and move, and have our being (Acts 17:28a; cf. Rom 11:36; 1Tim 6:13).

- **God is sovereign.** He "*hath most sovereign dominion over [every creature], to do by them, for them, or upon them, whatsoever Himself pleaseth.*" God's creatures, whether angels, men, animals or inanimate objects do not and cannot live or move independently from God. He does not only give them existence and life, He sustains their life and determine all their motions and changes.

- **God's knowledge and understanding is infinite**. "*In His sight all things are open and manifest, His knowledge is infinite, infallible, and independent upon the creature, so as nothing is to Him contingent, or uncertain.*" He is all-knowing or omniscient. Nothing adds to his knowledge. Nothing is hid from Him—even if it is future. There is no such thing as chance or luck. God is never surprised. "Known unto God are all his works from the beginning of the world" (Acts 15:18; cf. Heb 4:13; Rom 11:33–34; Ps 147:5; Ezk 11:5). This is so because it is God who ordained all things that comes to pass.

- **God is the standard of rightness and holiness**. "*He is most holy in all His counsels, in all His works, and in all His commands.*" All things that come to past, including the unholy and wicked deeds of His moral creature, and natural disasters are determined by His sovereign will. Yet God is always right and holy. He is not the author of sin. All He does is holy. All He commands is holy.

- **God is alone is worthy of all praise and honour.** *To Him is due from angels and men, and every other creature, whatsoever worship, service, or obedience, He is pleased to require of them.* To worship is to ascribe worthiness. Man and angels must worship God with a moral consciousness. All other creatures are made to ascribe glory to their Creator according to their nature (cf. Rev 5:12-14).

The Triunity of God

2.3 In the unity of the Godhead there be three persons, of one substance, power, and eternity; God the Father, God the Son, and God the Holy Ghost:[1] the Father is of none, neither begotten, nor proceeding; the Son is eternally begotten of the Father;[2] the Holy Ghost eternally proceeding from the Father and the Son.[3]

[1] 1 Jn 5:7; Mt 3:16–17; 28:19; 2 Cor 13:14; [2] Jn 1:14, 18; [3] Jn 15:26; Gal 4:6.

- It is manifestly not helpful to try to explain the doctrine of the Trinity using earthly and material illustrations such as the three states of water; the clover leaf; the roles of a person as father, son and uncle; or the sun with its heat, light and warmth. Each of these tends to promote a heretical thinking related to the doctrine such as Sabbellian Modalism, which denies the distinct subsistences (Persons) within the Godhead.

- Nevertheless, it is helpful to illustrate the Trinity using a word diagram such as the following:

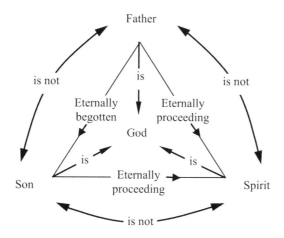

- **The Father is God**. There are numerous passages in the Old Testament that speaks of God as the Father (e.g. Isa 63:16; 64:8), but these may not be referring specifically to the first person in the Trinity. However, in the New Testament, there are numerous references to "God the Father" in distinction to Christ the Son (eg. Rom 1:7; 15:6; 1 Cor 1:3; 8:6; 15:24; 2Cor 1:2, 3; 11:31; Gal 1:1, 3; 2

Jn 1:9; Jude 1:1). These verses clearly speak of a distinct Person within the Godhead, especially when we see that Christ the Son is God in our next point. In fact, in His high priestly prayer, the Lord Jesus Christ addresses Him as "Father" (Jn 17:1) and "the only true God" (Jn 17:3). So the Father is God.

- **The Son is God**:

  (a) He has divine attributes: (i) Eternality (1Jn 1:2; Heb 1:2–3; Jn 17:5; 1:1); (ii) Omniscience (e.g., Mt 16:8; 22:18; Mk 2:8; Lk 5:22; Rev 2:18, 23); (iii) Omnipresence (e.g., Mt 18:20; 28:20); and (iv) Omnipotence (e.g., Mt 28:18).

  (b) He has divine titles, such as "the mighty God, The everlasting Father" (Isa 9:6), "Immanuel" (Isa 7:14), "JEHOVAH OUR RIGHTEOUSNESS" (Jer 23:6); and "KING OF KINGS, LORD OF LORDS" (Rev 19:16).

  (c) He has divine works and offices: (i) Creation (Jn 1:3; Heb 1:2); (ii) Providence (Heb 1:3); (iii) Judgment (Jn 5:22, 9:39; Rom 14:10; 2 Cor 5:10); and (iv) Forgiveness of sin (Mt 9:6).

  (d) He is identified with Jehovah as the stone of stumbling or rock of offence (Isa 8:13–14; cf. Rom 9:32–33; 1 Pet 2:8).

  (e) He received Thomas' worship (Jn 20:28; cf. Acts 10:25–26; Rev 22:8–9).

  (f) He identifies Himself as the Son of God, so making Himself equal with God (see John 5:18).

  (g) He identifies Himself as the "I am" (see John 8:58; 18:6).

  (h) Other clear NT references: e.g., "Christ came, who is over all, God blessed forever" (Rom 9:5); "God was manifest in the flesh" (1 Tim 3:16); "...Christ Jesus: who, being in the form of God..." (Phil 2:5–6); "in him dwelleth all the fulness of the Godhead bodily" (Col 2:9); "This is the true God, and eternal life" (1 Jn 5:20); and "...the Church of God, which he hath purchased with his own blood" (Acts 20:28).

- **The Holy Spirit is God**:

  (a) He has divine attributes: (i) Eternality (Heb 9:14); (ii) Omnipresence (Ps 139:7–8); (iii) Omniscience (1 Cor 2:10–11); (iv) Omnipotence (Lk 1:35a); and (v) Sovereignty (1 Cor 12:11).

  (b) He has divine works and offices: (i) creation (Gen 1:2; Job 33:4); (ii) directing missions (Acts 16:7); (iii) regeneration and sanctification (Tit 3:5); (iv) miracles (Mt 12:28); (v) bestowing wisdom and illumination (1 Cor 2:10–16); (vi) inspiring the Scripture (2 Pet 1:21); and (vi) resurrection (Rom 8:11).

  (c) He is ascribed equality with God, e.g., we are the temple of God because His Spirit indwells us (1 Cor 3:16) and Peter rebuking Ananias for lying against the Holy Spirit declares that his sin is "not ... unto men, but unto God" (Acts 5:3–4).

- **The Holy Spirit is a Person not a force**.

  (a) He is called the Comforter not a comfort (Jn 14:26, 15:26, 16:7).

  (b) The New Testament, despite grammatical inconsistency, frequently makes use of masculine pronouns for the Holy Spirit although 'spirit' (Gk. *pneuma*) is neuter in the Greek (1 Cor 2:10–11; Jn 16:13).

  (c) He possesses attributes of a Person: (i) He has a mind (Jn 14:26; Rom 8:27); (ii) He works according to His own will (Acts 16:7; 1 Cor 12:11); (iii) He can be grieved (Eph 4:30); (iv) He can be vexed (Isa 63:10); (v) He can be tested (Acts 5:9); (vi) He can be lied to (Acts 5:3); and (vii) He can be blasphemed (Mt 12:31).

  (d) He performs works of a Person: (i) He creates and gives life (Job 33:4); (ii) He appoints and commissions ministers (Isa 48:16; Acts 13:2; 20:28); (iii) He directs ministers where and what to preach (Acts 8:29; 10:19–20, etc.); (iv) He spoke in, and by, the prophets (Acts 1:16; 1 Pet 1:11–12; 2 Pet 1:21); (v) He strives with sinners (Gen 6:3); (vi) He reproves (Jn 16:8); (vii) He comforts (Acts 9:31); (viii) He helps our infirmities (Rom 8:26); (ix) He intercedes on our behalf (Rom 8:26); (x) He teaches (Jn 14:26; 1 Cor 12:3); (xi) He guides (Jn 16:13); (xii) He sanctifies

(Rom 15:16; 1 Cor 6:11); (xiii) He testifies of and glorifies Christ (Jn 15:26; 16:14); and (xiv) He searches all things (Rom 11:33–34; 1 Cor 2:10–11).

- **The Persons in the Godhead are not only distinguishable but distinct**: The ancient heresy of Sabellian Modalism (or Monarchaism) insists that "God appears at different times in three different modes." If so, the Persons of the Godhead are indistinct. But it is clear from Scripture that this is not the case. The Persons of the Godhead are irrefutably distinct, for:

  (a) It is hinted in the Old Testament when God spoke with the plural first person personal pronoun, —"Let us make man in our image, after our likeness" (Gen 1:26). This clearly suggests a plurality in the Godhead.

  (b) It is seen very clearly at the time of Jesus' baptism where the Son was being baptised, the Holy Spirit descended like a dove and the Father spoke from heaven (Mt 3:16–17).

  (c) It can be deduced from Scripture in that: (i) The Son is distinguished from the Father in that He, but not the Father, descended to Earth; and it was not the Father who died and rose again, but His Son. (ii) The Spirit is distinguished from the Father since He "proceedeth from the Father" (Jn 15:26). (iii) The Spirit is distinguished from the Son since the Son calls Him "another Comforter" (Jn 14:16).

  (d) It can be seen in the personal properties of the divine Persons in the Godhead: (i) God the Father *exists* of Himself (Jn 5:26); (ii) God the Son is *eternally begotten* of the Father (Jn 1:18; 3:16; Gal 4:4) and (iii) God the Holy Spirit is *eternally proceeding* from both the Father and the Son (Jn 14:26; 15:26).

- **There is unity of essence in the Godhead**: if the Persons of the Godhead have separate existence, then God would not be mono-theistic but of tri-theistic. Thus, if it can be shown that the Bible teaches that the persons of the Godhead exist separately, then it would contradict the biblical assertion that there is only one living and true God. But this is not the case; the Bible is clear that though there are three persons in the Godhead, they are one in essence, e.g.:

(a) 1 John 5:7, "There are three that bear record in heaven, the Father, the Word, and the Holy Ghost: and these three are one";

(b) Matthew 28:19, "... baptising them in *the name* of the Father, and of the Son, and of the Holy Ghost." In the formula we see that baptism is to be made in the name (singular) of the one God who subsists in three Persons, namely the Father, Son and Spirit;

(c) Compare Isaiah 6:5, where Isaiah saw "the King, the LORD of hosts," with John 12:41 where Isaiah is said to have seen Christ, with Acts 28:25 where He who spoke to Isaiah is noted as the Holy Spirit.

Augustine puts it succinctly: "Christ, considered in Himself is called God; but with relation to the Father, He is called the Son. The Father, considered in Himself is called God; but with relation to the Son, He is called the Father. ... They who are severally called the Father and the Son are the same God." We may add: "The Holy Spirit, considered in Himself is called God; but in relation to the Father and the Son, He is called the Spirit of God and the Spirit of Christ."

- **The Father is of none, neither begotten, nor proceeding**: In the Scriptures, we find that the Father, unlike the Son is never spoken of as being *'begotten'*, and unlike the Spirit is never spoken of as *'proceeding.'*

- **The Son is eternally begotten of the Father**: This is the doctrine of *filiation*. The Scriptures speaks of Christ as being "the only begotten Son" (e.g. Jn 1:18; Gal 4:4; Heb 1:1-3). This description, — together with the facts that (1) Christ is eternal and pre-existent (Jn 1:1); and (2) Christ himself declared: "For as the Father hath life in himself; so hath he given to the Son to have life in himself" (Jn

5:26), —shows that we must think of Christ as being *eternally begotten*.

- **The Holy Ghost [is] eternally proceeding from the Father and the Son**: This is the doctrine of *spiration*. In the first place, the word 'Spirit' (רוּחַ [*rûach*] in the OT and πνεῦμα [*pneuma*] in the NT) when used in a genitive construct with God or the Lord (Spirit of God, or Spirit of the Lord), suggests a breath proceeding from God or the Lord. In the second place, the Lord describes the Holy Spirit as the "Spirit of truth, which proceedeth [lit. is proceeding] from the Father" (Jn 15:26). In the third place, the Holy Spirit, is known in the Scriptures as "Spirit of [God's] Son" (Gal 4:6) and "the Spirit of Christ" (Rom 8:9, 1 Pet 1:11), which suggests quite strongly that the Spirit does not only proceed from the Father, but also the Son.

WCF 03: OF GOD'S ETERNAL DECREE

We come now to a chapter in the Westminster Confession of Faith that marks it out as distinctly Calvinistic, not that there are many non-Calvinistic Protestant Creeds to begin with. But the contrast between Calvinism and Arminianism; or Augustinianism and Pelagianism is nowhere more pronoun than in the doctrine of the sovereignty of God and His decree. Augustinians and Calvinists insist that the Bible teaches us that God decreed everything that comes to pass in creation, providence and redemption; and that God is sovereignly bringing to past day by day, moment by moment all that He has decreed. This doctrine differs sharply from fatalism in that we believe God is control of all things, and that God is a hearer and answerer of prayers. Pelagians and Arminians (i.e. Semi-Pelagians) do not appreciate that, and accuse Augustinians and Calvinists of fatalism, of making God the author of sin, and of making men mere automatons. This chapter, if studied carefully, will prove otherwise.

God's Decree in General

3.1 God from all eternity did, by the most wise and holy counsel of His own will, freely, and unchangeably ordain whatsoever comes to pass:[1] *yet so, as thereby neither is God the author of sin,*[2] *nor is violence offered to the will of the creatures, nor is the liberty or contingency of second causes taken away, but rather established.*[3]

[1]Eph 1:11; Rom 11:33; Heb 6:17; Rom 9:15, 18; [2]Jas 1:13, 17; 1 Jn 1:5; [3]Acts 2:23; Mt 17:12; Acts 4:27–28; Jn 19:11; Prov 16:33.

- God has from all eternity, a plan with reference to His creation. "Remember the former things of old: for I am God, and there is none else; I am God, and there is none like me, Declaring the end from the beginning, and from ancient times the things that are not yet done, saying, My counsel shall stand, and I will do all my pleasure" (Isa 46:9–10).

- This plan comprehends and determines all things and events of every kind—whether great or small, whether good or evil—that come to pass. Even things that appear to happen by chance have been decreed: "The lot is cast into the lap; but the whole disposing thereof is of the LORD" (Prov 16:33). So even disasters and the acts of the wicked are ordained of God: "I form the light, and create darkness: I make peace, and create evil [i.e., disaster]: I the LORD do all these things" (Isa 45:7; cf. Amos 3:6b); "The LORD hath made all things for himself: yea, even the wicked for the day of evil" (Prov 16:4).

- This plan is consistent with God's infinite wisdom and holiness. This is how it can be said "And we know that ALL things work together for good to them that love God, to them who are the called according to his purpose" (Rom 8:28). So Joseph explained to his brothers: "But as for you, ye thought evil against me; but God meant it unto good, to bring to pass, as it is this day, to save much people alive" (Gen 50:20).

- God's absolute ordination of all things that comes to pass does not violate the freedom and responsibility of His creatures. Thus, James says, "Let no man say when he is tempted, I am tempted of God: for God cannot be tempted with evil, neither tempteth he any man" (Jas 1:13). So Judas is condemned though it was decreed that Christ would be delivered by him: "The Son of man goeth as it is written of him: but woe unto that man by whom the Son of man is betrayed! it had been good for that man if he had not been born" (Mt 26:24). Peter, in his sermon at Pentecost, similarly charged the Jews for their wickedness of slaying the Lord: "Him, being delivered by the determinate counsel and foreknowledge of God, ye have taken, and by wicked hands have crucified and slain" (Acts 2:23; see also Acts 4:28).

- This is so because God does not violate the freedom of His creatures which are free agents. The decisions and actions of such free agents are contingent upon secondary causes, which are ordained by God. God does not manipulate the heart or will. The will of a free agent is dependent on what it determines to be most attractive at the point of decision. Thus, when a rational free agent sins, he is fully responsible for his sin. The divines express this idea beautifully: *"Neither is God the author of sin, nor is violence offered to the will of the creatures."*

- Similarly, God's absolute ordination does not mean that *"the liberty or contingency of second causes [is] taken away, but rather established."* What are second causes? Second causes are simply 'means' to accomplish an end. God has ordained all things that will come to pass. But in general, especially in the physical realm, He does not directly bring about what was ordained by a direct intervention. He does so in the spiritual realm in such acts as regeneration; but in the physical realm it is seldom done except during the periods in Redemptive History when God would display His power through miracles, such as during the Lord's earthly ministry. Indeed, miracles are events or acts that are brought about directly by God's power contrary to the laws of nature and without second causes. But miracles are rare, for God has chosen normally to bring about what He has ordained through means or second causes.

Although the way that a second cause functions has also been ordained, we must see that it has been ordained according to its nature. So if God has ordained that you pass an examination, He would also have ordained that you study hard; get to school on time; the questions asked are those which you can answer; your pen works; the script marker likes your answer, etc, etc. All these second causes must concur to bring about the event in consideration (namely your passing of your examination). This is what we must understand by the phrase, *"the liberty or contingency of second causes [is not] taken away, but rather established."*

God's Decree is Unconditional

3.2 Although God knows whatsoever may or can come to pass upon all supposed conditions;[1] yet hath He not decreed any thing because He foresaw it as future, or as that which would come to pass upon such conditions.[2]

[1]*Acts 15:18; 1 Sam 23:11–12; Mt 11:21, 23;* [2]*Rom 9:11, 13, 16, 18.*

- This paragraph addresses one of the main points of debate between Luther and Erasmus during the 16th Century Reformation. This was the debate that gave rise to Luther's famous work, *The Bondage of the Will*. Erasmus had insisted that God decreed what comes to pass only in the sense that He foresaw everything that would come to pass down the corridor of time. Luther countered that God foresaw because He decreed everything.

- We must insist with Luther, that God's decree is not at any point dependant on God's foresight of what will happen. It may, in fact, be said that God knows all things future because He decreed whatsoever comes to pass, or that God is omniscient because He is absolutely sovereign. This must be so not only because God's sufficiency would otherwise be contradicted, but because God alone is an independent being. All God's creatures have their being in Him (Acts 17:28a). Socinians and Rationalists err by saying that God cannot foresee the free actions of His creatures, or else they would not be free. Arminians agree that He foresees their actions, but deny that He determines them. But Scripture plainly teaches that, "Known unto God are all his works from the beginning of the world" (Acts 15:18), because He "worketh all things after the counsel of his own will" (Eph 1:11).

- Bearing this in mind, we see that the decree of God will definitely come to pass in all its details and it is in no aspect conditional. In other words, whatever comes to pass is not merely one of multiple possible outcomes that depend on some intervening conditions. Every step of the way is ordained of God. It is true that some aspects of God's decree have an appearance of coming to pass only upon certain (supposed) conditions. For example, God revealed to Paul that He would save him and his companions on the ship to Rome, but only on condition that the sailors remain in the ship (Acts 27:24, 31). Thus, we may say that God decreed to save them only on condition that the sailors remain in the ship. This gives the appearance that God's plan could be frustrated by the sailors. But the reality is that God has not only decreed that all in the ship would be saved, but that the sailors would be prevented from fleeing. This intermediate decree is not made known to the centurion and the sailors, at least not as a plan of God, but as a requirement of God, so that they are held responsible for their actions.

Likewise, God has chosen to save His elect from the wrath to come, but He decreed to save them only through repentance and faith in Christ. We take note that both faith and repentance are gifts of God (Eph 2:8; Acts 11:18), and so we know that whether they will be saved or not is not conditioned upon a free response to the Gospel which could go either way. Yet, God has decreed that the salvation of his elect is to be conditioned upon their repentance and faith, and therefore the duty to repent and believe is given that the elect may know their responsibility towards the Lord.

This is how we must understand our duty to pray: God has decreed to provide for our various needs, but He also decreed that these needs be sought through prayer. So we see that prayer does not change anything in that God's decree is not conditional. Yet, we are encouraged to pray as a revealed duty, for God has ordained that He will provide our needs in answer to our prayers.

God's Decree in Relation to the Eternal Destinies of His Rational Creatures

3.3 By the decree of God, for the manifestation of His glory, some men and angels[1] are predestinated unto everlasting life, and others foreordained to everlasting death.[2]

[1] *1 Tim 5:21; Mt 25:41;* [2] *Rom 9:22–23; Eph 1:5–6; Prov 16:4.*

3.4 These angels and men, thus predestinated, and foreordained, are particularly and unchangeably designed; and their number is so certain and definite, that it cannot be either increased or diminished.[1]

[1] *2 Tim 2:19; Jn 13:18.*

The first two paragraphs of this chapter speak about the sovereign decree of God in general. The current two paragraphs apply the doctrine to God's rational creatures, —namely men and angels, —for which God has ordained to have everlasting existence. We note (1) that there are only two destinies for such creatures, even everlasting life or everlasting death; (2) that the numbers destined for either destiny are absolutely fixed; and (3) that the destiny for each creature is determined individually and unchangeably.

We note also the careful wordings of the divines: those who are to be granted everlasting life are said to be "*predestinated* unto everlasting life." On the other hand, those who are to be condemned to everlasting death are said to be "*foreordained* to everlasting death."

The next three paragraphs will explain the difference between the two terms, namely that for the elect, some extraordinary and supernatural acts are provided for their salvation; while the rest are passed by. The choice of language suggests an infralapsarian leaning, although William Twisse, the first president of the Westminster Assembly was a supralapsarian. Supralapsarianism is, however, not condemned by the assembly.

The distinction between infralapsarianism and supralapsarianism has to do with the logical order or arrangement of the aspects in God's eternal decree, and not the timing of individual decrees as some suppose. Or to put it more bluntly, it is a gross error to say that infralapsarians believe God decreed election after the Fall took place. No, no; all Calvinists believe that the decree (or decrees if we look at the constituent parts separately, cf. *WSC* 7 & 8) was made before the foundation of the world (Eph 1:4). It is one decree which many aspects logically inter-related to one another. The question is: Which aspect of the decree comes first, and which follows? Or in particular, does the decree of election logically precedes or follows the decree pertaining to the Fall? We are of course speaking of decrees here in reference to the aspects of the one decree. Is the will of God to have an elect people to enjoy and glorify Him the primary focus of the decree; or is the will of God to create the world the primary focus of the decree? If it is the former, then, the decree of election must logically precede the decree pertaining to the Fall; if the latter, then the decree of election must logically follow the decree pertaining to the Fall.

Very briefly, *Infralapsarianism* is an order of the decrees, in which the arrangement reflects the order in which the decrees work out in history, and so it may be said to be developed upon a historical principle. Since the providential out-working of the decree of salvation is in the order creation, then fall, then redemption, it is deemed that the decree to redeem the elect must follow the decree that all men should fall into sin. So the order may be presented as follows:

1. The decree to create the world and (all) men

2. The decree that (all) men would fall

3. The election of some fallen men to salvation in Christ (and the reprobation of the others)

4. The decree to redeem the elect by the cross work of Christ

5. The decree to apply Christ's redemptive benefits to the elect.[7]

This scheme is held by most Calvinists today and is implicitly adopted by the *Canons of Dort*, and arguably by the *Westminster Confession of Faith*. In this scheme, the reprobates are viewed as being passed-by and condemned because of their sin, though most who hold to this scheme are careful not to portray the decree to allow the Fall as bare permission, which is Arminianism.

It is suggested that one of the reasons, many Calvinists hold to this view is that over against the commonly held *supralapsarian* view, it presents God as gracious and tender towards the elect sinner while holy and just toward the reprobate sinner. The common *supralapsarian* view, it is noted, suggests that in the decree of election and reprobation, God is contemplating man not as sinners but as unfallen persons. It is felt that such a scheme makes God appear to be arbitrary and even to be the author of sin. And moreover, when the apostle Paul while discussing election and reprobation appeal God's word to Moses "I will have mercy on whom I will have mercy" (Rom 9:15), he seems to be suggesting that God is contemplating man as fallen when He elected some to life.

---

[7] Reymond, *op cit.*, 480. Take note that the Amyraldians transpose no. 3 and 4, while asserting that the decree to redeem is for all men and not just for the elect.

The problem with this scheme, however, is that it is no better than the Amyraldian scheme in explaining why each step should lead to the next; and neither does it do justice to a number of passages in Scripture such as Romans 9:19-24 which teaches us that God did indeed sovereignly (or if you like, 'arbitrarily'), make of the same lump of clay some vessels of honour and some vessels of dishonour.[8]

The *Supralapsarian View*, on the other hand, seeks to draw out an order of the decrees based on God's ultimate goal for all history or providence; and so it may be said to be developed upon a *Teleological* (from *telos*: end or goal) principle. To illustrate how this principle works, we may think the planning involved in the mind of, say, a young engineer who has a singular aspiration to serve as a pastor. He has no alternative goal. His singular goal is to enter the pastoral ministry! How does he go about planning to achieve his goal? He must plan by working backward! In order that he might enter the ministry, he must be called. In order that he might be called, he must first be trained for the ministry. In order that he might be trained, he must enroll in a seminary. In order that he might enroll in a seminary, he must first quit his job, etc. The man will, no doubt, execute his plan in reverse order, but he must develop his plan from the goal backwards in order to arrive at the various intermediate steps that he must take.

What is the ultimate goal of God in history or providence (and so the ultimate goal for His decrees)? We may infer from several passages in Scripture that it is that there may be a body of saints (the church) to enjoy and glorify Him fully forever (see for example, Eph 1:4, 3:10). The question of how this goal may be achieved through subordinate steps has lead theologians such as Reymond, Hoeksema, Clark, and possibly Zanchius to come up with a consistent *supralapsarian* order of decree as follows:

1. The election of some sinful men to salvation in Christ (and the reprobation of the rest of sinful man in order to make known the riches of God's gracious mercy to the elect)

---

[8] See *ibid.*, p. 481-8 for further objections.

2. The decree to apply Christ's redemptive benefits to the elect sinners

3. The decree to redeem the elect sinners by the cross work of Christ

4. The decree that men should fall

5. The decree to create the world and men.[9]

Take note that in this scheme (unlike the more commonly held *supralapsarian* scheme), God is represented as discriminating among men viewed as sinners rather than simply as men. This answers the objection of *infralapsarians* based on Roman 9:15, mentioned above; and does not contradict Romans 9:21, for the lump of clay is clearly representing sinners, rather than neutral humanity, else why are the elect spoken of as vessels of *mercy* (Rom 9:23). Or to put it in another way, the ultimate goal of God for providence that is revealed in Scripture is not just to have saints enjoying and glorifying him, but to have saints who are sinners redeemed in Christ enjoying and glorifying Him forever! For such sinners to fully appreciate the extent of God's mercy, it is necessary that there should also be the existence of the reprobate who would experience God's justice and wrath (cf. Rom 9:22).

Whichever position we take, we must be careful not to deny the doctrine of reprobation as is fashionable for some so-called Calvinist to do. Calvinism is simply 'Paulism' systematised. Paul teaches us that God moulded one lump of clay into a vessel of honour while, while another He moulds into a vessel of dishonour (Rom 9:21). He did not say that God mould some lumps of clay into vessels of honour, but passed by the rest of the lumps and left them to take their own shape!

Read Berkhof's *Systematic Theology*, pages 118–125; or even better Robert Reymond's *A New Systematic Theology of the Christian Faith*, pages 475-502 for an excellent treatment of the subject. Understanding the difference between the two positions helps us to think clearly on the decree of God.

---

[9] See *ibid.*, p. 489.

God's Decree with Reference to His Elect

3.5 Those of mankind that are predestinated unto life, God, before the foundation of the world was laid, according to His eternal and immutable purpose, and the secret counsel and good pleasure of His will, hath chosen, in Christ, unto everlasting glory,[1] out of His mere free grace and love, without any foresight of faith or good works, or perseverance in either of them, or any other thing in the creature, as conditions, or causes moving Him thereunto;[2] and all to the praise of His glorious grace.[3]

[1]*Eph 1:4, 9, 11; Rom 8:30; 2 Tim 1:9; 1 Th 5:9;* [2]*Rom 9:11, 13, 16; Eph 1:4, 9;* [3]*Eph 1:6, 12.*

Arminians believe that God chose the elect on account of His foreknowledge that they would believe in Christ, do good works and persevere in their faith. In other words, election, as far as the Arminian is concerned, is to be understood retrospectively. Our *Confession* teaches otherwise. The elect are chosen "*according to His eternal and immutable purpose, and the secret counsel and good pleasure of His will*" and "*out of His mere free grace and love.*" This doctrine is expressly taught in Scripture:

a. Election is conditioned on the good pleasure of God's will:

    "Having predestinated us unto the adoption of children by Jesus Christ to himself, according to the good pleasure of his will … In whom also we have obtained an inheritance, being predestinated according to the purpose of him who worketh all things after the counsel of his own will" (Eph 1:5, 11 cf. Mt 11:25–26; Jn 15:16, 19).

b. If election is based on foreknowledge of good works, then it is no more gracious:

    "… there is a remnant according to the election of grace. And if by grace, then is it no more of works: otherwise grace is no more grace. …" (Rom 11:5–6). "[God] hath saved us, and called us with an holy calling, not according to our works, but according to his own purpose and grace, which was given us in Christ Jesus before the world began" (2 Tim 1:9).

c. Faith and Repentance are the fruits of election and so cannot be conditions:

"For we are his workmanship, created in Christ Jesus unto good works, which God hath before ordained that we should walk in them" (Eph 2:10; cf. Eph 1:4). "All that the Father giveth me shall come to me; and him that cometh to me I will in no wise cast out" (Jn 6:37). "But ye believe not, because ye are not of my sheep, as I said unto you" (Jn 10:26). "… and as many as were ordained to eternal life believed" (Acts 13:48b).

d. Regeneration is wholly a work of God which must precede faith since man is by nature dead in trespasses and sin:

"For by grace are ye saved through faith; and that not of yourselves: it is the gift of God" (Eph 2:8). "Except a man be born again, he cannot see the kingdom of God" (Jn 3:3). Since regeneration is not conditioned on faith and repentance, it must be conditioned on God's decree.

e. God claims to have the sovereign prerogative to elect whom He will:

"As it is written, Jacob have I loved, but Esau have I hated. … So then it is not of him that willeth, nor of him that runneth, but of God that sheweth mercy. … Hath not the potter power over the clay, of the same lump to make one vessel unto honour, and another unto dishonour? " (Rom 9:13, 16, 21).

3.6 As God hath appointed the elect unto glory, so hath He, by the eternal and most free purpose of His will, foreordained all the means thereunto.[1] Wherefore, they who are elected, being fallen in Adam, are redeemed by Christ;[2] are effectually called unto faith in Christ by His Spirit working in due season; are justified, adopted, sanctified,[3] and kept by His power, through faith, unto salvation.[4] Neither are any other redeemed by Christ, effectually called, justified, adopted, sanctified, and saved, but the elect only.[5]

[1]1 Pet 1:2; Eph 1:4–5; 2:10; 2 Th 2:13; [2]1 Th 5:9–10; Tit 2:14; [3]Rom 8:30; Eph 1:5; 2 Th 2:13; [4]1 Pet 1:5; [5]Jn 17:9; Rom 8:28–39; Jn 6:64–65; 10:26; 8:47; 1 Jn 2:19.

Two important truths are taught in this paragraph:

a. God's design of redemption is particular: for the elect only. This is stated twice: (1) Positively, that *"God hath appointed the elect unto glory"* and that *"they who are elected... are redeemed by Christ."* And (2) negatively, that *"[none] other [are] redeemed by Christ... but the elect only."* This truth is clearly taught in Scripture: "As the Father knoweth me, even so know I the Father: and I lay down my life for the sheep" (Jn 10:15). It is also the only logical view.

    A.A. Hodge is certainly right when he says: "A purpose to save all and a purpose to save only some could not co-exist in the divine mind."[10] If God willed to save all, all will be saved. Otherwise, salvation becomes contingent upon man's response, —which our Confession repudiates; or God's will be no more sovereign, — which is blasphemous. Christ's atonement was therefore definite and particular in design.

b. As God has chosen the elect and appointed them to glory, He has also predestined the means by which the elect will be brought into His kingdom and to progress unto glory.

• Since man is totally dead in trespasses and sin, the only way that the elect may be saved is to be regenerated and *"effectually called unto faith in Christ by His Spirit working in due season."*

• But God's work of salvation does not end there. The Scripture teaches that the elect "are kept by the power of God through faith unto salvation ready to be revealed in the last time" (1 Pet 1:5; cf. Phil 1:6, 2:13). The salvation of the elect is from beginning to eternity a work of the Lord: "... whom he did predestinate, them he also called: and whom he called, them he also justified: and whom he justified, them he also glorified" (Rom 8:30).

• Our Confession draws on other passages (such as 1 Peter 1:2; Ephesians 1:4-5; 2:10) as well to explain that those who are

---

[10] AA Hodge, *The Confession of Faith* (Edinburgh: The Banner of Truth Trust, reprinted 1922 [1869]), 74.

effectually called unto faith in Christ *"are justified, adopted, sanctified, and kept by His power through faith unto salvation."* Salvation, in other words, is not seen in the Confession merely as an event that happens at a point, but as being a process that culminates with the glorification of the elect. This is an important point to note when studying the *Westminster Confession* and *Catechisms*.

God's Decree with Reference to the Reprobate

3.7   The rest of mankind, God was pleased, according to the unsearchable counsel of His own will, whereby He extendeth or withholdeth mercy as He pleaseth, for the glory of His sovereign power over His creatures, to pass by, and to ordain them to dishonour and wrath for their sin, to the praise of His glorious justice.[1]

[1]Mt 11:25–26; Rom 9:17–18, 21–22; 2 Tim 2:19–20; Jude 4; 1 Pet 2:8.

There are some professedly Calvinistic theologians who would deny that there is such a thing as reprobation though they affirm election.

- But both election and reprobation are taught in the Scripture: "Hath not the potter power over the clay, of the same lump to make one vessel unto honour, and another unto dishonour? What if God, willing to shew his wrath, and to make his power known, endured with much longsuffering the vessels of wrath fitted to destruction" (Rom 9:21–22; cf. 2 Tim 2:19–20; Jude 4; 1 Pet 2:8).

- Moreover the one thing unavoidably follows the other. If God has only chosen some, —not all, —to life, then it necessarily follows that He has chosen not to show grace to the rest.

- Furthermore, just as He has chosen to show the elect mercy— though they also deserve damnation, —He has chosen to treat the reprobate according to the principles of strict justice.

Our Confession is very carefully worded so that we may understand that the damnation of the reprobate is not unjust. In fact, they are ordained to dishonour and wrath *for their sin*. This is consistent with Paul's answer to the query, "Is there unrighteousness [or unfairness] with God?" (Rom 9:14): "For he saith to Moses, I will have mercy on whom I will have mercy, and I will have compassion on whom I will have compassion" (Rom 9:15). Thus, in *WCF* 3.5, we are told that the salvation of the elect is *"to the praise of His glorious grace"*; while here we are taught the damnation of the reprobate is *"to the praise of His glorious justice"* (*WCF* 3.7).

Election and Reprobation may be compared in the following table:

	Election	Reprobation
When?	Eternity 'Past'	Eternity 'Past'
Remote/Ultimate Cause	God & His secret counsel	God & His secret counsel
Proximate Cause	God & His grace	Man & his sin
Providential Execution	Predestination to Life	Condemnation to Death
How does it glorify God?	It magnifies His Grace	It magnifies His Justice

Counsel and Caveat Regarding this Doctrine

3.8   The doctrine of this high mystery of predestination is to be handled with special prudence and care,[1] that men, attending the will of God revealed in His Word, and yielding obedience thereunto, may, from the certainty of their effectual vocation, be assured of their eternal election.[2] So shall this doctrine afford matter of praise, reverence, and admiration of God,[3] and of humility, diligence, and abundant consolation, to all that sincerely obey the Gospel.[4]

[1]*Rom 9:20; 11:33; Dt 29:29;* [2]*2 Pet 1:10;* [3]*Eph 1:6; Rom 11:33;* [4]*Rom 11:5–6, 20; 2 Pet 1:10; Rom 8:33; Lk 10:20.*

Robert Shaw summarizes this beautifully:

"The doctrine of predestination is, indeed, a high mystery—one of the deep things of God, which our feeble intellects cannot fully comprehend. In our inquiries about it, we ought to repress a vain curiosity, and not attempt to be wise above what is written. But, since the doctrine is revealed by God in His Word, it is a proper subject for sober investigation, and ought to be published from the pulpit and from the press."[11]

Calvin, who is often accused of overstretching the doctrine of God's decree, is actually extremely cautious. He warns:

"... we should not investigate what the Lord has left in secret, [but] we should not neglect what He has brought into the open, so that we may not be convicted of excessive curiosity on the one hand, or of excessive ingratitude on the other."[12]

Note how our Confession carefully distinguishes between the revealed will and secret will of God. Predestination is a high mystery: it represents the secret will of God and is not designed to govern our lives but to "afford matter of praise, reverence, and admiration of God, and of humility, diligence, and abundant consolation, to all who sincerely obey the Gospel." The principles to govern our lives is the Gospel and "the will of God revealed in His Word." Thus, in the preaching of the Gospel, the unsaved is to be addressed not as elect or reprobate but as sinners ready to perish. All without distinction must be commanded to repent and believe in the Lord Jesus Christ. It is an obligation that rests equally on all, and all are to be encouraged with the same words of our Lord: "All that the Father giveth me shall come to me; and him that cometh to me I will in no wise cast out" (Jn 6:37).

It is, nevertheless, the duty and privilege of the believer to make the fact of His eternal calling and election sure (2 Pet 1:10) by working out his salvation with fear and trembling (Phil 2:12).

---

[11] Robert Shaw, *An Exposition of the Westminster Confession of Faith* (Ross-shire: Christian Focus Publications, 1992 [1845]), 58-9.

[12] *ICR* 2.21.4.

WCF 04: OF CREATION

We saw in the previous chapter what are the decree(s) of God. "The decrees of God," in brief, are "His eternal purpose, according to the counsel of His will, whereby, for his own glory, He hath fore-ordained whatsoever comes to pass" (*WSC* 7). But how does God execute his decrees? Simply stated in the words of our catechism, "God executeth His decrees in the works of creation and providence" (*WSC* 8).

All of God's decree pertains to the created world, both physical and spiritual, and therefore the first thing that God did to execute His decrees was to create the world. Now, this seems straightforward enough so that it would appear that no one at the time of the Assembly disputed the doctrine that is contained in this chapter. This is, unfortunately, no longer so. Many believers including those who would claim to subscribe to the doctrine of our Confession would actually dispute what we are taught in the very first paragraph of this chapter. But these disagreements have arisen, it appears, not so much through a study of the Scripture, but from influence of so-called science of evolution and geological age of the earth. From a purely biblical- exegetical basis our fathers in the faith would have uniformly held that the earth was created in six literal days and is less than 10,000 years old.

Today, there are various views. The old view is now known as "Young Earth Creationism." Those who hold to this view do not deny micro-evolution (which explains for example, the different species of finches that Charles Darwin observed), but would deny macro-evolution that man evolved from apes and whales from wolves, etc.

But some feel that the evidence for the geologic age of the earth is indisputable, and therefore they proposed various theories that are consistent with an old (4.5 billion years old) earth. These theories may be known as Old Earth Creationism. There are three main types: (1) Gap Creationism holds that there is a gap between Genesis 1:1 (which they claim is about the original creation which failed), and Genesis 1:2 (which begins to describe the creation of the present world). It does not believe in macro-evolution. (2) Day-Age Creationism holds that the days in Genesis 1 should be interpreted as ages which may last millions of years. These usually would usually reject macro-evolution but hold to micro-evolution as occurring over millions of years. (3) Progressive Creationism rejects macro-evolution to explain the origin of the species but replace it with an idea that God intervenes at specific moments in history to effect the creation of new species, such as man from apes. These hold that Genesis 1 is to be interpreted symbolically, poetically, metaphorically or literarily (e.g. Framework Hypothesis).

Then there are others hold to Theistic Evolution of various sorts. They believe that God is in control over creation, but that he created the world through the process of evolution so that for all intents and purposes the claims of atheistic scientists are correct except that they (the atheistic scientists) deny the place of God in the process.

It should be noted that the only view that is consistent with our Confession of Faith is Young Earth Creationism. All other views require not only a reading of anti-biblical theories into Scripture, but a re-interpretation of our Confession in ways which are clearly contrary to the intent of the Assembly.

On the Creation of the World

4.1 It pleased God the Father, Son, and Holy Ghost,[1] for the manifestation of the glory of His eternal power, wisdom, and goodness,[2] in the beginning, to create, or make of nothing, the world, and all things therein whether visible or invisible, in the space of six days, and all very good.[3]

[1] Heb 1:2; Jn 1:2–3; Gen 1:2; Job 26:13; 33:4; [2] Rom 1:20; Jer 10:12; Ps 104:24; 33:5–6; [3] Gen 1; Heb 11:3; Col 1:16; Acts 17:24.

- *Participants of Creation*: The Triune God, all three Persons of the Godhead. The Scripture attributes creation to:

  (1) God absolutely, without distinction of person: "In the beginning God created the heaven and the earth" (Gen 1:1).

  (2) The Father: "There is but one God, the Father, of whom are all things" (1 Cor 8:6).

(3) The Father through the Son: "[God] hath in these last days spoken unto us by his Son, whom he hath appointed heir of all things, by whom also he made the worlds" (Heb 1:2).

(4) The Son: "All things were made by him; and without him was not any thing made that was made" (Jn 1:3).

(5) The Father through the Holy Spirit: "Thou sendest forth thy spirit, they are created: and thou renewest the face of the earth" (Ps 104:30).

(6) The Holy Spirit: "And the earth was without form, and void; and darkness was upon the face of the deep. And the Spirit of God moved upon the face of the waters" (Gen 1:2); "By his spirit he hath garnished the heavens" (Job 26:13a).

- *Purpose of Creation*: "*for the manifestation of the glory of His eternal power, wisdom, and goodness.*" "For the invisible things of him from the creation of the world are clearly seen, being understood by the things that are made, even *his eternal power* and Godhead; so that they are without excuse" (Rom 1:20); "He hath made the earth *by his power*, he hath established the world *by his wisdom*, and hath stretched out the heavens *by his discretion*" (Jer 10:12); "He loveth righteousness and judgment: *the earth is full of the goodness of the LORD. By the word of the LORD were the heavens made; and all the host of them by the breath of his mouth*" (Ps 33:5–6 cf. Ps 104:24). The chief end of creation, as with the chief end of man, is therefore to glorify God (cf. *WSC* 1, *WLC* 1, Col 1:16; Prov 16:4).

- *Duration of Creation*: Six Days: "And God saw every thing that he had made, and, behold, it was very good. And the evening and the morning were the sixth day. … And on the seventh day God ended his work which he had made; and he rested on the seventh day from all his work which he had made" (Gen 1:31; 2:2).

- *Objects of Creation*: All things—visible and invisible. "For by him were all things created, that are in heaven, and that are in earth, visible and invisible …" (Col 1:16a; cf. Acts 17:24). The angelic host was probably created on the first day (Gen 1:1) since they were present when God laid the foundations of the world: "Where wast thou when I laid the foundations of the earth? ...When the morning stars sang together, and all the sons of God shouted for joy?"(Job 38:4, 7).

- *Source or Material for Creation*: Nothing (*Ex nihilo*). "Through faith we understand that the worlds were framed by the word of God, so that things which are seen were not made of things which do appear" (Heb 11:3). That there was nothing before God began to create is attested by: (1) Christ's reference to a time when the world was absolutely non-existent: "And now, O Father, glorify thou me with thine own self with the glory which I had with thee before the world was" (Jn 17:5); (2) The Hebrew verb used in Genesis 1:1 is best translated "create out of nothing"; and (3) If anything were not created by God, they must be pre-existent and must exist in and of themselves, which would contradict Romans 11:36, "For of him, and through him, and to him, are all things: to whom be glory for ever. Amen."

  Note the distinction between *creatio prima*—the first creation of the elementary substance of things and *creatio secunda*—combining of elements in the formation of things. We are referring to the former when we say that God created *ex nihilo*.

- *Condition of universe at Creation*: "very good" (Gen 1:31). This does not mean absolute perfection, for God alone is absolutely perfect. But Adam had original righteousness. Sin had not entered into the world; neither had diseases, deformity, disability, disasters, accidents, etc which came about due to sin.

On Creation of Man

4.2 After God had made all other creatures, He created man, male and female,[1] with reasonable and immortal souls,[2] endued with knowledge, righteousness, and true holiness, after His own image,[3] having the law of God written in their hearts,[4] and power to fulfill it;[5] and yet under a possibility of transgressing, being left to the liberty of their own will, which was subject unto change.[6] Beside this law written in their hearts, they received a command not to eat of the tree of the knowledge of good and evil;[7] *which while they kept, they were happy in their communion with God, and had dominion over the creatures.*[8]

[1] Gen 1:27; [2] Gen 2:7; Eccl 12:7; Lk 23:43; Mt 10:28; [3] Gen 1:26; Col 3:10; Eph 4:24; [4] Rom 2:14–15; [5] Eccl 7:29; [6] Gen 3:6; Eccl 7:29; [7] Gen 2:17; 3:8–11, 23; [8] Gen 1:26, 28.

- Man was created male and female (Gen 1:27). Adam was formed out "of the dust of the ground" (Gen 2:7), Eve was crafted out of a rib from Adam (Gen 2:22).

- Man was also created with a body and a soul. Some argue that the Scripture distinguishes between the soul (Heb: *nephesh*; Grk: *psuchê*) and spirit (Heb: *ruach*; Grk: *pneuma*) and that trichotomy is clearly taught in Hebrews 4:12 and 1 Thessalonians 5:23. These arguments are, however, invalid. Although the Scripture does speak of the soul as well as the spirit of man, the two terms are often used interchangeably in Scripture, for example Matthew 6:25; 10:28 speak of man as comprising of body and soul, while Ecclesiastes 12:7 and 1 Corinthians 5:3, 5 speak of man as comprising of body and spirit. Moreover, death is sometimes described as giving up the soul (e.g., Gen 35:18; Acts 15:26) and sometimes as giving up the spirit (e.g., Ps 31:5; Acts 7:59); and the immaterial essence of the dead is sometimes describe as the soul (e.g., Rev 20:4) and sometimes as the spirit (e.g., Heb 12:23). Furthermore, Hebrews 4:12 does not imply any more that soul and spirit are distinguishable entities than that thoughts and intents are distinguishable; also, if 1 Thessalonians 5:23 teaches trichotomy, then Luke 10:27 must teach quadratomy. Paul is emphasising the whole person rather than differentiating his parts. We conclude, therefore, that the Reformed position that man is dichotomic (2-part) is correct. 'Soul' and 'spirit' are synonymous.

- The *Imago Dei*. Man was created after God's own image:
  i. In the **comprehensive** (or wider) sense this refers to man's natural image in that he is made a spiritual being with rationality, morality or conscience (*vide infra*), spirituality, immortality and creativity. These things make us like God and distinguish us from animals. Man today still posses this image

of God. Though this image is defaced, it was not completely erased by the Fall. We have not lost immortality, morality, rationality, spirituality or creativity. Thus, our having the *imago dei* is not spoken of in the past tense in Scripture (cf. 1 Cor 15:49; Jas 3:9). It is on account of this aspect of the image of God that man is given, and continue to have, dominion over the lower creation: "And God said, Let us make man in our image, after our likeness: and let them have dominion over the fish of the sea, and over the fowl of the air, and over the cattle, and over all the earth, and over every creeping thing that creepeth upon the earth" (Gen 1:26; cf. Gen 8:15–9:7; Ps 8:4–9). It is also on this account that the death penalty is instituted for murder: "Whoso sheddeth man's blood, by man shall his blood be shed: for in the image of God made he man" (Gen 9:6).

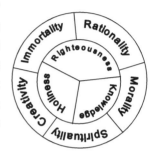

ii. In the **restricted** (or narrower) sense, this refers to the spiritual qualities that God has created man with, namely, true knowledge, righteousness, and holiness. Man was created with true knowledge. Unlike animals, he was created to know God and to know what is right and what is wrong according to God's standard. Man was also created with original righteousness. Unlike animals, he was created with an innate inclination to do right. Man was also created with true holiness. Thus, unlike animals, man was holy or separated unto God. Animals will merely live their lives according to their nature. Man was created in such a way that he desires to serve and glorify God. He feels his life to be meaningless and empty unless he is serving God. At least, that was until the Fall.

With the Fall, this image was lost because of sin.[13] But thank God it was restored by Christ: "And [ye] have put on the new

---

[13] The apostle Paul says: "There is none righteous, no, not one. There is none that understandeth, there is none that seeketh after God" (Rom 3:10-11). Understanding is knowledge applied. True knowledge must include understanding. If this is the case than, fallen man, having no understanding, cannot have any degree of true knowledge—even though the

man, which is renewed in knowledge after the image of him that created him" (Col 3:10); "And that ye put on the new man, which after God is created in righteousness and true holiness" (Eph 4:24). Regenerate man will, however, only possess the original perfection of knowledge, righteousness and holiness when his sanctification is complete.

- The soul of man is immortal or everlasting. "And the LORD God formed man of the dust of the ground, and breathed into his nostrils the breath of life; and man became a living soul" (Gen 2:7); "Then shall the dust return to the earth as it was: and the spirit shall return unto God who gave it" (Ecc 12:7; cf. Lk 23:43). Since man is not an independent being, his existence must be sustained by God forever for him to be immortal.

- Man is not only distinguished from animals by his rationality, but also by his morality, or his having a conscience. This is so because the law of God is written in his heart: "For when the Gentiles, which have not the law, do by nature the things contained in the law, these, having not the law, are a law unto themselves: Which shew the work of the law written in their hearts, their conscience also bearing witness, and their thoughts the mean while accusing or else excusing one another" (Rom 2:14–15). In that man was made upright (Ecc 7:29a), he also had the power to fulfil the Law written in his heart. And since he was created a free agent, and left to the liberty of his will which was subject to change or to influence by external causes, he was also under a possibility of transgressing the Law.

Before the Fall, man was *posse peccare, posse non peccare* (able to sin, able not to sin); after the Fall, unregenerate man is *non posse non peccare* (unable not to sin), regenerate man is *posse non peccare* (able not to sin) and glorified man is *non posse peccare*

---

works of the law is written in his heart. In other words, as long as we understand that true knowledge is inseparable from right understanding, we could say that fallen man has lost original knowledge completely. Likewise, 'true holiness' (Eph 4:24) must include seeking after God. Therefore, since there is none that seek after God, and seeking after Him is a *sine qua non* of true holiness, we may say that despite the religious sense that fallen man has, it would be more accurate biblically to say that man has lost original holiness altogether.

(unable to sin). (Note: subject of Original Righteousness will be dealt with in chapter 6, while Freewill will be dealt with in chapter 9).

- Adam and Eve were, furthermore, given a positive commandment "not to eat of the tree of the knowledge of good and evil." This command, —which involves something indifferent in itself, —is in a sense a summary or representative of the Moral Law of God inscribed in their heart. Our Confession does not here say that Adam and Eve would have been *rewarded* with eternal life as A.A. Hodge:

    In this state He subjects them to a moral test for a time. If they stand the test, the reward is that their moral characters are confirmed and rendered infallible, and they are introduced into an inalienable blessedness forever. If they fail, they are judicially excluded from God's favour and communion forever, and hence morally and eternally dead.[14]

The Confession is carefully worded, rather, that: "*while they kept [the commandment not to eat of the forbidden fruit], they were happy in their communion with God, and had dominion over the creatures.*" WSC 12 is similarly carefully worded perhaps to avoid the notion of reward for works or obedience: "When God had created man, He entered into a Covenant of Life with him, upon condition of perfect obedience; forbidding him to eat of the tree of the knowledge of good and evil, upon the pain of death" (cf. WLC 20).

However, the Confession does not deny Hodge's view, which is an old view dating to the time of the Reformation.[15] In fact, by the time we come to chapter 7 and deal with the subject of God's covenant with man, we will see that what Hodge has to say is, in fact, consistent with the doctrine of the covenant taught in our Standards, when viewed as a whole.

---

[14] Hodge, *Confession,* 105-6.

[15] See Francis Turretin, *Institute of Elenctic Theology,* 1.578 (Topic 9, Q. 3, para 17).

WCF 05: OF PROVIDENCE

The word 'providence' comes from the Latin *providentia* which means "foresight or forethought." But it is not only about God's foreknowledge as the etymology of the term may suggest. Rather, it speaks of God seeing to all things planned before hand, or of God bringing to pass all that He has decreed would happen in Creation. That is to say, the work of creation answers to God's eternal decree to bring into existence (out of nothing) all things in this universe. Providence, on the other hand, answers to God's eternal decree by which He did "unchangeably foreordained whatsoever comes to pass in time" (*WLC* 12).

The Holy Scripture teaches us about God sovereign providence from various angles.

- *Firstly*, it affirms that all things in this universe continue to exist (or have being) because they are upheld by God in Christ, "by the word of His power" (Heb 1:3).

- *Secondly*, it affirms that all things live and move by God's power: "For in him [i.e. God] we live, and move, and have our being" (Acts 17:28a).

- *Thirdly*, it declares that "all things work together for good to them that love God, to them who are the called according to his purpose" (Rom 8:28). Obviously for *all* things to work for the good of those who love God, God must be in sovereign control over all things that happen in this world, no matter how insignificant they may appear in our sight.

- *Fourthly*, God's work of providence at the micro level is illustrated in numerous ways. For example, we are taught that not a sparrow will fall to the ground without the heavenly Father's 'permission' (Mt 10:29); and, in fact, not one of our hairs can grow or drop without His bringing it to pass, for even our hair are all numbered (Mt 10:30). Nothing happens by chance. Even such as appears to be random in our perception are purposefully brought about by God's providence, for as Solomon declares: "The lot is cast into the lap; but the whole disposing thereof is of the LORD" (Prov 16:33).

- *Fifthly* and finally, the Scripture also illustrate God's providence at a macro level. For example, we are told that the patriarch Joseph was delivered into Egypt through the wicked acts of his brothers, in order that he might be instrumental in saving alive the fledging church under-age during a great famine that God was going to bring about (Gen 45:7). Indeed, even the crucifixion of the Lord Jesus Christ was by God's providence, for we are told that He was "delivered by the determinate counsel and foreknowledge of God" (Acts 2:23).

Our present chapter builds on these biblical data, to provide a systematic and theological study of the doctrine of providence.

On God's Providence Over the World

5.1 God, the great Creator of all things, doth uphold,[1] direct, dispose, and govern all creatures, actions, and things,[2] from the greatest even to the least,[3] by His most wise and holy providence,[4] according to His infallible foreknowledge,[5] and the free and immutable counsel of His own will,[6] to the praise of the glory of His wisdom, power, justice, goodness, and mercy.[7]

[1]Heb 1:3; [2]Dan 4:34–35; Ps 135:6; Acts 17:25–26, 28; Job 38; 39; 40; 41; [3]Mt 10:29–31; [4]Prov 15:3; Ps 104:24; 145:17; [5]Acts 15:18; Ps 94:8–11; [6]Eph 1:11; Ps 33:10–11; [7]Isa 63:14; Eph 3:10; Rom 9:17; Gen 45:7; Ps 145:7.

- Having created all the substance of the universe and forming the first things—organic and inorganic, God continues to uphold and sustain what He has made. There are four common theories on how this is done:

  (1) *Deism*: God has created the world, set its first series of cause and effect in motion, and then left it to run on itself. That this is false is obvious: "Behold, he that keepeth Israel shall neither slumber nor sleep" (Ps 121:4).

  (2) *Pantheism*: Every phenomena in the universe is a manifestation of the mode of existence of the one eternal substance: God. This is

also false, for the Scripture clearly distinguishes God from His creation.

(3) *Creatio Continua*: God's power is exerted in continually creating every individual thing again and again every fraction of duration. This has been held by some eminent theologians such as Jonathan Edwards and John Gerstner. But the problem with such a view is that God becomes the immediate cause of all things, including all evil passion, wicked thoughts and acts. Also the freedom and consciousness of free agencies are no longer real.

(4) *Creator and Governor View*: God has given all that He created, —material and spiritual, —real and permanent existence as entities exterior to Himself. These truly possess all the properties and attributes that God has severally endued them with, so that they exert real and not merely apparent second causes. Yet, as creatures, they are not self-existent. The ground of their continued existence is in God and not in them: "In Him we … have our being…" (Acts 17:28).

- Moreover, it is God who directs all the actions of all His creatures according to their respective nature and modes of actions: "…by him all things consist" (Col 1:17); "[Christ is] upholding all things by the word of his power" (Heb 1:3). "In Him we live, and move, and have our being…" (Acts 17:28).

- The Scripture also declares that God has absolute providential control over:

(1) *The natural world*: "Whatsoever the LORD pleased, that did he in heaven, and in earth, in the seas, and all deep places. He causeth the vapours to ascend from the ends of the earth; he maketh lightnings for the rain; he bringeth the wind out of his treasuries" (Ps 135:6–7; cf. Job 37:6–13; Ps 104:14; Ps 147:15–18). Also, "Are not two sparrows sold for a farthing? and one of them shall not fall on the ground without your Father" (Mt 10:29).

(2) *Events that appear fortuitous*: "The lot is cast into the lap; but the whole disposing thereof is of the LORD" (Prov 16:33).

(3) *The circumstances and affairs of men*: "And he changeth the times and the seasons: he removeth kings, and setteth up kings: he giveth wisdom unto the wise, and knowledge to them that know understanding" (Dan 2:21; cf. Isa 10:12–15). "The LORD killeth, and maketh alive: he bringeth down to the grave, and bringeth up. The LORD maketh poor, and maketh rich: he bringeth low, and lifteth up. He raiseth up the poor out of the dust, and lifteth up the beggar from the dunghill, to set them among princes, and to make them inherit the throne of glory: for the pillars of the earth are the LORD's, and he hath set the world upon them" (1 Sam 2:6–8; cf. Jas 4:13–15).

(4) *All the actions of men, whether good or evil*: "There are many devices in a man's heart; nevertheless the counsel of the LORD, that shall stand" (Prov 19:21; cf. Ex 12:36; Ps 33:14–15; Prov 21:1; Phil 2:13). "Surely the wrath of man shall praise thee: the remainder of wrath shalt thou restrain" (Ps 76:10; cf. Acts 4:27–28).

- This providential control is in all respect the consistent execution of God's eternal, immutable, and sovereign purpose, which is ultimately to manifest God's own glory: "In whom also we have obtained an inheritance, being predestinated according to the purpose of him who worketh all things after the counsel of his own will" (Eph 1:11); "Known unto God are all his works from the beginning of the world" (Acts 15:18). "For the scripture saith unto Pharaoh, Even for this same purpose have I raised thee up, that I might shew my power in thee, and that my name might be declared throughout all the earth" (Rom 9:17). "For of him, and through him, and to him, are all things: to whom be glory for ever. Amen" (Rom 11:36).

On Second Causes in Providence

5.2   Although, in relation to the foreknowledge and decree of God, the first Cause, all things come to pass immutably and infallibly;[1] yet, by the same providence, He ordereth them to fall out according to the nature of second causes, either necessarily, freely, or contingently.[2]

[1]Acts 2:23; [2]Gen 8:22; Jer 31:35; Ex 21:13; Dt 19:5; 1 Kgs 22:28, 34; Isa 10:6–7.

- God as the First Cause has immutably decreed all things that will come to pass, and all will indeed come to pass: "The counsel of the LORD standeth for ever, the thoughts of his heart to all generations" (Ps 33:11; cf. Job 23:13; Lam 2:17). How are these brought to pass? Our Confession teaches us that, they will be brought about by second causes in God's providence. Second causes are anything in the created universe that produces effects in one way or another. Every effect must have a cause. Only God is the uncaused Cause.

- The sun and the rotation and revolution of the earth are examples of necessary second causes that brings about different weather types and harvest seasons (cf. Gen 8:22; Jer 31:35; Isa 55:10). A loose axe head or a stray arrow which "by chance" killed someone is an example of free second cause (cf. Ex 21:13; Dt 19:5; 1 Kgs 22:28, 34). Isaiah 10:6–7 demonstrates another kind of free second cause. In verse 6 we are told that the Lord will use Assyria as a rod against a hypocritical nation, but in verse 7, we are told that Assyria has no idea about God's decree: she was pursuing her own purpose! Prayers which are answered accordingly are examples of contingent second causes. When Paul announced to the centurion on the ship to Italy that all in the ship would survive only if the sailors remained in the ship, he essentially made the condition a contingent second cause to God's purpose of preserving all in the ship.

- It is to be noted again that the manner in which God controls His creatures and their actions is always consistent with the nature of the creature and its mode of action. We know this to be true from experience—that we are conscious of acting freely according to the law of our constitution as free agents. In the same way, God's control of inanimate objects is always consistent with the properties of the substances that make up the objects. We know this to be true from empirical science.

5.3   God, in His ordinary providence, maketh use of means,[1] yet is free to work without,[2] above,[3] and against them,[4] at His pleasure.

[1]Acts 27:31, 44; Isa 55:10–11; Hos 2:21–22; [2]Hos 1:7; Mt 4:4; Job 34:10; [3]Rom 4:19–21; [4]2 Kgs 6:6; Dan 3:27.

- What §5.2 calls 'second causes,' this section calls 'means.' This section, essentially, teaches us that God occasionally 'intervenes' directly, sovereignly or miraculously, in the ordinary course of nature in order to accomplish His purpose. This does not mean that God sets aside His original decrees since miracles would also be comprehended in the eternal and immutable plan of God.

- The adjectives 'without,' 'above' and 'against' the ordinary means, are specially chosen to reflect scriptural illustrations. (1) *Without*: "But I will have mercy upon the house of Judah, and will save them by the LORD their God, and will not save them by bow, nor by sword, nor by battle, by horses, nor by horsemen" (Hos 1:7). (2) *Above*: "And being not weak in faith, he considered not his own body now dead, when he was about an hundred years old, neither yet the deadness of Sarah's womb: He staggered not at the promise of God through unbelief; but was strong in faith, giving glory to God; And being fully persuaded that, what he had promised, he was able also to perform" (Rom 4:19–21). (3) *Against*: "the iron did swim" (2 Kgs 6:6), "[their] bodies the fire had no power, nor was an hair of their head singed, neither were their coats changed, nor the smell of fire had passed on them" (Dan 3:27).

On God's Providence in Relation to Sinful Actions

5.4 The almighty power, unsearchable wisdom, and infinite goodness of God, so far manifest themselves in His providence, that it extendeth itself even to the first fall, and all other sins of angels and men,[1] and that not by a bare permission,[2] but such as hath joined with it a most wise and powerful bounding,[3] and otherwise ordering, and governing of them, in a manifold dispensation, to His own holy ends;[4] yet so, as the sinfulness thereof proceedeth only from the creature, and not from God; who, being most holy and righteous, neither is nor can be the author or approver of sin.[5]

[1]*Rom 11:32–34; 2 Sam 24:1; 1 Chr 21:1; 1 Kgs 22:22–23; 1 Chr 10:4, 13–14; 2 Sam 16:10; Acts 2:23; 4:27–28;* [2]*Acts 14:16;* [3]*Ps 76:10; 2 Kgs 19:28;* [4]*Gen 50:20; Isa 10:6–7, 12;* [5]*Jas 1:13–14, 17; 1 Jn 2:16; Ps 50:21.*

- This section addresses, —without attempting to explain, —the nature of God's providential action as it concerns the origin and control of sinful actions of His creature. There are two, —apparently paradoxical, —main propositions:

  a. Sinful acts are not only permitted, but directed and controlled by God for His own purpose. This is the clear teaching of Scripture: "Surely the wrath of man shall praise thee: the remainder of wrath shalt thou restrain" (Ps 76:10); "But as for you, ye thought evil against me; but God meant it unto good, to bring to pass, as it is this day, to save much people alive" (Gen 50:20); and "Him, being delivered by the determinate counsel and foreknowledge of God, ye have taken, and by wicked hands have crucified and slain" (Acts 2:23).

  b. God is neither the author nor approval of sin: "Let no man say when he is tempted, I am tempted of God: for God cannot be tempted with evil, neither tempteth he any man: But every man is tempted, when he is drawn away of his own lust, and enticed. … Every good gift and every perfect gift is from above, and cometh down from the Father of lights, with whom is no variableness, neither shadow of turning" (Jas 1:13–14, 17; cf. 1 Jn 2:16; Ps 50:21).

- These two facts cannot be reconciled due to the limitation of the human mind. We can at the most say that God does not do violence to the heart or will of his free agents. Free agents act according to what is perceived to be the most attractive course of actions. God ordained the external causes that contribute to the creature's perception, and He ordains the creatures' actions, but the motive for the actions come from the creatures themselves. Robert Shaw explains beautifully:

  > To solve the difficulty connected with this point [of difficulty], theologians distinguish between an action and its quality. The action, abstractly considered, is from God, for no action can be performed without the concurrence of Providence; but the sinfulness of the action proceeds entirely from the creature. As to the manner in which the providence of God is concerned

about the sinful actions of creatures, it is usually stated that God permits them, that He limits them, and the He overrules them for the accomplishment of His own holy ends. But the full elucidation of this abstruse subject, so as to remove every difficulty, surpasses the human faculties. We are certain that God is concerned in all the actions of His creatures; we are equally certain that God cannot be the author of sin; and here we ought to rest.[16]

5.5   *The most wise, righteous, and gracious God, doth oftentimes leave, for a season, His own children to manifold temptations, and the corruption of their own hearts, to chastise them for their former sins, or to discover unto them the hidden strength of corruption and deceitfulness of their hearts, that they may be humbled;[1] and to raise them to a more close and constant dependence for their support upon Himself, and to make them more watchful against all future occasions of sin, and for sundry other just and holy ends.[2]*

[1]*2 Chr 32:25–26, 31; 2 Sam 24:1;* [2]*2 Cor 12:7–9; Ps 73; 77:1, 10, 12; Mk 14:66–72; Jn 21:15–17.*

We saw in the previous paragraph that sinful actions are not only permitted, but providentially ordered and governed by God for His own holy purposes. But what are these purposes? In this and the next paragraph we will be looking at these purposes in regard (1) to God's children or elect, and (2) to the wicked and ungodly, or the reprobate, respectively.

We can glean from the Scripture that amongst God's purposes for "permitting" sin in His own children are:

(1) "*to chastise them for their former sins*";

(2) "*to discover unto them the hidden strength of corruption and deceitfulness of their hearts, that they may be humbled*";

(3) "*to raise them to a more close and constant dependence for their support upon Himself,*" i.e., to more fervent prayer against sin and corruption;

---

[16] Shaw, *op. cit.*, 70.

(4) *"to make them more watchful against all future occasions of sin"*;

(5) *"for sundry other just and holy ends."*

Thus, the Lord allowed Hezekiah to sin by showing off his riches to the ambassadors of Babylon, so "that he might know all that was in his heart" (2 Chr 32:31), namely his pride. Similarly, the children of Israel were chastised for their sin when God "moved David against them to say, Go, number Israel and Judah" (2 Sam 24:1). Again, Peter was allowed to fall into grievous sin of denying the Lord so that he might discover his arrogance and the deceitfulness of his heart (cf. Mk 14:29, 66–72 and Jn 21:15).

5.6 As for those wicked and ungodly men, whom God as a righteous Judge, for former sins, doth blind and harden,[1] from them He not only withholdeth His grace, whereby they might have been enlightened in their understandings, and wrought upon in their hearts;[2] but sometimes also withdraweth the gifts which they had,[3] and exposeth them to such objects as their corruption makes occasion of sin;[4] and withal, gives them over to their own lusts, the temptations of the world, and the power of Satan:[5] whereby it comes to pass, that they harden themselves, even under those means which God useth for the softening of others.[6]

[1]Rom 1:24, 26, 28; 11:7–8; [2]Dt 29:4; [3]Mt 13:12; 25:29; [4]Dt 2:30; 2 Kgs 8:12–13; [5]Ps 81:11–12; 2 Th 2:10–12; [6]Ex 7:3; 8:15, 32; 2 Cor 2:15–16; Isa 8:14; 1 Pet 2:7–8; Isa 6:9–10; Acts 28:26–27.

- While God allows His elect to fall sin for the purpose of exposing the sinfulness of their sin to them, He punishes the sin of the *"wicked and ungodly"* or the reprobate by blinding and hardening them. This is clearly taught in the Scripture: "Wherefore God also gave them up to uncleanness through the lusts of their own hearts, to dishonour their own bodies between themselves" (Rom 1:24; cf. Rom 1:26, 28); "What then? Israel hath not obtained that which he seeketh for; but the election hath obtained it, and the rest were blinded (According as it is written, God hath given them the spirit of slumber, eyes that they should not see, and ears that they should not hear;) unto this day" (Rom 11:7-8).

- But we must be careful to note that God does so not by infusing any wickedness into their hearts or by any direct manipulation or influence of their soul to render them obstinate. Rather, it is: (1) by withholding grace that is necessary to enlighten their understanding or to soften their hearts that they may see the sinfulness of their sins: "Yet the LORD hath not given you an heart to perceive, and eyes to see, and ears to hear, unto this day" (Dt 29:4); (2) by withdrawing *"the gifts which they had"* (see Mt 13:12, 25:29)—which gifts refer to opportunities of hearing the Gospel and opportunities of repentance, etc.; (3) by exposing them to *"such objects as their corruption makes occasion of sin"*: thus God is said to harden the heart of Sihon king of Heshbon by directing the children of Israel to pass through his land—knowing that he would not allow them to pass through peaceably (cf. Dt 2:30, 24); (4) by giving them *"over to their own lusts, the temptations of the world, and the power of Satan"*: "So I gave them up unto their own hearts' lust: and they walked in their own counsels" (Ps 81:12, see also v. 11), "And for this cause God shall send them strong delusion, that they should believe a lie: That they all might be damned who believed not the truth, but had pleasure in unrighteousness" (2 Th 2:11–12).

- Indeed, the wicked harden themselves, *"even under those means which God useth for the softening of others."* Thus, Pharaoh hardened his heart even though the plagues would have had an opposite effect on others; and as the hardening of his heart was God's original purpose in sending the plagues, God is said to harden Pharaoh's heart (Ex 7:3; 8:15, 32; Rom 9:17). Thus, preachers and the preaching of the Word of God is *"a sweet savour of Christ"* of life unto life for the elect, but a savour of death unto death unto the reprobate (2 Cor 2:15–16; cf. Isa 6:9 and Acts 28:26–27). Thus, Christ is a sanctuary and a precious corner stone for those who believe but a stone of stumbling for those who reject Him (Isa 8:14; 1 Pet 2:7).

- We note, then, that God has a very different purpose in permitting sin in His elect and in the reprobate. For His elect, it ultimately magnifies His grace; whereas for the reprobate, it ultimately displays His justice.

On General and Special Providence

5.7 As the providence of God doth, in general, reach to all creatures; so, after a most special manner, it taketh care of His Church, and disposeth all things to the good thereof.[1]

[1] *1 Tim 4:10; Amos 9:8–9; Rom 8:28; Isa 43:3–5, 14.*

- The providence of God may be considered as general and as special. His general providence is exercised over all His creatures, whereas His special providence is exercised, in a particular manner, for His Church and His people. Indeed, God constantly have the interest of His own people in view in the outworking of His providence, so that all things, —whether prosperous or adverse, — are made to co-operate in promoting their good (Rom 8:28).

- Also, as God exercises special providential care over Israel, —His Church under-age in the Old Covenant (Amos 9:8–9; Isa 43:3–5, 14), —so God continues to exercise a special providential care over His Church under the New Covenant. Thus, while God sometimes permit His Church to be persecuted and reduced to very low condition, the means by which His enemies intend for her destruction always become a means of edification and enlargement of the Church under the overruling providence of God. This explains why the Early Church grew because of the persecution she experienced (Acts 8:4).

WCF 06: OF THE FALL OF MAN, OF SIN, AND OF THE PUNISHMENT

Man was created in the image of God. But Adam our first Father fell into sin, and with him all mankind descending from him by natural generation. Why did it happen? What are the consequences, effects and results of the Fall? These are the questions that will be addressed in this chapter.

On the Fall

6.1 Our first parents, being seduced by the subtilty and temptation of Satan, sinned in eating the forbidden fruit.[1] This their sin, God was pleased, according to His wise and holy counsel, to permit, having purposed to order it to His own glory.[2]

[1]Gen 3:13; 2 Cor 11:3; [2]Rom 11:32.

- This section presents for us the facts pertaining to the Fall of Adam and Eve. They fell by the sovereign will of God under temptation of Satan. A number of questions remain unanswered and cannot be answered by finite minds, and therefore the Westminster divines make no attempt to answer at all. These are: (1) How did Satan (and his cohorts) fall in the first place when they were created holy and good? (2) How could Adam and Eve who had a perfectly righteous nature fall under the temptation of Satan, seeing that the will is always bounded to the prevailing affection and desire of the heart and mind (cf. Mt 12:33, 35), which in the case of Adam must be holy and righteous? and (3) Why did God allow Satan, Adam and Eve to fall into sin in the first place?

- Though these questions are commonly asked, we should refrain from attempting to answer them. Great theologians have attempted and made no headway. Like a great horse trying to pull a cart out of the mud, the more they try the deeper they get stuck!

- The most we could say is with the divines: *"God was pleased, according to His wise and holy counsel, to permit, having purposed* to order it to His own glory." Or we may say with the Apostle Paul: "What if God, willing to shew his wrath, and to make his power known, endured with much longsuffering the vessels of wrath fitted to destruction: And that he might make known the riches of his glory on the vessels of mercy, which he had afore prepared unto glory" (Rom 9:22–23). Our response to this doctrine should be one of profound reverence as that of our Lord: "Even so, Father; for so it seemed good in thy sight" (Lk 10:21b).

On the Consequence of the Fall

6.2 By this sin they fell from their original righteousness, and communion with God,[1] and so became dead in sin,[2] and wholly defiled in all the faculties and parts of soul and body.[3]

[1]Gen 3:6–8; Eccl 7:29; Rom 3:23; [2]Gen 2:17; Eph 2:1; [3]Tit 1:15; Gen 6:5; Jer 17:9; Rom 3:10–18.

- When God issued the prohibition to Adam and Eve, He said: "But of the tree of the knowledge of good and evil, thou shalt not eat of it: for in the day that thou eatest thereof thou shalt surely die" (Gen 2:17). This threat includes four kinds of death (cf. §6.6), viz.: (1) *Bodily* death in that Adam and Eve could no longer use their body to do good as they before. (2) *Temporal* death, consisting of the dissolution of the union between the body and the soul. Adam and Eve began the process of dying in this sense immediately after they fell. (3) *Spiritual* death, consisting in the loss of the image of God (in the narrower sense of true knowledge, righteousness and holiness) and the loss of communion and favour with God. This is the aspect highlighted in our Confession; and Adam and Eve experienced it to the full the moment they fell. (4) *Eternal* death, consisting in everlasting separation of both body and soul from God.

- Robert Shaw explains:

  The very day in which our first parents sinned, the sentence of death, though not immediately executed in its fullest extent, began to lay hold upon them. They became mortal, and were exposed to the disorders of a vitiated constitution; the principle of spiritual life was extinguished in their souls, and they were bound over to eternal wrath; and had not a Mediator been provided, not only would they have returned to the dust, but they would have been "punished with everlasting destruction from the presence of the Lord, and from the glory of His power."

- The result of the Fall is that man "became dead in sin, and wholly defiled in all the faculties and parts of soul and body."

Firstly, to be dead in sin is to be spiritually dead. It includes an inclination to sins and trespasses, and a totally inability to do what is good in the eyes of God. Paul expressed this in Ephesians 2:1, "And you hath he quickened, who were dead in trespasses and sins" (Eph 2:1). We may call this Radical Depravity (from Latin 'radix', i.e., 'root') to emphasise that fallen man is corrupt to the core, and so no good can possibly come out of him. The Scripture speaks of the radical depravity of man: "every imagination of the thoughts of his heart was only evil continually" (Gen 6:5b). His heart is "deceitful above all things, and desperately wicked" (Jer 17:9). This does not mean that unregenerate man is totally unable to seek after God, if we mean by seeking the reading of God's Word, the hearing of sermons, prayer and the turning away from outward acts of grosser sins. But it does mean that these acts are sinful in the eyes of God (though they may not be as sinful as a failure to seek). This must be how Edwards' distinction between natural and moral ability must be understood.

Secondly, to be wholly defiled is to be totally, pervasively, not partially or apparently, depraved. He is defiled in all the parts and faculties of the soul and body, and it speaks of Pervasive Depravity. A fallen man is sinful in all that he thinks, says or does. Thus, the understanding is darkened, the passion roused, the affections alienated, the conscience hardened and deceitful, the actions hypocritical, etc. Note that this does not mean that an unregenerate man is less intelligent than a regenerate man. Some of the world's greatest scientists were not Christians. But it does mean that the unregenerate mind is unable to apprehend spiritual things with approval. Also, when it is exercised in the matters of the world it is never with the glory of God in mind. Neither does it mean that the unregenerate men are less healthy than the Christians, but it does mean that the unregenerate men use their bodies constantly to serve sin.

- Note also that the issue is not whether fallen man is as bad as he can be, but that every unregenerate man is sinning constantly. Indeed, even when he does what may appear to be benevolent and good in the eyes of the world, he is sinning against God. His heart is depraved and has no place for God, and therefore cannot glorify God by his actions. Paul expresses this in no uncertain terms: "There is none righteous, no, not one: There is none that understandeth, there is none that seeketh after God. They are all gone out of the way, they are together become unprofitable; there is none that doeth good, no, not one. Their throat is an open sepulchre; with their tongues they have used deceit; the poison of asps is under their lips: Whose mouth is full of cursing and bitterness: Their feet are swift to shed blood: Destruction and misery are in their ways: And the way of peace have they not known: There is no fear of God before their eyes" (Rom 3:10–18). No unregenerate man can do anything that is pleasing to God, seeing that he falls short of the glory of God: "For all have sinned, and come short of the glory of God" (Rom 3:23).

  What about the commonly proposed idea that "Total Depravity does not mean that man is as bad as he can be"? To answer this question, we must realise that man is indeed as bad as he can be in his nature. He is perfectly capable of doing the worst atrocities imaginable. The reason why he is not doing it is simply due to physical and mental limitation and the restrain placed upon him due to the threat of the law of God and of the land, as well as, the fear of the disapproval of society, etc. For this reason, he is not as wicked as can be in his practice. But even then, we must remember that even his most perfect work is tainted with sin and sinful in the eyes of God (Isa 64:6).

- Finally, note that the phrase "*original righteousness*," occurring here in the Confession for the first and only time, clearly distinguishes the Westminster Assembly as Augustinian and Calvinistic. The opposing view about man's original state (which is sometimes unwarily adopted by those who profess to be Calvinistic) is Pelagianism which teaches that there is no such thing as original righteousness, and that Adam had the perfect freewill to do what he chose. His heart was like a clean slate and so are the hearts of all babies born by natural generation. In opposition, to this view, the Augustinan/Calvinistic view is that Adam had Original Righteousness, i.e., an inclination to holiness, but having lost it through the Fall he is now possesses Original Sin with an inclination towards evil.

6.3 They being the root of all mankind, the guilt of this sin was imputed,[1] and the same death in sin and corrupted nature conveyed to all their posterity, descending from them by ordinary generation.[2]

[1]Gen 1:27–28; 2:16–17; Acts 17:26; Rom 5:12, 15–19; 1 Cor 15:21–22, 45, 49; [2]Ps 51:5; Gen 5:3; Job 14:4; 15:14.

6.4 From this original corruption, whereby we are utterly indisposed, disabled, and made opposite to all good,[1] and wholly inclined to all evil,[2] do proceed all actual transgressions.[3]

[1]Rom 5:6; 8:7; 7:18; Col 1:21; [2]Gen 6:5; 8:21; Rom 3:10–12; [3]Jas 1:14–15; Eph 2:2–3; Mt 15:19.

- Theologians call the sinful state and condition in which men are born: Original Sin. Original Sin, it must be remembered, does not refer to the sin of eating of the forbidden fruit, but to the consequence of that sin. It is so called because: (1) It is derived from the original root of the human race; (2) It is present in the life of every individual at the time of birth; and (3) It is the inward root of all the actual sins that defile the life of man.

- These two paragraphs deal with the two elements of Original Sin, namely: (1) original guilt, and (2) original corruption or pollution together with the actual transgressions that proceed from it. These two aspects of Original Sin are well expressed in *WSC* Q. 18: *"Wherein consists the sinfulness of that estate whereinto man fell?"* Answer: *"The sinfulness of that estate whereinto man fell, consists in (1) the guilt of Adam's first sin, (2) [negatively,] the want of original righteousness, and [positively,] the corruption of his whole nature, —which is commonly called Original Sin; together with all actual transgressions which proceed from it."*

- *WCF* 6.3 explains how the guilt of Adam is imputed to us, and how we inherited his corrupt nature. *WCF* 6.4 enlarges on this original corruption to explain how we became sinners in actual words, deeds and thoughts.

- The guilt of Adam's first sin was imputed or credited to his posterity by natural generation, because (1) Adam was the Covenant or Federal Representative of all men (*WCF* 7.2); and (2) because they were seminally present in Adam (cf. Heb 7:9–10 and Acts 17:26) and therefore "sinned in him...in his first transgression" (*WSC* 16, *WLC* 22). Paul expresses this doctrine in Romans 5:12, "Wherefore, as by one man sin entered into the world, and death by sin; and so death passed upon all men, for that all have sinned" (Rom 5:12). Some believe that the phrase "for that all have sinned" (Grk. ἐφ᾽ ᾧ πάντες ἥμαρτον, *eph hô pantes hēmarton*) may be translated "in whom all sinned." This is possible, but not necessary. I believe both seminalism (that we were present in Adam's loins and so we are participants in the sin) and federalism (that we were represented by Adam so we are accounted sinners) are involved.

- Moreover, because we inherit Adam's nature, our souls also are devoid of Original Righteousness and are wholly corrupted. We sin because we are sinners; we do not become sinners because we sin. Thus, our Confession speaks about actual transgression as proceeding from original corruption. David expressed this idea in his penitential Psalm: "Behold, I was shapen in iniquity; and in sin did my mother conceive me" (Ps 51:5). Job also understood this to be the case: "Who can bring a clean thing out of an unclean? not one" (Job 14:4). His friend Eliphaz correctly concurred: "What is man, that he should be clean? and he which is born of a woman, that he should be righteous?" (Job 15:14). We are by nature and so by birth, *"utterly indisposed, disabled, and made opposite to all good, and wholly inclined to all evil."* It is therefore inevitable that actual transgressions proceed from us. We must, however, remember that both the inherited aspect of Original Sin, namely the corrupt inclinations of the soul, and actual transgression are violation of God's Law. Thus, a baby who has not actually transgressed the Law of God by any act is also to be regarded as guilty on account of Original Sin.

- Note that in saying that we inherit Adam's sin nature by virtue of our being born by natural generation, I am saying that I am inclined towards traducianism (that we receive both our physical nature and soul from our parents) rather than creationism (that we receive our bodies from our parents, but our souls are separately created by God) to explain the origin of our souls. The Westminster divines were clearly traducianists by their use of Acts 17:26 in this section. But the divines do not deny immediate (direct) imputation of Adam's guilt upon his posterity. Our depravity is inherited (or "conveyed"), our guilt is imputed.

On the Effect of Regeneration

6.5 This corruption of nature, during this life, doth remain in those that are regenerated:[1] and although it be through Christ pardoned, and mortified, yet both itself, and all the motions thereof, are truly and properly sin.[2]

[1]1 Jn 1:8, 10; Rom 7:14, 17–18, 23; Jas 3:2; Prov 20:9; Eccl 7:20; [2]Rom 7:5, 7–8, 25; Gal 5:17.

- We have ascertained that all man born by ordinary generation is born with a corrupt nature, so that all he does is sinful. But the question is: What about the Christian? What if he is regenerate? Does regeneration remove the natural corruption of fallen man?

- This section confirms the biblical assertion that regeneration does not rid a person of the corruption of his nature. As long as he lives in this life, the regenerate person remains liable to fall into sin. John highlights this doctrine by a rhetoric statement: "If we say that we have no sin, we deceive ourselves, and the truth is not in us. …If we say that we have not sinned, we make him a liar, and his word is not in us" (1 Jn 1:8, 10).

- Though the sin of the regenerate is pardoned, and though his nature is being gradually brought into subjection and being mortified by the work of the Holy Spirit in sanctification, the corruption of his nature and all the motions of it remain truly and properly sin. This is to refute the Romish teaching that Original Sin is taken away in regeneration through baptism, so that when a baptised person recognises a corrupt disposition in himself, he is told that that it has nothing to do with Original Sin, but stems out of concupiscence (covetous desires and lust), which is not by itself sinful. But the Apostle Paul teaches clearly that concupiscence or lust is sin: "I had not known sin, but by the law: for I had not known lust, except the law had said, Thou shalt not covet" (Rom 7:7).

On the Wages of Sin

6.6 Every sin, both original and actual, being a transgression of the righteous law of God, and contrary thereunto,[1] doth, in its own nature, bring guilt upon the sinner,[2] whereby he is bound over to the wrath of God,[3] and curse of the law,[4] and so made subject to death,[5] with all miseries spiritual,[6] temporal,[7] and eternal.[8]

[1]1 Jn 3:4; [2]Rom 2:15; 3:9, 19; [3]Eph 2:3; [4]Gal 3:10; [5]Rom 6:23; [6]Eph 4:18; [7]Rom 8:20; Lam 3:39; [8]Mt 25:41; 2 Th 1:9.

- The phrase translated "transgression of the law" in 1 John 3:4, is only one word in the Greek (ἀνομία, *anomia*) which may be rendered "lawlessness." Sin is lawlessness. It is not just a positive breaking of the Law (as taught by Pelagius), but includes the failure to meet up to the standards of the Law. Thus, the answer to *WSC* 14 reads, "*Sin is any want of conformity unto, or transgression of, the Law of God.*" It is the Law that defines sin, and those who fail to conform to the Law or transgress it are guilty before God: "Now we know that what things soever the law saith, it saith to them who are under the law: that every mouth may be stopped, and all the world may become guilty before God" (Rom 3:19). This guilt is attended with "the wrath of God" (Eph 5:6) and the curse (opposite of blessing) of the law: "Cursed is every one that continueth not in all things which are written in the book of the law to do them" (Gal 3:10; cf. Dt 27:26). This curse is manifested in death and miseries of three sorts: *spiritual, temporal* and *eternal.* The Larger Catechism speaks of punishments in this world and in the world to come:

> WLC 28. *What are the punishments of sin in this world?*
>
> A. *The punishments of sin in this world are either inward, as blindness of mind, a reprobate sense, strong delusions, hardness of heart, horror of conscience, and vile affections; or outward, as the curse of God upon the creatures for our sakes, and all other evils that befall us in our bodies, names, estates, relations, and employments; together with death itself.*
>
> WLC 29. *What are the punishments of sin in the world to come?*
>
> A. *The punishments of sin in the world to come, are everlasting separation from the comfortable presence of God, and most grievous torments in soul and body, without intermission, in hell-fire for ever.*

- What do we say to these things? Listen to the counsel of Robert Shaw:

"When we reflect on the loss which Adam sustained by his fall, and on the guilty and corrupt state in which we are thereby involved, and on the manifold miseries to which we are liable, both here and hereafter, let us be deeply impressed with a sense of the dreadful malignity and demerit of sin, —the source of all our woe. Let us not dare to repine against God, or to impeach His goodness or equity, for permitting sin to enter into the world, and making us responsible for the transgression of the first Adam; but rather let us admire the divine wisdom and grace displayed in providing the Second Adam, by whose obedience we may be made righteous, as by the disobedience of the first we were made sinners. Let us cordially receive the Lord Jesus Christ, that, being found in Him, we may not only be acquitted from the guilt of the first man's transgression, but may be brought, through 'the abundance of grace, and of the gift of righteousness, to reign in life by one,' even by Jesus Christ, our Lord" (p. 83).

WCF 07: OF GOD'S COVENANT WITH MAN

The term 'covenant' has become quite controversial in many modern churches partly because it sounds so 'profound' and 'theological', and partly because of its confrontational connotations. It is in a certain sense confrontational because those who affirm 'Covenant Theology' would often do so in contra distinction to 'Dispensational Theology' which has become rather popular in conservative churches because it is widely promoted in Study Bibles such as Scofield Study Bible; Ryrie Study Bible; KJV Study Bible, etc.

But the essence of "Covenant Theology" has always been taught since the early days of the New Testament Church, though its present systematic form can be traced back largely to the 16th Century Reformation.

This chapter of our Confession presents the systematic and developed form of Covenant Theology as held by the Reformed and Presbyterian Churches in the tradition of John Calvin. This form, we believe, is fully consistent with Biblical data and presents in a systematic way the mind of God in regard to the framework with which He would want us to think of His relationship with us.

Why Covenant?

7.1 The distance between God and the creature is so great, that although reasonable creatures do owe obedience unto Him as their Creator, yet they could never have any fruition of Him as their blessedness and reward, but by some voluntary condescension on God's part, which He hath been pleased to express by way of covenant.[1]

[1] *Isa 40:13–17; Job 9:32–33; 1 Sam 2:25; Ps 113:5–6; 100:2–3; Job 22:2–3; 35:7–8; Lk 17:10; Acts 17:24–25.*

The distance between God as Creator and man as creature is a theme that is frequently emphasised in Scripture (see proof-texts above). Because of this distance, and the fact that man's existence is dependent on God, man owes God his absolute obedience and therefore cannot expect to be rewarded by Him. So our Lord, pointing out to His disciples that a master does not thank his slave for doing his duties, teaches us: "So likewise ye, when ye shall have done all those things which are commanded you, say, We are unprofitable servants: we have done that which was our duty to do" (Lk 17:10). The Lord has nevertheless condescended to relate to man by way of covenant so that man may have some *"fruition [or enjoyment] of Him as their blessedness and reward."*

What is a covenant? Palmer Robertson defines it as "bond-in-blood, committing the participants to loyalty on pain of death."[17] We may put it this way: "A covenant is a bond of friendship governed by a sworn statement."

Think of marriage. Marriage is not just a contract. It is a bond of friendship. It is friendship, but it is not just friendship because the husband and wife make a sworn agreement with each other. They are more than friends. They made a vow to love each other exclusively and for the rest of their life. They promise not to have any other man or woman in their life. If they keep their vows, then they would enjoy the blessings of each other's company including having children together. But if they fail to keep their vows, then the consequences are severe. They cannot just part company. They will suffer the penalty in various ways such as lost of peace, lost of face, lost of property, or lost of custody of the children, etc.

In the Ancient Near Eastern Culture, a covenant is a treaty or contract that generally has five elements (of which the first four are essential):

- *Two parties*. Both parties are sometimes represented by an individual in the Scripture. In Abraham's covenant with Abimelech, the contracting parties were really Abraham's family and Abimelech and his descendants (Gen 21:23).

- *A condition or stipulation*. This is the statement or oath of the covenant. This is usually stated either in clear writing (Ex 34:27–28) or verbally (Gen 21:23–24, 31–32; Ex 19:8; 24:3, 7), and can be

---

[17] O Palmer Robertson, *The Christ of the Covenants* (Phillipsburg, New Jersey: Presbyterian and Reformed Publishing, 1980), 11.

ratified by (a) offering a sacrifice (Ps 50:5); (b) sprinkling of blood (Ex 24:8); (c) passing under the rod (Ezk 20:37); (d) passing through path of divided animals (Gen 15:10, 18); etc.

- *A blessing or promise*. This refers to the pledge or guarantee of blessing when the stipulations of the covenant are kept. In bilateral covenant, the promise is often implied rather than explicitly spelt out. In Abraham's covenant with Abimelech, for example, the promise implied was that Abraham and his descendants would be allowed to dwell in peace at Beersheba (see Gen 21:22–23).

- *A curse or penalty*. This refers to the punishment that will be inflicted when the stipulation of the covenant is broken. Again, this is often implied as in the covenant between Abraham and Abimelech.

- *A sign and seal* (or sacrament). This refers to the token or symbol that points to the substance of the covenant, to remind the covenanting parties of the covenant that has been made. It can take a variety of forms such as: (a) a gift (Gen 21:27–32); (b) a meal (Gen 31:54); or (c) a memorial (Gen 31:44ff; Josh 24:27).

A divine covenant may also be understood according to these five elements. It may be defined as "a bond-in-blood sovereignly administered" (*ibid,* 15), or as I prefer, "a bond of love governed by divine oath and sovereignly administered.' This means divine covenants are unilateral, i.e., God dictates the terms, and man has no right to bargain.

The Covenant of Works

7.2 The first covenant made with man was a covenant of works,[1] wherein life was promised to Adam; and in him to his posterity,[2] upon condition of perfect and personal obedience.[3]

[1] Gal 3:12; [2] Rom 10:5; 5:12–20; [3] Gen 2:17; Gal 3:10.

It is often objected that the word *covenant* does not appear in Genesis 1 to 3 and therefore it is unbiblical to speak of a Covenant of Works.

However, there are three good reasons to believe that God did make a covenant with Adam:

a. The Hebrew of Hosea 6:7 is better rendered: "They like *Adam* have transgressed the covenant" rather than "They like *men* have transgressed the covenant." Firstly, the Hebrew אָדָם (*âdâm*) is singular. Secondly, if Israel did not transgress the covenant "like men" how else would they have transgressed it, since they are men? Thirdly, the same Hebrew word translated "like men" (כְּאָדָם, *ke-adam*) is translated "as Adam" in Job 31:33, "If I covered my transgressions as Adam, by hiding mine iniquity in my bosom."

b. The parallel which the Apostle Paul draws between Adam and Christ in Romans 5:12–21, in connection with justification, can only be explained on the assumption that Adam, like Christ, is the head of a covenant. Just as Adam's sin was imputed on his posterity whom He represented, Christ's righteousness is imputed on the elect whom he represented.

c.   All the essential elements of a covenant are present.

   i.   *The Contracting Parties*

   These are:

   (1) The Triune God, the Creator and Sovereign Lord; and
   (2) Man, His dependent creature. Note their relationship:-

   —Naturally: Creator and Creature. Creature is duty bound to keep the laws of the Creator. Transgression deserves punishment, Obedience deserves nothing.

   —Covenantally: Adam was the representative and head of the whole human race. He was under probation: Would he subject his will to the will of God? Transgression deserves punishment; Obedience obtains eternal life (by grace).

   ii.   *The Condition or Stipulation*

   This is implied, namely: Perfect, personal, perpetual obedience to the Moral Law of God. Adam had the Moral Law written in the tablets of his heart: "For when the Gentiles, which have not the law, do by nature the things contained in the law, these, having not the law, are a law unto themselves: Which shew the work of the *law written in their hearts*, their conscience also bearing witness, and their thoughts the mean while accusing or else excusing one another" (Rom 2:14–15). The Moral Law of God is summarised in the Ten Commandments, but in a different form. The Ten Commandments in Exodus 20 is predominantly negative because it pre-supposes knowledge of sin. But Adam knew no sin, so the Law inscribed in his heart must have been entirely positive. Moreover, since he knew no sin, it would have been natural, effortless and reasonable for him to obey these commandments. Therefore, God deemed it necessary to add a negative commandment that is in some sense arbitrary and indifferent: "But of the tree of the knowledge of good and evil, thou shalt not eat of it: for in the day that thou eatest thereof thou shalt surely die" (Gen 2:17). By itself it was not a moral evil, but it was a test of pure obedience on the part of Adam. Would Adam obey God, or would he follow the guidance of his own judgment? In that sense, the demands of the law is concentrated on one point. If Adam obeyed, he would receive the blessings of the covenant, if he failed, he will experience the curses.

iii. *The Promise or Blessing of the Covenant*

Most Reformed theologians believe that it is a promise of eternal life (Hoeksema asserts that it is a natural earthly life). Although the promise is not explicit, it is implied since death— temporal, spiritual and eternal, —results from disobedience. Although there is no mention of eternal life, we know that Adam already had eternal life in so far as the quality is concerned since eternal life is life in communion with God: "This is life eternal, that they might know thee the only true God, and Jesus Christ, whom thou hast sent" (Jn 17:3).

But Adam could lose that by sin. So it cannot be eternal or everlasting. However, Scripture suggests that if he continued on and stood the test, he would be lifted to a higher plane after an indefinite period—just as the good angels have been confirmed in righteousness. Adam would have been raised above the possibility of erring, sinning and dying. That is the implicit promise.

The life promised under the Covenant of Works is referred to in numerous places in Scripture:

Rom 7:10   And the commandment, which was ordained to life, I found to be unto death. I.e., "The law was designed and adapted to secure life, but became in fact the cause of death" (Charles Hodge).

Rom 10:5   For Moses describeth the righteousness which is of the law, That the man which doeth those things shall live by them.

Lev 18:5   Ye shall therefore keep my statutes, and my judgments: which if a man do, he shall live in them: I am the LORD.

Gal 3:12   And the law is not of faith: but, The man that doeth them shall live in them.

Lk 10:25–28 And, behold, a certain lawyer stood up, and tempted him, saying, Master, what shall I do to *inherit eternal life*? He said unto him, What is written in the law? how readest thou? And he answering said, Thou shalt love the Lord thy God with all thy heart, and with all thy soul, and with all thy strength, and with all thy mind; and thy neighbour as thyself. And he said unto him, Thou hast answered right: *this do, and thou shalt live*.

Ezk 20:11   And I gave them my statutes, and shewed them my judgments, which if a man do, he shall even live in them (cf. Ezk 20:13, 21).

iv. *The Penalty*

"But of the tree of the knowledge of good and evil, thou shalt not eat of it: for in the day that thou eatest thereof *thou shalt surely die*" (Gen 2:17). This refers to death: physical, spiritual and eternal (cf. *WCF* 6.6).

- Physical death: That is, Adam and Eve would become mortal and begin the process of bodily decay which would eventually lead to necrosis. "In the sweat of thy face shalt thou eat bread, *till thou return unto the ground; for out of it wast thou taken: for dust thou art, and unto dust shalt thou return*" (Gen 3:19). "But now is Christ risen from the dead, and become the firstfruits of them that slept. For since by man came death, by man came also the resurrection of the dead. *For as in Adam all die*, even so in Christ shall all be made alive" (1 Cor 15:20–22).

- Spiritual death: That is, Adam and Eve would henceforth not be able to do good in the sight of God whatsoever. They would become "dead in trespasses and sin" (Eph 2:1); and all their righteousness would be as "filthy rags" (Is 64:6) in the eyes of God. This spiritual death is referred to in Romans 5:17, "For if by one man's offence death reigned by one; much more they which receive abundance of grace and of the gift of righteousness shall reign in life by one, Jesus Christ."

- Eternal death: That is, Adam and Eve would no longer be able to enjoy fellowship with God and would upon their bodily death experience the full wrath of God forever and ever. This death is symbolised in Genesis 3:24, "So he drove out the man; and he placed at the east of the garden of Eden Cherubims, and a flaming sword which turned every way, to keep the way of the tree of life." This is the death referred to in Romans 6:23, "For the wages of sin is *death*; but the gift of God is *eternal life* through Jesus Christ our Lord" and in Roman 5:18-19, "Therefore as by the offence of one judgment came upon all men to condemnation; even so by the righteousness of one the free gift came upon all men unto justification of life. For as by one man's disobedience many were made sinners, so by the obedience of one shall many be made righteous."

When Adam fell, he experienced spiritual death immediately, and had begun to feel both the corruption of physical death and the effects of eternal death. But God, as we shall see, immediately introduced an economy of grace and restoration, even the Covenant of Grace (Gen 3:15).

v. *The Sign and Seal*

Although the sign and seal is an optional element in a covenant, most Reformed theologians, such as Francis Turretin see the Tree of Life as the sign and seal of the Covenant of Works. He says: "[The Tree of Life] was a sacrament and symbol of the immortality which would have been bestowed upon Adam if he had persevered in his first state. Augustine says, 'He had nourishment in other trees; in this, however, a sacrament.' Now this signification can have a threefold relation. (1) With respect to past life, it was a symbol putting him in mind of the life received from God. As often as he tasted its fruit, he was bound to recollect that he had life not from himself, but from God. (2) With respect to future life, it was a declarative and sealing sign of the happy life to be passed in paradise and to be changed afterwards into a heavenly life, if he had continued upright. (3) With respect to the state of grace, it was an illustrious type of the eternal happiness prepared for us in heaven; also a type of Christ himself who acquired and confers it upon us and who is therefore called 'the tree of life in the midst of the paradise of God' (Rev 2:7); 'the tree of life yielding her fruit twelve times every month, whose leaves are for the healing of the nations' (Rev 22:2)."[18]

Since Adam was the federal head of the human race, the result of his fall was that (1) His posterity is imputed with his sin: "Wherefore, as by one man sin entered into the world, and death by sin; and so death passed upon all men, for that all have sinned" (Rom 5:12). (2) His

---

[18] *Institutes of Elenctic Theology*, 1.581

posterity inherits his sin nature: "Behold, I was shapen in iniquity, and in sin did my mother conceive me" (Ps 51:5). See also *WCF* 6.2, 6.3.

The Covenant of Grace

7.3 Man, by his fall, having made himself incapable of life by that covenant, the Lord was pleased to make a second,[1] commonly called the Covenant of Grace: wherein He freely offereth unto sinners life and salvation by Jesus Christ, requiring of them faith in Him, that they may be saved;[2] and promising to give unto all those that are ordained unto eternal life His Holy Spirit, to make them willing and able to believe.[3]

[1]*Gal 3:21; Rom 8:3; 3:20–21; Gen 3:15; Isa 42:6;* [2]*Mk 16:15–16; Jn 3:16; Rom 10:6, 9; Gal 3:11;* [3]*Ezk 36:26–27; Jn 6:44–45.*

Many Reformed theologians including some of the Puritans such as Owen, Charnock, Flavel, etc., speak of two covenants connected with the salvation of fallen men, namely: (1) the Covenant of Redemption which is made between the persons of the Godhead in eternity, and (2) the Covenant of Grace which is made with sinners in time. In such a scheme, the Covenant of Grace is generally regarded as being conditioned upon faith, i.e. only those who exercise faith enters into a covenant relation with God. This faith is provided to the elect as a gift that comes with the Covenant of Redemption.

Our Confession, on the other hand, speaks only of one covenant, which combines the covenant between the persons of the Godhead and God's covenant with the elect. In this scheme, the Covenant of Grace (note the slight difference in meaning with the understanding of those who speak of a Covenant of Redemption) is a covenant between God and His elect, with Christ, the God-Man as their representative.

The Larger Catechism, Q. 31 makes it clear: "*With whom was the Covenant of Grace made?*" Answer: "*The Covenant of Grace was made with Christ as the second Adam, and in Him with all the elect as His seed.*" The Covenant of Works was made with Adam as a representative of all mankind, and so it was made with him for his posterity. In the same way, the Covenant of Grace is made with Christ, the second Adam, as the representative of His elect, and so it was made with Him for His seed (see Gal 3:16; Rom 5:15ff.; Isa 53:10–11).

It is as such an unconditional covenant as far as the elect is concerned, although it is, in a sense, conditioned upon Christ's fulfilment of the Covenant of Works as well as payment of the debt of sin on the behalf of the elect.

This is elaborated in the confessional statement above, which may be comprehended in the following 9 propositions:

1. This Covenant was made between God the Father, representing the entire Godhead, and His co-eternal Son, who was to assume, in the fullness of time, a human element into His Person, and to represent all His elect as their Mediator and Surety. This is taught in various passages in the Scripture:

   Psalm 89:3, 4: "I have made a covenant with my chosen, I have sworn unto David my servant, Thy seed will I establish for ever, and build up thy throne to all generations." This psalm, —as all the psalms, —refers to David as a type of Christ, the Greater David or the "Root of David" (Rev 5:5). The Scripture clearly intimates that the covenant was made with Christ rather than merely with David, for long after David was dead and buried, Ezekiel prophesied, "And I will set up one shepherd over them, and he shall feed them, even my servant David; he shall feed them, and he shall be their shepherd. … And David my servant shall be king over them; and they all shall have one shepherd: they shall also walk in my judgments, and observe my statutes, and do them" (Ezk 34:23, 37:24; cf. Jer 30:9; Lk 24:44).

   Isaiah 42:6–7: "I the LORD have called thee in righteousness, and will hold thine hand, and will keep thee, and give thee for a covenant of the people, for a light of the Gentiles; To open the blind eyes, to bring out the prisoners from the prison, and them that sit in darkness out of the prison house." This verse clearly refers to Christ (cf. Isa 42:1–3 with Mt 12:18–21). It teaches us that the Covenant is a covenant of redemption of sinners from sin and Satan.

   2. This Covenant was made with Christ, as the head or representative of His spiritual seed. This is clearly taught by the

Apostle Paul in his comparisons between Adam and Christ: "Wherefore, as by one man sin entered into the world, and death by sin; and so death passed upon all men, for that all have sinned: ...But not as the offence, so also is the free gift. For if through the offence of one many be dead, much more the grace of God, and the gift by grace, which is by one man, Jesus Christ, hath abounded unto many. ... Therefore as by the offence of one judgment came upon all men to condemnation; even so by the righteousness of one the free gift came upon all men unto justification of life" (Rom 5:12, 15, 18). Just as Adam, as a public person, represented his posterity in death, so Christ represent His elect in life. Christ may, in fact, be called the "Second Adam": "And so it is written, The first man Adam was made a living soul; the last Adam was made a quickening spirit. ... The first man is of the earth, earthy: the second man is the Lord from heaven" (1 Cor 15:45, 47).

Furthermore, the identity of Christ and His Church through covenant union is clearly taught in the Scripture. The covenant people and Christ are identified by the same name: "And said unto me, Thou art my servant, O Israel, in whom I will be glorified" (Isa 49:3). Though Saul persecuted the Church, the Lord asked him: "Saul, Saul, why persecutest thou me?" (Acts 9:4).

Christ is also called the Surety of the Covenant: "By so much was Jesus made a surety of a better testament" (Heb 7:22). A surety is a person who takes upon himself the legal obligations of another. And the promises of the Covenant were primarily made with Him: "Now to Abraham and his seed were the promises made. He saith not, And to seeds, as of many; but as of one, And to thy seed, which is Christ" (Gal 3:16). These promises were not made when the covenant was enacted in Genesis 15. They were made before the foundation of the world: "In hope of eternal life, which God, that cannot lie, promised before the world began" (Tit 1:2).

3. This Covenant was established from eternity. The Covenant of Grace is called a "second" covenant in our *Confession* because it is second in respect to *manifestation* and *execution* when compared with the Covenant of Works. Yet, in respect to the period or the

order in which it was made, it is the first covenant. Christ, —the embodiment of Wisdom, — says, "I was set up from everlasting, from the beginning, or ever the earth was" (Prov 8:23); i.e., "he was set apart to his mediatory office and work, —in other words, to be the head of his spiritual seed in the Covenant of Grace from everlasting."[19] Thus, Christ in His earthly ministry made constant reference to a previous commission He had received of His Father (Jn 10:18, 17:4–5; Lk 22:29). Thus, Paul tells us that eternal life was "promised before the world began" (Tit 1:2); and thus the Covenant of Grace is called an "everlasting covenant" (Heb 13:20).

4. This Covenant originated in the good pleasure of His sovereign will of God and is completely gratuitous. "Blessed be the God and Father of our Lord Jesus Christ, who hath blessed us with all spiritual blessings in heavenly places in Christ: According as he hath chosen us in him before the foundation of the world, that we should be holy and without blame before him in love: Having predestinated us unto the adoption of children by Jesus Christ to himself, according to the good pleasure of his will, To the praise of the glory of his grace, wherein he hath made us accepted in the beloved" (Eph 1:3–6).

5. While the Covenant of Grace seen from the standpoint of it being a relationship between God and the elect is unilateral (will be kept by God) and unconditional (to man), when seen as an agreement between God and the Son, it is neither unilateral nor unconditional. The conditions or requirements of this Covenant are:

    a. That Christ should fulfil the Covenant of Works on behalf of His elect. In this sense the Covenant of Grace is the continuation of the Covenant of Works. In this regard, He would assume human nature with its present infirmities, yet without sin, by being born of a virgin. This is seen in Galatians 4:4–5, Hebrews 2:10 and 4:15. He would also place Himself under the Law, to keep it perfectly and so merit salvation on behalf of His elect.

---

[19] Shaw, Op. Cit., 90–91; cf. Ps 2:6–8.

This is seen in Matthew 5:17–18, "Think not that I am come to destroy the law, or the prophets: I am not come to destroy, but to fulfil. For verily I say unto you, Till heaven and earth pass, one jot or one tittle shall in no wise pass from the law, till all be fulfilled" (cf. Ps 40:8; Jn 8:29).

b. That Christ should bear their iniquities by dying a propitiatory death on behalf of His elect—thus receiving upon Himself the curse due them for the violation of the Covenant of Works. This is clearly taught in Isaiah 53:10–11: "Yet it pleased the LORD to bruise him; he hath put him to grief: when thou shalt make his soul an offering for sin, he shall see his seed, he shall prolong his days, and the pleasure of the LORD shall prosper in his hand. He shall see of the travail of his soul, and shall be satisfied: by his knowledge shall my righteous servant justify many; for he shall bear their iniquities." Verse 10 has been paraphrased beautifully as: "If His soul shall make a propitiatory sacrifice, he shall see a seed which shall prolong their days; and the gracious purpose of Jehovah shall prosper in His hands" (cited by Shaw, 90). See also John 10:17–18.

c. That Christ should apply His merits to His elect by regenerating them, endowing them with faith, and sanctifying them through the monergistic work of the Holy Spirit, thus securing the consecration of their lives to God. That this is the work of Christ is clearly seen in John 17:19–22: "And for their sakes I sanctify myself, that they also might be sanctified through the truth. Neither pray I for these alone, but for them also which shall believe on me through their word; That they all may be one; as thou, Father, art in me, and I in thee, that they also may be one in us: that the world may believe that thou hast sent me. And the glory which thou gavest me I have given them; that they may be one, even as we are one." That it is worked through the Holy Spirit is seen in John 16:13–15.

6. The promises of the Covenant, which the Father makes on behalf of the entire Godhead, include:

a. That He would prepare for Him a body uncontaminated by sin (Heb 10:5), and would anoint Him by giving Him the Spirit without measure, thus qualifying Him for the Messianic office (Isa 42:1–2; 61:1; Jn 3:34).

b. That He would support Him in His work (Isa 42:6–7; Lk 22:43).

c. That He would deliver Him from the power of death, and highly exalt Him over all power in heaven and earth (Ps 16:8–11; Acts 2:25–28; Phil 2:9–11).

d. That He would enable Him, on account of His fulfilment of the conditions of the Covenant to send out the Holy Spirit for the formation of His spiritual body by regeneration and sanctification of His elect; and for the instruction, guidance and protection of His Church so constituted (Jn 6:37, 39–40, 44–45, 14:26; 15:26; 16:13–14). This is the aspect emphasised in our Confession, which notes that God promises *"to give unto all those that are ordained unto life His Holy Spirit, to make them willing and able to believe."*

7. In the administration of this Covenant, God *"freely offereth unto sinners life and salvation by Jesus Christ, requiring of them faith in Him, that they may be saved."* It must be carefully noted that the faith in Christ that is referred here is, strictly speaking, not a condition, stipulation or requirement of the Covenant—if we understand such condition, stipulation or requirement as *meritorious*. Rather, faith is presented here as the instrument or means of obtaining the salvation already procured by Christ. The condition of the Covenant is wholly fulfilled by Christ. It is true that *WLC* 32 speaks of *"requiring faith as the condition to interest them in Him."* But this must be read carefully in context, for it a participle clause to the phrase, "promiseth *and giveth His Holy Spirit to all His elect, to work in them that faith, with all other saving graces....*" In other words, the emphasis in the statement is the work of the Spirit. The present section in the Confession says the same: *"promising to give unto all those that are ordained unto eternal life His Holy Spirit, to make them willing, and able to*

believe." It is the Arminian doctrine that faith is a condition of the Covenant of Grace. But if this is the case, it is no longer a gracious covenant, for however much easier it is for the sinner to repent and believe in Christ (as the Arminians claim), it is still a work or obedience on the part of the sinner.

Note, however, that there is a sense, —from the human standpoint, —in which faith and obedience is required on the part of Christ's elect. This requirement is not meritorious, but instrumental and preceptive, namely, that (1) they accept the Covenant and its promises by faith, and therefore enter upon the life of the Covenant; and (2) that from the principle of new life born within them according to the promise, they consecrate themselves to God in new obedience as His people. We highlight this to point out that being in the Covenant of Grace does not imply being without responsibility. But from the standpoint of divine purpose the faith and obedience of the covenant people belongs to the promissory part of the Covenant rather than its stipulations.

8. The penalty of failure to fulfil the requirements of the Covenant is implied in Hebrews 6:17–18, "Wherein God, willing more abundantly to shew unto the heirs of promise the immutability of his counsel, confirmed it by an oath: That by two immutable things, in which it was impossible for God to lie, we might have a strong consolation, who have fled for refuge to lay hold upon the hope set before us." This passage refers to Genesis 15 when God cut a covenant with Abraham—which is really a graphic re-affirmation of the Covenant of Grace already in force. In that display, God alone passed through the pieces of the animals, signifying that He would be destroyed if He fails to keep His covenant, which is of course impossible. The two immutable things which the author of Hebrews refer to are probably the Father represented by the smoking furnace (cf. Mt 13:42) and Christ represented by the burning lamp (Jn 1:9).

9. The Sign and Seal of the Covenant of Grace are, in the Old Testament, Circumcision and the Passover, and in the New Testament, Baptism and the Lord's Supper. We will see more of this in chapters 27–29.

Covenant Versus Testament

7.4 This covenant of grace is frequently set forth in Scripture by the name of a Testament, in reference to the death of Jesus Christ the Testator, and to the everlasting inheritance, with all things belonging to it, therein bequeathed.[1]

[1]*Heb 9:15–17; 7:22; Lk 22:20; 1 Cor 11:25.*

- The words 'testament' and 'covenant' in the Authorised Version translate the same word in the Greek (διαθήκη, *diathēkē*). The word 'testament' refers to a will in which the testator bequeath an inheritance to his heirs. A covenant is related to a testament in that death is involved in both. In the case of a covenant, death stands at the beginning of the relationship between two parties, as the curse factor of the covenant. Death is not strictly necessary unless the covenant is broken. In the case of a testament, however, death stands at the end of a relationship between two parties to actualise an inheritance. Death is strictly necessary in a testament. [20]

- The meaning of 'testament' is clearly intended in Hebrews 9:16–17, "For where a testament is, there must also of necessity be the death of the testator. For a testament is of force after men are dead: otherwise it is of no strength at all while the testator liveth." However, I believe that in all other cases (Heb 9:15, 7:22; Lk 22:20; 1 Cor 11:25), the word 'covenant' is probably more appropriate. Christ died to pay for the penalty of covenant breakers, not really as a testator. However, since the Greek word allows for both meaning, the author of Hebrews appears to employ the second meaning of the word, i.e., 'testament,' to emphasis the necessity of the death of Christ in God's sovereign design of the Covenant of

---

[20] See discussion in Robertson, *Christ in the Covenants*, 11–14.

Grace. A parallel can be seen in Paul's reference to the singularity of the word 'seed' in Galatians 3:16, when the Hebrew word, though singular, can in fact have a plural meaning, namely descendants. There, the choice of word 'seed' points to Christ being the representative of the elect. Here the choice of word '*diathêkê*' points to Christ being the covenant head who would die for His people before they can be adopted as children of God, and so heirs of the promise.

- It would probably be more meaningful for us to understand "Old Testament" as "Old Covenant" and "New Testament" as "New Covenant" whenever we see the two former phrases employed in the Confession.

The Covenant of Grace in the Old and New Testaments

7.5 This covenant was differently administered in the time of the law, and in the time of the gospel:[1] under the law it was administered by promises, prophecies, sacrifices, circumcision, the paschal lamb, and other types and ordinances delivered to the people of the Jews, all fore-signifying Christ to come;[2] which were, for that time, sufficient and efficacious, through the operation of the Spirit, to instruct and build up the elect in faith in the promised Messiah,[3] by whom they had full remission of sins, and eternal salvation; and is called the Old Testament.[4]

[1] 2 Cor 3:6–9; [2] Heb 8; 9; 10; Rom 4:11; Col 2:11–12; 1 Cor 5:7; [3] 1 Cor 10:1–4; Heb 11:13; Jn 8:56; [4] Gal 3:7–9, 14.

There is only one Covenant of Grace which is administered differently in the Old and New Testaments. They are called 'old' and 'new' to indicate their differences with respect to the incarnation. But in all essential respects, they are the same:

(a) Christ is the Saviour of men before and after His advent, and He saves them in the same way, by grace through faith in Him. So Christ is said to be "the Lamb slain from the foundation of the world" (Rev 13:8). And He is a propitiation also for the sins committed under the old covenant (Rom 3:25; Heb 9:15). Thus, Christ was exhibited typically in all the ceremonial, but especially in the sacrificial, system of the tabernacle and temple (Col 2:17; Heb 10:1–10). And these Old Testament sacrifices and ceremonies are *"sufficient and efficacious, through the operation of the Spirit"* on the basis of their sacramental union to the incarnational work of Christ.

(b) Faith in Christ was the *instrumental* cause of salvation in the old and new covenants: "the just shall live by his faith" (Hab 2:4; cf. Ps 2:12; Rom 1:17; Gal 3:11; Heb 10:38). This is why the Old Covenant believers can be set forth as examples of faith (see Romans 4 and Hebrews 11). The same gracious promises of spiritual grace and eternal blessedness were administered then and now (cf. Gen 17:7 with Mt 22:32; Gen 22:18 with Gal 3:16; see also Isa 43:25–27; Ezk 36:27; Job 19:25–27; Dan 12:2–3).

This covenant of Grace was administered in the Old Testament in types and shadows which pointed to Christ. It was also worked out or displayed through several subordinate covenants (or more accurately, administration of the Covenant of Grace), each one continuing in the same theme of redemption, but increasing in fullness and clarity:

- The Adamic Covenant

  (Commencement; Genesis 3:15—the Messiah was promised)

- The Noahic Covenant

  (Preservation; Genesis 9—the religious significance of blood (for atonement) is announced (Cf. Genesis 9:4; Lev 17:11) to point to the procurement of salvation by propitiatory death of a Messiah; and the rainbow is given as sign of covenant)

- The Abrahamic Covenant

  (Promise; Genesis 12, 15—the sacrament of circumcision is appointed as a sign and seal of the covenant introduced to mark out covenant people; and land inheritance is set as a type eternal spiritual inheritance)

- The Mosaic Covenant

(Law; Exodus 19ff—The Ceremonial Law (Ex 24–30) is set in place; and the Moral Law (Ex 19-20) as way of life for God's people is summarised and codified)

- The Davidic Covenant

(Kingdom; 2 Samuel 7:12–13; Kingship of Christ is made obvious)

The unity of all these subordinate covenants can be seen in two ways. Firstly, we see each one building on the previous one. This is known as structural unity. Next, we see a constant theme in each of the covenants. This is known as thematic unity.

a. With reference to structural unity, (a) we see at the inauguration of the Mosaic Covenant, that the Lord remembers the Abrahamic Covenant (see Exodus 6:3–8); (b) we see David who is directly in the Davidic Covenant charging Solomon to keep the Mosaic Law (see 1 King 2:3); and (c) we see in Ezekiel 37:24–26 most of the subordinate covenants mentioned in a breath: "And David my servant shall be king over them; and they all shall have one shepherd [an allusion to the Davidic Covenant]: they shall also walk in my judgments, and observe my statutes [Mosaic], and do them. And they shall dwell in the land that I have given unto Jacob my servant, wherein your fathers have dwelt; and they shall dwell therein, even they, and their children [Abrahamic], and their children's children for ever: and my servant David shall be their prince for ever. Moreover I will make a covenant of peace with them; it shall be an everlasting covenant with them: and I will place them, and multiply them, and will set my sanctuary in the midst of them for evermore."

b. With reference to thematic unity, we see the same theme, "I shall be your God; you shall be my people," in each of the subordinate covenants. For example, in Adamic Covenant, see Genesis 3:15; cf. 4:25–5:32 and 4:16–24; in Abrahamic Covenant, see Genesis 17:7; in Mosaic Covenant, see Exodus 6:6–7; and in the Davidic Covenant, see 2 Kings 11:17.

7.6 Under the gospel, when Christ, the substance,[1] was exhibited, the ordinances in which this covenant is dispensed are the preaching of the

Word, and the administration of the sacraments of Baptism and the Lord's Supper:² which, though fewer in number, and administered with more simplicity and less outward glory, yet, in them, it is held forth in more fullness, evidence, and spiritual efficacy,³ to all nations, both Jews and Gentiles;⁴ and is called the New Testament.⁵ There are not therefore two covenants of grace differing in substance, but one and the same under various dispensations.⁶

¹Col 2:17; ²Mt 28:19–20; 1 Cor 11:23–25; ³Heb 12:22–27; Jer 31:33–34; ⁴Mt 28:19; Eph 2:15–19; ⁵Lk 22:20; ⁶Gal 3:14, 16; Acts 15:11; Rom 3:21–23, 30; Ps 32:1; Rom 4:3, 6, 16–17, 23–24; Heb 13:8.

The Covenant of Grace is administered in the New Testament (known here as the 'gospel') in greater simplicity, clearness and fulness since Christ, the anti-type, has completed His work of redemption. The New Testament dispensation is superior to the old dispensation for the following reasons:

a. It is administered by Christ, the Son, rather than servants such as Moses (Heb 3:5–6).

b. Before, the truth was partly hid, partly revealed in types and symbols, but now it is revealed in clear history of the incarnation and didactic teaching.

c. The old administration was largely external, carnal and ceremonial—involving land, temples, sacrifices, rituals and feasts. But under the new administration, all these are done away with and the administration of the covenant is largely internal and spiritual.

d. It was confined to one people, but now it embraces the whole earth without racial or geographic distinction.

e. The New Covenant involves internalisation of the Law, regeneration and indwelling of the Holy Spirit. Jeremiah 31:33, "But this shall be the covenant that I will make with the house of Israel; After those days, saith the LORD, I will put my law in their inward parts, and write it in their hearts; and will be their God, and they shall be my people" (cf. Ezk 11:19). Under the old economy, the Law of God was external on tablets of stones. And the Jews, — ordinarily, —had no power to keep them. It was not part of the covenant features. But with the New Covenant, covenant children have the Law of God inscribed in their hearts. This is a graphic way of saying that the New Covenant includes regeneration and indwelling of the Holy Spirit. Under the New Covenant, God's children are not only regenerated, and thus enabled to keep the Law, but also have the Holy Spirit indwelling them so that they can discern spiritual things, since spiritual things are spiritually discerned. This is what is meant by Jeremiah 31:34: "And they shall teach no more every man his neighbour, and every man his brother, saying, Know the LORD: for they shall all know me, from the least of them unto the greatest of them, saith the LORD." Jeremiah is, of course, employing a hyperbole: it does not really mean that we will know perfectly. But with the illuminating help of the Holy Spirit we do indeed know much more than the average person under the old economy.

But does it mean that there was no Holy Spirit's regenerative activity in the Old Testament? John Calvin answers: "... the Fathers, who were formerly regenerated obtained this favour through Christ, so that we may say, that it was as it were transferred to them from another source. The power then to penetrate into the heart was not inherent in the law, but it was a benefit transferred to the law from the Gospel."[21] Palmer O. Robertson concurs: "Nothing under the Old Covenant had the effectiveness necessary actually to reconcile the sinner to God. Only in anticipation of the finished work of Christ could an act of heart-renewal be performed under the provisions of the Old Covenant."[22]

---

[21] Calvin, *Comm. On Jeremiah 20:47*

[22] Robertson, op. cit., 292.

WCF 08: OF CHRIST THE MEDIATOR

The whole of Christianity is centred on Christ. All biblical history and prophecies centre on Christ. Our relationship with God and one another as believers is founded upon Christ. Our redemption is built upon the work of Christ and enjoyed because of Christ. Nothing in the Christian life and nothing in Christian theology can be divorced from Christ and considered apart from him. Whether we are studying theology proper, anthropology, soteriology, ecclesiology, pneumatology or eschatology, we cannot leave out Christ without falling into imbalance in one way or another.

In this chapter, we shall study what the Scripture has to teach us about Christ in His central role as our Saviour, our Covenant Head, or as our Mediator.

On the Mediatorial Offices of Christ

8.1 It pleased God, in His eternal purpose, to choose and ordain the Lord Jesus, His only begotten Son, to be the Mediator between God and man;[1] the Prophet,[2] Priest,[3] and King;[4] the Head and Saviour of His Church;[5] the Heir of all things;[6] and Judge of the world:[7] unto whom He did from all eternity give a people, to be His seed,[8] and to be by Him in time redeemed, called, justified, sanctified, and glorified.[9]

[1]Isa 42:1; 1 Pet 1:19–20; Jn 3:16; 1 Tim 2:5; [2]Acts 3:22; [3]Heb 5:5–6; [4]Ps 2:6; Lk 1:33; [5]Eph 5:23; [6]Heb 1:2; [7]Acts 17:31; [8]Jn 17:6; Ps 22:30; Isa 53:10; [9]1 Tim 2:6; Isa 55:4–5; 1 Cor 1:30.

We have already seen two facts referred to in this section: (1) God has from eternity chosen a definite number of people to be His people, the elect, the seed of Christ (*WCF* 3.3–6); (2) God the Father, representing the entire Godhead has made a Covenant of Grace with God the Son in which the Father promises the Son the elect to be His seed, —through calling, justification, sanctification and glorification, —on condition of His fulfilment of the conditions of the Covenant.

In this section, we learn that Christ entered the Covenant not as the Second Person of the Godhead, but as the *theanthropos* (God-man) who has been appointed to the following offices:

a. *The Mediator between God and man*. A mediator is a person who intervenes between two parties at variance for the sake of making reconciliation. Before the Fall, there was no need for a mediator between God and man since there was no variance between them though their distance in nature was very great. But after the Fall, man was alienated from God by his sin and subjected to God's judicial wrath. A mediator became absolutely necessary. Christ was appointed for that purpose: "there is one God, and one mediator between God and men, the man Christ Jesus" (1 Tim 2:5). This appointment was, of course, "set up from everlasting" (Prov 8:23) and "foreordained before the foundation of the world" (1 Pet 1:20).

To fulfil His role as the Mediator of the elect, Christ functioned as their Prophet, Priest and King. In this way, Christ qualifies as the Head and Saviour of the Church, the Heir of all things and the Judge of the World.

b. *A Prophet*. A prophet is a man who declares the will of God to man. The prophetic office of Christ is clearly taught in the Scripture. He was the Prophet like unto Moses (Dt 18:15, 18; cf. Acts 3:22–23, 7:37). He was known as "the messenger of the covenant" (Mal 3:1). It was the "spirit of Christ" who revealed the plan of redemption to the prophets of old (1 Pet 1:11). In the New Testament, Christ declares that He alone reveals the Father (Mt 11:27); He was the "teacher come from God" (Jn 3:2); and He alone "hast the words of eternal life" (Jn 6:68). Thus, the Apostle John calls Him "the Word" (Jn 1:1) and the Apostle Paul calls the Psalms, "the word of Christ" (Col 3:16).

How does Christ execute the office of a Prophet? The *WLC* 43 answers: "*Christ executeth the office of a prophet, in His revealing to the Church, in all ages, by His Spirit and Word, in divers ways of administration, the whole will of God, in all things concerning their edification and salvation.*" In other words, Christ declares to His Church, through all ages, including those under the Old Covenant, the whole counsel of God, or whatever God would have us know, believe and do as it pertains to our salvation.

c. *A Priest*. While a prophet is God's representative to men, a priest is a man who represents men to God by offering up sacrifices and making prayers on their behalf (Heb 5:1; 8:3). This is what Christ, as the Great High Priest, does for His Church throughout the ages. Indeed, even in the Old Testament, when the Aaronic priesthood was still functioning, the entire order of priests and the ceremonial system were typical of Christ. "Even he [The BRANCH, i.e., Christ] shall build the temple of the LORD; and he shall bear the glory, and shall sit and rule upon his throne; and *he shall be a priest upon his throne*: and the counsel of peace shall be between them both" (Zech 6:13; cf. Isa 53:10; Dan 9:24–25).

How does Christ execute the office of a priest? The *WSC* 25 answers beautifully: "*Christ executeth the office of a priest, in his once offering up of Himself a sacrifice to satisfy divine justice, and reconcile us to God, and in making continual intercession for us.*"

The author of Hebrews tells us that this was one of the chief reasons why Jesus took on the nature of man rather than of angels, for only as man can He represent us as a merciful high priest (Heb 2:16–17). But how could Jesus be a priest when He is descended from Judah rather than Levi? The answer lies in the fact that He was anointed a priest in the order of Melchizedek with an oath (Heb 5:6; 7:15–17; cf. Ps 110:4). By design, the Melchizedek priesthood is already a higher priesthood than the Aaronic priesthood since Abraham who is the ancestor of Levi gave tithes to Melchizedek (see Heb 7:1–10). But more than that, Jesus' priestly ministry is far superior to the ministry of the Aaronic priests.

- **Firstly**, He needs not offer any sacrifice for Himself since He is without sin though He was in all points tempted like as we are (Heb 4:15; 7:27).

- **Secondly**, rather than offering animal sacrifices which were but shadows and types which cannot take away sins (Heb 10:4), Jesus offered Himself, the antitype which all the OT sacrifices were pointing to (Heb 9:14, 28; Col 2:17). In doing so, He not only propitiated the wrath of God by vicariously taking the punishment for sin that is due us upon Himself, but reconciles us to God (Heb 2:17; Eph 2:16).

- **Thirdly**, unlike the Aaronic priests, Jesus continues ever to make intercession for us (Heb 7:24–25; 12:24–25). Moreover, He does not intercede for us on earth as the Aaronic priest would have, rather, He is exalted to the right hand of God the Father, and He intercedes for us there (Rom 8:34). What does He intercede for? As our Advocate, He pleads with God that, on account of the merit of His death, our sins may be pardoned; our consciences quieted and our souls preserved: "If any man sin, we have an advocate with the Father, Jesus Christ the righteous" (1 Jn 2:1). As our Mediator, Christ beautifies our prayers by removing all impurities and sin, and then, presenting them to the Father, pleads that such as made in His name and in the will of God may be answered: "If ye shall ask any thing in my name, I will do it" (John 14:14).

e. *A King.* A king is the ruler of a kingdom. Christ is such a King. His kingship was early prophesied in the OT, when Jacob blessed Judah by saying: "The sceptre shall not depart from Judah, nor a lawgiver from between his feet, until Shiloh come; and unto him shall the gathering of the people be" (Gen 49:10). Shiloh refers to the one to whom tribute belongs, i.e., an ultimate king. This prophesy was made a little more specific by Nathan the prophet in his delivery of God's promise to David: "And when thy days be fulfilled, and thou shalt sleep with thy fathers, I will set up thy seed after thee, which shall proceed out of thy bowels, and I will establish his kingdom. He shall build an house for my name, and I will stablish the throne of his kingdom for ever" (2 Sam 7:12–13). Although this prophesy appears to refer directly to Solomon (cf. 1 Chr 28:6), a comparison of Scripture shows us that it actually refers to him only as a type of Christ (Cf. 2 Sam 7:14 with Ps 2:7; cf. Ps 2:7 with Heb 1:5b; cf. 2 Sam 7:12-14, 16 with Lk 1:32). Moreover, the fact that the kingdom will be forever suggests to us a King who will be eternal (cf. Isa 55:3; Acts 13:34). Thus, David, under inspiration of the Holy Spirit, recognised that this King is his Lord: "The LORD said unto my Lord, Sit thou at my right hand, until I make thine enemies thy footstool. The LORD shall send the rod of thy strength out of Zion: rule thou in the midst of thine enemies" (Ps 110:1–2).

Under the ministry of the writing prophets, the prophecy of the coming King became more and more distinct. For example, Jeremiah calls Him "a righteous Branch" and "THE LORD OUR RIGHTEOUSNESS" (Jer 23:5–6; cf. Acts 13:23). Isaiah is even more specific. He not only calls Him the Branch and Root of Jesse (Isa 11:1ff, 10; cf. Rom 15:12); but makes it clear that He is God, and to dwell among man, He would be born of a virgin: "For unto us a child is born, unto us a son is given: and the government shall be upon his shoulder: and his name shall be called Wonderful, Counsellor, The mighty God, The everlasting Father, The Prince of Peace. Of the increase of his government and peace there shall be no end, upon the throne of David, and upon his kingdom, to order it, and to establish it with judgment and with justice from henceforth even for ever" (Isa 9:6–7; cf. Isa 7:14).

Under the NT, the kingship of Christ is unveiled completely and proclaimed openly. It becomes clear that His Kingdom is not an earthly, political one, but one in which His subjects are the elect or redeemed people of God (Mt 5:5–10; 6:33; 13:38; Lk 17:20; Jn 1:49; 3:3; 1 Cor 15:50, etc.). This does not mean that Christ is not rightly the King of His and their enemies. He is (Ps 110:2), but His absolute dominion is not presently evident, and will one day become manifest (1 Cor 15:25; Phil 2:9–11; Rev 11:15, etc.).

In the meantime, Christ executes His kingship in three ways.

- *Firstly*, He subdues us to Himself by making us willing to obey Him (Col 1:21; Ps 110:3; Acts 15:14–16). This, He does so by effectually calling us by His Word and Spirit and then working in our heart a disposition to yield to Him the obedience He requires (Phil 2:13; Eph 3:16–19; 2 Cor 3:3).

- *Secondly*, He rules and defends us by giving us laws to guide and protect us (Isa 33:22; 32:1–2); and then to implement these laws.

He appoints officers in the Church not only to proclaim the law but to exercise Church discipline where necessary (Mt 16:19).

- **Thirdly**, He currently restrains and finally puts down all who oppose us and Him, including Satan and the world (1 Cor 15:25; Ps 110). See also *WLC* 45.

f. *The Head and Saviour of the Church*: "For the husband is the head of the wife, even as Christ is the head of the church: and he is the saviour of the body" (Eph 5:23).

g. *The Heir of all things*: "Hath in these last days spoken unto us by his Son, whom he hath appointed heir of all things, by whom also he made the worlds" (Heb 1:2). To be heir of all things is to have the dominion and possession of all things.

h. *The Judge of the World*: "Because he hath appointed a day, in the which he will judge the world in righteousness by that man whom he hath ordained; whereof he hath given assurance unto all men, in that he hath raised him from the dead" (Acts 17:31). This subject will be covered in *WCF* 33.

On the Person of the Lord Jesus Christ

8.2 The Son of God, the second person of the Trinity, being very and eternal God, of one substance, and equal with the Father, did, when the fullness of time was come, take upon Him man's nature,[1] with all the essential properties, and common infirmities thereof, yet without sin;[2] being conceived by the power of the Holy Ghost, in the womb of the virgin Mary, of her substance.[3] So that two whole, perfect, and distinct natures, the Godhead and the manhood, were inseparably joined together in one person, without conversion, composition, or confusion.[4] Which person is very God, and very man, yet one Christ, the only Mediator between God and man.[5]

[1]Jn 1:1, 14; 1 Jn 5:20; Phil 2:6; Gal 4:4; [2]Heb 2:14, 16–17; Heb 4:15; [3]Lk 1:27, 31, 35; Gal 4:4; [4]Lk 1:35; Col 2:9; Rom 9:5; 1 Pet 3:18; 1 Tim 3:16; [5]Rom 1:3–4; 1 Tim 2:5.

The deity of Christ has already been taught in *WCF* 2.3. Section 8.2 teaches that Christ, the eternal son of God, in the fullness of time, took to Himself human nature with a true body and a reasonable soul, and so became the God-Man—one Person with two natures.

Although the doctrine of the Person and Nature of Christ can be derived quite easily from the Scripture, in the first 400–500 years, the New Testament Church battled with numerous heresies on the subject. It was only in A.D. 451, during the Council of Chalcedon where 630 Church Fathers met, that a definitive statement of the Person and Nature of Christ that does not admit to any misinterpretation was written. That statement was that, "Christ, Son, Lord, Only-begotten, [is] to be acknowledged in two natures, without confusion, without change, without division, without separation." This statement settled most of the Christological conflicts that the Church had to endure in those days.

The following table describes the heresies

Party	Time	Human Nature	Divine Nature	Remarks	Condemned by
Docetists	1st C.	Denied	Affirmed	Jesus only appeared to be a man. He did not really come in the flesh	1 Jn 4:1-3
Ebionites	2nd C.	Affirmed	Denied	Generally denied Christ's pre-existence, and so His deity.	Irenaeus, etc.
Arians	4th C.	Affirmed	Reduced	Christ is the greatest created being. He is similar, but not the same in nature to God. *Homoiousious* but not *homoousious*.	Nicea, 325
Apollinarians	4th C.	Reduced	Affirmed	Jesus has a human body and human soul. The human nature is so elevated as to be scarcely human.	Constantinople, 381
Nestorians	5th C.	Affirmed	Affirmed	Christ was 2 distinct persons, one eternal Son of God; the other the human Jesus.	Ephesus, 431
Eutychians	5th C.	Reduced	Reduced	Christ had one mixed, half-human, half-divine nature.	Chalcedon, 451

| Orthodox | - | Affirmed | Affirmed | Christ is one Person with 2 natures one fully human, the other fully divine, in hypostatic union. | Chalcedon, 451 |
| Monothelites | 5th C. | Reduced | Reduced | Variant of Eutychianism. Conceded that Christ has two natures, but insists He has one will. | Constantinople III, 680 |

Orthodox View (Creed of Chalcedon, A.D. 451):

a. Jesus Christ is *one* Person (contra Nestorianism).

b. He has a *fully* divine nature (contra Ebionites, Arians, Euthychians, Monothelites) and a *fully* human nature (contra Docetists, Apollinarians, Euthychians, Monothelites); the two natures are *without confusion* (contra Eutychianism), without *change, without division* (contra Nestorianism), *without separation*.

c. He had *two* wills, one divine and the other human (contra Monothelites)

With this in mind, the assertions of our Confessional statement can be proven as follows:

1. *The full humanity of Christ* is shown in the Scriptures from three angles. Firstly, Christ is called "the Son of Man" (e.g., Mt 8:20) or "man" (1 Tim 2:5) in the Scripture. Secondly, the Scripture ascribes the attributes of an human being to Him: He has a body (Mt 26:12; 27:58, etc.); He grew in stature and wisdom (Lk 2:52); He ate and drank (Mt 11:19, etc.); He experienced the feelings of the body, such as thirst (Jn 19:28), hunger (Lk 4:2), pain and tiredness (Lk 8:23; Jn 4:6); and He had feelings which a reasonable human soul has, such as agony (Lk 22:44), grief (Mk 3:5; Jn 11:35), compassion (Mt 9:36, etc.) and anger (Mt 21:12). Thirdly, we note that the human body of Christ was not extraordinarily created. Rather, like us, He was conceived and developed in a womb. Thus, Christ is contrasted to angels who were individually created: "For verily he took not on him the nature of angels; but he took on him the seed of Abraham" (Heb 2:16; see also Gen 3:15; Gal 4:4, etc.).

2. *The full deity of Christ* has already been shown in *WCF* 2.3. Christ has always existed in His divinity: "Before Abraham was, I am" (Jn 8:58); "In the beginning was the Word, and the Word was with God, and the Word was God" (Jn 1:1). The humanity of Christ was added in the fullness of time when He took to Himself a true body and a reasonable soul: "The Word was made flesh" (Jn 1:14); "Who, being in the form of God, thought it not robbery to be equal with God: But made himself of no reputation, and took upon him the form of a servant, and was made in the likeness of men" (Phil 2:6–7).

3. *The distinction between these two natures* is seen in the fact that Scripture clearly attributes acts and attributes of humanity to Christ (see above); and also acts and attributes of divinity to Him. Also, in many passages in the Scripture, it can be seen quite clearly which of His two natures is in focus. For example, Christ was probably referring to His human nature when He says: "But of that day and that hour knoweth no man, no, not the angels which are in heaven, neither the Son, but the Father" (Mk 13:32). But when He saw Nathanael under the fig tree (Jn 1:48), His divinity was in focus. Theologically and logically, moreover, it is impossible for the two natures to be mixed or confused: For if the human nature is made infinite, self-existent, eternal and absolutely perfect, then it would be no more human; and then the obedience, suffering and death of Christ would be meaningless. On the other hand, if the divine nature were to take any of the limitations of the human nature, then it would cease to be divine. If Christ were to have a mixed nature, He would be neither man nor God, which would contradict the Scriptural assertions of His humanity and deity.

4. *The sinlessness of Christ* is clearly stated in Scripture: "For we have not an high priest which cannot be touched with the feeling of our infirmities; but was in all points tempted like as we are, yet without sin" (Heb 4:15); "[He] did no sin, neither was guile found in his mouth" (1 Pet 2:22); "In him is no sin" (1 Jn 3:5); He is "holy" and "undefiled" (Heb 7:26). He did not have Original Sin because (a) The power of the Holy Ghost overshadowed Mary in her

conception and bearing of the child, so that He did not inherit her corrupt nature: "And the angel answered and said unto her, The Holy Ghost shall come upon thee, and the power of the Highest shall overshadow thee: therefore also that holy thing which shall be born of thee shall be called the Son of God" (Lk 1:35). (b) He was born of a virgin, and therefore was neither seminally present in Adam nor represented by Adam.

5. *The unipersonality of Christ*, or the hypostatic (inseparable, indivisible) union between His divine nature and His human nature, and therefore His possessing a community of divine and human attributes, is taught in section 8.7. Scripturally, it can be seen **firstly**, in the fact that the Scripture does not anywhere attribute any action, word, or attribute to Christ which suggests that He is other than a singular individual. **Secondly**, Scripture does not use the plural pronoun for Christ, unlike the reference to the Triune God. **Thirdly**, there are passages in which Christ is designated by a divine title while an attribute or action that properly belongs to His human nature is being describes. Thus, we read of "the church of God, which he hath purchased with his own blood" (Acts 20:28); and "crucified the Lord of glory" (1 Cor 2:8). **Fourthly**, there are passages in which the reverse is true, e.g.: "No man hath ascended up to heaven, but he that came down from heaven, even the Son of man which is in heaven" (Jn 3:13). **Fifthly**, there are passages in which both divine and human attributes and actions are predicated to the same person, e.g.: "In whom we have redemption through his blood, even the forgiveness of sins: Who is the image of the invisible God, the firstborn of every creature: For by him were all things created..." (Col 1:14–16a); "For in him dwelleth all the fulness of the Godhead bodily" (Col 2:9).

It must be noted that the unipersonality of Christ is a mystery which cannot be fully grasped. It may be weakly illustrated in the unity between the soul and body in man, but note that the human nature is finite while the divine nature is infinite. Also, in the unity of Christ there are two spiritual natures—God as spirit and a human soul, whereas in man there is only one. Our *Confession* again makes no attempt to explain the mystery.

On Christ's Qualification for the Mediatorial Office

8.3 The Lord Jesus, in His human nature thus united to the divine, was sanctified, and anointed with the Holy Spirit, above measure;[1] having in Him all the treasures of wisdom and knowledge;[2] in whom it pleased the Father that all fullness should dwell:[3] to the end, that being holy, harmless, undefiled, and full of grace and truth,[4] He might be thoroughly furnished to execute the office of a Mediator and Surety.[5] Which office He took not unto Himself, but was thereunto called by His Father;[6] who put all power and judgment into His hand, and gave Him commandment to execute the same.[7]

[1]Ps 45:7; Jn 3:34; [2]Col 2:3; [3]Col 1:19; [4]Heb 7:26; Jn 1:14; [5]Acts 10:38; Heb 12:24; 7:22; [6]Heb 5:4–5; [7]Jn 5:22, 27; Mt 28:18; Acts 2:36.

This section teaches us that the Father not only prepared a body for the Son (Heb 10:5) that He might be capable of suffering and dying; but He also conferred upon His human nature the gifts and graces of the Holy Spirit in an immeasurable degree that He be thoroughly furnished to execute His mediatorial office. The Scripture reveals this in the following verses:

- Psalm 45:7, —"Thou lovest righteousness, and hatest wickedness: therefore God, thy God, hath anointed thee with the oil of gladness above thy fellows";

- John 3:34—"God giveth not the Spirit by measure unto him"; and

- Colossians 1:19—"For it pleased the Father that in him should all fulness dwell."

The result of this fullness is that Christ is fitted for His work, being *"holy, harmless, undefiled, and full of grace and truth."*

Without going into a lot of details, it may be seen that the Westminster divines see the unity of the human and divine natures as the basis for the Holy Ghost anointing and sanctification without measure. What this means is that because the human nature is united to the divine nature, it is from the first moment of its existence adorned with all kinds of rich and glorious gifts, particularly of intellect, will and power. As such the human nature of Christ is exalted far above any other creature.

For this reason, Christ as a person becomes worthy of worship, and, — as most theologians believe, —*non posse peccare* (not possible to sin). Some theologians (e.g., Gerstner, Sproul) believe that Christ in so far as His human nature is concerned was *posse peccare, posse non peccare*. The reasoning is that unless this is so, the temptations of Christ would be quite meaningless (Heb 4:15). This is helpful apart from the fact that because of the union of the two natures, Christ would never have sinned.

On the Humiliation and Exaltation of Christ

8.4 This office the Lord Jesus did most willingly undertake;[1] which that He might discharge, He was made under the law[2] and did perfectly fulfill it;[3] endured most grievous torments immediately in His soul,[4] and most painful sufferings in His body;[5] was crucified, and died;[6] was buried, and remained under the power of death, yet saw no corruption.[7] On the third day He arose from the dead,[8] with the same body in which He suffered,[9] with which also He ascended into heaven, and there sitteth at the right hand of His Father,[10] making intercession;[11] and shall return to judge men and angels at the end of the world.[12]

[1]Ps 40:7–8; Heb 10:5–10; Jn 10:18; Phil 2:8; [2]Gal 4:4; [3]Mt 3:15; 5:17; [4]Mt 26:37–38; Lk 22:44; Mt 27:46; [5]Mt 26; 27; [6]Phil 2:8; [7]Acts 2:23–24, 27; 13:37; Rom 6:9; [8]1 Cor 15:3–4; [9]Jn 20:25, 27; [10]Mk 16:19; [11]Rom 8:34; Heb 9:24; 7:25; [12]Rom 14:9–10; Acts 1:11; 10:42; Mt 13:40–42; Jude 6; 2 Pet 2:4.

In the previous section, we are taught that Christ took not the office of a Mediator and Surety upon Himself, but that He was commissioned and commanded by the Father. This is clearly seen in Scriptures:

> "And no man taketh this honour unto himself, but he that is called of God, as was Aaron. So also Christ glorified not himself to be made an high priest; but he that said unto him, Thou art my Son, to day have I begotten thee" (Heb 5:4–5).

So we read that the Father "hath given him authority to execute judgment" (Jn 5:27) and that "all power … in heaven and in earth" is given to Him (Mt 28:18).

This section begins by teaching us that Christ, being same in substance and equal in power and glory with the Father, "did most willingly undertake" the office. This has to be the case not only because it would otherwise be manifestly unjust to punish Him for the sins He did not commit, but also because He Himself has declared:

> "Sacrifice and offering thou wouldest not, but a body hast thou prepared me: In burnt offerings and sacrifices for sin thou hast had no pleasure. Then said I, Lo, I come (in the volume of the book it is written of me,) to do thy will, O God" (Heb 10:5–7).

Then in regards to His laying down His life in propitiatory death, He says:

> "No man taketh it from me, but I lay it down of myself. I have power to lay it down, and I have power to take it again. This commandment have I received of my Father" (Jn 10:18).

This section goes on to teach how Christ discharged His duties both in the estate of humiliation and exaltation.

- *WSC* 27. Wherein did Christ's *humiliation* consist?

  A. Christ's humiliation consisted in His *being born*, and that in a *low condition*, made *under the law*, undergoing the *miseries of this life*, the *wrath of God*, and the *cursed death* of the CROSS; in being *buried*, and *continuing under the power of death* for a time.

  There is a very popular uninspired hymn by Charles Wesley, "And Can it be That I Should Gain," which contains a very pietistic phrase which had often moved me to tears. This statement declares that Christ "emptied Himself of all but love, and bled for Adam's helpless race." Apart from the fact that this statement must have been intended by Wesley to teach universal atonement (though it can be sung with Calvinistic filters), it contains another pernicious error (though perhaps not intended), namely, that in the incarnate Christ, emptied Himself of His deity too! This idea is known as the *kenosis* theory, and is derived from a false interpretation of Philippians 2:6–8.

What then did Christ empty Himself of? Not His deity, else His death would not be sufficient for us all. Christ emptied Himself, rather of His position, glory and dignity. Christ was the Son of God, and very God Himself, but He "made himself of no reputation, and took upon him the form of a servant, and was made in the likeness of men," and as such was made a vicarious sacrifice for us. Theologically, the process that Christ went through for our sakes is known as His humiliation. Christ's humiliation may be understood in three stages: in His birth, life and death.

1. *Christ's humiliation in His birth* comprises: (1) His being born, in the first place, though He is infinite and eternal; and (2) His being born in a low condition, not in a rich and regal family, but in a poor family with a stable for His nativity and manger for his crib, though He is the eternal Son of God and owns the cattle upon a thousand hills.

2. *Christ's humiliation in His life* comprises: (1) His being made subject to the law, though He is the Law-Giver; and (2) His suffering the sorrows of this life, though He not only created the world, but upholds the universe. It should be noted that Christ's earthly sufferings was not a result of sin, but are the natural infirmities of the flesh, such as weariness, hunger, thirst, and the like (cf. Jn 4:6; Mt 4:2); and the affliction of the soul such as grief and sorrow: "He is ... a man of sorrows, and acquainted with grief" (Isa 53:3).

3. *Christ's humiliation in His death* comprises: (1) His suffering an intense separation from His Father and enduring the infinite wrath of God's judgment on the sin of all the elect throughout the ages, which was imputed on Him—though He is eternally beloved of the Father; (2) His being crucified; a cruel, painful and lingering form of punishment reserved for the accursed criminals—though He did not sin at all; (3) His being buried; and (4) His remaining in the grave for three days—though He raised Lazarus and others.

- *WSC* 28. Wherein consisteth Christ's *exaltation*?

A. Christ's exaltation consisteth in His *rising again from the dead* on the third day, in *ascending up into heaven*, in SITTING AT THE RIGHT HAND OF GOD *the Father*, and in *coming to judge the world* at the last day.

Christ's exaltation refers to His being raised to a position of high dignity and glory with a Name that is above every name. Four steps are involved:

1. *His Resurrection. Firstly*, it occurred on the third day (in Jewish reckoning) after Jesus was buried (1 Cor 15:4). This is why Christians keep the Sabbath on the first day of the week (cf. Ps 118:22–24; Acts 4:10–11). *Secondly*, it involves the human soul of Christ reuniting with His body. When Christ died, His divine nature did not separate from His human nature, but His soul was separated from His body. His body was left behind and then buried in the tomb while His soul entered Paradise (Lk 23:43). At the resurrection, His soul was reunited with His body. *Thirdly*, the body that was raised was the same body that was laid in the tomb, but it is now healed of all the blows, stripes and wounds that it suffered and is no longer encumbered with the limitations of the earthly body, including mortality (Rom 6:9). *Fourthly*, His resurrection was testified by "many infallible proofs" (Acts 1:3), including 500 witnesses (1 Cor 15:5–6). *Fifthly*, His resurrection fulfilled OT prophesies (1 Cor 15:4; Isa 53:10; cf. Ps 16:10 and Acts 2:31; 13:35). *Sixthly*, His Resurrection is necessary not only that He may be the captain of our salvation (Heb 2:10; 1 Cor 15:17, 20), but that He may fulfil His Mediatorial office (cf. Ps 110:4; Heb 7:23–25). *Seventhly*, Christ Himself is the author of His own resurrection. He said, "Destroy this temple, and in three days I will raise it up" (Jn 2:19; cf. Jn 10:17).

2. *His Ascension. Firstly*, it occurred forty days after His resurrection, during which time, He confirmed the faith of His disciples (Acts 1:3). *Secondly*, He ascended visibly in His physical body (Lk 24:50–51; Acts 1:9). *Thirdly*, He ascended in triumph as a glorious conqueror (Eph 4:8; Ps 47:5). *Fourthly*, He

ascended that He might be glorified as God-Man with the original glory that He had (Jn 17:5). *Fifthly*, He ascended that He might, as head of the Church, take possession of heaven on behalf of His Church (Jn 14:2; Heb 6:20).

3. *His Enthronement*, or His sitting on the right hand of the throne of God. *Firstly*, it must be noted that the phrase "the right hand of God" (Heb 1:3; Mk 16:19; Eph 1:20; cf. 1 Pet 3:22) must be taken metaphorically as meaning a position of highest majesty and honour (cf. Phil 2:9–10). *Secondly*, in that position, Christ is making continual intercession for us (Rom 8:27, 34; Heb 7:25).

4. *His Return. Firstly*, Christ's return will be visible to all (Acts 1:11; Mt 24:30), glorious (Lk 9:26; Mk 13:26); and sudden (Mt 24:37–39; 1 Th 5:2). *Secondly*, His return will be on the very last day of this present world (2 Pet 3:10). *Thirdly*, He will come to judge the world (Acts 17:31; 2 Cor 5:10).

On the Work of Redemption

8.5 The Lord Jesus, by His perfect obedience and sacrifice of Himself, which He through the eternal Spirit, once offered up unto God, has fully satisfied the justice of His Father;[1] and purchased not only reconciliation, but an everlasting inheritance in the kingdom of heaven, for all those whom the Father has given unto Him.[2]

[1]Rom 5:19; Heb 9:14, 16; 10:14; Eph 5:2; Rom 3:25–26; [2]Dan 9:24, 26; Col 1:19–20; Eph 1:11, 14; Jn 17:2; Heb 9:12, 15.

This section teaches us the effect of Christ's mediatorial work on earth:

1. Christ made satisfaction on behalf of "all those whom the Father has given unto Him," namely the elect, by: (a) His "perfect obedience", —sometimes called His Active Obedience, —by which He fulfilled the demands of the Law in the Covenant of Works, and so purchased an "everlasting in-heritance in the kingdom of heaven" for them. "For as by one man's disobedience many were made sinners, so by the obedience of one shall many be made righteous" (Rom 5:19). (2) His "sacrifice of Himself", —sometimes called His Passive Obedience, —by which He took upon Himself the

sin of His people, and offered up Himself to satisfy divine justice, to propitiate the wrath of God and so purchased reconciliation on their behalf. "For by one offering he hath perfected for ever them that are sanctified" (Heb 10:14; cf. Eph 5:2; Rom 3:25). We have also seen this in our commentary on *WCF* 7.3.

2. Christ's work of redemption was perfectly sufficient. *Firstly*, we note that Christ did not die as an ordinary person. He died as the God-Man, the infinite and transcendently glorious Person of the eternal Son of God. This is why Paul referred to the Church as being purchased by God's own blood: "Take heed therefore unto yourselves, and to all the flock, over the which the Holy Ghost hath made you overseers, to feed the church of God, which he hath purchased with his own blood" (Acts 20:28). Christ's death is therefore of infinite value and sufficiency. His death fully satisfied God, and no more payment of any kind is needed. *Secondly*, it follows that Christ's death purchased eternal life for the elect rather than simply making it possible for sinners to be reconciled to God on condition of faith. This is the uniform testimony of Scripture: "[Christ] gave himself for our sins, *that he might deliver us from this present evil world*, according to the will of God and our Father" (Gal 1:4); NOT: "to make it possible for us to be delivered...." "But when the fulness of the time was come, God sent forth his Son, made of a woman, made under the law, *To redeem them that were under the law, that we might receive the adoption of sons*" (Gal 4:4–5); NOT: "to make the initial down payment so that it is much easier for all to pay the rest and receive the adoption of sons." "Not by works of righteousness which we have done, but according to his mercy he saved us, by the washing of regeneration, and renewing of the Holy Ghost; Which he shed on us abundantly through Jesus Christ our Saviour" (Tit 3:5–6).

8.6 Although the work of redemption was not actually wrought by Christ till after His incarnation, yet the virtue, efficacy, and benefits thereof were communicated unto the elect in all ages successively from the beginning of the world, in and by those promises, types, and sacrifices, wherein He was revealed and signified to be the Seed of the woman, which should bruise the serpent's head, and the Lamb slain from the beginning of the world, being yesterday and to-day the same, and for ever.[1]

[1]*Gal 4:4–5; Gen 3:15; Rev 13:8; Heb 13:8.*

This section teaches us that though Christ's work of redemption was accomplished only after His incarnation, yet the full benefits of it was already available and applied to the elect throughout the ages, including those who lived under the Old Covenant. This is why Christ is said to be "the Lamb slain from the foundation of the world" (Rev 13:8). Indeed, Christ is explicitly said to be a propitiation also for the sins committed under the Old Covenant:

- "Whom God hath set forth to be a propitiation through faith in his blood, to declare his righteousness for the remission of sins that are past, through the forbearance of God" (Rom 3:25).

- "And for this cause he is the mediator of the New Testament, that by means of death, for the redemption of the transgressions that were under the first testament, they which are called might receive the promise of eternal inheritance" (Heb 9:15).

See commentary on *WCF* 7.5–6.

8.7 Christ, in the work of mediation, acteth according to both natures; by each nature doing that which is proper to itself:[1] *yet, by reason of the unity of the person, that which is proper to one nature is sometimes in Scripture attributed to the person dominated by the other nature.*[2]

[1]*Heb 9:14; 1 Pet 3:18;* [2]*Acts 20:28; Jn 3:13; 1 Jn 3:16.*

We saw in *WCF* 8.2 that though Christ has two natures and two wills, He is one person and not two persons. And neither does He act sometimes as God and sometimes as man. It is always as the God-Man. We have already seen the biblical proof of His unipersonality, including what is highlighted in this paragraph, namely that in certain places of Scripture Christ is referred to as God, but recorded as doing something that only man is capable of, such as dying and shedding his blood (cf. Acts 20:28; 1 Jn 3:16); and vice verse when He is referred to as man, but recorded as doing something that only God is capable of, such as coming from heaven and being in heaven while He is on earth (Jn 3:13).

A failure to understand this doctrine has led to the errors of Nestorianism where Christ is spoken of as dying as man; or loving as God. But if Christ died only as man, then His death could not have been sufficient for us. No; no, he suffered and died for us as the God-Man. Likewise, it is wrong to say that Christ loved the rich young man (Mk 10:21) as man, but not as God; or to say that God desires to save the reprobate because Christ spoke of His desire to gather the unbelieving in Jerusalem (Lk 13:34).

Christ indeed has two wills, but let us remember that His human will is completely sanctified and concurs completely with His divine will so that whatever He does, He does as the God-Man.

However, we must at the same time insist the two natures of Christ are united in one person in such a manner that each retained its own properties. Nevertheless, under some circumstances during His earthly ministry, His Divine nature was in, —as Calvin puts it, —"a state of repose" such that it did not at all exert itself.

One such circumstance would be as Christ headed to the Cross, for we remember how He cried out in the Garden of Gethsemane: "Saying, Father, if thou be willing, remove this cup from me: nevertheless not my will, but thine, be done" (Lk 22:42). In distinguishing between His will and His Father's will, He is, in fact, distinguishing between His divine will and His human will, for we must remember that His Father's will is really His divine will, for He and His Father are one in essence. There is only one will in the Godhead.

Apparently, as Christ headed to the Cross, the Divine nature, as it were, went deeper and deeper into "a state of repose," until our Lord cried out on the Cross: "My God, my God, why hast thou forsaken me?" (Mt 27:46). Christ, the God-Man could say these words because at that moment on the Cross, His consciousness of divine nature was, as it were, completely eclipsed by a sense of the wrath of God.

Another circumstance in which the divine nature was, in a sense, "in a state of repose," would be when Christ was a child, and growing and waxing string in spirit (Lk 2:40). While the Scripture does not explicitly say that the child grew in knowledge, it does appear that His interaction with the scholars in the temple (Lk 2:46) was a process of learning. If this is so, it would appear that Christ the God-Man actually grew in knowledge. That is: As God He was omniscient; but as the God-Man his knowledge had to be acquired. Of course, as the perfect man, no errors could ever be entertained in his mind, and no knowledge acquired would ever be lost.

If this is true, then certain knowledge that is propriety of the divine nature might not be made known to Christ the God-Man during His earthly ministry. I believe that as soon as He ascended to heaven after His resurrection, He attained to the fullness of knowledge as the God-Man. But during His earthly ministry, He was not omniscient. But He knew whatever the divine nature actively brought to His consciousness as the God-Man. It is in this way that He "knew all things" (Jn 21:17).

It is for this reason that in Mark 13:32, we are told that the Son, the God-Man did not know the day of His return. The knowledge of this when this day would be, had, —by the appointment of God, —not surfaced from the divine nature of our Lord into His consciousness as the God-Man.

8.8 To all those for whom Christ has purchased redemption, He doth certainly and effectually apply and communicate the same;[1] making intercession for them;[2] and revealing unto them, in and by the Word, the mysteries of salvation;[3] effectually persuading them by His Spirit to believe and obey; and governing their hearts by His Word and Spirit;[4] overcoming all their enemies by His almighty power and wisdom, in such manner, and ways, as are most consonant to His wonderful and unsearchable dispensation.[5]

[1]Jn 6:37, 39; 10:15–16; [2]1 Jn 2:1–2; Rom 8:34; [3]Jn 15:13, 15; Eph 1:7–9; Jn 17:6; [4]Jn 14:16; Heb 12:2; 2 Cor 4:13; Rom 8:9, 14; 15:18–19; Jn 17:17; [5]Ps 110:1; 1 Cor 15:25–26; Mal 4:2–3; Col 2:15.

This section expounds the mediatorial functions of Christ as Priest, Prophet and King, which we have already seen above. Take note again how our Confession once again reiterate that Christ's entire mediatorial work is intended for the salvation of the elect and no one else(see *WCF* 3.5–7, 5.6, 7.3, 8.1, 8.5, *WLC* 59). Christ not only suffered and died on behalf of the elect, but made sure that they would come unto salvation by the application of His Holy Spirit. He did not die for all to make salvation possible for all. Neither did He die for the elect, and then woo all to salvation by His Spirit.

WCF 09: OF FREE WILL

One of the fundamental differences between Calvinism and Arminianism, or between Reformed Theology and Liberal Theology rests on the question of what the free will of man is and whether man has free will. This is a question of utmost importance, for a failure to understand what the Scripture teaches on the subject could lead either to the error of fatalism (Calvinism gone awry) on the one hand or to some form of humanistic atheism (Arminianism gone awry) where man, not God, is ultimately sovereign in regard to his eternal destiny.

In this chapter, the framers of our Confession present one of the most succinct and biblically balanced treatments of the subject ever to appear in Reformed creeds.

On the Liberty of Free Agent

9.1 God hath endued the will of man with that natural liberty, that it is neither forced, nor by any absolute necessity of nature determined, to good or evil.[1]

[1]*Mt 17:12; Jas 1:14; Dt 30:19.*

- One of the most common questions asked about the doctrine of predestination is: "Does not absolute predestination make us robots?" This question is a valid one if we understand predestination and providence as the Westminster divines did, viz.: *"God from all eternity did, by the most wise and holy counsel of His own will, freely and unchangeably ordain whatsoever comes to pass"* (*WCF* 3.1), *"God, the great Creator of all things, doth uphold, direct, dispose, and govern all creatures, actions, and things, from the greatest even to the least..."* (*WCF* 5.1), and *"The almighty power, unsearchable wisdom, and infinite goodness of God so far manifest themselves in His providence, that it extendeth itself even to the first fall, and all other sins of angels and men, and that not by a bare permission..."* (*WCF* 5.4).

- This section anticipates the question and answers simply: God does not force the will of man, nor is man created with a nature that must necessarily do good or evil. In other words, the doctrine of absolute predestination and providence does not make us robots. All our actions considered abstractly, —apart from the goodness or badness of them, —are foreordained and ordered by the providence of God. But the quality, motive or morality of the action belongs to us. Thus, the actions as a whole rightly belong to us as individual moral creatures. Predestination is a remote cause. It does not manipulate us as do electrical signals that manipulate robots. Unless we are suffering from some mental disorder, we would normally be fully conscious of every one of our free actions as being determined by ourselves —according to our intellectual and emotional state, to our desire and affection, and to what we perceive to be the best course of action at the moment of decision. Even if we are held at gun-point and demanded of our money or our life, we make a decision based on what we deem to be best at that moment. To put it in yet another way, the immediate cause of an action in a robot is the controller of the robot or, at the most, a sophisticated program which runs it, —robots do not have feelings nor minds of their own! The immediate cause of our action is our own will, —we do have a mind of our own! God is the remote cause of our actions by way of foreordination and providence; but he is not the immediate cause. Thus, we are responsible for our actions.

- This conclusion is not without scriptural warrant, for Christ taught: "Out of the abundance of the heart the mouth speaketh. A good man out of the good treasure of the heart bringeth forth good things: and an evil man out of the evil treasure bringeth forth evil things" (Mt 12:34–35). Or if the thought in this profound statement is too obvious, consider the expostulation of Solomon in regard to the freedom of man: "The preparations of the heart [belongs to] man, [but] the answer of the tongue, is from the LORD. All the ways of a man are clean in his own eyes; but the LORD weigheth the [motives]" (Prov 16:1-2; paraphrased with a few word-replacements to clarify what Solomon is saying). What Solomon is saying is exactly what our *Confession* is saying, namely that while all actions, including speech is ordained, by the LORD, man does or speak according his own desires and is therefore held responsible by the LORD for his actions.

On Free Will in the Fourfold State of Man

9.2 Man, in his state of innocency, had freedom and power to will and to do that which was good and well pleasing to God;[1] but yet mutably, so that he might fall from it.[2]

[1]Eccl 7:29; Gen 1:26; [2]Gen 2:16–17; 3:6.

9.3 Man, by his fall into a state of sin, hath wholly lost all ability of will to any spiritual good accompanying salvation;[1] so as, a natural man, being altogether averse from that good,[2] and dead in sin,[3] is not able, by his own strength, to convert himself, or to prepare himself thereunto.[4]

[1]Rom 5:6; 8:7; Jn 15:5; [2]Rom 3:10, 12; [3]Eph 2:1, 5; Col 2:13; [4]Jn 6:44, 65; Eph 2:2–5; 1 Cor 2:14; Tit 3:3–5.

9.4 When God converts a sinner, and translates him into the state of grace, He freeth him from his natural bondage under sin,[1] and, by His grace alone, enables him freely to will and to do that which is spiritually good;[2] yet so as that, by reason of his remaining corruption, he doth not perfectly nor only will that which is good, but doth also will that which is evil.[3]

[1]Col 1:13; Jn 8:34, 36; [2]Phil 2:13; Rom 6:18, 22; [3]Gal 5:17; Rom 7:15, 18–19, 21, 23.

9.5 The will of man is made perfectly and immutably free to do good alone in the state of glory only.[1]

[1]Eph 4:13; Heb 12:23; 1 Jn 3:2; Jude 24.

These four sections describe the will of man in his four states, namely: (1) state of innocence; (2) natural corrupt state; (3) state of grace; (4) state of glory. It must be understood that the will considered by itself remains the same in all four states. Or, to put it in another way, the *liberty* of the will remains the same today as before the Fall. But the will of man is bounded to the heart or soul of man, and since the condition of the heart or soul of man differs in the four states, the freedom and power, —or *ability*, —of the will is affected.

The four states may be summarised as follows:

State	Natural Inclination	Nature inherently mutable?[23]	Will's relation to sin
Innocency	Only Good	Yes	Able to Sin; Able not to Sin
Sin	Only Evil	No; needs regeneration	Not able not to Sin
Grace	Good & Evil	No; needs glorification	Able not to Sin
Glory	Only Good	No; perfected	Not able to Sin

These four states, correspond to the four states of man in relation to sin enumerated by Augustine of Hippo: (a) able to sin, able not to sin (posse peccare, posse non peccare); (b) not able not to sin (non posse non peccare); (c) able not to sin (posse non peccare); and (d) unable to sin (non posse peccare).

A few remarks are in order for each of the four states:

1. *State of Innocency* (¶ 2)

    Cf. *WCF* 6.1–2. Man was created with Original Righteousness: "God hath made man upright" (Eccl 7:29). How then could Adam and Eve fall into sin? The divines answer: their nature was mutable. How? The divines make no attempt to explain. A.A. Hodge speculates: Adam was "liable to be seduced by external temptation, and by the inordinate excitement of the propensions of his animal nature, such as in their proper degree and due subordination are innocent" (p. 162).

2. *State of Sin* (¶ 3)

    Cf. *WCF* 6.3–4. "*Spiritual good accompanying salvation*" refers to anything that can be considered good in the eyes of God. The

---

[23] I.e., whether the natural inclination of the nature in the state can change without supernatural intervention?

Roman Catholic Church teaches that salvation is by faith and works accompanying, but the Reformed Church teaches that all our works are as filthy rags in the eyes of God. The natural man is dead, not sick in sin. Thus, the natural man is unable to convert himself. This contrasts with the assertion of Arminianism, that the Holy Spirit will woo, but the sinner must make his own decision. Moreover, the sinner is unable *"to prepare himself"* for his conversion. Most of the Puritans taught that sinners should seek salvation. Since conversion or regeneration is wholly a work of God, it was deemed by many of the Puritans that sinners should wait for God to convert them, so that they may say that they have wholehearted trust in Christ. But they should not remain idle while waiting, since they are able to read the Bible, attend church, hear sermons, etc. Yet, these actions are not meritorious: there is no guarantee that God will convert them when they engage in such activities. However, many misunderstood that they taught that these actions were absolutely essential and efficacious, and that they actually prepare the sinners for grace. (Many of the Puritans did indeed use the word 'prepare' when they meant 'seek,' and that could have given rise to the misunderstanding). The divines were in a sense correcting this false notion. There is no way that the natural man can prepare himself for grace. Even his seeking is not truly seeking after God, but after the comforts and benefits of salvation. Such seeking is selfish and sinful, though, as Edwards taught, less sinful.

The inability of the soul to convert itself is clearly taught in the Scripture in its insistence:

a. That the natural man is "dead in trespasses and sins" (Eph 2:1); is afflicted with blindness of heart and darkness of understanding (Eph 4:18); is a slave of sin (Rom 6:16, 20); and is a captive of Satan (2 Tim 2:26).

b. That the natural man cannot change himself: "Can the Ethiopian change his skin, or the leopard his spots? then may ye also do good, that are accustomed to do evil" (Jer 13:23). "No man can come to me, except the Father which hath sent me draw him" (Jn 6:44a). See also Romans 9:16; 1 Corinthians 2:14.

c. That a sovereign intervention by way of God is necessary for a man to enter into the kingdom of God: "Except a man be born again, he cannot see the kingdom of God" (Jn 3:3). Thus, the act of conversion is called creation (Eph 2:10) and resurrection (Jn 5:21).

d. That the conversion of sinners is God's own work: "And I will give them one heart, and I will put a new spirit within you; and I will take the stony heart out of their flesh, and will give them an heart of flesh: That they may walk in my statutes, and keep mine ordinances, and do them: and they shall be my people, and I will be their God" (Ezk 11:19–20; 36:26–27; Jer 31:33). "And a certain woman named Lydia, a seller of purple, of the city of Thyatira, which worshipped God, heard us: whose heart the Lord opened, that she attended unto the things which were spoken of Paul" (Acts 16:14).

e. That the increase of faith and holiness in Christians is a work of God: "Being confident of this very thing, that he which hath begun a good work in you will perform it until the day of Jesus Christ" (Phil 1:6); "For it is God which worketh in you both to will and to do of his good pleasure" (Phil 2:13).

3. *State of Grace* (¶ 4)

The state of grace is entered into by a sinner upon regeneration. In the act of regeneration, two things happen, first, negatively, God *"freeth [the sinner] from his natural bondage under sin."* The regenerate man is not longer a captive or a slave to sin and Satan. "Jesus answered them, Verily, verily, I say unto you, Whosoever committeth sin is the servant of sin. … If the Son therefore shall make you free, ye shall be free indeed" (Jn 8:34, 36). To put it in another way, the sinner is now enabled not to sin. Secondly, positively, God *"by His grace alone, enables him freely to will and to do that which is spiritually good."* We learn from the next chapter (*WCF* 10) that this is effected by the Holy Spirit changing the heart or implanting a new spiritual principle, habit or tendency, in the affections of the soul.

God has, however, deemed it fit that while in this life, the corruption of nature of the regenerate will not be fully eradicated. Thus, by reason of the remaining corruption, the regenerate does not will only that which is good, but also wills that which is sinful. And even when he wills what is good, it is mixed with sin. "For the flesh lusteth against the Spirit, and the Spirit against the flesh: and these are contrary the one to the other: so that ye cannot do the things that ye would" (Gal 5:17; cf. Rom 7:15–23).

We will see more on this subject in *WCF* 13, On Sanctification.

4. *State of Glory* (¶ 5)

This is the state that the elect enters into when he passes from this present world into eternity, at which point he is "*made perfect in holiness*" (*WSC* 37), and will sin no more. In terms of his will, he is in this state of glory "*made perfectly and immutably free to do good.*" He might do good after he was regenerated. However, his good works are never perfect, for they are always tainted with sin. But now, he will forever be able to do good, and to do good perfectly. He is unable to sin.

But take note that when we say that a glorified man is "unable to sin," we do not mean that he is, therefore, no more a free agent. What it does mean is that the old corrupt tendencies are completely eradicated, and the soul is perfectly sanctified (Eph 4:13; Heb 12:23) so that it has an immutable holy disposition. There is no longer any desire to do anything sinful. While he remains in this world, the remnant of corruption may deceive the regenerate man by making sin and its fruits seem attractive. But now the remnant of corruption is eradicated, and therefore the glorified man hates sin and will never choose ever again to sin. It is in this sense that glorified men are unable to sin.

WCF 10: OF EFFECTUAL CALLING

Reformed theologians frequently speak about the *ordo salutis*, or the logical order of God's work, in the salvation of a soul. The Reformed *ordo salutis* is radically different from that of an Arminian. Although conscientious theologians disagree sometimes in minor details, a common Reformed order is: election, predestination, external call, regeneration, internal (or effectual) call, conversion: repentance and faith, justification in time, sanctification, initial glorification, resurrection and final glorification. Our *Confession* follows this order, by using a slightly different terminology. In particular, the *Confession* speaks of regeneration as being an essential part of effectual calling rather than separately. We may think of effectual calling as an inwardly perceived command of God which requires a response on our part; and regeneration as what God does in our heart to enable us to respond to the command.

On the Nature of the Effectual Call

10.1 All those whom God hath predestinated unto life, and those only, He is pleased, in His appointed and accepted time, effectually to call,[1] by His Word and Spirit,[2] out of that state of sin and death, in which they are by nature, to grace and salvation by Jesus Christ;[3] enlightening their minds spiritually and savingly to understand the things of God;[4] taking away their heart of stone, and giving unto them an heart of flesh;[5] renewing their wills, and by His almighty power determining them to that which is good;[6] and effectually drawing them to Jesus Christ;[7] yet so as they come most freely, being made willing by His grace.[8]

[1]Rom 8:30; 11:7; Eph 1:10–11; [2]2 Th 2:13–14; 2 Cor 3:3, 6; [3]Rom 8:2; Eph 2:1–5; 2 Tim 1:9–10; [4]Acts 26:18; 1 Cor 2:10, 12; Eph 1:17–18; [5]Ezk 36:26; [6]Ezk 11:19; Phil 2:13; Dt 30:6; Ezk 36:27; [7]Eph 1:19; Jn 6:44–45; [8]Song 1:4; Ps 110:3; Jn 6:37; Rom 6:16–18.

a. There is such a thing as an effectual or internal call which differs from the external call. This is clear from Scripture. The internal call is taught in passages such as Romans 8:30, "Moreover whom he did predestinate, them he also called: and whom he called, them he also justified: and whom he justified, them he also glorified." All who are called effectually will be justified. Not so for the external call, which for all intends and purpose is the audible call unto repentance and faith of preaching. Thus, the Lord teaches: "For many are called, but few are chosen" (Mt 22:14). Commenting on this verse, Calvin states: "...there are two species of calling—for there is a universal call, by which God through the external preaching of the Word, invites all men alike, even those whom He designs the call to be a savour of death [cf. 2 Cor 2:16], and the ground of a severer condemnation. The other kind of call is special, which He deigns for the most part to give to the believers alone, while by the inward illumination of His Spirit He causes the preached Word to dwell in their hearts."[24]

b. The effectual call is issued to all the elect and only to the elect. Those who are effectually called will be saved. Since God has from eternity definitely and unchangeably determined who should be saved and the means to their salvation (*WCF* 3.3–5), it is clear that only the elect will be effectually called. Thus, the Scripture declares that our effectual calling is based on our election: "Who hath saved us, and called us with an holy calling, not according to our works, but according to his own purpose and grace, which was given us in Christ Jesus before the world began" (2 Tim 1:9; cf. 2 Th 2:13–14). Thus, the Scripture affirms that those who are elect will be called, and will be justified and eventually glorified (Rom 8:30).

c. The timing of the effectual call is under the direction and sovereign will and pleasure of God. Thus, our *Confession* speaks of the "*appointed and accepted time.*" In the Parable of the Vineyard (Mt 20:1–16), some are called early, some at the third hour, some at the sixth, some at the ninth and the rest at the eleventh hour. We may also add that there is also a difference in the manner in which the Lord calls. Some are sweetly and gently drawn to the Saviour over a period of time, so that they can scarcely say with confidence when the change in heart began (e.g., many children who were catechised from young). Others experienced dramatic conversion under powerful preaching (e.g., Saul of Tarsus; those under the

---

[24] *ICR* 3.24.8.

ministry of Whitefield). Still others underwent a time of terror and burden of guilt under the Law before they find relief in the Gospel (e.g., Bunyan and many under the ministry of Edwards).

d. The effectual call is effected by the Word and Spirit. The Holy Spirit is always the efficient agent in the effectual call: "Jesus answered and said unto him, Verily, verily, I say unto thee, Except a man be born again, he cannot see the kingdom of God. ... I say unto thee, Except a man be born of water and of the Spirit, he cannot enter into the kingdom of God. ...The wind bloweth where it listeth, and thou hearest the sound thereof, but canst not tell whence it cometh, and whither it goeth: so is every one that is born of the Spirit" (Jn 3:3, 5, 8). But the Holy Spirit ordinarily always employ the Word as the instrument or means of calling: "For our gospel came not unto you in word only, but also in power, and in the Holy Ghost, and in much assurance; as ye know what manner of men we were among you for your sake" (1 Th 1:5). The Word and the Spirit always operate together so that the power of the preaching is not derived from the piety or eloquence of the preacher. Thus, Paul testifies to the Corinthians: "And my speech and my preaching was not with enticing words of man's wisdom, but in demonstration of the Spirit and of power" (1 Cor 2:4). In the same way, apart from extraneous circumstances (e.g., see ¶ 3), the Holy Spirit does not call or regenerate a person apart from the Word. Using the Law, the Spirit convinces the sinner of his guilt and the utter insufficiency of his own works of righteousness as the ground of acceptance before God. Using the Gospel, the Spirit enlightens the mind of the sinner in the knowledge of Christ, —especially, His perfect righteousness, the fulness of His grace, His ability to save and His willingness to receive all who truly come to Him. At the same time, the Holy Spirit also takes away his heart of stone and replaces it with a heart of flesh so that he is now able to embrace and trust Christ (Eph 2:8), and indeed find Him to be irresistible.

e. In the effectual call, no violence is offered to the will. This is most beautifully explained by Robert Shaw:

While the Spirit effectually draws sinners to Christ, He deals with them in a way agreeable to their rational nature, "so as they come most freely, being made willing by His grace." The liberty of the will is not invaded, for that would destroy its very nature; but its obstinacy is overcome, its perverseness taken away, and the whole soul powerfully, yet sweetly, attracted to the Saviour. The compliance of the soul is voluntary, while the energy of the Spirit is efficient and almighty: "Thy people shall be willing in the day of thy power" (Ps 110:3).[25]

The implication is that a believer is not dragged in kicking and screaming (remember C.S. Lewis); neither is the door into the kingdom of God locked. It is always open, but sinners will not enter because they hate God and prefer Satan. The effectual call is irresistible because it involves a radical, permanent change in the entire moral nature of the subject, enlightening his mind, sanctifying his affection, renewing his will and giving new direction to his actions. This change is what causes the soul to step into the kingdom of God. Regeneration precedes faith.

f.   The elect, as all others, may actively resist the common operation of the Holy Spirit, but in the effectual call, the operation of the Holy Spirit is irresistible. In the Arminian scheme, the Holy Spirit only woos the sinner, giving him sufficient grace to be able to comply with the call of the Gospel and no further. The ultimate success of the Spirit's work therefore is dependent on the sinner's free will. This is a doctrine that is contrary to Scripture which affirms: "So then it is not of him that willeth, nor of him that runneth, but of God that sheweth mercy" (Rom 9:16).

It is true that there are common operations of the Spirit which are extended to all men in a greater or lesser degree, which do not involve any change in principle or disposition of the soul, but only in heightening the conscience, increasing the natural emotions of the heart in view of sin, duty and self-interest. This is sometimes called 'conviction,' in Puritan language. Such influence are spoken

---

[25] Shaw, Op. Cit., 121

of in the Scripture and are resistible: "For it is impossible for those who were once enlightened, and have tasted of the heavenly gift, and were made partakers of the Holy Ghost, And have tasted the good word of God, and the powers of the world to come" (Heb 6:4–5; cf. Mt 7:22; 13:20). Those who come under conviction of sin do not necessarily proceed on to regeneration. We may say that the common operations of the Holy Spirit acts upon, but not in, the heart of the unbeliever.

10.2 This effectual call is of God's free and special grace alone, not from any thing at all foreseen in man;[1] who is altogether passive therein, until, being quickened and renewed by the Holy Spirit,[2] he is thereby enabled to answer this call, and to embrace the grace offered and conveyed in it.[3]

[1] 2 Tim 1:9; Tit 3:4–5; Eph 2:4–5, 8–9; Rom 9:11; [2] 1 Cor 2:14; Rom 8:7; Eph 2:5; [3] Jn 6:37; Ezk 36:27; Jn 5:25.

In addition to the propositions already made in the first paragraph, we must also be clear of two additional verities regarding the effectual call:

a. Firstly, the effectual call is of *"God's free and special grace alone"*, rather than *"from anything at all foreseen in man"* (cf. 2 Tim 1:9). God does not give His elect the blessing of the effectual call in response to anything that he (the elect) does, nor on the basis or anything that God foresees he would do. All the positive responses of the elect, including repentance, faith and good works, —flow from the effectual call, which God graciously and freely bestows. Therefore, for all intends and purposes, it is impossible to see whom God would gift the effectual call. Thus, it is wrong to ask God to reward someone with the effectual call on the basis of his observed 'good' works.

b. For in the second place, in the effectual calling, the sinner is *"altogether passive... until [he is] quickened and renewed by the Holy Spirit."* Before regeneration or effectual calling, a sinner may do many things which may be reckoned as activities of seeking salvation. He comes to church, he talks to believers, he listens to sermons, he reads the Bible, and he sometime prays. He may even feel conviction of sin, and turn away from the grosser sins in his life. But none of these activities are meritorious or righteous in the eyes of God. The Scripture teaches us that even such a person is dead in trespasses and sin. Indeed, although, experience teaches us that God normally regenerates those who are seeking, none of these activities contribute to the effectual calling of the sinner, which is entirely by grace. It is only after a sinner is regenerated, that the Holy Spirit begins to convert or sanctify him. The child of God, in conversion, has the responsibility of making use of the means of grace. Thus, he is in a sense, no longer entirely passive. Nevertheless, the sinner acts as he is acted upon by God, for as Paul insists: "For it is God which worketh in you both to will and to do of his good pleasure" (Phil 2:13).

On the Effectual Call of those Incapable of being Outwardly Called

10.3 Elect infants, dying in infancy, are regenerated, and saved by Christ through the Spirit,[1] who worketh when, and where, and how He pleaseth.[2] So also are all other elect persons, who are incapable of being outwardly called by the ministry of the Word.[3]

[1]Lk 18:15–16; Acts 2:38–39; Jn 3:3, 5; 1 Jn 5:12; Rom 8:9; [2]Jn 3:8; [3]1 Jn 5:12; Acts 4:12.

In the previous two sections, we saw that the Holy Spirit normally works by means of the Word preached or read. This means that a sinner should first experience the outward call, and then only the inward or effectual call. But what about infants dying in infancy and adults who are mentally incapable of being called by the Word, or those who are unable to hear or understand the Gospel?

The Westminster divines have provided, perhaps the most judicious and biblically defensible answer: those who are elect will be *"regenerated and saved by Christ, though the Spirit, who worketh when, and where, and how He pleaseth."* By this answer, the divines recognise: (1) That all men, including infants in the womb, deserve damnation for imputed guilt; (2) God's election is not conditioned on the physical ability or length of life of the individual; (3) God can regenerate without the means if He chooses to; and (4) There is no scriptural warrant to believe that all infants dying in infancy will be saved.

It is true that the Westminster position does not afford much comfort for grieving parents, which is why many theologians choose to believe on very flimsy ground that all infants dying in infancy will be saved. Indeed, when Spurgeon edited the *Baptist Confession of Faith* of 1689, which is based on the *WCF*, for his church to use, he actually dropped the word 'elect' while retaining the rest of the wordings in this section. This edition of the *BCF* is currently subscribed to by many Reformed Baptist Churches especially in the UK. But what comfort can be derived from a statement that has little scriptural support?

In any case, with the biblical position which we are given to hold, we acknowledge that while the church will have a warrant to speak of the child who is baptized as belonging to the Lord, the parents of a child who dies in infancy may not derive much assurance that the child is regenerated. Nevertheless, comfort may always be sought in the fact that God is merciful and that all He does is right. A bereaved mother may indeed pray at the grave side:

> Lord, in Thy name I have brought forth a child. And from Thy hand I have received it. I have consecrated it to Thee, in order that it should be a child for Thy covenant. And now Thou hast taken the child away from me. In that same faith wherein I consecrated him to Thee, I leave him with Thee, without being filled with anxious doubts concerning the salvation and election of this child, but knowing that Thou, according to Thy good pleasure, which by faith to me is always good, dost save Thy children out of my seed.[26] ().

On those who are not Effectually Called

10.4 Others not elected, although they may be called by the ministry of the Word,[1] and may have some common operations of the Spirit,[2] yet they never truly come unto Christ, and therefore cannot be saved:[3] much less can men not professing the Christian religion be saved in any other way whatsoever, be they never so diligent to frame their lives

---

[26] Herman Hoeksema, *Believers and Their Seed: Children in the Covenant* (Grandville: Reformed Free Publishing, 1997), 166

according to the light of nature, and the laws of that religion they do profess;[4] and to assert and maintain that they may, is very pernicious, and to be detested.[5]

[1]Mt 22:14; [2]Mt 7:22; 13:20–21; Heb 6:4–5; [3]Jn 6:64–66; 8:24; [4]Acts 4:12; Jn 14:6; Eph 2:12; Jn 4:22; 17:3; [5]2 Jn 9–11; 1 Cor 16:22; Gal 1:6–8.

- After asking the question of salvation of those incapable of faith, the divines now turn to two other questions: (1) Is it possible for those who come under the ministry of the Word and experience some of the common operations of the Spirit, to be not elected? (2) What about those who have never heard the Gospel? Can they be saved?

- The answer for the first question is 'Yes,' it is possible for a person to be part of a church, involved actively in the life of the church and experiencing the common operations of the Spirit, —of conviction under the preaching of the Law and joy under the preaching of the Gospel, —to be nevertheless not elected. Such a person does not come truly to Christ and may even profess faith hypocritically. Such a person cannot be saved. But it must be noted that the responsibility of unbelief lies not in God, but in the unbeliever. This is why Dr Gerstner preaches that the deepest part of hell is reserved for the sinner who walks to it through the aisles of the church. This is why every Christian has a responsibility to examine himself to see whether he is in the faith (2 Cor 13:5). No discriminatory preaching, —on the marks of regeneration, —can hurt the elect, though their trust in their own righteousness can be shaken. Thus, we must not be presumptuous of our faith if we possess none of the marks of faith and are living in wilful sins. Indeed, if this be the case, we ought rather to doubt our salvation and come to Christ afresh, pleading forgiveness and faith in Him.

- The answer to the second question is 'No,' it is not possible for a person who has never heard the gospel, or who has a different religion to be saved, —even if he lives in all sincerity according to the dictates of his conscience or according to rules of his religion. *First* of all, all men are guilty in Adam. *Secondly*, all men are born with a corrupt nature so that no matter how well they may heed their conscience and live according to the light of nature, they are living in sin. *Thirdly*, although God has given general revelation of Himself so that all man "are without excuse," yet without special revelation it is impossible to come unto salvation (*WCF* 1.1). *Fourthly*, Christ has declared: "I am the way, the truth, and the life: no man cometh unto the Father, but by me" (Jn 14:6). This is why Peter asserts: "Neither is there salvation in any other: for there is none other name under heaven given among men, whereby we must be saved" (Acts 4:12). Thus, Paul is emphatic about the necessity of preaching if anyone were to be saved: "For whosoever shall call upon the name of the Lord shall be saved. How then shall they call on him in whom they have not believed? and how shall they believe in him of whom they have not heard? and how shall they hear without a preacher?" (Rom 10:13–14).

WCF 11: OF JUSTIFICATION

Justification refers to the divine affirmation of a person as legally righteous and therefore not liable for condemnation. The doctrine of Justification holds a most important place in the Christian Church. During the time of the Reformation, Martin Luther apparently declared it the *articulus standis vel cadentis ecclesiæ*—the article on which the Church stands or fall. It was the prominent issue that led to the Reformation.

Today, a proper understanding of the subject is crucial not only to guard against erroneous conceptions concerning our salvation and state before the Lord, but to give us comfort and assurance in the face of the real struggles that confront anyone who seeks honestly to walk with the Lord.

It is to this end that this chapter presents us with the classic Protestant or Reformed understanding of the subject.

On the Nature of Justification

11.1 Those whom God effectually calleth He also freely justifieth;[1] not by infusing righteousness into them, but by pardoning their sins, and by accounting and accepting their persons as righteous: not for anything wrought in them, or done by them, but for Christ's sake alone; nor by imputing faith itself, the act of believing, or any other evangelical obedience, to them as their righteousness; but by imputing the obedience and satisfaction of Christ unto them,[2] they receiving and resting on Him and His righteousness by faith: which faith they have not of themselves, it is the gift of God.[3]

[1]Rom 8:30; 3:24; [2]Rom 4:5–8; 2 Cor 5:19, 21; Rom 3:22, 24–25, 27–28; Tit 3:5, 7; Eph 1:7; Jer 23:6; 1 Cor 1:30–31; Rom 5:17–19; [3]Acts 10:44; Gal 2:16; Phil 3:9; Acts 13:38–39; Eph 2:7–8.

The apostle Paul declares, "whom [God] did predestinate, them he also called: and whom he called, them he also justified" (Rom 8:30). The word translated "justified" is the Greek verb δικαιόω (*dikaioō*), which is derived from the adjective δίκαιος (*díkaios*), which means "righteous." Thus, to justify someone is either to make him righteous or to declare him to be righteous. Justification is an act of God that involves both making a sinner righteous and declaring him to be righteous. Theologians call these two aspects of justification *Actual Justification* and *Declarative Justification*.[27] Our *Confession* does not overtly mention the distinction, but speaks of the *actual* basis upon which God *declares* His elect righteous.

With this in mind, we may draw the following five things about justification:

a. The *price* of Justification: *"It is the gift of God"* which is *"freely"* given. It is entirely gratuitous to us. The apostle Paul emphatically insists on this truth repeatedly. He reminds us, for example, that we are "justified freely by [God's] grace through the redemption that is in Christ Jesus" (Rom 3:24). Even faith itself, the instrument of justification, is a gracious gift of God (Eph 2:8). This means that we are justified not by our own works or righteousness, "otherwise grace is no more grace" (Rom 11:6). Thus, the Reformation watchword: *Sola Gratia*.

b. The *scope* of justification: Only those whom *"God effectually calleth."* In other words, only the elect, are justified since only the elect are effectually called (Rom 8:30). And so conversely, those who are justified are elect. This is so obvious the apostle could ask rhetorically and answer firmly: "Who shall lay anything to the charge of God's elect? It is God that justifieth" (Rom 8:33).

---

[27] see James Buchanan, *The Doctrine of Justification: An Outline of Its History in the Church and of Its Exposition from Scripture* (Grand Rapids: Baker Books, 1970), 233-9. A case may be made that our Confession deals only with *Actual* Justification, i.e. the imputation of Christ's righteousness upon the sinner, the imputation of the sinner's guilt upon Christ, and reconciliation through the blood of Christ. The is no direct reference to *Declarative* Justification in which God declares the sinner to be just (by which "his acceptance is proved or attested, so as to be made manifest to his own conscience, or to his fellow-men" [ibid, 234]), unless we consider all references to the terms, 'justified' and 'justification' in this chapter as having exactly that meaning. In other words, instead of speaking of the two aspects of justification as Buchanan does, our Confession simply deals with it as one by speaking of its *ground* as being inalienably a part of that one act of justification in which God declares His elect to be righteous in His sight.

c. The *nature* of justification: It is a judicial act of God that does not include a change of the sinner's nature, but rather a change of the sinner's legal status in relation to God's Law. Thus, we are given to confess that God justifies the elect *"not by infusing righteousness into them, but by pardoning their sins, and by accounting and accepting their persons as righteous."* In other words, it is a forensic act involving a judicial declaration. And this agrees with the fact that justification is frequently, in the Scripture, set in opposition to condemnation, which is a declaration of guilt. Paul says, for example: "And not as it was by one that sinned, so is the gift: for the judgment was by one to condemnation, but the free gift is of many offences unto justification" (Rom 5:16; cf. Rom 8:33–34). This is why we insist that the justification of the elect is *"not by infusing righteousness into them."* Thus, a Christian, as Luther insisted, is *simul justus et peccator*—simultaneously just and a sinner (cf. Rom 4:5).

d. The *basis* of justification: *"for Christ's sake alone,"* or more precisely, *"the obedience and satisfaction of Christ."* In other words, the righteousness of Jesus Christ and His atoning death is the sole ground of a sinner's justification before God. This is essentially what Paul is declaring when he says, "Therefore as by the offence of one judgment came upon all men to condemnation; even so by the righteousness of one the free gift came upon all men unto justification of life. For as by one man's disobedience many were made sinners, so by the obedience of one shall many be made righteous" (Rom 5:18-19).

e. The *method* of Justification: By *"imputing the obedience and satisfaction of Christ"* rather than by infusing or imparting righteousness to the elect. It is true that in our conversion, God's Spirit works righteousness or an inclination to do good in our heart. However, God's Spirit indwells and sanctifies on the basis of, rather than for the purpose of, our justification. Thus, we are given to confess that the justification of the elect cannot be *"for anything wrought in them, or done by them." Indeed,* no man can be justified before God, in whole or in part, on the ground of personal righteousness of any kind, whether pre-conversion or post-conversion, for all our righteousnesses are filthy rags in God's eyes, which are purer than to behold evil (Isa 64:6, Hab 1:13). Even *"faith"* or the *"act of believing"* is not the ground, but the instrument of our justification.

The fundamental error of the Church of Rome is to confuse the *imparted* (or infused or inherent) righteousness of the regenerate with the *imputed* righteousness of the Redeemer. In other words, she confused sanctification with justification. The merits of Christ, according to Rome, was for the procuring of regenerating grace by which we are made righteous. For them, God's righteousness in Christ is not the sole and all-sufficient ground for our justification. The suffering and obedience on the part of the believer is necessary for justification. But this runs contrary to Scripture, which declares that the righteousness by which we are justified is not our own. Paul, for example, is clear that his desire is to "be found in [Christ], not having [his] own righteousness, which is of the law, but that which is through the faith of Christ, the righteousness which is of God by faith" (Phil 3:9). And furthermore, the Romish doctrine ultimately implies that it is how one lives that determines whether he is justified or not, which of course contradicts the Scripture, which teaches us that our justification is "Not of works, lest any man should boast" (Eph 2:9).

The doctrine of justification, so understood, distinguishes true Christianity from all false religions including Roman Catholicism. Christianity alone insists that salvation is by grace alone through faith alone in Christ alone. This is an extremely liberating theology for it frees us from the bondage of the fear of not being good enough and the hypocritical pride of being better than others, while humbling us to live for the glory of God out of gratitude and love for all that Christ has done for us.

11.2 Faith, thus receiving and resting on Christ and His righteousness, is the alone instrument of justification;[1] yet is it not alone in the person justified, but is ever accompanied with all other saving graces, and is no dead faith, but worketh by love.[2]

[1]Jn 1:12; Rom 3:28; 5:1; [2]Jas 2:17, 22, 26; Gal 5:6.

It is clear that we are justified by faith. What is faith? Faith, essentially is *"receiving and resting on Christ and His righteousness"* for our salvation. All branches and manifestations of Christianity agree that faith is necessary for our salvation. However, a failure to grasp the intricate relationship between faith and justification as taught in the Scripture has resulted in many groups veering away from true Christianity into legalistic religions that falsely claim to be Christian, or into forms of lawless Christianity that bring shame to the name of Christ. All such religions are powerless to save sinners even if they claim to be Christian.

But what is the correct understanding of the relationship between faith and justification? The present paragraph of our *Confession* highlights 3 things:

a. First of all, we are given to reaffirm that faith is not the basis or the *meritorious* cause of justification. When the Scripture speaks of the elect being "justified by faith" (Rom 3:28; 5:1) or "the just shall live by faith" (Rom 1:17; Hab 2:4), it does not mean that faith is the *meritorious* cause of justification. The meritorious cause of our justification is Christ, His atonement and His righteousness. Believers are justified by faith and through faith but never on account of faith. This must be carefully understood as it is one of the most common errors even amongst evangelical Christians today. Robert Haldane is surely right when he says, "Nothing, then, can be a greater corruption of the truth than to represent faith itself as accepted instead of righteousness, or to be the righteousness that saves the sinner. Faith is not righteousness. Righteousness is fulfilling of the law."[28]

b. Secondly, we are given to confess not only that faith is the instrumental cause of justification, but that it is the "*alone instrument of justification.*" This is what we mean when we say that we hold to *sola fides*. This contrasts sharply with the doctrine of Roman Catholicism that we are justified by faith *and* works together. When James says that "by works a man is justified and

---

[28] Robert Haldane, *Romans* (Edinburgh: Banner of Truth Trust, 1996 [1874]), 163.

not by faith only" (Jas 2:24), he is not talking about justification before God, but justification before man. Or to put it in another way, he is not speaking of "justified" in the theological sense of the word, but in the sense of "proved to be true" (cf. Lk 7:35). James is saying that good works proves that a Christian is for real.

c. Thirdly, we are given to insist that saving faith is *"not alone in the person justified."* It is *"ever accompanied with all other saving graces, and is no dead faith, but worketh by love."* In other words, justification is by faith alone, but the faith is not alone (*Sola fides justificat, sed fides non est sola*). "Faith, if it hath not work, is dead, being alone" (Jas 2:17), says James. This, of course, does not mean that justification is by faith plus works. Luther has well said: "Works are not taken into consideration when the question respects justification. But true faith will no more fail to produce them, than the sun can cease to give light." To put it in another way: a justified person will also receive sanctification in which righteousness is formed within him. Justification not accompanied by sanctification cannot be true. Justification and sanctification must be distinguished but not separated (cf. 1 Cor 6:11). There is a modern false teaching which may be known as Dispensational Antinomianism, which teaches that a person can be saved so long as he has received Christ as his Saviour, but not necessarily as Lord. Those who hold to this position teach that once a person prays to receive Christ, he will be saved even if he shows no evidence of conversion or sanctification. This is what our *Confession* is guarding against.

We may summarise:
Roman Catholic:	faith + works → justification
Antinomian:	faith → justification (− works)
Reformed:	faith → justification → works

11.3 Christ, by His obedience and death, did fully discharge the debt of all those that are thus justified, and did make a proper, real, and full satisfaction to His Father's justice in their behalf.[1] Yet, in as much as He was given by the Father for them,[2] and His obedience and satisfaction accepted in their stead,[3] and both, freely, not for any thing in them, their justification is only of free grace;[4] *that both the exact justice, and rich grace of God might be glorified in the justification of sinners.*[5]

[1]*Rom 5:8–10, 19; 1 Tim 2:5–6; Heb 10:10, 14; Dan 9:24, 26; Isa 53:4–6, 10–12;* [2]*Rom 8:32;* [3]*2 Cor 5:21; Mt 3:17; Eph 5:2;* [4]*Rom 3:24; Eph 1:7;* [5]*Rom 3:26; Eph 2:7.*

Herein we learn of the benefits and goals of justification.

a. The *benefits* of justification: This comprises two parts—pardon and acceptance. The *WSC* 33 teaches: "*Justification is an act of God's free grace, wherein he pardoneth all our sins, and accepteth us as righteous in his sight, only for the righteousness of Christ imputed to us, and received by faith alone.*"

The pardoning of our sins was accomplished by Christ's propitiatory atonement, i.e., His taking the punishment due us on Himself: "He shall see of the travail of his soul, and shall be satisfied: by his knowledge shall my righteous servant justify many; for he shall bear their iniquities" (Isa 53:11); "For he hath made him to be sin for us, who knew no sin; that we might be made the righteousness of God in him" (2 Cor 5:21; cf. Gal 3:13; Col 2:14). Christ bore our sins and "*did fully discharge the debt of all those that are thus justified, and did make a proper, real, and full satisfaction to His Father's justice in [our] behalf.*" This is sometimes known as Christ's *passive* obedience.

Our being accepted as righteous is not only because our sins have been atoned for, but also because the righteousness of Christ—in His perfect keeping of the Law throughout His earthly ministry as our covenantal representative, —is imputed to us (Rom 5:17–19). In this way, "*His obedience [is] accepted in [our] stead.*" This obedience is sometimes known as Christ's *active* obedience. We may say that Christ is the *meritorious* cause or ground of justification; and the imputation of Christ's righteousness by grace is the *formal* cause of justification.

b. The *goal* of justification: That God may be glorified as "*both the exact justice, and rich grace of God [are] glorified in the justification of sinners.*" That this is the biblically stated goal is clear: "To declare, I say, at this time his righteousness: that he might be just, and the justifier of him which believeth in Jesus" (Rom 3:26); and "That in the ages to come he might shew the exceeding riches of his grace in his kindness toward us through Christ Jesus" (Eph 2:7).

On the Timing of Justification

11.4 God did, from all eternity, decree to justify all the elect;[1] and Christ did, in the fullness of time, die for their sins, and rise again for their justification:[2] nevertheless they are not justified, until the Holy Spirit doth, in due time, actually apply Christ unto them.[3]

[1]*Gal 3:8; 1 Pet 1:2, 19–20; Rom 8:30;* [2]*Gal 4:4; 1 Tim 2:6; Rom 4:25;* [3]*Col 1:21–22; Gal 2:16; Tit 3:4–7.*

- What this section indicates is that there is a sense in which justification happens in eternity—with the immutable and sovereign decree of God to redeem the elect; and there is a sense in which it happens in time in the objective history of redemption when Christ died on the cross to pay for the sins of His elect; and there is also a sense in which it happens in the life of an individual child of God when the Holy Spirit applies to him the redemption purchased by Christ. It must be noted that in this chapter, it is the third or the subjective aspect of justification that is given emphasis. This is clearly the case since the elect are deemed *"not justified, until the Holy Spirit doth, in due time, actually apply Christ unto them"* (*WCF* 11.4). We may say that the elect were virtually justified from eternity, which is the basis for the love of God for the elect, but they are not actually and formally justified until they are vitally united to Christ by faith.

- However, it is important that we understand the threefold economic division in the work of redemption of the Triune God. An overemphasis on the decretive work of the Father leads to a one-sided doctrine of eternal justification that denies that there is a sense in which the elect are under the wrath of God prior to the organic application of redemption (see Eph 2:3). An overemphasis on the redemptive work of Christ in time and a failure to see that justification was already planned—sovereignly, irrevocably and immutably, and is therefore certain and in a sense actual from all eternity, will draw a sharp discontinuity between the Old and New Testaments and give rise to a doctrine of salvation by works for Old Testament saints. On the other hand, an overemphasis on the work of the Holy Spirit's work in justification without a realisation that the elect are beloved of God from eternity, and that Christ has satisfied divine justice on behalf of all His elect when He died on the cross, will give rise to an Arminian emphasis on faith and good works as the cause of justification, —which usually also give rise to the doctrine of resistible grace.

- James Buchanan puts it well:

  The one is the error of the Antinomians, who have spoken of Justification as being antecedent to, and independent of regeneration by the Holy Spirit, and have identified it sometimes with God's eternal election, —at other times with the redeeming work of Christ, —as if there were no difference between an eternal purpose to save, and the execution of that purpose in time, or between the procuring of redemption, and the actual application of it to the souls of men. The other is the error of Popish writers, and some of their followers in the Protestant Church, who have spoken of Justification as dependent, not on the finished work of Christ alone, but on our personal obedience.... But such difficulties will be found to resolve themselves into a more general and profound question; and can only be effectually removed, by falling back on God's eternal purpose of mercy towards sinners, which includes equally their redemption by Christ, and their regeneration by the Holy Spirit."[29]

On Justification and Forgiveness

11.5 God doth continue to forgive the sins of those that are justified:[1] and, although they can never fall from the state of justification,[2] yet they may by their sins fall under God's fatherly displeasure, and not have the light of His countenance restored unto them, until they humble themselves, confess their sins, beg pardon, and renew their faith and repentance.[3]

---

[29] Buchanan, *op. cit.*, 402–3.

This section essentially teaches that justification removes the guilt of the sinner with respect to all his sins—past, present and future. The justified man has *judicial* forgiveness. However, the Scripture teaches us that we can incur God's fatherly displeasure, and so we are taught to seek God *Fatherly* forgiveness by confession and repentance.

Robert Shaw explains well:

> As justification is an act completed at once, so those who are justified cannot come into condemnation: "There is now no condemnation to them that are in Christ Jesus" (Romans 8:1). The sins which they afterwards commit cannot revoke the pardon which God has graciously given them; but they may subject them to His fatherly displeasure, and to temporary chastisements (Psalm 89:30–33). Here we must advert to the well-known distinction between *judicial* and *fatherly* forgiveness. Though God, in the capacity of a judge, pardons all the sins of believers, in the most free and unconditional manner, in the day of their justification, yet that forgiveness which, as a Father, He bestows upon His justified and adopted children, is not, in general, vouchsafed without suitable preparation on their part for receiving and improving the privilege. They ought, therefore, to humble themselves before God, make ingenuous confession of their offences, renew their faith and repentance, and earnestly supplicate the removal of His fatherly displeasure, and the restoration of His paternal smiles.[30]

On Justification in the Old Testament

11.6 The justification of believers under the Old Testament was, in all these respects, one and the same with the justification of believers under the New Testament.[1]

[1]Gal 3:9, 13–14; Rom 4:22–24; Heb 13:8.

We have already treated this subject in our commentary on *WCF* 7.4–6. It is also clearly taught in the book of Hebrews which seeks to prove

---

[30] Shaw, *op. cit.*, 135-6.

that the Old Testament sacrifices were all shadows and types which point to Christ: "Jesus Christ the same yesterday, and to day, and for ever" (Heb 13:8).

Believers under the Old Testament were not justified by offering sacrifices or by faith in God but not in the Lord Jesus Christ as some claim. They were justified in exactly the same way as New Testament believers, namely, by grace through faith in the Lord Jesus Christ as their propitiatory sacrifice and mediator. The only difference between the saints of the Old Testament and the saints of the New Testament is that the former believed in the Messiah who was coming, whereas latter believed in the one and the same Messiah who has come.

WCF 12: OF ADOPTION

The benefit of justification, which we considered in the previous chapter, may be regarded as the core and foundation of the Christian life; and so the doctrine of justification is the article on which the Christian church stands or falls. For this reason, the doctrine of justification is often presented and taught in such precise theological language that it can be seen as cold and technical. Thankfully, however, justification never stands alone. It stands alongside the doctrine of regeneration or the new birth by which we are given faith with which to receive the blessings of redemption, including justification. Additionally, those who understand the doctrine of justification will know that we are justified not only so that we may have fellowship with God, but that we may be adopted as His sons and daughters. It is for this reason that our *Confession* begins to deal with the doctrine of adoption immediately after its treatment of justification. While justification is the foundation of the Christian life, adoption is the heart of the Christian life.

12.1 All those that are justified, God vouchsafeth, in and for His only Son Jesus Christ, to make partakers of the grace of adoption:[1] by which they are taken into the number, and enjoy the liberties and privileges of the children of God;[2] have His name put upon them,[3] receive the Spirit of adoption;[4] have access to the throne of grace with boldness;[5] are enabled to cry, Abba, Father,[6] are pitied,[7] protected,[8] provided for,[9] and chastened by Him as by a Father;[10] yet never cast off,[11] but sealed to the day of redemption,[12] and inherit the promises,[13] as heirs of everlasting salvation.[14]

[1]Eph 1:5; Gal 4:4–5; [2]Rom 8:17; Jn 1:12; [3]Jer 14:9; 2 Cor 6:18; Rev 3:12; [4]Rom 8:15; [5]Eph 3:12; Rom 5:2; [6]Gal 4:6; [7]Ps 103:13; [8]Prov 14:26; [9]Mt 6:30, 32; 1 Pet 5:7; [10]Heb 12:6; [11]Lam 3:31; [12]Eph 4:30; [13]Heb 6:12; [14]1 Pet 1:3–4; Heb 1:14.

- Adoption denotes the taking of a child, who is a stranger, into a family, and treating him as a member of it. In spiritual adoption, *"we are received into the number, —and have a right to all the privileges, —of the sons of God"* (*WSC* 34). Many theologians, e.g., Berkhof, would include adoption as part of justification. However, the *WCF* treats it separately, I believe, for two reasons. Firstly, while justification speaks about our state before God as a judge, adoption speaks about our relationship with God as our heavenly Father. Secondly, justification is purely declarative, but adoption includes not only a change in status, but a change in nature. In a sense therefore, adoption spans justification and regeneration and sanctification.

- Indeed, carefully considered, though justification is of utmost importance, it may be seen a means to an end, while adoption may be understood as one of the goals of our redemption. This is clearly taught in Scripture where Paul reminds us that we were "predestinated unto the adoption of children by Jesus Christ" (Eph 1:5) and that we are redeemed "that we might receive the adoption of sons" (Gal 4:5). This is why we are given to confess that *"all those that are justified, God vouchsafeth, in and for His only Son Jesus Christ, to make partakers of the grace of adoption."* Through Christ, His only begotten Son, God would receive many to be His adoptive children.

- Before our conversion, we were by nature the children of wrath and were strangers and foreigners of the household of God (Eph 2:3, 19). When we are translated into His kingdom, the Lord does not leave us to continue to live as aliens, or even as friends of the household of God. He makes us His children in two distinguishable acts. First, He regenerates us so that we may be conformed to the image of His only begotten Son (cf. Jas 1:18; Rom 8:29); secondly, He adopts us as His children.

- Like justification, adoption is an act of God's free grace whereby we are granted privileges which we had no right to. It is so amazing that though we were enemies of God, we have not only been reconciled to Him, but made His children that John exclaimed, "Behold, what manner of love the Father hath bestowed upon us, that we should be called the sons of God" (1 Jn 3:1a).

- As the adoptive children of God, we are not only *"taken into the number"* but given the right to all the *"liberties and privileges of the children of God"* such as:

  1. Having *"[God's] name put upon [us]"* so that we are recognised and may identify ourselves as God's sons and daughters (Rev 3:12; 2 Cor 6:18).

  2. Indwelling of the *"Spirit of Adoption"* by whom we have inward assurance that we are the children of God, and therefore can be sure of His fatherly love and care. Paul says: "For ye have not received the spirit of bondage again to fear; but ye have received the Spirit of adoption, whereby we cry, Abba, Father. The Spirit itself beareth witness with our spirit, that we are the children of God" (Rom 8:15–16).

  3. Fatherly audience and response to our prayers—"And this is the confidence that we have in him, that, if we ask any thing according to his will, he heareth us: And if we know that he hear us, whatsoever we ask, we know that we have the petitions that we desired of him" (1 Jn 5:14–15; cf. Eph 3:12).

  4. Fatherly pity in tribulation—"Like as a father pitieth his children, so the LORD pitieth them that fear him" (Ps 103:13).

  5. Fatherly protection through temporal and spiritual evils—"The LORD shall preserve thee from all evil" (Ps 121:7a; cf. Prov 14:26).

  6. Fatherly provision for the needs of our bodies and souls—"your heavenly Father knoweth that ye have need of all these things" (Mt 6:32b; cf. Ps 34:10).

  7. Fatherly chastisement when we stray—"For whom the Lord loveth he chasteneth, and scourgeth every son whom he receiveth" (Heb 12:6).

  8. A sure title sealed by the earnest of the Holy Spirit to the inheritance of the kingdom of heaven—"And if children, then heirs; heirs of God, and joint-heirs with Christ" (Rom 8:17; cf. 1 Pet 1:3–5, Eph 1:13-14).

WCF 13: OF SANCTIFICATION

To sanctify is to 'make holy.' Sanctification is the divine process by which we are made holy or righteous.

One of the major errors of Roman Catholicism is the confusion of justification with sanctification. Justification, we must remember, is declarative. It is righteousness imputed. Sanctification on the other hand involves actual change in our souls. It is righteousness infused.

One of the major errors of 'parachurch easy-believism' today is also a failure to understand the place of justification and sanctification in the Christian life. We are not saved simply by a sinner's prayer that makes us justified. Unless we are also sanctified and are being sanctified, we can have no assurance that we are justified.

In this chapter, these errors are dealt with by a positive biblical exposition of the doctrine of sanctification.

1. On the Nature of Sanctification

13.1 They who are once effectually called and regenerated, having a new heart, and a new spirit created in them, are farther sanctified really and personally, through the virtue of Christ's death and resurrection,[1] by His Word and Spirit dwelling in them;[2] the dominion of the whole body of sin is destroyed,[3] and the several lusts thereof are more and more weakened and mortified,[4] and they more and more quickened and strengthened in all saving graces,[5] to the practice of true holiness, without which no man shall see the Lord.[6]

[1] 1 Cor 6:11; Acts 20:32; Phil 3:10; Rom 6:5–6; [2] Jn 17:17; Eph 5:26; 2 Th 2:13; [3] Rom 6:6, 14; [4] Gal 5:24; Rom 8:13; [5] Col 1:11; Eph 3:16–19; [6] 2 Cor 7:1; Heb 12:14.

- We have seen effectual calling, regeneration, justification and adoption in the *ordo salutis* thus far. As the *Confession* comes to the subject of sanctification, notice that reference is not made to justification but to effectual calling and regeneration. The reason for this is that justification is a declarative act of God outside the sinner. The sinner is declared to be righteous by the imputation of Christ's righteousness upon him. He does not actually become righteous, but is given a status of righteousness on account of the work of Christ. Justification, therefore does not logically lead to sanctification, though those who are justified will immediately and inevitably begin the process of sanctification. On the other hand, effectual calling and regeneration have to do with a real change in the soul, —"*having a new heart and a new spirit created in them*" and so provide the logical and necessary beginning of sanctification.

- *WSC 35. What is sanctification?*

  A. Sanctification is the work of God's free grace,[1] *whereby we are renewed in the whole man after the IMAGE OF GOD,*[2] *and are enabled more and more to die unto sin, and live unto righteousness.*[3]

  [1]*2 Th 2:13;* [2]*Eph 4:23–24;* [3]*Rom 6:4, 6; 8:1.*

- It is instructive to compare the difference between sanctification and justification:

	Justification	Sanctification
Nature	A declarative act	An actual work on the soul
Matter	Righteousness of Christ Imputed	Inherent righteousness Imparted
Time Frame	Punctiliar, at once	Progressive, over a life time
Result	Title to heaven	Meetness for, and capacity of enjoying heaven.

- It is described in *WSC* 35 as a *work* rather than an *act* as with justification and adoption (*WSC* 33–34) because it is a continuous and gradual operation of God the Holy Spirit in the soul of the justified sinner. Paul tells us that we are chosen "to salvation through sanctification of the Spirit" (2 Th 2:13). Paul is, of course, speaking of salvation as a process leading to our glorification at the end of this life's journey.

- Positively, sanctification consists in our being "*renewed in the whole man after the image of God.*" In other words, we are being restored to the state that Adam and Eve were in, when they were first created in the image of God, in knowledge, righteousness and holiness. This is accomplished, in the words of our *Confession*, by our being *"more and more quickened and strengthened in all saving graces, to the practice of true holiness"* (cf. Col 1:11; Eph 3:16–19).

- Negatively, sanctification involves the destruction of the *"dominion of the whole body of sin"* and the progressive weakening and mortification (putting to death) of the sinful passions related to our body of sin (Rom 6:6; Gal 5:24; Rom 8:13). *WSC* 35 speaks of our being *"enabled more and more to die unto sin, and live unto righteousness."* In other words, we are more and more purified from the pollution of sin and made more and more to hate sin, while at the same time growing to love righteousness and finding it more and more in our nature to practise holiness.

1. On the Extent, Degree and Triumph of Sanctification

13.2 This sanctification is throughout in the whole man,[1] yet imperfect in this life; there abideth still some remnants of corruption in every part:[2] whence ariseth a continual and irreconcilable war; the flesh lusting against the Spirit, and the Spirit against the flesh.[3]

[1] Th 5:23; [2]1 Jn 1:10; Rom 7:18, 23; Phil 3:12; [3]Gal 5:17; 1 Pet 2:11.

- The *extent* of sanctification is the "whole man"—including all the faculties of the soul, such as the conscience, the intellect and the affections, and all the members of the body: "And the very God of peace sanctify you wholly; and I pray God your whole spirit and soul and body be preserved blameless unto the coming of our Lord Jesus Christ" (1 Th 5:23). Sanctification enlightens the blindness of our minds; softens the hardness of conscience; and subdues our sinful passions. "As our bodies are integral parts of our persons, their instincts and appetites act immediately upon the passions of our souls; and hence they must be brought subject to the control of the sanctified will, and all the members of the body, as organs of the soul, made instruments of righteousness unto God."[31] Thus,

---

[31] Hodge, *Confession*, 198.

Paul commands: "Neither yield ye your members as instruments of un-righteousness unto sin: but yield yourselves unto God, as those that are alive from the dead, and your members as instruments of righteousness unto God" (Rom 6:13; cf. 1 Th 4:4).

- The *degree* of sanctification, on the other hand, is limited and *"imperfect in this life"* so that *"some remnant of corruption"* remains *"in every part"* of the man. Thus, throughout the process of sanctification, a fierce struggle ensues between our flesh and the Spirit. Paul speaks of this struggle in Galatians 5:17, —

  "For the flesh lusteth against the Spirit, and the Spirit against the flesh: and these are contrary the one to the other: so that ye cannot do the things that ye would."

There is war, in other words, between the Spirit and the flesh. But what are the Spirit and the flesh? In the first place, Paul is not referring to a battle between the soul and the body. Those who teach that there is such a battle fall into the error of Gnostic dualism. No, no; our soul and body are one, they do not war against each other. It is with some perceptive decisiveness that our translators (and for that matter, all translators of modern Bible versions) capitalised the 'Spirit' in the translation. However, in the second place, I do not think that Paul is speaking about a direct battle between the Holy Spirit and our flesh (whatever the flesh is). If the Spirit is in direct battle, He will win instantly. I believe, rather, that the Spirit refers to the regenerate part of our nature that is under the influence of the indwelling Spirit, whereas the flesh refers to the remnant of our old nature.

Note that this does not mean that there are two natures in us, but that the regenerate man will constantly struggle against temptations that arise out of the remnant of corrupt nature.

13.3 In which war, although the remaining corruption for a time may much prevail,[1] yet, through the continual supply of strength from the sanctifying Spirit of Christ, the regenerate part doth overcome:[2] and so, the saints grow in grace,[3] perfecting holiness in the fear of God.[4]

[1]Rom 7:23; [2]Rom 6:14; 1 Jn 5:4; Eph 4:15–16; [3]2 Pet 3:18; 2 Cor 3:18; [4]2 Cor 7:1.

Notwithstanding the fierceness of the battle between the Spirit and the flesh, the *triumph* of sanctification can be seen in the Christian's victory over sin. Our *Confession* puts it this way: "*through the continual supply of strength from the sanctifying Spirit of Christ, the regenerate part does overcome, and so the saint grows in grace, perfecting holiness in the fear of the Lord.*" In other words, the Christian should normally be victorious in his struggle against sin. Though sin remains, it no longer reigns. Paul speaks about this victory in Romans 6:14, "For sin shall not have dominion over you: for ye are not under the law, but under grace." John confirms: "For whatsoever is born of God overcometh the world: and this is the victory that overcometh the world, even our faith" (1 Jn 5:4). A defeated Christian is a contradiction of terms. However, a Christian cannot attain perfection in this life because of the corruption of nature.

But to further clarify our understanding in regard to sanctification, we must understand that:

- The *impulsive* or moving cause of sanctification is the free grace of God: "Not by works of righteousness which we have done, but according to his mercy he saved us, by the washing of regeneration, and renewing of the Holy Ghost" (Tit 3:5).

- The *meritorious* cause is the death and resurrection of Christ: "Who gave himself for us, that he might redeem us from all iniquity, and purify unto himself a peculiar people, zealous of good works" (Tit 2:14).

- The *efficient* cause or Agency of sanctification is the Holy Spirit dwelling in believers: "And such were some of you: but ye are washed, but ye are sanctified, but ye are justified in the name of the Lord Jesus, and by the Spirit of our God" (1 Cor 6:11; cf. 2 Th 2:13; 1 Pet 1:2).

- Therefore, God, and not man, is the *author* of sanctification. But this does not mean that man is entirely passive in the process. He can and should actively participate in God's work of sanctification by the exercise of faith and the diligent use of the means that God has placed at his disposal. Thus, Paul urges the Philippian

Christians: "Work out your own salvation with fear and trembling. For it is God which worketh in you both to will and to do of his good pleasure" (Phil 2:12–13). Indeed ...

- Faith in Christ may be known as the *instrumental* cause of our sanctification. Thus, Peter, referring to the Holy Spirit's work in the hearts of the Gentiles, notes that He was "purifying their hearts by faith" (Acts 15:9). Similarly the Lord commissioned Paul to minister to the Gentiles, that they may have an inheritance among them which are sanctified by faith in Him (Acts 26:18).

- The *means* of grace, or of sanctification include:

  (1) The Word read and preached: "Sanctify them through thy truth: thy word is truth" (Jn 17:17; cf. 1 Pet 2:2);

  (2) The sacraments: Peter speaks of baptism as saving us by the resurrection of Christ as an "answer of a good conscience toward God" (1 Pet 3:21). Surely he is not teaching baptismal regeneration, but speaking of salvation as incorporating sanctification. Paul admonished the Corinthians for coming together for the Lord's Supper "not for the better, but for the worse" (1 Cor 11:17), which clearly implies the spiritual benefits of partaking the Lord's Supper;

  (3) Prayer: "And whatsoever ye shall ask in my name, that will I do, that the Father may be glorified in the Son. If ye shall ask any thing in my name, I will do it" (Jn 14:13–14);

  (4) Discipline of God's providence: "And not only so, but we glory in tribulations also: knowing that tribulation worketh patience; And patience, experience; and experience, hope" (Rom 5:3–4; cf. Jn 15:2; Heb 12:5–11).

- It is instructive also to understand the different errors pertaining to sanctification and compare them with what is taught in our *Confession*:

Pelagian View	Every man is able perfectly to do all that is required of him in the law since the law only regulates outward behaviour. (But

	see Rom 7:7).
Romish View	A sinner is justified by righteousness of Christ imputed and actual righteousness infused (sanctification). Concupiscence (tendency to sin and thoughts of sinning) is not sin; therefore, it is possible to attain perfection.
Antinomian view	Believers are sanctified only by the holiness of Christ imputed; no inherent holiness is imparted to them.
Wesleyan View	Believers can achieve "entire sanctification" or freedom from all wilful sin in this life (Teaches the same as RC on matter of concupiscence)
Keswick View	'Normal' Christians should have sustained victory over known sin. Many are unsurrendered Christians, they need a crisis experience to turn them back to God. But who can love the Lord and our neighbours perfectly? What sin is not wilful?
Pentecostal View	Every Christian must be baptised by the Holy Spirit subsequent to his initial conversion. This Baptism of the Spirit removes Original Sin or the tendency to sin entirely.
Dispensational View	The Christian has two natures (flesh and spirit) just like Christ has two nature (human and divine). These two natures are constantly at war until the flesh is eradicated at death. Sanctification is the Christian choosing more and more to act according to the new nature (which does not sin). A Christian can accept Jesus Christ as Saviour without accepting Him as Lord. Such a person is known as a carnal Christian.
Reformed (*WCF*) View	The Christian is in a state of grace; the image of God is being restored in him, but there is a remnant of corruption in him that will remain in him until he passes into glory at death. Throughout his life time, the new man (the growing new nature) will battle with the old man (the remnant of corruption) in that the Christian will struggle with sin. Nevertheless, he is growing in Sanctification and so the new man is getting stronger by the power of the Holy Spirit. Christ is both his Saviour and Lord from the moment of his new birth.

WCF 14: OF SAVING FAITH

We are in a section of our *Confession* that deals directly with the doctrine of salvation (*WCF* 10-18). In this section, we first considered the works and acts of God in translating us from the kingdom of darkness into the kingdom of light. We looked at effectual calling and regeneration (*WCF* 10); justification (*WCF* 11), adoption (*WCF* 12) and sanctification (*WCF* 13). In this and the next chapter, we shall consider our response in terms of faith (*WCF* 14) and repentance (*WCF* 15); and then we shall consider the effects of our salvation, namely, good works (*WCF* 16), perseverance (*WCF* 17) and assurance (*WCF* 18).

1. On the Nature of Faith

14.1 The grace of faith, whereby the elect are enabled to believe to the saving of their souls,[1] is the work of the Spirit of Christ in their hearts,[2] and is ordinarily wrought by the ministry of the Word:[3] by which also, and by the administration of the sacraments, and prayer, it is increased and strengthened.[4]

[1]Heb 10:39; [2]2 Cor 4:13; Eph 1:17–19; 2:8; [3]Rom 10:14, 17; [4]1 Pet 2:2; Acts 20:32; Rom 4:11; Lk 17:5; Rom 1:16–17.

- The most well-known biblical definition of faith is given in the book of Hebrews:

  "But we are not of them who draw back unto perdition; but of them that believe to the saving of the soul. Now faith is the substance of things hoped for, the evidence of things not seen. For by it the elders obtained a good report. Through faith we understand that the worlds were framed by the word of God, so that things which are seen were not made of things which do appear. … But without faith it is impossible to please him: for he that cometh to God must believe that he is, and that he is a rewarder of them that diligently seek him" (Heb 10:39–11:3, 6).

- From here, we note:

  (1) Faith is belief or believing. In fact, the phrase "of them that believe" in Hebrews 10:39 is just one word in the Greek and is

the same noun as the word translated 'faith' (πίστις, *pistis*) in Hebrews 11:1.

(2) Faith is necessary *(not robotic)* for our salvation. Hebrews 10:39b may be rendered literally "faith [is] unto salvation of [the] soul." Hebrews 11:6 tells us that "without faith it is impossible to please [God]." How then can there be salvation without faith? The Lord Himself declares: "He that believeth [i.e., has faith] and is baptised shall be saved; but he that believeth not [i.e., has not faith] shall be damned" (Mk 16:16).

(3) Faith has to do with an assurance (substance) and certainty (evidence) of the truth and reality of what cannot be perceived with the physical senses.

(4) Faith does not work independently of the intellect or the mind. Hebrews 11:3 tells us that it is "through faith we understand that the worlds were framed by the word of God." The word translated 'understand' (νοιέω, *noeô*) is a verb based on a noun which may be translated as 'mind' (νοῦς, *nous*). Faith, in other words, is not blind or irrational. How do we understand that the worlds were framed by the word of God, but that the Word of God declares it? Yet faith is different from knowledge. Knowledge is empirical, *factual verifiable* faith is revelational. We have knowledge that the earth is round, we have faith that God made the earth. We have knowledge about the properties of the human body; we believe the properties of the Triune God according to His own revelation.

- With this in mind, the saving faith that is expounded in this chapter may be defined as "that spiritual discernment of the excellence and beauty of divine truth, and that cordial embrace and acceptance of it, which is affirmed in our hearts by the Holy Ghost" (Hodge, 203). To put it in another way, saving faith refers to the wholehearted trust that one has of Christ, "*whereby we receive and rest upon Him alone for salvation, as He is offered to us in the gospel*" (*WSC* 86). This is the faith referred to as the gift of God in Ephesians 2:8.

- This section further teaches us that:

    a. The subjects of saving faith are elect sinners. This is clearly taught in the Scriptures: "All that the Father giveth me shall come to me; and him that cometh to me I will in no wise cast out" (Jn 6:37); "And when the Gentiles heard this, they were glad, and glorified the word of the Lord: and as many as were ordained to eternal life believed" (Acts 13:48).

        The Scripture also teaches false belief. Simon Magus believed (Acts 8:13) but was declared to be yet in bondage to sin (vv. 20–23). King Agrippa believed (Acts 26:27) and almost but did not become a Christian (v. 28). Many who saw Christ's miracles believed in the name of Jesus (Jn 2:23), "But Jesus did not commit himself unto them, because he knew all men" (v. 24). The hearers represented by the stony ground received the Word with joy (Mt 13:20), but soon withered away when the sun of persecution rose over them (Mt 13:21). Indeed, even the demons believe and tremble (Jas 2:19). In all these cases, the subjects are said to believe because they do assent to certain truths of Scripture, but they do not have true saving faith which is more than a belief in certain propositions of Scriptures, but a whole-hearted belief in all that is revealed in Scripture (see below under *WCF* 14.2).

    b. This faith is wrought in the hearts of the elect by the Holy Spirit. Since man, in his fallen state, "*has lost all ability of will to any spiritual good accompanying salvation*," it follows that faith cannot be self-generated. Thus, Paul speaks about faith being "a gift of God" (Eph 2:8). That it is specifically the third Person of the Godhead who grants faith is clear from the fact that He is called "the spirit of faith" (2 Cor 4:13); and faith is one of the "fruit of the Spirit" (Gal 5:22).

    c. This faith is ordinarily wrought in the hearts of the elect by the ministry or instrumentality of the Word: "So then faith cometh by hearing, and hearing by the word of God" (Rom 10:17). Thus, Lydia heard the preaching of Paul, but she had genuine faith because the Holy Spirit opened her heart (Acts 16:14).

d. This faith is increased and strengthened by the administration of the sacraments and prayer as means of grace.

2. On the Objects and Acts of Saving Faith

14.2 By this faith, a Christian believeth to be true whatsoever is revealed in the Word, for the authority of God Himself speaking therein;[1] and acteth differently upon that which each particular passage thereof containeth; yielding obedience to the commands,[2] trembling at the threatenings,[3] and embracing the promises of God for this life and that which is to come.[4] But the principal acts of saving faith are, accepting, receiving, and resting upon Christ alone for justification, sanctification, and eternal life, by virtue of the covenant of grace.[5]

[1]Jn 4:42; 1 Th 2:13; 1 Jn 5:10; Acts 24:14; [2]Rom 16:26; [3]Isa 66:2; [4]Heb 11:13; 1 Tim 4:8; [5]Jn 1:12; Acts 16:31; Gal 2:20; Acts 15:11.

a. *Generally*, the object of saving faith is the whole counsel of the Word of God. Paul was referring to this aspect of his faith when he declared that he believed "all things which are written in the law and in the prophets" (Acts 24:14). The believer takes the Word of God as the authoritative voice of God. He believes it to the exclusion of all traditions and doctrines of man that contradict the Scripture. And the believer responds appropriately to the Word of God: he yields obedience to the commands (Rom 16:26); trembles at the threatenings (Isa 66:2) and embraces the promises of God for this life (Heb 11:13; 1 Tim 4:8).

b. *Specifically* and personally, the object of saving faith is the Lord Jesus Christ. Thus, the Scripture constantly speaks of "faith in Jesus Christ" or "faith of Jesus Christ," e.g., "Knowing that a man is not justified by the works of the law, but by the faith of Jesus Christ, even we have believed in Jesus Christ, that we might be justified by the faith of Christ" (Gal 2:16; cf. Gal 2:20; 3:22, 26; Phil 3:9; Col 1:4; 2:5; 1 Tim 1:14; 3:13; etc.). Thus, the Lord Himself defines eternal life in this way: "And this is life eternal, that they might know thee the only true God, and Jesus Christ, whom thou hast sent" (Jn 17:3). But which proposition of the doctrine of Christ must be believed for salvation? This is a common question that is frequently asked because modern evangelism has subtly simplified faith in Christ to belief in certain propositional truth concerning the Lord Jesus Christ. Let Robert Shaw answer:

> It will not do to limit the object of saving faith to any one doctrinal proposition—such as, that Jesus is the Son of God or, that Jesus Christ is come in the flesh, or that Christ died for our sins according to the Scriptures. This, at the utmost, would only be giving credit to a certain *doctrine*; but saving faith is a believing on the *person* of Christ, or an appropriating of Christ Himself, with all the benefits and blessings included in Him.[32]

c. The principal acts of saving faith are accepting, receiving and resting upon Christ. Reformed theology has traditionally spoken of saving faith as having three elements, namely *notitia*, *assensus* and *fiducia*. It should be noted that these three elements do not correspond to three principal acts of saving faith noted in our *Confession*. Nevertheless, it is instructive for us to consider the three elements for a moment:

  i. *Notitia* or knowledge involves a positive recognition of the truth revealed in the Word of God. One who has *notitia* on the proposition, "Christ Jesus came into the world to save sinners," would agree that it is found in the Bible.

  ii. *Assensus* or assent involves a deep conviction of the veracity of a proposition in Scripture. One who has *assensus* to the same proposition, "Christ Jesus came into the world to save sinners," would affirm that Christ came to die for sinners.

  iii. *Fiducia* or faith involves a wholehearted belief in everything that is revealed in the Scriptures and therefore response volitionally (i.e. by his will) by accepting, receiving and resting on Christ as Saviour and Lord. One who has *fiducia* would not only believe the proposition "Christ Jesus came into the world to save sinners," but all other propositions from the Scripture

---

[32] Shaw, Op. Cit., 149.

that is known to him, including the truths that he himself is a sinner and that he needs a Saviour.

It may be noted that a sinner may possess *fiducia* only after regeneration, though he may have *notitia* and *assensus* before regeneration. It should also be noted that in a sense, the nature of *assensus* and *fiducia* are really the same. They differ only in the extent of what is believed. When one has *fiducia*, he believes (or assents to) everything that is revealed in the Word of God, and not just a few selected propositions. This does not mean that he who has *fiducia* must know everything, but simply that his heart is so changed by the Holy Spirit that whatever he is convinced is in the Scripture, he believes. Moreover, it is *fiducia* alone that gives rise to a will motivated by love to the service and worship of the Lord. Or to put it in another way, *fiducia* can only come about through a change of heart which makes the sinner recognises (in his intellect) the Scriptures as being the Word inspired by the God who is worthy of worship and love. This is accompanied by resolution of obedience (as it pertains to his volition) as well as confidence and affections (as it pertains to his emotion) for the God of the Word. Thus, one who has fiducia accepts, receives and rests upon Christ (as He is revealed in the Scriptures). In other word, his heart is now filled with confidence and love for the Lord and so would seek to live a life of gratitude and love towards the Lord.

Also, take note that while *assensus* may spawn a degree of obedience, it only be an outward, legalistic motion. Think of the five foolish virgins, or the hearts represented by the socky and thorny soils. It will never be an obedience that is motivated by the proposition: "This is the Lord worthy of my wholehearted sacrifice, confidence and love."

d. The true believer receives and rests on Christ *alone* for salvation. The true believer knows that all his righteousness are as filthy rags, and so he cannot trust in them one shred. He knows also that without Christ he cannot expect the mercy of God, for God is not only merciful, but holy and just.

e. The true believer receives and rests on Christ for *complete* salvation, viz. justification, sanctification and eternal life. "He trusts in Christ for salvation not only from wrath, but from sin—not only for salvation from the guilt of sin, but also from its pollution and power—not only for happiness hereafter, but also for holiness here."[33]

3. On the Degrees of Faith

14.3 This faith is different in degrees, weak or strong;[1] may be often and many ways assailed, and weakened, but gets the victory:[2] growing up in many to the attainment of a full assurance, through Christ,[3] who is both the author and finisher of our faith.[4]

[1] Heb 5:13–14; Rom 4:19–20; Mt 6:30; 8:10; [2] Lk 22:31–32; Eph 6:16; 1 Jn 5:4–5; [3] Heb 6:11–12; 10:22; Col. 2:2; [4] Heb 12:2.

Three propositions are taught in this section:

a. Faith may be of different degrees in different persons at different times. The notion that genuine faith can be weak is seen in the fact that Christ received those with weak faith without doubting the reality of their faith. He received the man who cried, "Lord, I believe; help thou mine unbelief" (Mk 9:24). And when Peter doubted and began to sink, the Lord rebuked him for his little faith, but did not reject him: "And immediately Jesus stretched forth his hand, and caught him, and said unto him, O thou of little faith, wherefore didst thou doubt?" (Mt 14:31).

b. True faith will always be finally victorious, —i.e., it will overcome temptation and it will not be obliterated, —though it may be *"often and many ways assailed and weakened."* Faith gets the victory because of the intervention of Christ: "And the Lord said, Simon, Simon, behold, Satan hath desired to have you, that he may sift you as wheat: But I have prayed for thee, that thy faith fail not: and when thou art converted, strengthen thy brethren" (Lk 22:31–

---

[33] Shaw, *Op. Cit.*, 195.

32). John affirms: "For whatsoever is born of God overcometh the world: and this is the victory that overcometh the world, even our faith. Who is he that overcometh the world, but he that believeth that Jesus is the Son of God?" (1 Jn 5:4–5).

c. In many, faith will grow up *"to the attainment of a full assurance through Christ."* This phrase is often disputed as theologians argue whether assurance is the essence of faith. This subject will be dealt with in chapter 18, but it suffices for us to note that the full assurance that the *Confession* speaks about here has to do with "assurance of sense" rather than "assurance of faith."

Assurance of faith has to do with the veracity of the Word of God. No one can be saved who is not assured that what is revealed in the Word of God is true. But many Christians may be assailed by doubts as to the authenticity of their own faith and so lack assurance of sense. By faith we believe the Scripture and embrace Christ for salvation; by sense, we feel that we are accepted of the Lord by the marks of salvation evident in our lives. Thus, a young believer may not have a strong assurance of sense, but as he experiences the Christian life, his assurance of faith is fortified with an assurance of sense and he attains full assurance through Christ.

WCF 15: OF REPENTANCE UNTO LIFE

Faith and repentance are the two most important responses that a believer must have to the work of salvation. Whether faith comes first or repentance comes first is a moot question. By the way in which the framers of our *Confession* put faith before repentance, it may appear that they believe that faith must come first. So, it suggests that until the sinner has a sight of the loveliness Christ, he shall not want to turn away from sin. However, others hold that if a man were to experience regeneration and therefore exercises faith and repentance unto life, he must first have a form of legal repentance. This legal repentance must precede faith in that a person must first turn away from sin and seek after the Lord for whatever reasons including self-preservation. Those who hold to the second opinion must be careful not to fall into the errors of Arminianism and suggest that somehow the sinner's seeking will contribute to their salvation. Those who insist on the first must be careful not to fall into the errors of antinomianism.

But whatever position is held, we must be careful not to fall into the error of modern parachurch Christianity that suggests that repentance and faith are concluded with a one-time act of 'praying to receive Christ.' This error has led to a most crass form of easy-believism as well as superstition in which is thought that all that is require for salvation is a sinner's prayer. No, no; faith and repentance are responses of conversion that every child of God, including the covenant child, must exercise throughout his life. It involves a conscious turning away from worldly ways and thinking, to follow after Christ.

On the Nature of Repentance

15.1 Repentance unto life is an evangelical grace,[1] the doctrine whereof is to be preached by every minister of the Gospel, as well as that of faith in Christ.[2]

[1]Zech 12:10; Acts 11:18; [2]Lk 24:47; Mk 1:15; Acts 20:21.

- Meaning of Repentance. The Greek words translated 'repentance' (μετάνοια, metanoia) and 'repent' (μετανοέω, metanoeô) literally mean "change of mind" or "to change one's mind." They are used in the New Testament particularly to refer to a change of mind concerning sin and so a turning away from sin. Thus, the Lord commanded the people: "repent ye, and believe the gospel" (Mk 1:15). *WSC* 87 teaches us that *"Repentance unto life is a saving grace, whereby a sinner, out of a true sense of his sin, and apprehension of the mercy of God in Christ, doth, with grief and hatred of his sin, turn from it unto God, with full purpose of, and endeavour after, new obedience."*

  Our *Confession* calls it an *"evangelical grace"* or *"saving grace"* (*WSC* 87) because firstly, it is entirely gratuitous. It is a free gift of God: "When they heard these things, they held their peace, and glorified God, saying, Then hath God also to the Gentiles granted repentance unto life" (Acts 11:18; cf. Jer 31:18–19). Secondly, it is inseparably connected with our enjoyment of eternal life. Thus, ...

- It is to be distinguished from Legal Repentance. Paul is comparing evangelical repentance with legal repentance when he says: "For godly sorrow worketh repentance to salvation not to be repented of: but the sorrow of the world worketh death" (2 Cor 7:10). Legal repentance flows from a dread of God's wrath and the temporal consequence of sin such as a lost of wealth, status and reputation. After Judas Iscariot had betrayed the Lord, he regretted his action. We are told he "repented himself, and brought again the thirty pieces of silver to the chief priests and elders" (Mt 27:3). His repentance was, however, not an evangelical repentance but a legal repentance. He was grieved for the consequence of his action, and perhaps even feared the punishment that would be due him for what he did. But he committed suicide as a graceless man.

- Evangelical repentance, on the other hand, flows from hatred of one's sin arising out of both reverence and love for God as well as a sense of God's mercy in Christ. Evangelical or true repentance in other words is never separated from saving faith though it is to be distinguished from it.

- The Necessity and Duty of Preaching Repentance. Antinomians insist that repentance ought not to be preached by any minister of the gospel as they believe that such preaching detracts from Christ, and proves hurtful and dangerous. However, this notion contradicts the Lord's own ministry, for He called for repentance and faith in the gospel (Mk 1:15). And He explained to His disciples "that repentance and remission of sins should be preached in his name among all nations, beginning at Jerusalem" (Lk 24:47). Thus, Paul testified that he spent his time in Ephesus "Testifying both to the Jews, and also to the Greeks, repentance toward God, and faith toward our Lord Jesus Christ" (Act 20:21).

15.2 By it a sinner, out of the sight and sense, not only of the danger, but also of the filthiness and odiousness of his sins, as contrary to the holy nature and righteous law of God, and upon the apprehension of His mercy in Christ to such as are penitent, so grieves for, and hates his sins, as to turn from them all unto God,[1] purposing and endeavouring to walk with Him in all the ways of His commandments.[2]

[1]Ezk 18:30–31; 36:31; Isa 30:22; Ps 51:4; Jer 31:18–19; Joel 2:12–13; Amos 5:15; Ps 119:128; 2 Cor 7:11; [2]Ps 119:6, 59, 106; Lk 1:6; 2 Kgs 23:25.

This beautiful paragraph on the doctrine of repentance, which should really be read together with the previous paragraph teaches us 3 important aspects of Repentance.

1. The Subject of Repentance: "*a sinner.*" The Lord said: "I came not to call the righteous, but sinners to repentance" (Lk 5:32). This has a twofold significance. Firstly, since "all have sinned, and come short of the glory of God" (Rom 3:23), repentance is universally necessary. Thus, we read that God "now commandeth all men everywhere to repent" (Acts 17:30). Secondly, although the call is issued generally, and all men may acknowledge themselves to be sinners in general terms, only those who are quickened will have a clear sight and sense of their sins and thus regard themselves as

sinners deserving damnation. Therefore, the call to repent will only be obeyed by the elect.

2. Grounds of Evangelical Repentance:

   a. It springs from a clear sight and sense of the filthiness and odiousness of one's sins and sinfulness. We note that only a regenerate person will have such an apprehension of guilt and grief. This apprehension comes from the Holy Spirit, whose work is to convince of sin: "And when he is come, he will reprove the world of sin, and of righteousness, and of judgment" (Jn 16:8). He does so by means of the Law: "for by the law is the knowledge of sin" (Rom 3:20b). Thus, when the Law is preached, the Holy Spirit enlightens the mind and quickens the conscience to see the purity and the demands of the Law and to convince the sinner of his inability to meet the Law's demands. And so he sees sin to be *"exceeding sinful,"* senses its danger and sees that it is contrary to the holy nature and righteous Law of God, and is therefore odious and abominable in the sight of God.

   b. It flows from an apprehension of the mercy of God in Christ to such as be penitent. Immediately as the (regenerate) sinner is given an apprehension of the odiousness of sin and of the grave danger that his soul is in, he is given an apprehension that God is, in Christ, truly merciful to all such as are genuinely penitent. This comes through a careful preaching of the gospel which includes references to the fact that God is ever ready to forgive any sinner who would come to Him in genuine repentance. It is at this point that repentance logically becomes faith as the sinner embraces Christ for His forgiveness.

   The Puritans used to call the preaching that is adapted to bring about the first aspect of repentance: *Law Works* or *Law Preaching*. This kind of preaching lays a heavy burden of the Law on the back of the sinner. The unregenerate are either hardened or may be brought to some form of legal repentance. The regenerate, on the other hand, will be brought irresistibly to evangelical repentance. The preaching that is adapted to the second aspect of repentance was frequently called: *Grace Works* or *Gospel Preaching*. Under such preaching, the mercy of God and the beauty of Christ are fervently emphasised.

The Gospel Preaching of the Puritans and Westminster divines must be carefully distinguished from the modern day 'Gospel' Preaching. The modern 'Gospel Preaching' emphasises the love of God for the world: "God loves you and offers a wonderful plan for you." This kind of preaching stirs up romantic feelings of the hearers with promises of happy life in heaven. The Puritans on the other hand emphasised the justice of God in condemning sin and sinners, and the mercy of God to forgive and receive those who are truly penitent. Thus, for the Puritans, the preaching of the Law must precede the preaching of the Gospel. Thus, in the Shorter Catechism, for example, we find that the questions pertaining to repentance and faith comes after the exposition of the Law. This approach of preaching is patterned after the arrangement of the Law (Old Testament emphasises on the Law) and the Gospel (New Testament emphasises on Grace) in the Bible. It is also consistent with the way in which sinners are called to salvation in the Scriptures.

The prophet Ezekiel thus preached: "Therefore I will judge you, O house of Israel, every one according to his ways, saith the Lord GOD. Repent, and turn yourselves from all your transgressions; so iniquity shall not be your ruin. Cast away from you all your transgressions, whereby ye have transgressed; and make you a new heart and a new spirit: for why will ye die, O house of Israel?" (Ezk 18:30–31). Notice that the 'invitation' to life is not without a strong warning of the consequence of sin. Isaiah preached in the same way: "Let the wicked forsake his way, and the unrighteous man his thoughts: and let him return unto the LORD, and he will have mercy upon him; and to our God, for he will abundantly pardon" (Isa 55:7).

Sadly many a modern evangelist would hardly call his unbelieving hearers wicked.

The preaching of the mercy and love of God must not be divorced from the doctrine of His holiness and justice. Thus, the Lord Himself declares about Himself: "The LORD, The LORD God, merciful and gracious, longsuffering, and abundant in goodness and truth, Keeping mercy for thousands, forgiving iniquity and transgression and sin, and that will by no means clear the guilty; visiting the iniquity of the fathers upon the children, and upon the children's children, unto the third and to the fourth generation" (Ex 34:6–7).

3. Essence of Evangelical Repentance.

   a. It includes grief, or deep contrition and godly sorrow for sin. False sorrow may be easily mistaken for genuine godly sorrow. But the key difference is that false sorrow is due to temporal personal loses and pains, whereas godly sorrow arises out of grief that we have rebelled against God. Thus, David, though he had sinned against Bathsheba, prayed to the Lord: "Against thee, thee only, have I sinned, and done this evil in thy sight: that thou mightest be justified when thou speakest, and be clear when thou judgest" (Ps 51:4)

   b. It includes a hatred for sin. While legal repentance may involve a hatred for the consequence of sin, true repentance involves a hatred for sin itself as something hateful and abominable to God. This hatred should not extend merely to some particular sin in our lives but to all sin and pollution of sin in ourselves and in others: "Then shall ye remember your own evil ways, and your doings that were not good, and shall lothe yourselves in your own sight for your iniquities and for your abominations" (Ezk 36:31). "Wherefore I abhor myself, and repent in dust and ashes" (Job 42:6). "Therefore I esteem all thy precepts concerning all things to be right; and I hate every false way" (Ps 119:128). "Rivers of waters run down mine eyes, because they keep not thy law" (Ps 119:136).

c. Includes a turning from sin unto God with a sincere purpose, and endeavour to walk with Him in all the ways of His commandments. The child of God is not only converted from the love of sin, but the practice of sin. In place of such practice, they now do "works meet for repentance" (Acts 26:20), i.e., they resolve to walk after God in new obedience. This sounds like saving faith and does lead to saving faith, but note that faith is about "resting upon Christ alone for [salvation]" whereas the positive aspect of repentance is about obedience to Christ.

On the Necessity and Efficacy of Repentance

15.3 Although repentance be not to be rested in, as any satisfaction for sin, or any cause of the pardon thereof,[1] which is the act of God's free grace in Christ;[2] yet it is of such necessity to all sinners, that none may expect pardon without it.[3]

[1]Ezk 36:31–32; 16:61–63; [2]Hos 14:2, 4; Rom 3:24; Eph 1:7; [3]Lk 13:3, 5; Acts 17:30–31.

- While the Protestant church emphasises 'repentance,' the Roman Catholic church emphasises 'penance.' By this designation, the Romanist teaches that certain acts or penances performed by an offender constitute compensation or satisfaction for his transgressions.[34] This doctrine totally contradicts the Scripture which not only teaches us that "all our righteousness are as filthy rags" (Isa 64:6), but that our pardon for sin is entirely by the grace of God alone (Rom 3:22–28).

- However, it must be noted that true repentance and pardon are inseparably connected. No one can expect pardon who is not repentant. Thus, the Lord admonished His disciples: "I tell you, Nay: but, except ye repent, ye shall all likewise perish" (Lk 13:3).

15.4 As there is no sin so small but it deserves damnation;[1] so there is no sin so great, that it can bring damnation upon those who truly repent.[2]

---

[34] See *Catechism of the [Roman] Catholic Church*, § 1459.

[1]Rom 6:23; 5:12; Mt 12:36; [2]Isa 55:7; Rom 8:1; Isa 1:16, 18.

- This section is again written in opposition to Rome which teaches that there are mortal sins deserving death, but there are venial sins,[35] which are so minor, they can be expiated by some temporary punishment in Purgatory.

- While we admit that there are varying degrees of severity of sinfulness so that some sins are more heinous in the sight of God than others (Lk 12:47; WSC 83), we must insist that every sin deserves eternal punishment. Paul teaches us that "the wages of sin is death" (Rom 6:23). He does not distinguish the degree of sin. In fact, the Lord Himself teaches us that we shall be judged for every idle word that we utter (Mt 12:36).

- Nevertheless, even the greatest sin can be pardoned if there is genuine repentance. David sinned so grievously when he committed adultery with Bathsheba and murdered her husband, yet he received pardon when he repented. Peter denied the Lord three times, and yet the Lord forgave him and restored him.

15.5 Men ought not to content themselves with a general repentance, but it is every man's duty to endeavour to repent of his particular sins particularly.[1]

[1]Ps 19:13; Lk 19:8; 1 Tim 1:13, 15.

Although the corruption of nature has made it impossible for man to know all his sins, it is still the duty of man to strictly and honestly examine his heart so as to discover his particular sins by which God is offended and dishonoured. David understood the need to confess his sins particularly and thus we see that in his confession he referred to the particular evil he has committed: "For I acknowledge my transgressions: and my sin is ever before me. Against thee, thee only, have I sinned, and done this evil in thy sight: that thou mightest be justified when thou speakest, and be clear when thou judgest" (Ps 51:3–4). David also recognised that though he may not have particular awareness of all his sin, yet he is responsible for them: "Who can

---

[35] See C[R]CC, § 1863

understand his errors? cleanse thou me from secret faults" (Ps 19:12). Thus, he also prays: "Search me, O God, and know my heart: try me, and know my thoughts: And see if there be any wicked way in me, and lead me in the way everlasting" (Ps 139:23–24).

On the Duty of Repentance

15.6 As every man is bound to make private confession of his sins to God, praying for the pardon thereof;[1] upon which, and the forsaking of them, he shall find mercy;[2] so he that scandalizeth his brother, or the Church of Christ, ought to be willing, by a private or public confession and sorrow for his sin, to declare his repentance to those that are offended;[3] who are thereupon to be reconciled to him, and in love to receive him.[4]

[1]*Ps 51:4–5, 7, 9, 14; Ps 32:5–6;* [2]*Prov 28:13; 1 Jn 1:9;* [3]*Jas 5:16; Lk 17:3–4; Josh 7:19; Ps 51;* [4]*2 Cor 2:8.*

- Although repentance is an inward act, if it is genuine, it will manifest itself in outward expressions. This expression does not include confession to priest and acts of penance. Only God can forgive (Mt 9:2–6). But it does include:

  a. Private confession to God: "If we confess our sins, he is faithful and just to forgive us our sins, and to cleanse us from all unrighteousness" (1 Jn 1:9; cf. Ps 51:4–7).

  b. Confession to the parties offended or injured. This is to be done privately if the offence is committed privately. But if the offence is committed publicly, then the confession must be made publicly. Though much neglected today, this aspect of repentance is scriptural: "Confess your faults one to another, and pray one for another, that ye may be healed. The effectual fervent prayer of a righteous man availeth much" (Jas 5:16). "Take heed to yourselves: If thy brother trespass against thee, rebuke him; and if he repent, forgive him. And if he trespass against thee seven times in a day, and seven times in a day turn again to thee, saying, I repent; thou shalt forgive him" (Lk 17:3–4).

- Interestingly, the *Confession* also insists that those who received apologies or confessions must forgive. This is again biblical. When Peter asked the Lord how many times he should forgive his brother who sin against him, He replied: "Until seventy times seven" (Mt 18:21–22). The immediate context (vv. 15–17) instructs us that Christ is referring to the forgiveness of one who comes confessing his fault and indicating his repentance. When this happens, we are always to take the confession at face value and forgive. Note, of course, that this forgiveness does not absolve the person of guilt. Only God can thus forgive. Our forgiveness only says: "I accept your apology. I forgive you. I will not pursue the matter; it will not hinder our relationship with each other. I undertake not to gossip about what wrong you did to me."

WCF 16: OF GOOD WORKS

Roman Catholicism and indeed practically all Christian cults and pagan religions place a lot of emphasis on good works. The reason for this emphasis is that man tends to be legalistic in his thinking by nature. Almost intuitively man assumes that he deserves to go to heaven rather than hell when his supposed good works outweigh his sinful deeds. Protestantism, in general, however, tends to de-emphasis good works both in reaction to the legalism of Rome, and in its emphasise the doctrine of justification by grace alone through faith alone.

It is undeniable that the doctrine of Monergistic Regeneration and Justification by grace through faith alone are biblical. However, it is also undeniable that good works are important for the believer. Two verses from the Scripture make this very clear.

First, the apostle Paul says in Ephesians 2:8-10—

> [8] For by grace are ye saved through faith; and that not of yourselves: *it is* the gift of God: [9] Not of works, lest any man should boast. [10] For we are his workmanship, created in Christ Jesus unto good works, which God hath before ordained that we should walk in them.

By these words, Paul teaches us that in God's plan, we are saved in order that we might do good works! I believe that works done out of a legalistic notion of meriting salvation or even out of a mere sense of duty or fear of God's wrath are not acceptable to God. God saves us by His grace that we might do good works in grateful response and love towards Him.

Secondly, James says in James 2:17:

> ...Faith, if it hath not works, is dead, being alone.

By this statement and his extended treatment of the subject, James makes it clear to us that such as have saving faith will have good works. This is because saving faith is not something that is endowed as an independent gift to the elect. Rather, it is endowed as part of the package that comes with regeneration. With regeneration, the sinner not only finds Christ irresistible, but finds in his heart gratitude and love for God that will naturally overflow with good works. Faith that does not have good works is not true saving faith.

For this reason, our *Confession of Faith* has devoted a whole chapter to "Good Works," which is unique among all the Reformed Confessions.

On the Nature of Good Works

16.1 Good works are only such as God hath commanded in His holy Word,[1] and not such as, without the warrant thereof, are devised by men, out of blind zeal, or upon any pretense of good intention.[2]

[1]*Mic 6:8; Rom 12:2; Heb 13:21;* [2]*Mt 15:9; Isa 29:13; 1 Pet 1:18; Rom 10:2; Jn 16:2; 1 Sam 15:21–23.*

- Our chapter begins by asking the question: "What, after all, are good works?" If we are going to talk about good works, we must have a good definition. The answer positively stated is that *"Good works are only such as God hath commanded [whether explicitly or implicitly] in His holy Word."*

- This doctrine is hinted in the Word of God. Paul says: "And be not conformed to this world: but be ye transformed by the renewing of your mind, that ye may prove what is that good, and acceptable, and perfect, will of God" (Rom 12:2). The author of Hebrews says: "Make you perfect in every good work to do his will, working in you that which is well-pleasing in his sight, through Jesus Christ; to whom be glory for ever and ever" (Heb 13:21). Both of these references refer to the 'will of God' as the principle on which we should conduct ourselves in a manner that pleases God. The will of God here referred to must be the revealed will, i.e., the Word of God.

- Negatively, whatever deeds are devised by men for whatever reason, including well-meaning intentions, that are not sanctioned in God's word may not be regarded as "good works." In other words, what is not commanded cannot be transformed into good works by the good intention of the doer, as Roman Catholicism teaches. The Prophet Samuel rebuked king Saul for thinking that he could please God by keeping some of the animals of the Amalekites to sacrifice to God: "Hath the LORD as great delight in burnt offerings and sacrifices, as in obeying the voice of the LORD? Behold, to obey is better than sacrifice, and to hearken than the fat of rams" (1 Sam 15:22). This statement implies that good intention does not make an action good. Similarly, the Lord rebuked the Pharisees for their services which they invented with the notion that they would be pleasing to God: "But in vain they do worship me, teaching for doctrines the commandments of men" (Mt 15:9).

- Note that this principle does not imply that we cannot do anything at all that is not commanded in the Word of God without sinning against God, otherwise, many of our day-to-day functions in the modern society cannot be engaged in without sinning against God. What it does teach is that only deeds that are commanded and sanctioned may be regarded as *good*. Other actions are either sinful or indifferent.

- This definition of good works must not be confused with the *Regulative Principle of Life* which states that "Whatever is not forbidden in the Word of God is allowed in day to day life." What is allowed because it is not forbidden is not necessarily a good work. We should not, for example, claim to be doing good work if we participate in a marathon to raise funds to cull kangaroos. It is of course permissible for us to participate in such an activity so long as it is not held on the Lord's Day, but it is simply not 'good work.'

- Neither must this definition of good works be confused with the *Regulative Principle of Worship* which states that "Whatever is not sanctioned in the Word of God forbidden in formal worship." All acts of worship covered under the *Regulative Principle of Worship* are indeed good works, but not all good works are permitted in worship.

- Note also that whether a work, —which when considered abstractly as good, —is actually good in the sight of God will depend on several factors which are highlighted in *WCF* 16.7. These are: (a) Whether it is performed by a justified person; (b)

Whether it is done with the right principle—faith working by love: "And though I bestow all my goods to feed the poor, and though I give my body to be burned, and have not charity, it profiteth me nothing" (1 Cor 13:3); and (c) Whether it is directed to the right end, —to glorify God (1 Cor 10:31).

16.2 These good works, done in obedience to God's commandments, are the fruits and evidences of a true and lively faith:[1] and by them believers manifest their thankfulness,[2] strengthen their assurance,[3] edify their brethren,[4] adorn the profession of the gospel,[5] stop the mouths of the adversaries,[6] and glorify God,[7] whose workmanship they are, created in Christ Jesus thereunto;[8] that, having their fruit unto holiness, they may have the end eternal life.[9]

[1]Jas 2:18, 22; [2]Ps 116:12–13; 1 Pet 2:9; [3]1 Jn 2:3, 5; 2 Pet 1:5–10; [4]2 Cor 9:2; Mt 5:16; [5]Tit 2:5, 9–12; 1 Tim 6:1; [6]1 Pet 2:15; [7]1 Pet 2:12; Phil 1:11; Jn 15:8; [8]Eph 2:10; [9]Rom 6:22.

Good works, we must remember, are not just any deeds which are beneficial to our neighbours. They are, as we are given to reiterate, works "*done in obedience to God's commandments.*" Such works serve several important purposes in the life of believers:

a. As "*fruits and evidences of a true and lively faith.*" They are borne out of living faith, and therefore offer evidence that the doer is a true believer. James is referring to the authenticating function of works when he says: "Yea, a man may say, Thou hast faith, and I have works: shew me thy faith without thy works, and I will shew thee my faith by my works" (Jas 2:18).

b. As means by which "*believers manifest their thankfulness.*" They are, we may say, suitable expression of gratitude to "[show] forth the praises of Him who has called [us] out of darkness into His marvellous light" (1 Pet 2:9).

c. To "*strengthen [the] assurance*" of grace of believers. The apostle John says in his *Test-of-Life Epistle*: "And hereby we do know that we know him, if we keep his commandments" (1 Jn 2:3). Properly understood, keeping of God's commandments is almost synonymous with doing good works.

d. To *"edify [fellow Christians]."* Thus, Paul commends the Corinthians: "Your zeal hath provoked very many" (2 Cor 9:2).

e. To *"adorn the profession of the gospel."* In other words, they accompany and beautify the testimony of believers. This is what the apostle Paul has in mind when urges Titus to teach the servants to be obedient "that they may adorn the doctrine of God our Saviour in all things" (Tit 2:10).

f. To *"stop the mouth of adversaries."* Peter highlights this when he says, "for so is the will of God, that with well doing ye may put to silence the ignorance of foolish men" (1 Pet 2:15). How does this happen? It happens by removing opportunity to charge believers of hypocrisy and also by making it unconscionable and uncomfortable to condemn them. It is not easy to condemn someone who is known to be doing good sincerely!

g. To *"glorify God."* This is what the Lord Jesus is testifying when He affirms: "Herein is my Father glorified, that ye bear much fruit; so shall ye be my disciples" (Jn 15:8).

These, then are the purposes of good works in the life of believers. So important are such works, that though they are not meritorious, they are indispensable for admission to everlasting life. Thus, we are given to confess at the end of the paragraph that we are *"God's workmanship... created in Christ Jesus [unto good works], that, having [our] fruit unto holiness, [we] may [attain unto] eternal life"* (cf. Eph 2:10, Rom 6:22).

On the Ability to do Good Works

16.3 Their ability to do good works is not at all of themselves, but wholly from the Spirit of Christ.[1] And that they may be enabled thereunto, beside the graces they have already received, there is required an actual influence of the same Holy Spirit, to work in them to will and to do of His good pleasure:[2] yet are they not hereupon to grow negligent, as if they were not bound to perform any duty unless upon a special motion of the Spirit; but they ought to be diligent in stirring up the grace of God that is in them.[3]

[1]Jn 15:4–6; Ezk 36:26–27; [2]Phil 2:13; 4:13; 2 Cor 3:5; [3]Phil 2:12; Heb 6:11–12; 2 Pet 1:3, 5, 10–11; Isa 64:7; 2 Tim 1:6; Acts 26:6–7; Jude 20–21.

- Good works are important. But the Scriptures also says that "there is none that doeth good, no, not one" (Rom 3:12, cf. Ps 14:1); that all our righteousness are as filthy rags in the sight of God (Isa 64:6); and that we all "fall short of the glory of God" (Rom 3:23). These propositions must be true even for regenerate and justified believers for our sanctification is not perfect in this life. If this is so, how can we do any good works at all?

- The answer, as we are given to confess, is that our "ability to do good works" is "*wholly from the Spirit of Christ,*" contra Pelagians, Romanists and Arminians. This is alluded to in Scripture: (a) by the Lord's assertion: "without me ye can do nothing" (Jn 15:5b); (b) by Paul's testimony: "Not that we are sufficient of ourselves to think anything as of ourselves; but our sufficiency is of God" (2 Cor 3:5); and (c) by the recorded prayers of the saints for strength to do the will of God (e.g., Heb 13:20–21).

- But how does the Spirit enable us to do good work? Again we are given to confess that He enables us both by graces bestowed at regeneration, as well as by *"an actual influence [upon our soul], to work in [us] to will, and to do, of His good pleasure."*

- This doctrine humbles us and makes us realise that we contribute nothing to our own salvation from beginning to end. Even our use of the means of grace which is necessary for our sanctification is possible because of the actual and continual operation of the Holy Spirit in our heart. This is why the apostle Paul says: "Work out your own salvation with fear and trembling" (Phil 2:12), but immediately adds: "For it is God which worketh in you both to will and to do of *his* good pleasure" (Phil 2:13).

- This doctrine of absolute dependence of our soul upon the Spirit of Christ must, nevertheless, not be perverted into occasions of indolence, or to reduce, to any degree, a sense of personal obligation. No one, for example, should refuse to do good by giving the excuse that the Spirit has not roused him to action. We are responsible to obey all the commands of the Lord, including to "work out our own salvation" (Phil 2:12). Inability does not nullify our responsibility. This is especially so in the matter of good works when an act for which the motive to begin with may be largely impure or legalistic (and therefore may not be a good work in the eyes of God) may result in the *"stirring up of the grace of God"* in the heart of the believer, that the continuance of it is sustained by the power of the Spirit of Christ thereby rendering it good.

On the Value of Good Works

16.4 They who in their obedience attain to the greatest height which is possible in this life, are so far from being able to supererogate, and to do more than God requires, as that they fall short of much which in duty they are bound to do.[1]

[1]Lk 17:10; Neh 13:22; Job 9:2–3; Gal 5:17.

- The Romish doctrine of supererogation teaches that extra good works not required for the salvation of the performer can be stored up for use by others who may pay for them by way of indulgences.[36]

- This highly perverted doctrine is refuted in this section and is clearly anti-scriptural since we can never do anything more than what God already commands us to do. We are always doing less than our duty; and our work is never up to standard before the holy eyes of God. How then can we expect to earn any merit by our work, not to mention extra merit for others? Our Lord's instruction about service for the Lord brings this reality home very clearly:

  "So likewise ye, when ye shall have done all those things which are commanded you, say, We are unprofitable servants: we have done that which was our duty to do" (Lk 17:10).

16.5 We cannot, by our best works, merit pardon of sin, or eternal life at the hand of God, by reason of the great disproportion that is between them and the glory to come, and the infinite distance that is between us and God, whom by them we can neither profit nor satisfy for the debt of our former sins;[1] but when we have done all we can, we have done but our duty, and are unprofitable servants;[2] and because,

---

[36] See C[R]CC, §1477–8.

as they are good, they proceed from His Spirit;[3] and as they are wrought by us, they are defiled, and mixed with so much weakness and imperfection, that they cannot endure the severity of God's judgment.[4]

[1]*Rom 3:20; 4:2, 4, 6; Eph 2:8–9; Tit 3:5–7; Rom 8:18; Ps 16:2; Job 22:2–3; 35:7–8;* [2]*Lk 17:10;* [3]*Gal 5:22–23;* [4]*Isa 64:6; Gal 5:17; Rom 7:15, 18; Ps 143:2; 130:3.*

- There are a few reasons why we cannot by our best works merit pardon of sin or eternal life by the hand of God.

- *First* of all, there is a *"great disproportion ...between [us] and the glory to come"* as well as an *"infinite distance ... between us and God, whom by them we can neither profit nor satisfy for the debt of our former sins."* In other words, since we all fall short of the glory of God (Rom 3:23), nothing we do, can by our own strength, ever please God or be sufficient to pay for our sin. This is why Paul asserts that "by the deeds of the law there shall no flesh be justified in [God's] sight" (Rom 3:20).

- *Secondly*, it is impossible for us to do anything extra to win any merit because whatever we can possibly do in this life that may be regarded as good are really part of our duty towards God our Creator and Redeemer (cf. Lk 17:10).

- *Thirdly*, all our works that may be regarded as good works proceed from the almighty agency of the Spirit of grace (Phil 2:13, cf. Zech 12:10).

- And *fourthly*, because of our corruption of nature, all that we do are always mingled with sin and therefore cannot be good enough to merit a payment or prize. All our righteousnesses are filthy rags in the eyes of God says Isaiah (Isa 64:6). *Thus*, we are given to confess regarding our good works: *"as they are wrought by us, they are defiled, and mixed with so much weakness and imperfection, that they cannot endure the severity of God's judgment."* Thus, even if God rewards us for our labours, it is always by grace (cf. Jas 3:2; 1 Jn 1:8; Lk 10:27, Rom 4:4).

- Thus, our good works do not contribute one iota the inestimable blessing of eternal life: "For by grace are ye saved through faith;

and that not of yourselves: it is the gift of God: Not of works, lest any man should boast" says Paul (Eph 2:8-9).

16.6 Yet notwithstanding, the persons of believers being accepted through Christ, their good works also are accepted in Him;[1] not as though they were in this life wholly unblamable and unreproveable in God's sight;[2] but that He, looking upon them in His Son, is pleased to accept and reward that which is sincere, although accompanied with many weaknesses and imperfections.[3]

[1]Eph 1:6; 1 Pet 2:5; Ex 28:38; Gen 4:4; Heb 11:4; [2]Job 9:20; Ps 143:2; [3]Heb 13:20–21; 2 Cor 8:12; Heb 6:10; Mt 25:21, 23.

Good works are not meritorious for even our most righteous deeds are *"accompanied with many weaknesses and imperfections"* and so are but filthy rags in the sight of God when considered by themselves. However, good works done in faith with an eye of gratitude and love unto Christ are accepted and graciously rewarded of God. Calvin puts it beautifully when he says:

> "However defective the works of believer may be, they are nevertheless pleasing to God through the intervention of pardon... Whilst, therefore, they reach forward and strive, reward is given to their efforts although imperfect, exactly as if they had fully discharged their duty; for, since their deficiencies are put out of sight by faith, God honours with the title of reward what He gratuitously bestows upon them."[37]

This is possible because believers are accepted as righteous in Christ (Eph 1:6), and therefore any work done by them out of love for Him is sprinkled, as it were, with His blood and cleansed. Or to put it in another way, because of the believers' union with Christ, God views their works through the purifying mediation of Christ, and therefore accepts them in Him. Or as we are given to confess, believers *"being accepted through Christ, their good works also are accepted in Him; not as though they were in this life wholly unblamable and unreproveable in God's sight; but that He, looking upon them in His*

---

[37] Calvin, *Comm.* on Leviticus 26:3.

Son" is please to accept and reward whatever is done with faith and love.

Thus, Abel's sacrifice was acceptable to God because it was done by faith in Christ as He to whom the sacrifice pointed to. This contrasted with Cain's bloodless offering which indicates faithlessness. So we are told: "By faith Abel offered unto God a more excellent sacrifice than Cain, by which he obtained witness that *he was righteous*, God testifying of his gifts: and by it he being dead yet speaketh" (Heb 11:4). Thus, the apostle Peter declares: "Ye also, as lively stones, are built up a spiritual house, an holy priesthood, to offer up spiritual sacrifices, *acceptable to God by Jesus Christ*" (1 Pet 2:5). For Christ's sake, God will accept and reward our good works, wrought out of sincere faith and love, even though they fall short of His glory in many ways.

Nevertheless, as we have highlighted before, any reward expected or received must be understood as graciously appointed. Therefore, they are no cause for boasting; nor should they be the primary motivating factor for doing good works. Our motivation to do good should always be gratitude to the Lord (2 Cor 5:14).

On the Works of the Unregenerate

16.7 Works done by unregenerate men, although, for the matter of them, they may be things which God commands, and of good use both to themselves and others;[1] yet, because they proceed not from an heart purified by faith;[2] nor are done in a right manner, according to the Word;[3] nor to a right end, the glory of God;[4] they are therefore sinful, and cannot please God, or make a man meet to receive grace from God.[5] And yet their neglect of them is more sinful, and displeasing unto God.[6]

[1]2 Kgs 10:30–31; 1 Kgs 21:27, 29; Phil 1:15–16, 18; [2]Gen 4:5; Heb 11:4, 6; [3]1 Cor 13:3; Isa 1:12; [4]Mt 6:2, 5, 16; [5]Hag 2:14; Tit 1:15; Amos 5:21–22; Hos 1:4; Rom 9:16; Tit 3:5; [6]Ps 14:4; 36:3; Job 21:14–15; Mt 25:41–43, 45; 23:3.

Rome teaches that the work of the unregenerate can be so pure as to be free from all sins, and so may obtain merit of congruity from God. This section refutes this doctrine by insisting that while an action may be theoretically or materially good when considered by itself, it cannot in reality be actually good when performed by fallible man, much less by unregenerate man, —because an action cannot be separated from the person performing it. Only a regenerate person is able fulfil all four criteria that makes a work truly good, namely: (1) right "*matter;*" (2) right "*manner;*" (3) right motivation, namely, "*faith;*" and (4) right "*end*" or purpose.

An unregenerate man may read and hear the Word of God, give to the poor, and pray. These are commanded of God, and considered by themselves, these actions are good and commendable. But unless done by a person accepted in the Beloved, they are sinful actions. "The sacrifice of the wicked is an abomination to the LORD: but the prayer of the upright is his delight" (Prov 15:8).

However, this does not mean that the wicked, therefore, should not read and hear sermons or pray. Neither does it mean that the wicked need not, in the final analysis, keep the laws of God. These are duties required of all men, and the neglect of them incurs greater judgement. Moreover, as Jonathan Edwards was wont to say: "God usually gives success to those who diligently, and constantly, and perseveringly seek conversion."[38]

---

[38] Jonathan Edwards, "Sermon on Hosea 5.15," in *Works* 2.87b.

WCF 17: OF THE PERSEVERANCE OF THE SAINTS

Can a Christian, once saved, fall out of grace and be lost ultimately? Does not experience show us that he can? Does not Scripture support the observation? These are the questions that are addressed in this chapter of our *Confession* under the title: "Of the Perseverance of the Saints."

The doctrine of the Perseverance of the Saints is very closely interconnected with the doctrine of Assurance, which is the subject of the very next chapter in the *Confession*. Indeed, it is impossible to maintain the doctrine of Assurance without first believing in the doctrine of Perseverance. *WCF* 17, thus, lays an important foundation for the next chapter.

But before we proceed to consider what is taught here, it is instructive for us to consider how the doctrine is spoken of under a variety of nomenclatures.

The term used in our *Confession*, namely "Perseverance of the Saints" came from the fifth head of the *Canons of Dort*. This was the document produced by the Synod of Dort in the Netherlands in 1618 as a response to the attempt by the followers of James Arminius to push Arminianism as sound theology. The Synod of Dort condemned it as heresy. The five heads of the *Canons of Dort* correspond to the five points of the *Remonstrantia*, the document produced by the Arminians. The *Canons* has been reordered by English theologians to fit the beautiful acronym TULIP, the last point of which is "Perseverance of the Saints." This phrase emphasises that all true believers will persevere diligently in faith, holiness and good works. Contrary to the Arminian charge, the doctrine of sovereign grace does not encouraged Christians to live in sin, carelessness and lawlessness.

Some Calvinists, such as RC Sproul, prefer to speak of "Preservation of the saints."[39] This emphasises the fact that it is God who preserves His

---

[39] RC Sproul, *Chosen By God* (Illinois: Tyndale House Publishers, 1986),174.

people from totally and finally falling away. God does not merely help believers to remain in the faith, He ensures it. The Lord Jesus makes this very clear when He declares: "And I give unto them eternal life; and they shall never perish, neither shall any man pluck them out of my hand. My Father, which gave them me, is greater than all; and no man is able to pluck them out of my Father's hand" (John 10:28–29).

Other Calvinist's such as AW Pink prefer to speak of "Eternal Security."[40] This emphasises the comfort and assurance that true believers may enjoy, i.e., that they are secure in their salvation both in this life, and in the life to come (cf. Rom 8:33–39). Sadly, however "eternal security" have often been abused by those who teach a form of carnal security where mere professors of faith are misled into thinking that all is well just because they once "prayed to receive Christ."

Linus Chua is certainly right when he says:

> "It is important to notice that the word '**Saints**' and not 'sinners' is used. The word 'saint,' when applied to believers, in itself, implies a person who is living and walking in holiness. A saint is not someone who lives continually in sin and whose life bears no marks of regeneration whatsoever. A popular teaching of many people today is the 'Carnal Christian' doctrine, which inevitably leads to what we would call "perseverance of sinners." The carnal Christian, according to leading dispensationalist Lewis Sperry Chafer, is characterised by a 'walk' that is on the same plane as that of the natural man. And such a "Carnal Christian," who persists in his carnality all his life, will still be saved at the end!"[41]

---

[40] See AW Pink, *Eternal Security* (Sovereign Grace Publishers, 2001), 128 pages.

[41] From the original class notes that formed the basis of this book. The present book, as mentioned in the preface, arose out of these class notes distributed to sabbath class students during the initial years of Pilgrim Covenant Church in Singapore. At that time, Pastor Linus Chua, who was then a ministerial student, was assigned to take one of the lectures in this series of studies. Knowing his love for the Puritans and his interest in the subject of perseverance and assurance, I had assigned him to present this and the next chapter on assurance. Over the years, as the class notes evolved into a book, much of the original material has been absorbed, reworded and reorganised; but I have retained some of the original wordings, both purposefully and unwittingly. –JJL.

On the Certainty of Perseverance

17.1 They whom God hath accepted in His Beloved, effectually called and sanctified by His Spirit, can neither totally nor finally fall away from the state of grace; but shall certainly persevere therein to the end, and be eternally saved.[1]

[1]Phil 1:6; 2 Pet 1:10; Jn 10:28–29; 1 Jn 3:9; 1 Pet 1:5, 9.

This statement sets forth the doctrine of the Perseverance of the Saints in no uncertain terms. It deals with the question of whether true believers will continue in their faith and in the state of salvation till the very end. Calvinists believe that all those whom God has elected in eternity will be saved forever; with no possibility of them being lost. Arminians on the other hand believe that it is possible for truly regenerate people to fall totally and finally from grace into eternal reprobation. In fact, the Roman Catholic Church, whose doctrine is semi-Pelagian as is Arminianism, declares in her authoritative statement, "If any one saith, that a man once justified [cannot] lose grace, and that he that falls and sins was never truly justified;... let him be anathema."[42]

A.A. Hodge summarise the reasoning behind the Arminian view this way:

> "Since neither the decree of God, nor the atonement of Christ, nor the grace of the Holy Ghost determines the certain salvation of any individual—since the application and effect of the atonement and of the renewing and sanctifying influences of the Spirit depend upon the free will of every man in his own case, it necessarily follows that the perseverance of any man in the grace once received must also depend entirely upon his own will. And since the human will is essentially fallible and capable of change,... it follows

---

[42] Council of Trent, Session 6, Canon 23. The full wordings, which contains a mixture of truth and error is: "If any one saith, that a man once justified can sin no more, nor lose grace, and that therefore he that falls and sins was never truly justified; or, on the other hand, that he is able, during his whole life, to avoid all sins, even those that are venial, --except by a special privilege from God, as the Church holds in regard of the Blessed Virgin; let him be anathema."

of course that the believer is at all times liable to total apostasy, and… to final perdition."[43]

Now, many Arminians today claim that they do believe the doctrine of perseverance and the statement, "once saved, always saved," holds true for them. Sadly, though, they fail to see how the doctrine of Perseverance is, in fact, inconsistent with every other point of Arminianism. At least, the original Arminians were more consistent than many of their present day adherents!

On the Basis of Perseverance

17.2 This perseverance of the saints depends not upon their own free will, but upon the immutability of the degree of election, flowing from the free and unchangeable love of God the Father;[1] upon the efficacy of the merit and intercession of Jesus Christ;[2] the abiding of the Spirit, and of the seed of God within them;[3] and the nature of the covenant of grace:[4] from all which ariseth also the certainty and infallibility thereof.[5]

[1]*2 Tim 2:18–19; Jer 31:3;* [2]*Heb 10:10, 14; 13:20–21; 9:12–15; Rom 8:33–39; Jn 17:11, 24; Lk 22:32; Heb 7:25;* [3]*Jn 14:16–17; 1 Jn 2:27; 3:9;* [4]*Jer 32:40;* [5]*Jn 10:28; 2 Th 3:3; 1 Jn 2:19.*

The basis of perseverance does not lie in the free will of man. Instead, the *Confession* gives us a fourfold ground of perseverance which is certain and infallible. They are:

a. *"The immutability of the eternal decree of election":* We saw in *WCF* 3 that God decreed the salvation of certain men, and that His decree is unchangeable and sure. Arminians cannot claim God's eternal decree in election as a sure ground of perseverance because, for in their reckoning, God's decree is based on His foreknowledge and not His foreordination.

b. *"The merit and intercession of Christ":* This was elaborated in *WCF* 8, where we considered the work of Christ as our Mediator and Redeemer. We noted how, through His active and passive obedience, He obtained eternal redemption for us and that He is

---

[43] Hodge, *Confession*, 233–4.

even right now making intercessions for His people on the basis of His finished work. Since the mediation of Christ cannot possibly fail, we can be sure that none of His people will ever be lost.

c. *"The abiding of the Spirit, and of the seed of God within them"*: The Lord had assured his disciples: "And I will pray the Father, and he shall give you another Comforter, that he may abide with you *forever"* (Jn 14:16). Accordingly, the Spirit of God dwells in every true believer and will never depart from us. As long as we have the Spirit of God abiding in us, we can be sure that we will never finally fall away from grace.

d. *"The nature of the covenant of grace"*: We have seen in *WCF* 7, that the Covenant of Grace of which the elect are beneficiaries is a sure covenant which can never be broken. Thus, all who come under this covenant cannot be lost.

On the Possibility of Backsliding

17.3 Nevertheless they may, through the temptations of Satan and of the world, the prevalency of corruption remaining in them, and the neglect of the means of their preservation, fall into grievous sins;[1] and, for a time, continue therein:[2] whereby they incur God's displeasure,[3] and grieve His Holy Spirit;[4] come to be deprived of some measure of their graces and comforts;[5] have their hearts hardened,[6] and their consciences wounded;[7] hurt and scandalize others,[8] and bring temporal judgments upon themselves.[9]

[1]Mt 26:70, 72, 74; [2]Ps 51:title, 14; [3]Isa 64:5, 7,9; 2 Sam 11:27; [4]Eph 4:30; [5]Ps 51:8, 10, 12; Rev 2:4; Song 5:2–4, 6; [6]Isa 63:17; Mk 6:52; 16:14; [7]Ps 32:3–4; 51:8; [8]2 Sam 12:14; [9]Ps 89:31–32; 1 Cor 11:32.

• Though a true believer will persevere in the faith forever, it is possible for him to *"fall into grievous sins; and for a time, continue therein."* There are several biblical examples of this. We think of Moses, David, and Peter. These all fell into some lamentable sin, even though they were true believers. Moses would not circumcise his second son until the LORD threatened to take his life. David did not repent until his sin was exposed by the prophet Nathan almost a year later. Peter denied the Lord with curses within the same day of assuring Him that he would never leave Him. Scripture records these failures no doubt to warn us to take heed lest we fall; for it is appointed of God that even true believers can fall so that we may remain humble till humility is etched in our hearts at the end of our pilgrimage.

- But what are the causes of such failures that we may watch out for them? Our *Confession* gives us four: (1) "*The temptation of Satan*"; (2) The enticements "*of the world*"; (3) "*The prevalency of corruption remaining*" in our nature; and (4) "*The neglect of the mean of [our] preservation,*" or in other words, the means of grace.

- What happens when we fall? Our *Confession* warns us of five possible consequences: (1) God is displeased and the Holy Spirit is grieved; (2) We are "*deprived of some measure of their graces and comforts*"; (3) Our hearts are "*hardened and [our] consciences [are] wounded*"; (4) Others around us may be "*hurt and scandalised,*" i.e. stumbled and grieved because of our sin; and (5) God may visit us with temporal judgment (see 1 Cor 11:30-31).

- What shall we do in view of all these warnings? Shall we not work out our salvation with fear and trembling (Phil 2:12)? Shall we not take heed to put on the full amour of God daily (Eph 6:11ff); and strive not to neglect the means of grace, be they reading and hearing of the Word, or the use of the sacraments, or prayer. The Lord Jesus exhorted his disciples, "Watch and pray, that ye enter not into temptation: the spirit indeed is willing, but the flesh is weak" (Mt 26:41).

And let us not despise the importance of the church as a means of our perseverance. Let us take heed to the exhortation of the apostle to the Hebrews:

"And let us consider one another to provoke unto love and to good works: [25] Not forsaking the assembling of ourselves together, as the manner of some *is;* but exhorting *one another:* and so much the more, as ye see the day approaching" (Heb 10:24-25).

WCF 18: OF THE ASSURANCE OF GRACE & SALVATION

When the Canons of Dort was formulated in 1618 against the doctrine of Jacobus Arminius, the fifth head of the Canon was entitled "Of the Perseverance of the Saints" This title and the doctrine that it heads bears testimony against two errors pertaining to the doctrine of salvation. The first relates to the false doctrine that believers can lose their salvation and therefore it is meaningless to have assurance of salvation. Those who hold to this error think that to have assurance of salvation is to be proud, presumptuous and carnally secured. The second error, on the other hand, supposes that salvation is to be seen as punctiliar, that is to say: it should be seen only as entering into a door. The journey that must immediately begin if the believer has entered the strait gate is minimised or completely ignored. Those who hold to this error believe that once a person prayed to receive Christ, he will attain to heaven no matter what. "Once saved, always saved!" they insist. Well, they are right theoretically. If a person is truly saved, he will persevere in salvation unto eternity. However, those who hold to this error also tend also to ridicule self-examination and speak of those who question their own salvation as doubting God.

This chapter of our *Confession*, which is founded squarely on the biblical doctrine of the Perseverance of the Saints already discussed in the previous chapter, strikes a straight course through these two opposing errors. It teaches us that while true believers cannot lose their salvation, they should be concerned about their assurance of salvation and that it is possible, on the one hand, for a believer to have full assurance, and on the other hand, to lose that assurance of salvation.

On True and False Assurance

18.1 Although hypocrites, and other unregenerate men, may vainly deceive themselves with false hopes and carnal presumptions of being in the favour of God and estate of salvation;[1] which hope of theirs shall perish;[2] yet such as truly believe in the Lord Jesus, and love Him in sincerity, endeavouring to walk in all good conscience before Him, may in this life be certainly assured that they are in the state of grace,[3] and may rejoice in the hope of the glory of God; which hope shall never make them ashamed.[4]

[1]*Job 8:13–14; Mic 3:11; Dt 29:19; Jn 8:41;* [2]*Mt 7:22–23;* [3]*1 Jn 2:3; 3:14, 18–19, 21, 24; 5:13;* [4]*Rom 5:2, 5.*

- This section basically distinguishes between true and false assurance of salvation.

It is true that the blessing of assurance of salvation can be abused for it is possible for an unregenerate person to be very assured of his "salvation," but in actual fact, have no salvation to be assured of! Such a person is what our *Confession* calls a 'hypocrite'.

However, we must not, —because of this possibility of abuse, — deny that it is possible for a person who is truly saved to be certainly assured of his salvation.

These then are the two errors we must steer clear off: (a) that it is not possible to be assured of one's salvation; and (b) that assurance is a given as we should never question our salvation.

a. Roman Catholicism holds that "no one can know with a certainty of faith, which cannot be subject to error, that he has obtained the grace of God."[44] In other words, no one can ordinarily know for sure that he is indeed a child of God. In fact, Rome teaches that it is neither possible nor desirable that any one should attain such assurance without a special supernatural revelation. Therefore, to claim assurance is to boast of vain self-confidence and pride.

b. Much of modern-day evangelism, on the other hand, teaches "easy-believism." This leads to a real distortion and dilution of the biblical doctrine of assurance. People are called to pray a so-called sinner's prayer, and then told that they have been saved and from then on, they must never doubt their salvation no matter what. This kind of doctrine results in many churches

---

[44] *Council of Trent*, On Justification, chap. 9.

today being filled with hypocrites as well as sincere but unregenerate people, who vainly deceive themselves with false hopes and carnal presumptions of being in favour with God; which hope of theirs shall surely perish. Let us be very careful of such false doctrines and false prophets, who as in the days of Jeremiah cry, "Peace, peace"; when there is no peace (Jer 6:14).

2. How do we know that assurance is attainable in this life?

   Firstly, many passages in Scripture teach us directly that such assurance is attainable in this life, e.g., Romans 8:16, 2 Peter 1:10, 1 John 2:3, 1 John 5:13. *Secondly*, there are scriptural examples of its attainment, e.g., 2 Timothy 1:12, 4:7–8. *Thirdly*, there are numerous examples of Christians, through the ages, who have enjoyed a full assurance of their personal salvation and whose life vindicated the genuineness of their faith.

3. But how can we distinguish between true and false assurance? A.A. Hodge gives us four tests:

   (a) True assurance begets unfeigned humility; false assurance begets spiritual pride (1 Cor 15:10; Gal 6:14); (b) True assurance leads to increased diligence in the practice of holiness; false assurance leads to sloth and self-indulgence (Ps 51:12–13, 19); (c) True assurance leads to candid self-examination and to a desire to be searched and corrected by God; false assurance leads to a disposition to be satisfied with appearance and to avoid accurate investigation (Ps 139:23–24); (d) True assurance leads to constant aspirations after more intimate fellowship with God (1 Jn 3:2–3).[45]

On the Grounds of True Assurance

18.2 This certainty is not a bare conjectural and probable persuasion, grounded upon a fallible hope;[1] but an infallible assurance of faith*,

---

[45] Hodge, *Confession*, 239.

* i.e. Assurance of the reality of faith, or the assurance of sense and hope of salvation. See comments under *WCF* 18.3.

founded upon the divine truth of the promises of salvation,[2] the inward evidence of those graces unto which these promises are made,[3] the testimony of the Spirit of adoption witnessing with our spirits that we are the children of God:[4] which Spirit is the earnest of our inheritance, whereby we are sealed to the day of redemption.[5]

[1]Heb 6:11, 19; [2]Heb 6:17–18; [3]2 Pet 1:4–5, 10–11; 1 Jn 2:3; 3:14; 2 Cor 1:12; [4]Rom 8:15–16; [5]Eph 1:13–14; 4:30; 2 Cor 1:21–22.

This section is very important as it lays down the foundation or ground of assurance. This ground may be divided into two categories, namely, a primary objective ground, viz.—"*the divine truth of the promises of salvation*") and two secondary subjective grounds, viz.—"*the inward evidences of those graces unto which these promises are made*" and "*the testimony of the Spirit of adoption witnessing with our spirits.*" When all these three grounds of assurance are combined together, they form an infallible or full assurance of salvation.

1. Primary Objective Ground: The Divine Truth of the Promises of Salvation

   The first ground of assurance is the promise given in the Scripture that all who repents of their sin and all who embrace Christ, —believing that He lived and died on behalf of sinful man, and that He rose again, and that He is seated at the right hand of the throne of God interceding for His own, —will be saved and preserved in their faith. Prof John Murray's explanation can hardly be bettered:

   "Every believer is assured of God's reality and the truth of the Gospel. These are the certainties which constitute the ground of faith itself [which] does not exist except as it entertains the assurance of these certitudes. Faith is not compatible with uncertainty as to its object, though it may consist with uncertainty as to the possession of the salvation which is the result of faith. Neither does it mean that there is any insecurity in the salvation of those who believe. The security does not rest upon the stability of the assurance the believers entertains of that security; the security resides in the faithfulness of the Saviour."[47]

---

[47] John Murray, *Collected Writings* (Edinburgh: The Banner of Truth Trust, 1977), 2:266-7

In other words, the promise of salvation is not only the objective ground of assurance, but the primary ground as well. It is the bedrock on which the other two grounds of assurance rest. Or to put it in another way, you may only have assurance of salvation, if you know and understand the Gospel, and believe in its promises such as: John 3:36, "He that believeth on the Son hath everlasting life...." And John 6:37b, "him that cometh to me I will in no wise cast out."

A person who does a lot of work in a church, but has no appreciation of the Gospel, is, —in the final analysis, —an unbeliever trying to attain salvation by works. Such a person ought to re-examine his foundation. Similarly, a person who claims to have experiences of the Holy Spirit, but have no desire to know what the Scripture teaches is simply fooling himself or is deluded by an unholy spirit. On the other hand, a person whose heart has been changed by the Holy Spirit, such that he knows in his heart of hearts that all that the Scripture says is true and therefore trusts and obeys the Lord may have the confidence that he is a child of God.

2. First secondary subjective ground: Inward Evidence of Grace

    It is one thing for me to believe and another thing for me to believe that I believe. It is here that the secondary subjective grounds help us examine whether our faith is genuine.

    The first of the two secondary grounds is that of the evidence of inward grace. The Puritans, including the Westminster Divines, distinguish between two closely related aspects of the evidence of inward grace.

    - The first has to do with the existence and improvement of the marks of grace in the soul such as genuine love, meekness, poverty of spirit (or humility), hatred for sin and hunger and thirst for righteousness, etc (cf. Gal 5:22-23; Mt 5:3-6).

    - The second has to do with good works which flows from a heart of love and obedience (cf. Mt 7:16; Heb 6:10).

    In other words, the first is invisible to others, the second is visible. The

Puritans speak of these two aspects in terms of a "mystical syllogism" and a "practical syllogism."[48] Basically, they mean that since the Scripture presents these marks as the evidences of regeneration, we may conclude that we are regenerate, if we can honestly detect them in our lives. It is true that when the Puritans were addressing this aspect of assurance, they did enjoin introspection. But they did not end there. Jonathan Edwards, for example, made it clear:

> "Although self-examination be a duty of great use and importance, and by no means to be neglected; yet it is not the *principal* means by which the saints do get satisfaction of their good estate. Assurance is not to be obtained so much by *self-examination* as by *action*."[49]

In other words, we must not think that we may obtain assurance merely by inward examination. True assurance may only be found in children of God who are walking in the straight and narrow way of life, and actively obeying the will of God given in the Moral Laws. "Hereby we do know that we know Him, if we keep His commandments" says the apostle John (1Jn 2:3).

In any case, how should we evaluate ourselves? John Gerstner suggests 3 steps—(i) Introspection, (ii) Retrospection, (iii)

---

[48] "The practical syllogism was based largely on the believer's *sanctification and good works as evidenced in practical, daily life*. It tended to accent the believer's life of new obedience which expressed and confirmed his experience of grace. It went something like this. *Major Premise*: According to Scripture, only those who possess saving faith will receive the Spirit's testimony that their lives manifest fruits of sanctification and good works. *Minor Premise*: I cannot deny that by the grace of God I have received the Spirit's testimony that I may manifest fruits of sanctification and good works. *Conclusion*: Consequently, I may be assured that I am a partaker of saving faith.

The mystical syllogism was based largely on the believer's *internal exercises and progress in the steps of grace*. It tended to focus on the inward man and went something like this. *Major Premise*: According to the Scripture, only those who possess saving faith will experience the Spirit's testimony confirming inward grace and godliness, such that self will decrease and Christ will increase. *Minor Premise*: I cannot deny that by the grace of God I may experience the Spirit's testimony confirming inward grace and godliness such that self decreases and Christ increases. *Conclusion*: Consequently, I may be assured that I am a partaker of saving grace" (Joel R. Beeke, *Assurance of Faith: Calvin, English Puritanism, and the Dutch Second Reformation* [New York: Peter Lang Publishing, 1991], 160).

[49] Jonathan Edwards, *Works* (BOT), 1.263

Extrospection. Introspection has to do with looking into our hearts to see if indeed a work of grace has begun, and whether we see those visible marks of regeneration are present. Retrospection has to do with looking back to the past to see if there has been any spiritual growth since we first came to Christ and made a profession of faith. Just as it is a sure sign that a plant is alive when it grows and bears fruits, so also, it is a clear evidence that a person has the new life in him if he grows and matures in it. Lastly, extrospection has to do with what other godly believers have to say about us. Do they observe in us the marks of grace? Can they see Christ in us?

3. Second secondary subjective ground: The Witness of the Spirit

This third ground for assurance is taken directly from Paul's words in Romans 8:15–16, "… but ye have received the Spirit of adoption, whereby we cry, Abba, Father. The Spirit itself beareth witness with our spirit, that we are the children of God."

Dr Joel Beeke has noted that the Westminster divines were not all agreed on what this means. The first group with divines such as Jeremiah Burroughs, Anthony Burgess, and George Gillespie believe that the Spirit works through the conscience in the context of the syllogisms (above). The second group with divines such as Samuel Rutherford, Henry Scudder, William Twisse, William Bridge holds that the Spirit sometimes witness to the believer's spirit by direct application of the Word. The third group led by Thomas Goodwin holds that this is an extraordinary testimony of the spirit of God in the spirit of believers to give them full assurance of the love of God and to grant them joy unspeakable.[50]

Which of these is correct? I am inclined to agree with the second group without discounting the first. In other words, I believe that the third ground of assurance is distinguishable from the second. I would

---

[50] Beeke, *Op. Cit.*, 170. Note that difference between the first two groups. "The [first group] leaves in its wake the self-conscious conviction, "I am a child of God," and on the basis of such Spirit-worked syllogisms finds freedom to approach the Father. The [second group] speaks [of] the Spirit's pronouncement on behalf of the Father, "You are a child of God," and on the basis of hearing its sonship from God's own Word by the Spirit, proceeds to approach Him with the familiarity of a child" (ibid.).

not discount the experiences of those in the third group, but I believe these experiences are really heightened experience of the illuminating work of the Holy Spirit. In other words, I do not believe that we should not expect any extraordinary revelation from God to assure us of our salvation. I believe that the Holy Spirit bears witness with our spirits that we are the sons of God by assuring us of the Fatherly love of God as we read the Scripture or meditate on Scripture already memorised. When this assurance of love floods our hearts, our natural response is to cry call out unto God, calling Him "Abba, Father." We must remember that such illuminations are not "extraordinary revelation" (see *WCF* 18.3, *WLC* 81). If, then, you would have such additional testimony of the Spirit, you must read and meditate on the Word rather than expect some mystical experience.

Joel Beeke summarised this section very well when he wrote:

"At every point in true assurance, the activity of the Spirit is essential. Without the application of the Spirit, the promises of God lead to self-deceit and fruitless lives. Without the enlightening of the Spirit, self-examination tends to introspection, bondage, and legalism. The witness of the Spirit, divorced from the promises of God and from scriptural self-examination, is prone to reap unbiblical mysticism and excessive emotionalism."[51]

On the Growth of Assurance

18.3 This infallible assurance does not so belong to the essence of faith, but that a true believer may wait long, and conflict with many difficulties, before he be partaker of it:[1] yet, being enabled by the Spirit to know the things which are freely given him of God, he may, without extraordinary revelation, in the right use of ordinary means, attain thereunto.[2] And therefore it is the duty of every one to give all diligence to make his calling and election sure;[3] that thereby his heart may be enlarged in peace and joy in the Holy Ghost, in love and thankfulness to God, and in strength and cheerfulness in the duties of obedience,[4] the

---

[51] *Ibid.*, 173.

proper fruits of this assurance: so far is it from inclining men to looseness.[5]

[1] 1 Jn 5:13; Isa 1:10; Mk 9:24; Ps 88; 77:1–12; [2] 1 Cor 2:12; 1 Jn 4:13; Heb 6:11–12; Eph 3:17–19; [3] 2 Pet 1:10; [4] Rom 5:1–2, 5; 14:17; 15:13; Eph 1:3–4; Ps 4:6–7; Ps 119:32; [5] 1 Jn 2:1–2; Rom 6:1–2; Tit 2:11–12, 14; 2 Cor 7:1; Rom 8:1, 12; 1 Jn 3:2–3; Ps 130:4; 1 Jn 1:6–7.

- In the chapter on "Saving Faith" (*WCF* 14) we noted the difference between "assurance of faith" and "assurance of sense." We made this distinction really for the purpose of clarifying the answer to the question: "Does assurance belong to the essence of faith?" In this paragraph of our *Confession*, we shall see that assurance does not belong to the essence of faith. However, continental Reformed theologians such as Calvin would tend to answer the question in the affirmative. How do we explain the difference between the *WCF* view and the continental view? The difference lies in the fact that the continental Reformers were thinking of faith in terms of the objective truth of the word. If so, then indeed, in order for a person to be saved, he must be assured of faith. In our *Confession*, however, when the phrase, "assurance of faith" is used, it is really referring to faith as in believing, not as in objective truth. Or to put it in another way, the phrase "assurance of faith" (*WCF* 18.2) refers to "assurance of the reality of faith," which we may, more precisely, call "assurance of sense," rather than the "assurance of the truth of the God's revelation." The former is not of the essence of faith, whereas the latter is of the essence of faith, for it is really faith itself.

Assurance of the faith (as objective truth) has to do with the assurance that God's Word is true and that all that He says in His Word will surely come to pass. For example, no one can be saved who is not fully convinced and assured that the blood of Christ is able to cleanse us from all our sins and that those who believe in Him shall certainly be saved. Assurance of sense, on the other hand, has to do with a confidence of whether one has truly believed unto salvation or not. And so, assurance in this sense is really the fruit of a well-developed faith.

- Having distinguished between the possession of saving faith and of developed assurance, the *Confession* then tells us that it is possible for a person to wait for a period of time and even undergo much difficulty before he comes to enjoy a deeper sense of assurance. Thus, the prophet Isaiah says,

  "Who is among you that feareth the LORD, that obeyeth the voice of his servant, that walketh in darkness, and hath no light? let him trust in the name of the LORD, and stay upon his God" (Isa 50:10).

  God is sovereign with respect to the duration of this period of darkness, but He especially uses difficulties, trials, and doubts to strengthen and mature the faith of a believer.

3. Although God is ultimately sovereign in His bestowing of assurance, nevertheless He normally bestows it through "*the right use of ordinary means*." In fact, as Christians, it is our duty to use these means of grace for the obtaining of assurance. This is essentially what the writer of Hebrews means when he says:

   "And we desire that every one of you do shew the same diligence to the full assurance of hope unto the end: That ye may not be slothful, but followers of them who through faith and patience inherit the promises" (Heb 6:11–12).

   What are the means of grace? The reading and meditating of God's Word and promises, the attendance to the sacraments and earnest prayer. Earlier, we mentioned that God often uses trials to strengthen our faith. That is also a means of grace and although only God can send trials into our lives, yet, when they come, we are to pray for wisdom (Jas 1:5), and trust that in God's hand, they are ultimately for our own benefit (Rom 8:28).

4. Finally, assurance bears fruits. The *Confession* describes for us what they are. Positively, it produces peace and joy in the Holy Ghost, love and thankfulness to God, strength and obedience in duty with cheerfulness. Negatively, it turns us away from sin, carelessness and "loose" living. The more a person is assured of his salvation, the more he will love God and strive to walk in obedience to His laws.

On the Renewal of Assurance

18.4 True believers may have the assurance of their salvation divers ways shaken, diminished, and intermitted; as, by negligence in preserving of it; by falling into some special sin, which woundeth the conscience, and grieveth the Spirit; by some sudden or vehement temptation; by God's withdrawing the light of His countenance, and suffering even such as fear Him to walk in darkness, and to have no light:[1] yet are they never utterly destitute of that seed of God, and life of faith, that love of Christ and the brethren, that sincerity of heart and conscience of duty, out of which, by the operation of the Spirit, this assurance may in due time be revived,[2] and by the which, in the mean time, they are supported from utter despair.[3]

[1]*Song 5:2–3, 6; Ps 51:8, 12, 14; Eph 4:30–31; Ps 77:1–10; Mt 26:69–72; Ps 31:22; 88; Isa 1:10;* [2]*1 Jn 3:9; Lk 22:32; Job 13:15; Ps 73:15; 51:8, 12; Isa 1:10;* [3]*Mic 7:7–9; Jer 32:40; Isa 54:7–10; Ps 22:1; 88.*

- Because this infallible assurance is not of the essence of faith, it may be lost, weakened or even unreachable for a certain period of time. Our *Confession* identifies two causes for this lack of assurance in a true believer, namely: (a) the sin and backsliding of the believer, (b) God's temporary withdrawing of the light of His countenance.

  a. A believer who is negligent in preserving this grace of assurance, who falls into some special sin and yields to sudden or vehement temptation, will no doubt suffer a lack of assurance. The Christian cannot enjoy high levels of assurance when he persists in low levels of obedience. Assurance is very closely related to sanctification. The more we grow in the grace of sanctification, the more we will experience assurance of salvation. The more we see ourselves dying to sin and living unto righteousness, the more we'll have the assurance that we are truly the children of God. Now if a true sense of assurance could still remain on a high note even though a believer's obedience was minimal, that would no doubt make him take for granted the great privilege of being a child of God, and result in him growing spiritually lazy. This truth that backsliding diminishes assurance ought to make us watchful and active in searching our souls. When assurance turns into presumption through our backsliding, it is most healthy that our doubts and fears would spur desires in our heart to seek afresh for assurance.

b. The second reason for a believer's lack of assurance may lie in God and not so much in the believer himself. God, in His wisdom and sovereignty, may decide to withdraw His gracious presence from us for a season such that we lack assurance and feel God to be very distant. But why would God do something like that? The Puritan Thomas Brooks gives us a several reasons, for example: (i) For the exercise of our grace, (ii) Because we seek assurance more for ourselves, than we do for His honour and glory, (iii) That when we may have it, we may the more highly prize it, (iv) That we may be kept humble and low in our own eyes. [52]

Now it may not be possible for us to know all the reasons for God's "withdrawment." In fact, we may not know the reason for God's withdrawing until eternity. Nevertheless, we can be sure that God does it for His own glory and for the ultimate good of His people. William Gurnal says, "The Christian must trust in a with-drawing God."[53] Again, Joel Beeke summarises this point very well when he says,

"...both God's withdrawing of His countenance and His placing of sudden or vehement trials in the path of the believer are motivated, first, by His *fatherly discipline*, which teaches "right walking"; second, by His *fatherly sovereignty*, which teaches us dependence; and third, by His *fatherly wisdom*, which teaches that He knows and does what is best for His own."[54]

---

[52] See Thomas Brooks, *Works*, 2.330-4.

[53] William Gurnal, *The Christian in Complete Armour* (Edinburgh: Banner of Truth Trust, 1974), 2.145.

[54] Beeke, *Op. Cit.*, 188.

- The final part of this section tells us that a believer may lose his assurance but he will never lose his faith. No matter what happens, a true believer will never cease to be a child of God even though he may not be fully assured of his sonship. Samuel Rutherford writes, "Deserted souls not conscious of the reflex act of believing and longing for Christ, think themselves apostates, when they are advancing in their way...."[55]

- It is through the Spirit of God that we are supported from utter despair and it is by His operation in our hearts that our assurance may in due time be revived. On our part, we, who desire to have our assurance revived, are to use the means of grace diligently, repent of our sins and humbly cast ourselves afresh upon the gracious promises of Christ.

[Several paragraphs in this and the previous chapter were originally contributed by Pastor Linus Chua. See footnote under our introduction for the commentary of WSC 17: On Perseverance of the Saints]

---

[55] Samuel Rutherford, *The Trials and Triumph of Faith* (BOT, 2001), 139-40.

WCF 19: OF THE LAW OF GOD

It is a sad observation that many modern Christians hate doctrine. But these same professors of faith would often quote Paul's word in Roman 6:14—"for ye are not under the law, but under grace." If we would read Paul's words in context, we will quickly realise that he is not saying what the modern easy-believists take him to say, namely that Christians are not under any obligation to keep any law. "God is love," they say, "and to demand anything of anyone would be contrary to the principle of love." They forget the words of the apostle John: "For this is the love of [i.e. for] God, that we keep his commandments: and his commandments are not grievous" (1Jn 5:3). God's love for us demands a grateful response of love; and that response of love must manifest itself in the keeping of God's commandments or laws.

This Law is presented throughout the Scripture, although it is summarised in the Ten Commandments.

On the Moral Law as a Perpetual Rule of Life

19.1 God gave to Adam a law, as a covenant of works, by which He bound him, and all his posterity, to personal, entire, exact, and perpetual obedience; promised life upon the fulfilling, and threatened death upon the breach of it; and endued him with power and ability to keep it.[1]

[1]*Gen 1:26–27; 2:17; Rom 2:14–15; 10:5; 5:12, 19; Gal 3:10, 12; Eccl 7:29; Job 28:28.*

- Much of the content of this paragraph has already been dealt with under *WCF* 4.2 and *WCF* 7.2. In *WCF* 4.2, we are taught that man, created in the image of God, has "the law of God written in their hearts, and power to fulfil it" (cf. Rom 2:14–15). On the other hand, *WCF* 7.2, teaches that Adam was under a Covenant of Works wherein life was promised upon perfect and personal obedience to that Law (cf. Rom 10:5, 5:12, 19).

- This Law is commonly known as the Moral Law (see *WCF* 19:3) because it was the revelation of the will of God as man's moral Governor; and so it is the standard and rule of man's moral actions and character. In other words, what is moral or immoral is not defined by the majority view or even by consensus of society, but by God through His Law.

- This Law, we should note, is not really the Covenant of Works, but the condition of the covenant. A failure to meet this condition incurs eternal death under the terms of the covenant. Nevertheless, we are given presently to speak of it as a *covenant of works* because it was, and is, the essence of the Covenant of Works. Man, as we shall see in the next paragraph, is still required to keep it as the perfect rule of righteousness by which he may obtain life.

- But what exactly is involved in the personal and perfect obedience required in the Covenant of Works? *Personal* obedience means that it is an obedience that may be attributable to the individual. It does not rule out obedience by a representative; but he must be a divinely appointed representative. What about *perfect* obedience? Perfect obedience is flawless obedience which may be described as *"entire, exact, and perpetual obedience."*

- It must be *entire* in that it must not be partial, whether it has to do with the scope of obedience, or the quality of obedience. That is to say, every statement of the law must be obeyed in its letter and its spirit; as well as, in what it demands and in what it forbids. And moreover, the person obeying must obey with his entire being: in his heart, soul, strength and mind.

- It must be *exact* in that it must be objective and absolute in God's eyes, and does not allow for subjectivity, nor mitigations based on weaknesses of man, extenuating circumstances or ignorance. God is "purer eyes than to behold evil, and canst not look on iniquity" (Hab 1:13).

- It must be *perpetual* in that it must be a constant and unwavering obedience that is not affected by the passage of time.

- Is it possible for man to obey so perfectly? Well, Adam, as we are given to confess, was originally *"endued... with power and ability to keep*" the Law in such a way. The Fall made it impossible. But since the perfect obedience required in the Covenant of Works is based upon God's unchanging nature, God cannot accept any less from fallen man without destroying His holiness.

19.2 This law, after his fall, continued to be a perfect rule of righteousness; and, as such, was delivered by God upon Mount Sinai, in ten commandments, and written in two tables;[1] the first four commandments containing our duty towards God, and the other six, our duty to man.[2]
[1]Jas 1:25; 2:8, 10–12; Rom 13:8–9; Dt 5:32; 10:4; Ex 24:1; [2]Mt 22:37–40.

- *"This law*," that is, the Moral Law was imposed by God not only for Adam, but also for his posterity, as the perfect rule of righteousness. All lack of conformity, or transgression of the Moral Law is, therefore, unrighteousness or sin.

- The Moral Law was able to function as *"a perfect rule of righteousness*" before the fall because it was inscribed on the heart of Adam since he was created in the image of God. Had Adam, not fallen into sin, all his descendants would also have the Moral Law written in their heart. However, because of the Fall, the fair copy of the Law inscribed in his heart is defaced to such an extent that it is no longer understood as it ought to be. The apostle Paul says: "There is none righteous, no, not one: There is *none that understandeth*, there is none that seeketh after God" (Rom 3:10-11). What remains in the heart of fallen man is like footprints in sand. When we see footprints along a beach, we know that a person or an animal has walked by, but we do not know much more than that. We may know whether it's a person or animal; we may know roughly what kind of animal it is, and perhaps how heavy it is. But we can't really say much more about it. This is perhaps why Paul speaks of the Gentiles as having "the *work* of the law written in their hearts" (Rom 2:15).

The Law is not totally obliterated from the heart of fallen man, but it is no longer sufficient for achieving righteousness. It is now only sufficient to enable him to function as a moral being with his conscience steering him; as well as to condemn him of unrighteousness (Rom 2:12-15).

- This is why men everywhere, and of every age, and culture continue to have a religious and moral sense. Thus, every people group, no matter how backward or civilised have some form of religion. Man created in the image of God knows in his heart of hearts that there is a God, and He must be worshipped. Likewise, hardly any persons, regardless of race or societal development will disagree that murder and theft are crimes, and that parents must be honoured and obeyed. Indeed, in some societies, such as amongst the Chinese people, this obligation towards parents is carried to the extreme in the form of filial piety, which manifests itself in parental and ancestral worship.

We may say that the works of the law in the heart makes the natural man moral sinners, but not righteous saints.

- Nevertheless, since God has appointed that the Moral Law should remain as *"a perfect rule of righteousness"* for man, He, in the fulness of time, revealed it in summary form to His covenant people. This summary is the *"Ten Commandments."* This *"was delivered by God upon Mount Sinai"* audibly, with thundering, and lightning, and trumpets, and earthquake, and smoke, in the hearing of his entire covenant people whom He had just recently redeemed from Egypt (Ex 19:18; 20:18-19).

- Then to emphasise its importance, and for the better preservation of it, God personally inscribed these commandments on *"two tables"* of stone (Ex 31:8). So important are these Ten Commandments that when Moses destroyed the first copy of it, God condescended to write it a second time with his own fingers (Ex 34:1, 28b). Moses, we may remember, destroyed the first copy due to his rage against the people for making and worshipping a golden calf while he was up in the mount. God could have instructed Moses to write it, the second time, but He did not.

- Why does the Scripture and our Confession highlight that the Ten Commandments was presented in *"two tables"*? Many modern scholars believe that the Ten Commandments were given in duplicate as was done when covenants were made in the Ancient Near Eastern culture: ten on one slab as God's copy and ten on the other slab as Israel's copy. But whether this is right or not is not really as important as how the Ten Commandments may be logically divided.

The Westminster divines, following John Calvin, divided the Ten Commandments logically into two tables with *"the first four commandments containing our duty towards God; and the other six, our duty to man"*.

The Roman Catholic Church and the Lutherans divide the Ten Commandments into three on one table and seven on the other table. This is done by combining what we know as the 1st and 2nd Commandments together and breaking up what we know as the 10th Commandment. So their 9th Commandment is "Thou shalt not covet thy neighbour's house" and their 10th Commandment is "Thou shalt not covet thy neighbour's wife, ..." This division is not only absurd (as Calvin observes), but has no scriptural basis. More than that, such a division appears to be an artificial attempt to eradicate the regulative principle of worship which is taught in the 2nd Commandment. Calvin and all Reformed persons believe that the 2nd Commandment is not about worshipping other gods (as Lutherans and Romanists hold), but about how the Living and True God is to be worshipped.

- Briefly, the Ten Commandments may summarised as follows:

Our duty to God (out of wholehearted love for Him):

I   Thou shalt have no other gods before me.
- → Love the Living and True God wholeheartedly.
- → To worship God alone and none other.

II   Thou shalt not make unto thee any graven image....
- → Love God's appointed mode or manner of worship.
- → To worship God in the manner prescribed by Him.

III   Thou shalt not take the name of the LORD thy God in vain...

- → Love God's name and all that He puts His name upon.
- → To have sincere reverence for God's name and ordinances

IV   Remember the Sabbath day, to keep it holy.
- → Love God's Day of worship.
- → To keep the Sabbath holy.

Our duty to our fellow men (out of sincerely love for our neighbour):

V   Honour thy father and thy mother.
- → Out of love, respect and obey all God's representatives.
- → To honour our parents and all God-appointed authorities.

VI   Thou shalt not kill.
- → Out of love, respect the sanctity of human lives.
- → To avoid angry passions and reverence human lives.

VII   Thou shalt not commit adultery.
- → Out of love, respect the sanctity of marriage and sex.
- → To be pure in heart, language and conduct.

VIII   Thou shalt not steal.
- → Out of love, respect the ownership of personal property.
- → To be honest and industrious.

IX   Thou shalt not bear false witness against thy neighbour.
- → Out of love, respect the sanctity of truth.
- → To tell the truth.

X   Thou shalt not covet....
- → Out of love, respect what God has assigned to everyone.
- → To be content with what the Lord has given us.

On the Threefold Division of the Law of God

A cursory reading of the Bible will immediately reveal that God did not give only the Moral Commandments. The Law of God, which is revealed in the Word of God, can be classified broadly into three categories: Moral, Ceremonial and Judicial.

The next two paragraphs of our Confession deal with the Ceremonial Law and Judicial Law respectively.

19.3 Besides this law, commonly called Moral, God was pleased to give to the people of Israel, as a church under age, ceremonial laws, containing several typical ordinances; partly of worship, prefiguring Christ, His graces, actions, sufferings, and benefits;[1] and partly, holding forth divers instructions of moral duties.[2] All which ceremonial laws are now abrogated, under the New Testament.[3]

[1] Heb 9; 10:1; Gal 4:1–3; Col 2:17; [2] 1 Cor 5:7; 2 Cor 6:17; Jude 23; [3] Col 2:14, 16–17; Dan 9:27; Eph 2:15–16.

- The Law which God first gave to man for his obedience is *"commonly called Moral."* This is because it is understood that God has determined that the goodness or wickedness of man's thoughts, words and actions, is to be determined according to their degree of conformity or violation of these laws.

- The Ceremonial Law is so called not because it is only about ceremonies, but because it pertains to ceremonial purity and behaviour.

- The Ceremonial Law was given to the people of Israel, as a church under age. The nation of Israel in the Old Covenant, in other words, was God's church in her childhood. She was still being tutored, and led to Christ, in a way that is apposite to her immaturity (Gal 3:23-24).

- Ceremonial laws are appointed as part of this strategy. These laws contain *"several typical ordinances,"* such as the sacrificial system, the holy days, the priesthood and the dietary rules. These are known as *"typical ordinances"* because they are ordained of God, and have typical or symbolic spiritual meaning that will find their fulfillment in Christ in the New Covenant. We may say that they are all shadows and types pointing to Christ and His redemptive work. They pointed the Old Testament saints to Christ.

- How did these ceremonial laws serve their purpose? We are given to confess that they did so, largely, in two ways.

- First of all, they prescribed how God was to be worshipped, in a way that *"prefigur[ed] Christ, His graces, actions, sufferings, and benefits*." Thus, for example, the Tabernacle taught God's people that God would take on flesh to dwell in the midst of His people in the fullness of time (see Jn 1:14). Likewise, the animal sacrifices, and the atonement that they depicted, pointed to Christ's substitutionary atonement on behalf of His people (see Heb 9; 10).

- Secondly, the ceremonial laws also "*[held] forth diverse instructions of moral duties.*" For example, the ceremonial prohibition of leaven during the feast of unleavened bread taught God's people that scandalous sin must not be allowed to fester in the covenant community (cf. 1 Cor 5:7). Likewise, the prohibition of plowing with an ox and an ass yoked-together (Dt 22:10) taught God's people that they must not be yoked-together with unbelievers in the work of the Kingdom (2 Cor 6:14-16).

- These ceremonial laws were, however, appointed to be observed by God's people only in the old covenant times. They are, as such, as a whole, "now *abrogated*," and no longer to be observed by New Testament believers. They were, as a whole, a candle showing God's people who Christ is and what He would do on their behalf. But Christ, the Son of God, the Sun of Righteousness, has risen with healing in His wings and there is no more need for the candle. This is the clear teaching of Scripture both in the Old and New Testaments (cf. eg. Dan 9:27; Eph 2:15; Epistle to the Hebrews).

- Thank God for the Lord Jesus Christ who fulfilled the Ceremonial Law for us! Thank God that the middle wall of partition that separate between the Jews and Gentiles has been broken down. Thank God that we no longer have to offer bloody sacrifices in worship; or to cultivate holiness by avoiding pork, or crabs and prawns! But thank God also for the Ceremonial Laws. We could not properly understand the work of Christ unless we know the ceremonial laws. We cannot fully appreciate Christ's sacrifice, but that the ceremonial laws had animals sacrificed. We could not fully appreciate why John says that Christ tabernacled in our midst, but that the Ceremonial Law had a Tabernacle.

19.4 To them also, as a body politic, He gave sundry judicial laws, which expired together with the State of that people; not obliging any other now, further than the general equity thereof may require.[1]

[1] *Ex 21; 22:1–29; Gen 49:10; 1 Pet 2:13–14; Mt 5:17, 38–39; 1 Cor 9:8–10.*

- In the previous paragraph of our *Confession*, we noted how the nation of Israel under the Old Covenant was "*a church under age.*" She comprised the external people of God who were being taught about Christ, and led to Him through the shadows and types of the Ceremonial Law, in view of the fact that He had not yet come. If we think of the New Testament Church as the bride of Christ, then Israel of Old was the same bride in her growing-up years.

- But the nation of Israel was also, as we see in our present paragraph, "*a body politic.*" That is to say, she was a nation, or a society of people that was organised under a governmental authority. But as they were "the people of God" (Jdg 20:2; 2 Sam 14:13), God gave them "*sundry judicial laws*" to regulate their life as a nation dwelling and functioning together in the Land of Israel.

- Since this was the purpose of these laws, they naturally ceased to be authoritative as soon as the people of Israel ceased to be the holy people of God; or we may say, when they ceased to be the "church under age." Thus, we are given to confess that these laws "*expired together with the State of that people.*"

- Judicial laws are laws pertaining to judgements relating to the behaviour or conduct of the people dwelling together in the land. They regulate how the people are to conduct their life; how they are to relate to one another; and the penalties that should be inflicted upon those who fail to observe the appointed boundaries. But given the fact that the Church of God is no longer confined to a particular nation or locality, the divinely appointed Judicial Law can no longer be enforced, and is no longer binding upon anyone. Instead, the apostle Paul says: "Let every soul be subject unto the higher powers. For there is no power but of God: the powers that be are ordained of God" (Rom 13:1). New Testament believers must submit to the judicial laws of the land where they reside, even if the government is not Christian, or even anti-Christian, as the Roman government was.

- In any case, the judicial laws given in the Scriptures are not entirely irrelevant to New Testament believers. Notice how carefully our *Confession* is worded in this regard: for as we are given to confess that the judicial laws have expired with the state of Israel as the people of God, we are reminded that these same laws do *"not [oblige] any other now, further than the general equity thereof may require."* In other words, while they have *expired*, they continue to serve as useful guides for judgement and fairness. This is what our *Confession* is referring to by the phrase *"general equity thereof."*

  This being the case, all civil governments in the world ought to pattern their laws after the Old Testament Judicial Law. Since the biblical Judicial Law reveals the mind of God, we can have no doubt that human laws patterned after it are likely to be much more effective. For example, under the Judicial Law of God, if you steal, you will have to return what you stole, plus extra. If you stole an ox, you would have to pay back five oxen. If you stole a sheep, you would have to pay back four sheep (Ex 22:1). This would certainly be more effective than using prison sentences which sap tax-payers' money, and do little to compensate for the loss suffered by the victim.

- That said, since the Old Testament Judicial Law has expired, so long as we are not required to sin against God, believers should submit to the law of the land, even if it differs from the Old Testament Judicial Law. Thus, if the Judicial Law of our land prescribes imprisonment for parents who spank their children, then we must not be unwilling to suffer imprisonment if we are found guilty of breaking the Law of the land. The legislators of the land would sin against God by introducing such a law, but as long as the law stands, we must willingly submit to its penal sanction. Likewise, if say, the judicial law of the Land prescribe a fine, and nothing more, for murder, then our legislators would be answerable to God for refusing to follow the pattern He has laid down; but as private citizens, we may not insist on the death penalty; or take matters into our own hand on any pretext that this is required in the Old Testament Judicial Law.

- We should add, by way of clarification, that Judicial Law includes Civil Law and Criminal Law.

Civil Law deals with private disputes between individuals occasioned by debts, divorce, inheritance, or other relationships issues. In civil cases, the guilty party is generally asked to compensate the victim in an appropriate way.

By contrast, Criminal Law deals with crimes. That is, it concerns actions that the state prohibits, and takes steps to punish, such as: murder, treason, or theft.

The distinction between Civil and Criminal Law was, however, quite foreign to the biblical Jews. Nearly all offences were matters for private prosecution. If someone was murdered, his relatives were responsible for killing the murderer, or chasing him to the nearest city of refuge, where a trial would be held.

Nevertheless, all offences in Israel had a religious dimension: theft or adultery was not merely an offence against one's neighbour, but was a sin against God. This means that, in theory, every Israelite would be shocked by such behaviour and would want it punished. If such acts continued, God Himself might step in to punish the individual, his family, or even the whole nation. This religious dimension gave an aura of criminality to every offence, even though in most cases, prosecution was left in the hands of individuals.

Moreover, some serious religious offences, such as Sabbath-breaking (Num 15:32–36) or idolatry (Dt 13) were regarded as so heinous, that the whole nation was responsible for prosecuting and punishing the offenders. These offences thus correspond more closely to the modern understanding of crime.

19.5 The moral law doth for ever bind all, as well justified persons as others, to the obedience thereof;[1] and that, not only in regard of the matter contained in it, but also in respect of the authority of God, the Creator, who gave it.[2] Neither doth Christ in the Gospel any way dissolve, but much strengthen this obligation.[3]

[1] *Rom 13:8–10; Eph 6:2; 1 Jn 2:3–4, 7–8;* [2] *Jas 2:10–11;* [3] *Mt 5:17–19; Jas 2:8; Rom 3:31.*

- We have seen how the Ceremonial Law and the Judicial Law of the Old Testament are no longer binding to anyone *"in regard to the matter contained in it."* They served their purpose as legislation, and expired with the status of Israel as the Church underage.

- In the present paragraph of our *Confession*, however, we are given to affirm the authority, perpetuity and universality of the Moral Law of God. It is perpetual in that it is always applicable and binding. It is universal in that not only *"justified persons"*, but *"others"*, i.e., Christians, as well as, non-Christians, are obliged to keep it; and will be judged by it.

- These qualities of the Moral Law, in distinction to the Ceremonial and Judicial Laws, are founded upon the fact that it was given by *"God the Creator,"* to all mankind created in His image; and not only to any particular people living at any period of time. Therefore, as long as mankind persists, the Moral Law will remain authoritative *"not only in regard of the matter contained in it, but also in respect of the authority of God the Creator, who gave it."*

- Some Christians, such as those who hold to Classical Dispensationalism or Antinomianism, do not agree with this argument. They insist that Christians are not under the law, but under grace; and therefore, we are not obliged to keep the Law. This is due to a misinterpretation of verses such as Romans 6:15; Galatians 3:1-5; and 2 Corinthians 3:6-17. However, a careful study of the theology of the apostle Paul makes it clear that such a view would contradict with his explicit statements scattered throughout his writings. We think of Romans 2:12-13 where he says: "For as many as have sinned without law shall also perish without law: and as many as have sinned in the law shall be judged by the law; (For not the hearers of the law are just before God, but the doers of the law shall be justified." Or Romans 3:31 which reads—"Do we then make void the law through faith? God forbid: yea, we establish the law." Indeed, Paul makes direct appeals to the Moral Law on numerous occasions. We think of 1 Corinthians 10:14; Galatians 5:19-21; Colossians 3:5 and Ephesians 6:1-2.

- Bearing all these in mind, we can be certain that when Paul says "*we are not under the law, but under grace*" (Rom 6:15), he is not saying that we are not obliged to keep the law; but rather that we cannot obtain salvation by the law. This does not mean that the law is no longer relevant for the believer. Likewise, when Paul admonishes the Galatians by saying: "Are ye so foolish? having begun in the Spirit, are ye now made perfect by the flesh?" (Gal 3:3), he is not at all implying that the law has no place in Christian life. Rather, obedience to the Law is not a means of sanctification. It is our duty. Disobedience to the law hinders our sanctification, no doubt, but it is the Spirit who sanctifies us as we walk by faith in the use of all the appointed means of grace. Again, Paul is not saying in 2 Corinthians 3:6-17 that the Moral Law has been abolished; but rather that the ministry of condemnation of the Old Covenant pales in comparison to the ministry of righteousness under the New Covenant. The Old Covenant emphasized the failure of the people to keep the law, and thereby shut them up to Christ. The New Covenant emphasizes the power of the Spirit and forgiveness in Christ to enable God's people to walk in righteousness. Part of walking in righteousness is to walk in grateful obedience to the law. "If ye love me, keep my commandments" (Jn 14:15).

- Moreover, the Lord Jesus says in His the Sermon on the Mount:

  "Think not that I am come to destroy the law, or the prophets: I am come not to destroy, but to fulfil. For verily I say unto you, Till heaven and earth pass, one jot or one tittle shall in no wise pass from the law, till all be fulfilled. Whosoever therefore shall break one of these least commandments, and shall teach men so, he shall be called the least in the kingdom of heaven: but whosoever shall do and teach them, the same shall be called great in the kingdom of heaven" (Mt 5:17–19).

- It is clear that the Lord Jesus did not come to abrogate the Law, but rather to fulfil it. Indeed, in so far as the Moral Law is concerned, He not only fulfils it on behalf of His elect, but enables them, by the power of His Spirit to live by it. Sin, we must remember is lawlessness (1 Jn 3:4); whereas righteousness is conformity to the Law (cf. Rom 6:18, 20). Thus Paul says: "if Christ be in you, the body is dead because of sin; but the Spirit is life because of righteousness" (Rom 8:10). Similarly the apostle John says: "he that keepeth his commandments dwelleth in him, and he in him. And hereby we know that he abideth in us, by the Spirit which he hath given us" (1 Jn 3:24).

- Therefore, we heartily confess as we are given to do: "*Neither doth Christ, in the Gospel, any way dissolve, but much strengthen this obligation*" to keep God's Moral Law.

On the Uses of the Moral Law

19.6a Although true believers be not under the law as a covenant of works, to be thereby justified or condemned;[1] yet is it of great use to them, as well as to others; in that, as a rule of life, informing them of the will of God and their duty, it directs and binds them to walk accordingly;[2] discovering also the sinful pollutions of their nature, hearts, and lives;[3] so as, examining themselves thereby, they may come to further conviction of, humiliation for, and hatred against sin;[4] together with a clearer sight of the need they have of Christ, and the perfection of His obedience.[5]...

[1]Rom 6:14; Gal 2:16; 3:13; 4:4–5; Acts 13:39; Rom 8:1; [2]Rom 7:12, 22, 25; Ps 119:4–6; 1 Cor 7:19; Gal 5:14, 16, 18–23; [3]Rom 7:7; 3:20; [4]Jas 1:23–25; Rom 7:9, 14, 24; [5]Gal 3:24; Rom 7:24–25; 8:3–4.

- Notice the very careful wordings of the *Confession*: "*True believers [are] not under the law as a covenant of works, to be thereby justified or condemned.*" Since believers are justified in Christ, they will not be condemned or justified by the Law. What about unbelievers? In a sense unbelievers are under the Law as a Covenant of Works. They are unable to be justified by it because all men fell in Adam, but they will be condemned by it—not only because they are represented by Adam, but because they do actually transgress the Law personally.

- In any case, the Law *"of great use to them [true believers], as well as to others [unbelievers]."* Thus, the *Confession* is here speaking of the general uses of the Law for the regenerate and the unregenerate:

    a. It shows the will of God, or the duty that God requires of them: "Thou hast commanded us to keep thy precepts diligently. O that my ways were directed to keep thy statutes!" (Ps 119:4–5).

    b. It reveals the sinful pollutions of their nature, heart and life: "What shall we say then? Is the law sin? God forbid. Nay, I had not known sin, but by the law: for I had not known lust, except the law had said, Thou shalt not covet" (Rom 7:7); "Therefore by the deeds of the law there shall no flesh be justified in his sight: for by the law is the knowledge of sin" (Rom 3:20).

    c. It drives them to conviction and humiliation, and hatred for sin: "For I was alive without the law once: but when the commandment came, sin revived, and I died. … For we know that the law is spiritual: but I am carnal, sold under sin. … Now if I do that I would not, it is no more I that do it, but sin that dwelleth in me" (Rom 7:9, 14, 20).

    d. It leads them to Christ by showing them their need for a Saviour: "Wherefore the law was our schoolmaster to bring us unto Christ, that we might be justified by faith" (Gal 3:24). "O wretched man that I am! who shall deliver me from the body of this death? I thank God through Jesus Christ our Lord. So then with the mind I myself serve the law of God; but with the flesh the law of sin" (Rom 7:24–25).

19.6b ...It is likewise of use to the regenerate, to restrain their corruptions, in that it forbids sin;[1] and the threatenings of it serve to show what even their sins deserve, and what afflictions in this life they may expect for them, although freed from the curse thereof threatened in the law.[2] The promises of it, in like manner, show them God's approbation of obedience, and what blessings they may expect upon the performance thereof,[3] although not as due to them by the law as a covenant of works:[4]...

[1]Jas 2:11; Ps 119:101, 104, 128; [2]Ezra 9:13–14; Ps 89:30–34; [3]Lev 26:1–14; 2 Cor 6:16; Eph 6:2–3; Ps 37:11; Mt 5:5; Ps 19:11; [4]Gal 2:16; Lk 17:10.

- The Law also has specific uses for the regenerate only:

  a. It restrains their corruption. It does so by forbidding sin and showing what chastisement they may expect for their sins, even though they may be freed from the curse of the Law: "If his children forsake my law, and walk not in my judgments; If they break my statutes, and keep not my commandments; Then will I visit their transgression with the rod, and their iniquity with stripes. Nevertheless my lovingkindness will I not utterly take from him, nor suffer my faithfulness to fail. My covenant will I not break, nor alter the thing that is gone out of my lips" (Ps 89:30–34).

  b. It encourages them to obedience. It does so by showing what blessings may be expected from obedience (though not due them as a Covenant of Works): "Moreover by them is thy servant warned: and in keeping of them there is great reward" (Ps 19:11).

- The more astute student of Historical Theology will recognise that these uses of the Law correspond roughly to the Three Uses of the Law presented by John Calvin in his *Institutes*.[56] We may simplify Calvin's three uses thus:

→ *Firstly*, the Law shows God's righteousness or the righteousness alone acceptable to God. And in so doing, it warns, informs, convicts, and lastly condemns, every man of his own unrighteousness.[57] Calvin calls this the *theological use* of the Law. The Law as such is like:

---

[56] *ICR* 2.7.6–12.

[57] See *ICR* 2.7.6

(a) A *portrait*, picturing our Creator and His righteousness (Rom 7:7), and also

(b) A *mirror*, displaying our unrighteousness (cf. Rom 3:20; Jas 1:23–25).

→ *Secondly*, it restrains (particularly) the unregenerate by its dire threats and compels them to Christ.[58] This is known as the *civil or pedagogical use* of the Law. As such the Law is like:

(a) A *leash*, retraining sin (cf. Rom 2:14–15) and

(b) A *cane* leading the unregenerate to seek Christ (cf. Gal 3:24).

→ *Thirdly*, the Law shows believers the nature of the Lord's will, confirms in them their understanding of it, and urges them on in well-doing.[59] We may call this the *moral or didactic use* of the Law. In this regard, it is like:

(a) A *lamp* unto our feet and a light unto our path (Ps 119:105), as well as

(b) A *goad* to prod us on in our Christian walk (cf. Eccl 12:11).

- Can you see how these three uses are presented in our *Confession* with a little re-ordering?[60]

On the Relation of the Law to Grace

19.6c ...So as a man's doing good, and refraining from evil, because the law encourageth to the one, and detereth from the other, is no evidence of his being under the law, and not under grace.[1]

[1]*Rom 6:12, 14; 1 Pet 3:8–12; Ps 34:12–16; Heb 12:28–29.*

- Because Christians are no longer under the Law as a Covenant of Works, it would appear that anyone who is striving to keep the Law of God is not under grace but under the Law. This conclusion is, however, unwarranted since it is the proper functions of the Law

---

[58] See *ICR* 2.7.10–11.

[59] See *ICR* 2.7.12.

[60] Note how the *Civil Use* with respect to the unregenerate is not mentioned in our *Confession*; and instead, restrain from sin is included under the *Moral Use* relative to the regenerate.

of God to encourage believers to obedience and restraint from evil. Thus, there is no basis for declaring a person to be unregenerate or living under Law just because he seeks to conform to the Law. In fact, a person who is freely and cheerfully seeking to be obedient to the Law of God is more likely a regenerate man, being enabled by the Spirit of Christ to new obedience.

19.7 Neither are the forementioned uses of the law contrary to the grace of the Gospel, but do sweetly comply with it;[1] the Spirit of Christ subduing and enabling the will of man to do that freely, and cheerfully which the will of God revealed in the law requireth to be done.[2]

[1]*Gal 3:21;* [2]*Ezk 36:27; Heb 8:10; Jer 31:33.*

The Law and the Gospel are often set in opposition to each other by those who wish to de-emphasise the role of the Law in the Christian Church. By contrast, we are given to confess, and we should do so wholeheartedly, that the *"uses of the law… do sweetly comply with [the grace of the Gospel]."* Though the Law and the Gospel should be distinguished, they should never be dichotomised or set at variance against each other.

- *Firstly*, it is the Law that shows the necessity of the Gospel. The gospel of salvation is necessary because of sin, and "by the law is the knowledge of sin" (Rom 3:20). So Paul declares: "But the scripture hath concluded all under sin, that the promise by faith of Jesus Christ might be given to them that believe" (Gal 3:22). Without the Law, there will be no sin, and no knowledge of sin; and therefore, no place for the gospel.

- *Secondly*, by the gospel, a sinner is saved from sin. This includes freedom from: not only the condemnation of sin; but also the bondage of sin. Thus, a Christian, having been quickened by the Spirit, is one who *"freely, and cheerfully"* does the will of God by obeying His laws. This is why both Ezekiel and Jeremiah gave emphasis to obedience to the Law when they prophesied about the New Covenant:

"And I will put my spirit within you, and cause you to walk in my statutes, and ye shall keep my judgments, and do them" (Ezk 36:27).

"But this shall be the covenant that I will make with the house of Israel; After those days, saith the Lord, I will put my law in their inward parts, and write it in their hearts; and will be their God, and they shall be my people" (Jer 31:33).

- It is no wonder that the apostle John declares:

"By this we know that we love the children of God, when we love God, and keep his commandments. For this is the love of God, that we keep his commandments: and his commandments are not grievous" (1Jn 5:2-3).

True believers not only love God, but desire to keep God's commandments, and find that it is not burdensome to do so.

WCF 20: OF CHRISTIAN LIBERTY, & LIBERTY OF CONSCIENCE

The human soul knows the value of freedom. When the devil tempted Adam and Eve in the Garden of Eden, he was appealing to their love for freedom. They, of course, had freedom. They were created to live within the bounds of freedom which God intended for them: for outside of this bound, they would die, —just as a fish out of its watery bounds will die. But Satan managed to persuade them to jump out of the water; and bondage and death came upon then and all men descending from them by natural generation.

Christ came to set us free. But it pleases God not only (1) to leave a remnant of corruption in us so that we do not have perfect freedom by ourselves to do His will; but also (2) that we should dwell in this sinful world with all its encroachments upon our liberty due to the demands of sinful man upon one another. For this reason, while on this side of eternity, we shall experience much of the tugs and shoves of the conflict between freedom and bondage in all aspects of our lives.

This chapter deals with this subject. It teaches us about the freedom that has been purchased for us by Christ, and of how we may enjoy freedom within the bounds of liberty ordained of God for us; and how we may escape the bondage imposed by sinful demands.

On the Aspects of Christian Liberty

20.1a The liberty which Christ hath purchased for believers under the Gospel, consists in their freedom from the guilt of sin, the condemning wrath of God, the curse of the moral law;[1] and in their being delivered from this present evil world, bondage to Satan, and dominion of sin,[2] from the evil of afflictions, the sting of death, the victory of the grave, and everlasting damnation;[3] as also in their free access to God,[4] and their yielding obedience unto Him, not out of slavish fear, but a child-like love and willing mind.[5]...

[1]Tit 2:14; 1 Th 1:10; Gal 3:13; [2]Gal 1:4; Col 1:13; Acts 26:18; Rom 6:14; [3]Rom 8:28; Ps 119:71; 1 Cor 15:54–57; Rom 8:1; [4]Rom 5:1–2; [5]Rom 8:14–15; 1 Jn 4:18.

This first part of the first paragraph teaches us what the liberty purchased by Christ comprises.

a. *Negatively* it comprises:

    i. "*Freedom from guilt of sin, the condemning wrath of God, and the curse of the Moral Law.*" This is clear from Scripture which teaches us that Christ "gave himself for us, that he might redeem us from all iniquity, and purify unto himself a peculiar people, zealous of good works" (Tit 2:14). In redeeming us, Christ was "made a curse for us" (Gal 3:13) and thus delivering us "from the curse of the law" (Gal 3:13a) and "from the wrath to come" (1 Th 1:10).

    ii. Freedom from "*bondage to Satan, and dominion of sin*" as well as attraction to the world. God the Father "hath delivered us from the power of darkness, and hath translated us into the kingdom of his dear Son" (Col 1:13). Before our conversion, we were unable not to sin. We were under Satan's bondage and the power of sin. By regenerating us with His Spirit, Christ frees us from this bondage so that we are now able not to sin and also able to resist the lure of the world and of worldliness.

    iii. Freedom from "*the sting of death*" and "*the evil of afflictions.*" We are freed from the sting of death because we shall be resurrected: "So when this corruptible shall have put on incorruption, and this mortal shall have put on immortality, then shall be brought to pass the saying that is written, Death is swallowed up in victory. O death, where is thy sting? O grave, where is thy victory? The sting of death is sin; and the strength of sin is the law. But thanks be to God, which giveth us the victory through our Lord Jesus Christ" (1 Cor 15:54–57). Christ does not grant believers exemption from all afflictions in this world, but He promises us to deliver us from the evil of the affliction. We are delivered from the evil of affliction not only because nothing can separate us from the love of God, but because affliction in this life is always beneficial for a Christian: "And we know that all things work together for good to them that love God, to them who are the called according to his purpose" (Rom 8:28).

b.   *Positively* it comprises:

   i.   Freedom of *"access to God."* "Therefore being justified by faith, we have peace with God through our Lord Jesus Christ: By whom also we have access by faith into this grace wherein we stand, and rejoice in hope of the glory of God" (Rom 5:1–2). "In whom we have boldness and access with confidence by the faith of him" (Eph 3:12).

   ii. Freedom of spirit to serve God. A child of God has a new willingness and desire to yield obedience to God: *"yielding obedience unto Him, not out of slavish fear, but a child–like love and willing mind."* This is the case because the child of God is both changed in heart and indwelt by the Holy Spirit. "For as many as are led by the Spirit of God, they are the sons of God. For ye have not received the spirit of bondage again to fear; but ye have received the Spirit of adoption, whereby we cry, Abba, Father" (Rom 8:14–15). "There is no fear in love; but perfect love casteth out fear: because fear hath torment. He that feareth is not made perfect in love" (1 Jn 4:18).

On the Advantage of the NT Saints over the OT Saints

20.1b ...All which were common also to believers under the law;[1] but under the new testament, the liberty of Christians is further enlarged in their freedom from the yoke of the ceremonial law, to which the Jewish Church was subjected,[2] and in greater boldness of access to the throne of grace,[3] and in fuller communications of the free Spirit of God, than believers under the law did ordinarily partake of.[4]

[1]*Gal 3:9, 14;* [2]*Gal 4:1–3, 6–7; 5:1; Acts 15:10–11;* [3]*Heb 4:14, 16; 10:19–22;* [4]*Jn 7:38–39; 2 Cor 3:13, 17–18.*

The liberty which has been described in the previous sub-paragraph is enjoyed by Old Testament believers, as well as New Testament believers. However, New Testament believers enjoy additional benefits such as:

a. *"Freedom from the yoke of the ceremonial laws."* The ceremonial laws comprise shadows and types pointing to Christ. Now that Christ has completed His work of redemption, there is no more need for the ceremonial laws. Thus, Peter chided some of the members of the council at Jerusalem for thinking that the ceremonial laws were applicable to the disciples of Christ: "Now therefore why tempt ye God, to put a yoke upon the neck of the disciples, which neither our fathers nor we were able to bear? But we believe that through the grace of the Lord Jesus Christ we shall be saved, even as they" (Acts 15:10–11).

b. *"Greater boldness of access to the Throne of Grace."* When Christ finished His work of substitutionary atonement on the cross of Calvary, the curtain that covered the Holy of holies in the temple was rent into two, symbolising that there is now free access to the Throne of Grace. The author of Hebrews seems to have this event in mind when he wrote:

> "Having therefore, brethren, boldness to enter into the holiest by the blood of Jesus, By a new and living way, which he hath consecrated for us, through the veil, that is to say, his flesh; And having an high priest over the house of God; Let us draw near with a true heart in full assurance of faith, having our hearts sprinkled from an evil conscience, and our bodies washed with pure water" (Heb 10:19–22; cf. Heb 4:14).

c. They have a *"fuller communication of the free Spirit of God."* "The Spirit had, no doubt, been dispensed to the Church under the Old Testament; but the more extensive and copious effusion of the Spirit was reserved to New Testament times."[61] This is why Christ spoke of the Spirit as being withheld until He is glorified: "He that believeth on me, as the scripture hath said, out of his belly shall flow rivers of living water. (But this spake he of the Spirit, which they that believe on him should receive: for the Holy Ghost was not yet given; because that Jesus was not yet glorified.)" (Jn 7:38–39). This greater outpouring of the Holy Spirit under the New Covenant was already prophesied in the Old Testament, e.g.:

---

[61] Shaw, *op. cit.*, 253.

"And it shall come to pass afterward, that I will pour out my spirit upon all flesh; and your sons and your daughters shall prophesy, your old men shall dream dreams, your young men shall see visions: And also upon the servants and upon the handmaids in those days will I pour out my spirit" (Joel 2:28–29; cf. Isa 44:3).

Thus, Paul, comparing the old dispensation and the new dispensation, likens the Old Covenant saints as being covered with a veil, whereas the New Covenant saints enjoy the privilege of liberty to behold the glory of the Lord in a mirror (2 Cor 3:13, 17–18).

On the Liberty of Conscience

20.2 God alone is Lord of the conscience,[1] and hath left it free from the doctrines and commandments of men which are in any thing contrary to His Word, or beside it, in matters of faith or worship.[2] So that to believe such doctrines, or to obey such commandments out of conscience, is to betray true liberty of conscience;[3] and the requiring of an implicit faith, and an absolute and blind obedience, is to destroy liberty of conscience, and reason also.[4]

[1]Jas 4:12; Rom 14:4; [2]Acts 4:19; 5:29; 1 Cor 7:23; Mt 23:8–10; 2 Cor 1:24; Mt 15:9; [3]Col 2:20, 22–23; Gal 1:10; 2:4–5; 5:1; [4]Rom 10:17; 14:23; Isa 8:20; Acts 17:11; Jn 4:22; Hos 5:11; Rev 13:12, 16–17; Jer 8:9.

- Conscience is the faculty by which we distinguish between the morally right or wrong. It is like a subordinate court which God has set in the heart of man. A conscience instructed and held captive to the Word of God must be taken as authoritative for the individual Christian. "*God is the Lord of the conscience*," i.e., God alone has the right to dictate the conscience, and so our conscience must be subjected to His authority alone and not to any traditions or doctrines of men.

- The carefully worded statement in our *Confession* teaches that our conscience must be "*free from*," i.e., not bounded to: (1) Doctrines and commandments *of men* pertaining to the Christian Life (cf. *WCF* 20.4, "*faith, worship, or conversation*"), which are in any way *contrary* to the Word of God; (2) Doctrines and commandments *of men* pertaining to faith and worship which are in any way *beside*, i.e., not sanctioned or taught in the Word of God.

- In other words, in cases of faith and worship, the conscience must only be bounded to what is explicitly taught in the Word of God. The Christian, for example, must not be bounded to any ceremonies or rituals not sanctioned in the Word of God. In 1551, John Knox became the chaplain to King Edward VI. At that time, the *Book of Common Prayer* of the Anglican church was being revised. It was already at the printers when Knox discovered that the liturgy required kneeling while partaking the elements of the Eucharist (i.e. the Lord's Supper). Knox recognised that the statement had no biblical basis and was a vestige of the Romish Mass, and that its inclusion would bind the conscience of believers to a matter of indifference. He spoke so vehemently on the subject that the king had an erratum sheet, known as the 'Black Rubric' inserted into the book to say that kneeling is not mandatory.

- In cases pertaining to the Christian's daily life, however, our *Confession* teaches us that where it is contrary to the Word of God, we must not be subject to it. However, if it is a matter of indifference, but required by the civil or ecclesiastical authority, then the Christian ought to submit to the demands of the law. Take, for example, a Christian in Singapore is bound to obey the anti-jay walking law which prohibits a pedestrian from crossing a road at a traffic junction when the red light for pedestrians is on, —even if there are no cars on the road. But a Christian must not submit to a law that will require the Christian to sin against God. If the government should forbid anyone from witnessing for Christ in public, the conscientious Christian must not be bounded by such a law. He ought, rather, to say with Peter and John: "Whether it be right in the sight of God to hearken unto you more than unto God, judge ye" (Acts 4:19; cf. 5:29).

- Such being the case, we may not believe such doctrines or obey such commandments, nor should we impose them upon others or to require of them implicit faith. Doing so would destroy the liberty of conscience.

On Licentiousness

20.3 They who, upon pretence of Christian liberty, do practice any sin, or cherish any lust, do thereby destroy the end of Christian liberty; which is, that being delivered out of the hands of our enemies, we might serve the Lord without fear, in holiness and righteousness before Him, all the days of our life.[1]

[1]*Gal 5:13; 1 Pet 2:16; 2 Pet 2:19; Jn 8:34; Lk 1:74–75.*

Christian liberty does not mean freedom from Moral Law of God as a rule and standard of life. In fact, our liberty from the bondage of sin is applied to our souls individually by an act of regeneration in which the soul is given a new desire and will to obey the Law of God. This is why both Ezekiel and Jeremiah emphasise a new ability and will to obey the Law when they spoke about regeneration as a benefit of the New Covenant (Ezk 36:27; Jer 31:33). This is why James calls the Moral Law, the "perfect law of liberty" (Jas 1:25). Since sin is lawlessness (1 Jn 3:4; 'transgression of the law' = Grk. ἀνομία [*anomia*] = 'lawlessness'), true liberty from sin must involve an ability to obey the Law.

Moreover, when the Ten Commandments, which summarises the Moral Law of God, was delivered by the LORD on Mount Sinai, He prefaced it with the words: "I am the LORD thy God, which have brought thee out of the land of Egypt, out of the house of bondage" (Ex 20:1–2). In other words, Israel was being enjoined to obey the Law on the basis of their deliverance from Egypt. The New Testament teaches us that this deliverance from Egypt was a type of our deliverance from the bondage of sin and Satan (cf. Lk 1:72–75; Gen 15:8–21; Heb 6:13–20; Rom 4:13; Gal 3:16ff). Thus, the preface of the Ten Commandments has a very important spiritual bearing for us, for it teaches us that *"because God is the Lord, and our God, and Redeemer, therefore we are bound to keep all His commandments"* (*WSC* 44).

A Christian is not only granted the ability and desire to obey the Law of God, but is obliged to obey it. But the Christian does not find obedience to the Law to be grievous (1 Jn 5:3). Indeed, he finds his liberty in obedience to the Law. His liberty is like that of a fish in water,

—swimming freely, rather than that of a fish out of water, —free from constraints but dying. In other words, a Christian may not plead liberty to practise any known sin. To do so, is to plead for licentiousness and to use his liberty "for an occasion to the flesh" (Gal 5:13). A married Christian man, for example, may not plead liberty to live with a woman who is not his wife. To do so, would be to sin against God.

Licentiousness destroys the goal of Christian Liberty, which is that *"we might serve the Lord without fear, in holiness and righteousness before Him, all the days of our life."*

On the Duty of a Church Member or a Citizen

20.4   And because the powers which God hath ordained, and the liberty which Christ hath purchased, are not intended by God to destroy, but mutually to uphold and preserve one another; they who, upon pretence of Christian liberty, shall oppose any lawful power, or the lawful exercise of it, whether it be civil or ecclesiastical, resist the ordinance of God.[1] And for their publishing of such opinions, or maintaining of such practices, as are contrary to the light of nature, or to the known principles of Christianity, whether concerning faith, worship, or conversation; or to the power of godliness, or such erroneous opinions or practices, as either in their own nature, or in the manner of publishing or maintaining them, are destructive to the external peace and order which Christ hath established in the Church, they may lawfully be called to account, and proceeded against by the censures of the Church,[2] and by the power of the civil magistrate.[3]

[1]Mt 12:25; 1 Pet 2:13–14, 16; Rom 13:1–8; Heb 13:17; [2]Rom 1:32; 1 Cor 5:1, 5, 11, 13; 2 Jn 10–11; 2 Th 3:14; 1 Tim 6:3–5; Tit 1:10–11, 13; 3:10; Mt 18:15–17; 1 Tim 1:19–20; Rev 2:2, 14–15, 20; 3:9; [3]Dt 13:6–12; Rom 13:3–4; 2 Jn 10–11; Ezra 7:23, 25–28; Rev 17:12, 16–17; Neh 13:15, 17, 21–22, 25, 30; 2 Kgs 23:5–6, 9, 20–21; 2 Chr 34:33; 15:12–13, 16; Dan 3:29; 1 Tim 2:2; Isa 49:23; Zech 13:2–3.

The section may be summarised in the following points:

a.   A church or the civil government of the land may make laws. These rules are to be obeyed as long as they do not contradict the Word of God. "Let every soul be subject unto the higher powers. For there is no power but of God: the powers that be are ordained of God" (Rom 13:1). "Submit yourselves to every ordinance of man for the Lord's sake: whether it be to the king, as supreme" (1 Pet 2:13; cf. Fifth Commandment).

b. Therefore, no one may claim to be exercising Christian liberty, if he fails to obey such rules. "Whosoever therefore resisteth the power, resisteth the ordinance of God: and they that resist shall receive to themselves damnation" (Rom 13:2). "As free, and not using your liberty for a cloak of maliciousness, but as the servants of God" (1 Pet 2:16).

c. A person may disrupt the external peace of the church or nation by disobedience or by publishing his opinions contrary to the principles of the nation or the church; or more broadly, by *"publishing of such opinions, or maintaining of such practices, as are contrary to the light of nature, or to the known principles of Christianity, whether concerning faith, worship, or conversation; or to the power of godliness."* Such a person may rightly be disciplined either by the church or by the state (depending on the offence). (Cf. Discipline of civil powers: Rom 13:3; Discipline of the church: Mt 18:15–17; 1 Cor 5:1–13; 2 Th 3:6, 14-15).

- Note carefully: "It is not sin as *sin*, but as *scandal*, or injurious to the spiritual interests of Christians, that is the proper object of Church censure; and it is not for sins as such, but for *crimes*, that persons become liable to punishment by magistrates."[62]

- What if a person disagrees with the practices or doctrine of the church? He may continue to be a member of the church, just as he may be a member of a nation though he may disagree with the laws of the nations. However, as long as he is a member, he is duty bound not to speak disparagingly against the doctrine of the church or the law of the nation or to act in a way that will disrupt the external peace of the church or nation. What if the church acts or teaches unconstitutionally or unbiblically? Then the member has a right, and perhaps even duty to protest. The same goes for a nation.

---

[62] Shaw, Op. Cit., 260.

WCF 21: OF RELIGIOUS WORSHIP AND THE SABBATH DAY

The Ten Commandments summarises the will of God for His people in regard to their thought, speech and behaviour. As such, if we love God and would live for God, we would shape our lives personally and corporately around the Ten Commandments. Sadly, there is a stark departure from the Law of God in the modern church. And this departure is nowhere more evident than where it touches the two commandments which are given the most emphasis by the LORD, if the length of the commandments is anything to go by. I am referring to the 2nd and the 4th Commandments. It may be observed that in the history of the church, these two commandments have served rather like the two banks through which the river of evangelicalism runs shallow or deep. When they were firmly taught, the true religion was deep and satisfying, producing long lasting and significant fruits. Such was the case during the days of the Reformers and the Puritans. But where one or both of the banks are eroded, then evangelicalism becomes broad and shallow as in our present day.

This chapter, which deals with the application of these two commandments, is therefore, of great importance, if we desire a reformation of lives unto the glory of Christ in our day.

On the Object and Manner of Worship

21.1a The light of nature showeth that there is a God, who hath lordship and sovereignty over all; is good, and doeth good unto all; and is therefore to be feared, loved, praised, called upon, trusted in, and served, with all the heart, and with all the soul, and with all the might.[1]
...

[1]*Rom 1:20; Acts 17:24; Ps 119:68; Jer 10:7; Ps 31:23; 18:3; Rom 10:12; Ps 62:8; Jos 24:14; Mk 12:33.*

We begin with three propositions that should lay to rest the question of whether the obligations presented in this chapter are only applicable to the church and those who have been instructed, and not to all men in general:

a. Nature teaches us that there is a God and that such a God must be glorious, powerful and good. Indeed, a moment's reflection should show that this God must be sovereign, or He would not be God. "For the invisible things of him from the creation of the world are clearly seen, being understood by the things that are made, even his eternal power and Godhead; so that they are without excuse" (Rom 1:20). "The heavens declare the glory of God; and the firmament sheweth his handywork" (Ps 19:1). What is taught in natural theology is, of course, confirmed in the Word of God.

b. Common sense teaches us that therefore we must fear Him, love Him, praise Him, call upon Him, trust in Him, and serve Him, which is again affirmed in the Word of God.

c. This must be done with *"with all the heart, and with all the soul, and with all the might"* since we are His creatures and He is our Creator. The Lord affirms this duty: "The first of all the commandments is, Hear, O Israel; The Lord our God is one Lord: And thou shalt love the Lord thy God with all thy heart, and with all thy soul, and with all thy mind, and with all thy strength: this is the first commandment" (Mk 12:29–30). "The chief object of life is to acknowledge and worship God" says Calvin.[63]

21.1b   …But the acceptable way of worshipping the true God is instituted by Himself, and so limited by His own revealed will, that He may not be worshipped according to the imaginations and devices of men, or the suggestions of Satan, under any visible representation, or any other way not prescribed in the Holy Scripture.[1]

[1]Dt 12:32; Mt 15:9; Acts 17:25; Mt 4:9–10; Dt 4:15–20; Ex 20:4–6; Col 2:23.

- While the light of nature teaches us that we are to worship God, the manner we ought to worship God is given in the Scripture, which, according to our *Confession*, teaches a principle of worship, which we may call the *Reformed Regulative Principle of Worship* (RPW). The Lutheran and Romish Principle, —sometimes called the *Normative Principle of Worship*, —is "Whatever is not forbidden is

---

[63] Calvin, *Comm. on Isa 3.368.*

allowed," or "Whatever is not appointed in Scripture is not necessarily forbidden." The Reformed Principle, which is given in our *Confession* is "Whatever is not appointed in the Word of God for His own worship is forbidden." Or more fully, God *"may not be worshipped according to the imaginations and devices of men, or the suggestions of Satan, under any visible representation, or any other way not prescribed in the holy Scripture."*

- John Calvin, the theologian *par excellence* of the Reformation, was so firmly persuaded of this principle, and taught it so vigorously, that anyone who claims to be Reformed or Calvinistic should for candour sake concede any dissent. Calvin taught: "The right rule then as to worship of God is, to adopt nothing but what He prescribes."[64] Commenting on Ezekiel 6:6, he expands his assertion: "There is no need of a long discussion if we desire to know how God is to be worshipped. For He rejects and excludes our works. If, therefore, we do not obtrude our works, but only follow what God demands, our worship will be pure, but if we add anything of our own, it is an abomination. We see, therefore, that useful instruction can be collected from one word, namely, that all worship is perverse and disapproved by God when men bring anything forward of themselves."[65]

- Is this a biblical principle?

The Second Commandment clearly forbids the use of any images in our worship of the living and true God (Ex 20:4–6). Romanists, indeed, not only combine the first and second commandments together, but teach that you can worship God by using images and that the honour they pay to their images is *eidôlatreia* (idol-service) and not *eidôdouleia* (idol-worship). This distinction is, however, a mere play of words.[66] The scriptural prohibition of the use of images to worship God is clearly expounded in Exodus 32 when Aaron made a golden calf for the people. This calf, we must

---

[64] Calvin, *Comm. on Jer 44:17*.

[65] Calvin, *Comm. on Ezk 6:6*.

[66] See *ICR* 1.11.11; 1.11.16.

remember, was not to represent other gods, but to represent Jehovah, the God of Israel. Thus, when Aaron presented the golden calf to the people, they said: "These be thy *elohim*, O Israel, which brought thee up out of the land of Egypt" (Ex 32:4). The Hebrew *elohim* can be translated as 'gods' or 'God.' But the fact the people spoke of it as having brought them out of Egypt suggests that they had in mind that it represented Jehovah. This is why after Aaron had built an altar, he made a proclamation saying, "Tomorrow is a feast to *Jehovah*" (Ex 32:5). This act of rebellion so angered God that He nearly wiped out the whole nation. Years later, after the reign of Solomon, when the Northern tribes broke away, King Jeroboam made two calves, setting one in Dan and the other in Bethel (1 Kgs 12:28–29). These calves were again images to represent Jehovah and it was considered a great sin so that every subsequent king in the North was condemned on account of their failure to remove the calves.

What about the general principle that only what is appointed is allowed? Is it a biblical principle? We believe that it is.

a. *Old Testament*. Many who do not believe in the Regulative Principle of Worship assert that we must not use the Old Testament to derive the principle because the Old Testament was a time of shadows and types, and the acts and elements of worship were minutely detailed. We grant the observation concerning Old Testament worship, and we agree that the specific commands are no longer applicable to us today. But we must insist that the principle of worship, on which those commands were based, has not changed since it is founded upon God's character and His sovereignty. And since God does not change (Mal 3:6), this principle which can be derived from the Old Testament must be applicable in the New Testament as well.

i. In Genesis 4, we read about the first acts of formal worship of God. Abel offered of his flocks, and his offering was accepted, but Cain offered of the ground, but his offering was rejected. Why? Fundamentally, it is because God must have instructed Adam and Eve they must always worship with a bloody sacrifice. Perhaps, He gave them this instruction when He made a coat of skin for them (Gen 3:21); and it is clear that this instruction was passed down, for we find that years later Noah would know exactly what to offer unto the Lord (Gen 8:20). Cain offered of the ground voluntarily and sincerely, but his offerings were rejected as they were not appointed by God.

ii. On surface reading, it appears that the Second Commandment (Ex 20:4-6) is merely about making and bowing to images representing God or any creature with religious significance. But we know that this cannot be the case because God instructed Moses to adorn the mercy seat of the ark of the covenant with two golden cherubims (Ex 25:18)! If the second commandment were merely about making of images, then God would be contradicting Himself by instructing Moses to violate His own commandment. Clearly Moses understood the Second Commandment to mean, as we are given to confess, that God "*may not be worshipped ...under any visible representation, or any other way not prescribed in the holy Scripture."* In other words, if God had instructed His people to make images of Him to worship Him, then they must worship Him with images!

iii. Nadab and Abihu had taken their censers, put fire into them and then put incense into them to offer unto the Lord. This appeared pious and reverential, but what they did was displeasing to God, for in a moment they were struck dead because they "offered strange fire before the LORD, which he commanded them not" (Lev 10:1–3). What was their sin? Jeremiah Burroughs, a member of the Westminster Assembly, answers:

"Their sin was offering strange fire, for the text says that they offered strange fire which God had not commanded them. But had God ever forbidden them to offer strange fire or appointed that they should offer only one kind of fire? There is no text of Scripture that you can find from the beginning of Genesis to this place where God had said in so many words expressly, 'You shall offer no fire but one kind of fire.' And yet here they are consumed by fire from God for offering strange fire. I find in Exodus 30:9 that they were forbidden to offer strange incense, but I do not find that they were forbidden to offer strange fire."[67]

What is strange fire? We are not told the details, but it is either fire taken from the wrong source or they had offered it at the wrong place or wrong time—a time, place or source not expressly sanctioned by God. In other words, they had not acted according to the prescription of the Law and as a result they were struck dead. This passage, very dramatically, demonstrates God's zeal for the purity of His own worship. He makes it clear that He must be worshipped strictly according to His own prescription. It also shows that the Lutheran principle: "what is not forbidden is allowed" is false. Rather, God must be worshipped exactly as He has appointed: nothing more, nothing less.

iv. Moses gave specific instructions pertaining to the manner of worship, and warned Israel against adopting the manner of worship of the people of the land (Dt 12:31). And he concludes: "What thing soever I command you, observe to do it: thou shalt not add thereto, nor diminish from it" (Dt 12:32). Someone may object to our using Cain and Abel, and Nadab and Abihu by saying that "in those cases, something was commanded, therefore, it must be done precisely, but what if there is no instruction on it? Wouldn't the act then be allowed? Since there is no instruction regulating or forbidding the lighting of candles or for the use of a choir in the New Testament church, shouldn't they

---

[67] Jeremiah Burroughs, *Gospel Worship* (Pittsburg: Soli Deo Gloria Publications, 1993 [1648]), 3.

be allowed?" This argument falls flat since Moses, under inspiration, tells us that we are not to add or diminish from God's commands concerning worship.

b. *New Testament*. Two of the most common objections against the Regulative Principle of Worship for today's church are: (1) that the New Testament does not teach such a principle; and (2) that the New Testament does not give specific commands on what to do. However, no one, who believes that God is immutable and holy, will assert that God has lowered the standard of behaviour that He requires of His children. Moreover, the New Testament does answer the two objections.

Consider first, how it teaches that the Regulative Principle is still applicable:

i. The Lord condemning the scribes and Pharisees for their extraneous acts of worship, quoted Isaiah 29:13 to show the vanity of their deeds: "But in vain they do worship me, teaching for doctrines the commandments of men" (Mt 15:9).

ii. The Lord told the Samaritan woman: "God is a Spirit: and they that worship him must worship him in spirit and in truth" (Jn 4:24). What did He mean by "in truth"? The only objective truth that God has given to man is His revealed Word, therefore to worship *in truth*, is to worship according to the prescription of His Word.

iii. Paul confirms this principle by warning the Colossians against will-worship: "Wherefore if ye be dead with Christ from the rudiments of the world, why, as though living in the world, are ye subject to ordinances,... after the commandments and doctrines of men? Which things have indeed a shew of wisdom in will worship, and humility, and neglecting of the body; not in any honour to the satisfying of the flesh" (Col 2:20–23). What is "will worship"? Calvin defines it as "fictitious modes of worship that men themselves device or receive from others, and all precepts whatsoever that they presume to deliver at their own hand concerning the worship of God."[68] Lighting of candles, dances, processions, dramas, song presentations, puppet shows, etc would all be regarded as *will worship* by Calvin and I believe, by the Apostle Paul.

The evidence is, I believe, compelling. This explains why from the time of the Reformation, every genuine Presbyterian and Reformed church has acknowledged it as true (more or less, though sometimes in practice these churches violate the principles). We are compelled to agree with Calvin in his treatise on the *True Method of Reforming the Church*: "All modes of worship devised contrary to His command, He not only repudiates as void, but distinctly condemns. Why need I adduce proofs in so clear a matter? Passages to this effect should be proverbial among Christians."[69]

21.2 Religious worship is to be given to God, the Father, Son, and Holy Ghost; and to Him alone;[1] not to angels, saints, or any other creature:[2] and, since the fall, not without a Mediator; nor in the mediation of any other but of Christ alone.[3]

[1]Mt 4:10; Jn 5:23; 2 Cor 13:14; [2]Col 2:18; Rev 19:10; Rom 1:25; [3]Jn 14:6; 1 Tim 2:5; Eph 2:18; Col 3:17.

- Worship is to be given to God alone; and since God is a Triune God, worship may be directed to all three persons of the Godhead: they being the same in essence, and equal in power and glory.

- But worship must not be directed to "*angels, saints, or to any other creatures.*" The Apostle Paul specifically forbids the worshipping of angels (Col 2:18). When Cornelius fell down at the feet of Peter in reverence, Peter straightaway took him up, and admonished him: "Stand up, I myself also am a man" (Acts 10:26). When Apostle John fell at the feet of the angel in Revelation 19 to worship him, probably by mistake, the angel prevented him, saying: "See thou do it not: I am thy fellowservant, and of thy brethren that have the

---

[68] *ICR* 4.10.8.

[69] Calvin, *Tracts*, 3.261.

testimony of Jesus: worship God: for the testimony of Jesus is the spirit of prophecy" (Rev 19:10).

- Since the fall of man, the distance between sinful man and the Holy God is so great that a Mediator is necessary for us to come to God. The Scripture declares emphatically that this man is Jesus and Jesus alone: "For there is one God, and one mediator between God and men, the man Christ Jesus" (1 Tim 2:5). The Lord himself declares: "I am the way, the truth, and the life: no man cometh unto the Father, but by me" (Jn 14:6).

- The Roman Catholic Church affirms that Jesus is the alone mediator of redemption, but insists that angels and saints are co-mediators of intercession with Christ. But nowhere does the Scripture teach such a distinction in the mediatorial office. Paul makes it clear that Christ is also the mediator of our intercession and worship: "For through him we both have access by one Spirit unto the Father" (Eph 2:18).

On the Elements of Worship

21.3 Prayer, with thanksgiving, being one special part of religious worship,[1] is by God required of all men;[2] and, that it may be accepted, it is to be made in the name of the Son,[3] by the help of His Spirit,[4] according to His will,[5] with understanding, reverence, humility, fervency, faith, love, and perseverance;[6] and, if vocal, in a known tongue.[7]

[1]Phil 4:6; [2]Ps 65:2; [3]Jn 14:13–14; 1 Pet 2:5; [4]Rom 8:26; [5]1 Jn 5:14; [6]Ps 47:7; Eccl 5:1–2; Heb 12:28; Gen 18:27; Jas 5:16; 1:6–7; Mk 11:24; Mt 6:12, 14–15; Col 4:2; Eph 6:18; [7]1 Cor 14:14.

21.4 Prayer is to be made for things lawful,[1] and for all sorts of men living, or that shall live hereafter;[2] but not for the dead,[3] nor for those of whom it may be known that they have sinned the sin unto death.[4]

[1]1 Jn 5:14; [2]1 Tim 2:1–2; Jn 17:20; 2 Sam 7:29; Ruth 4:12; [3]2 Sam 12:21–23; Lk 16:25–26; Rev 14:13; [4]1 Jn 5:16.

21.5 The reading of the Scriptures with godly fear;[1] the sound preaching,[2] and conscionable hearing of the Word, in obedience unto God, with understanding, faith, and reverence:[3] singing of psalms with grace in the heart;[4] as also the due administration and worthy receiving of the sacraments instituted by Christ; are all parts of the ordinary religious worship of God:[5] beside religious oaths[6] and vows,[7] solemn fastings,[8] and thanksgivings upon special occasions,[9] which are, in their several times and seasons, to be used in an holy and religious manner.[10]

[1]*Acts 15:21; Rev 1:3;* [2]*2 Tim 4:2;* [3]*Jas 1:22; Acts 10:33; Mt 13:19; Heb 4:2; Isa 66:2;* [4]*Col 3:16; Eph 5:19; Jas 5:13;* [5]*Mt 28:19; 1 Cor 11:23–29; Acts 2:42;* [6]*Dt 6:13; Neh 10:29;* [7]*Isa 19:21; Eccl 5:4–5;* [8]*Joel 2:12; Esth 4:16; Mt 9:15; 1 Cor 7:5;* [9]*Ps 107; Esth 9:22;* [10]*Heb 12:28.*

- These few paragraphs show us what the Scripture sanctions to be allowable in the worship of God in the New Testament Church. We should note carefully that divine warrant needs not necessarily require an explicit command by God. Michael Bushell has well stated:

  "When we say that each element of worship requires a divine warrant, we do not mean that an explicit command in a single text is required in every instance. Commandment in the narrow sense of the term is not necessary to establish divine prescription. Approved example or inference from relevant scriptural data is sufficient to determine the proper manner of worship."[70]

  This means, for example, that there is warrant to pattern our worship on the synagogue worship of the Jews during the days of the Lord, for the Lord and the Apostles sanctioned such manner of worship by attending them.

- We should also not confuse "worship ordinances" and "worship circumstances." Many who have spoken out against the *Reformed Regulative Principle of Worship* have charged that it is impractical since it does not sanction pews or even printed Bibles. Worship circumstances are things that attend to our worship which do not

---

[70] Michael Bushell, *The Songs of Zion: A Contemporary Case for Exclusive Psalmody* (Pennsylvania: Crown & Covenant Publications, 1993 [1997]), 122.

have spiritual significance such as pews, etc. The following table, adapted from a compilation by Brian Schwertley,[71] is helpful:

Worship Ordinances		Worship Circumstances	
Preaching from the Bible	Mt 26:13; Mk 16:15; Acts 9:20; 2 Tim 4:2; Acts 20:7; 17:10; 1 Cor 14:28	Structure in which the church meets	Acts 20:8, 17:10; 1 Cor 14:28
Reading the Word of God	Lk 4:16-20; Acts 13:15; 1 Tim 4:13; Rev 1:3; Acts 1:13, 16:13; 1 Cor 11:20	Location at which the church meets	Acts 1:13, 16:13; 1 Cor 11:20
Meeting on the Lord's Day	Acts 20:7; 1 Cor 16:2; Rev 1:10; Acts 20:7; 1 Cor 11:18	Time at which the church meets	Acts 20:7; 1 Cor 11:18
Administration of Sacraments	Mt 28:19; Mt 26:26-29; 1 Cor 11:24-25	Clothing worn to worship	1 Cor 11:13-15; Dt 22:5
Hearing the Word of God	Rom 10:14; Jas 1:22; Lk 4:20; Acts 20:9	Type of seating provided	Lk 4:20; Acts 20:9
Prayer to God	Mt 6:9; 1 Th 5:17; Heb 13:15,18; Phil 4:6; Jas 1:5; 1 Cor 11:13-15; Dt 22:5	Congregational use of printed Bibles and Psalters	
The Singing of Psalms	1 Chr 16:9; Ps 95:1-1; Ps 105:2; 1 Cor 14:26; Eph 5:19; Col 3:16	Incidental and co-ordinating instructions such as 'rise up', 'be seated,' 'turn to...' etc	

- Everything in the left column must be learnt from Scripture. Everything in the right column is circumstantial. But note how something that may be circumstantial may become illegal in worship. James Bannerman explains:

So soon as you attach a spiritual meaning, a sacred significance, to anything connected with worship, it becomes *eo ipso* a part of worship. It stands forthwith on a like footing with the typical

---

[71] Brian Schwertley, *Musical Instruments in the Public Worship of God* (Southfield: Reformed Witness, 1999), 36-38

ceremonies of the Old Testament, many of which were quite as insignificant in themselves as white surplice or a lighted candle.[72]

In other words, if there is a blackout and the minister lights a candle, that candle has no spiritual significance, and is circumstantial. But if the minister symbolically lights a candle when he comes on the pulpit (perhaps to represent the illumination of the Holy Spirit), then it takes a spiritual significance and is forbidden. In the same way the printed Bible and Psalters have no spiritual significance, but suppose each member of the congregation is required to lift up the Bible in the air, and then kiss it before reading it, then it becomes an element of worship, and becomes forbidden.

- Note that the context of each element of each element of worship, viz.: preaching, reading, prayer and singing, is either given in the Word or left to the freedom of the minister, apart from general guidelines. In so far as the *Westminster Confession of Faith* is concerned, the content for Scripture reading and psalm singing is provided in the Word of God and so nothing else should be read or sung (apart from what may be read as sermons or as part of sermons). The content of preaching and prayer is left to the minister, though there are biblical guidelines, such as the Lord's Prayer. However, the minister may read his sermon and prayer since they are left to his discretion.

- Beyond indicating what elements are allowable in worship, our *Confession* also gives us some useful guidelines on how each of the five regular elements of worship is to be carried out:

    a. *Prayer*: "Prayer is an offering up of our desires unto God for things agreeable to His will, in the name of Christ, with confession of our sins, and thankful acknowledgement of His mercies" (*WSC* 8). It should be:

    (1) Made with thankful heart.

---

[72] James Bannerman, *The Church of Christ: A Treatise on the Nature, Powers, Ordinances, Discipline, and Government of the Christian Church* (New Jersey: Mack Publishing Company, 1960 [1869]), vol. 1, 355, footnote 2

(2) Made in the name of the Son. This does not mean always intoning the name of Christ as if there is some magical power in the formula. None of the recorded prayers in the Bible ends with "In Jesus Name." What it does mean is that prayer must be made with the mediatorship of Christ in mind.

(3) Made according to God's will: "if we ask any thing according to his will, he heareth us" (1 Jn 5:14b). This is a reference to the Revealed Will of God. In other words, we must not pray for anything contrary to the Word of God and the teaching of the Word of God. We must only pray "for things lawful."

(4) Attended with understanding, reverence, humility, fervency, faith, love and perseverance.

(5) Offered in a known language if vocal (in public or in private).

(6) Made for all men living or shall live, i.e., including the future generation (1 Tim 2:1; Jn 17:20); but not for the dead or for those who are known to have committed the unpardonable sin (2 Sam 12:21-23; 1 Jn 5:16).

b. *Reading of the Scripture.* "Give attendance to reading" (1 Tim 4:13). This must be attended with godly fear. "Reading of the Word in the congregation, being part of the public worship of God (wherein we acknowledge our dependence upon Him, and subjection to Him), and one means sanctified by Him for the edifying of His people, is to be performed by the pastors and teachers. Howbeit, such as intend the ministry, may occasionally both read the Word, and exercise their gift of preaching in the congregation, if allowed by the presbytery thereunto."[73]

---

[73] *The Directory for the Publick Worship of God*, s.v. "Of Public Reading of the Holy Scriptures" in *Westminster Confession of Faith* (Glasgow: Free Presbyterian Publications, 1997 [1958, 1646]), 375.

c. *Preaching*. "Preach the word; be instant in season, out of season; reprove, rebuke, exhort with all longsuffering and doctrine" (2 Tim 4:2). This must be sound or doctrinally accurate.

d. *Hearing*. This must be attended conscientiously with (1) obedience (Jas 1:22); (2) understanding (Mt 13:19); (3) faith (Heb 4:2); and (4) reverence (Isa 66:2).

e. *Singing*. This must be done with grace in the heart. Notice that the *Confession* restricts the singing only to Psalms. What about hymns and spiritual songs (Col 3:16 and Eph 5:19). There is strong Biblical evidence that Paul was referring only to the Psalms as all three terms 'songs', 'hymns' and 'psalms' are used to describe the Psalms in the Septuagint translation of the Old Testament, which the Apostles and the early church used regularly. Moreover, the term 'spiritual' suggests 'Spirit-inspired,' which cannot be applied to any human compositions.

- The administration of the sacraments is also part of religious worship. Notice how the *Confession* separates it from the other five items. It is not considered necessary to administer the sacraments, or in particular the Lord's Supper, every week. We will look at this in *WCF* 27–29.

- Note that our *Confession* also teaches that "religious oaths [Neh 10:29] and vows [Ecc 5:4], solemn fastings [Joel 2:12; 1 Cor 7:5], and thanksgivings upon special occasions [Esth 9:22]," are sanctioned in the Word of God as part of religious worship. These may be used in a holy and religious manner when appropriate. Religious vows and oaths will be studied in the next chapter, but here we note that there is no warrant for religious holy days, —be it Easter, Good Friday or Christmas, —in the Scripture or in our *Confession*. However, on special occasions, brought about by divine providence, the church may set aside a day for thanksgiving or fasting as may be the case. There is therefore nothing wrong with having a church anniversary thanksgiving day.

On the Place of Worship

21.6   Neither prayer, nor any other part of religious worship, is, now under the Gospel, either tied unto, or made more acceptable by, any place in which it is performed, or towards which it is directed:[1] but God is to be worshipped every where[2] in spirit and truth;[3] as in private families[4] daily,[5] and in secret each one by himself;[6] so more solemnly in the public assemblies, which are not carelessly or willfully to be neglected or forsaken, when God, by His Word or providence, calleth thereunto.[7]

[1]Jn 4:21; [2]Mal 1:11; 1 Tim 2:8; [3]Jn 4:23–24; [4]Jer 10:25; Dt 6:6–7; Job 1:5; 2 Sam 6:18, 20; 1 Pet 3:7; Acts 10:2; [5]Mt 6:11; [6]Mt 6:6; Eph 6:18; [7]Isa 56:6–7; Heb 10:25; Prov 1:20–21, 24; 8:34; Acts 13:42; Lk 4:16; Acts 2:42.

Worship under the New Covenant is no longer restricted to, nor any more acceptable if engaged in, any particular place, not even a church building (cf. Jn 4:21). Worship in spirit and in truth may be carried out:

a. In private families daily: "And these words, which I command thee this day, shall be in thine heart: And thou shalt teach them diligently unto thy children, and shalt talk of them when thou sittest in thine house, and when thou walkest by the way, and when thou liest down, and when thou risest up" (Dt 6:6-7; cf. Jer 10:25).

b. In private personal devotions: "But thou, when thou prayest, enter into thy closet, and when thou hast shut thy door, pray to thy Father which is in secret; and thy Father which seeth in secret shall reward thee openly" (Mt 6:6).

c. In public with other brethren: "Not forsaking the assembling of ourselves together, as the manner of some is; but exhorting one another: and so much the more, as ye see the day approaching" (Heb 10:25).

On the Time of Worship—The Christian Sabbath

21.7 As it is the law of nature, that, in general, a due proportion of time be set apart for the worship of God; so, in His Word, by a positive, moral, and perpetual commandment binding all men in all ages, He hath particularly appointed one day in seven for a Sabbath, to be kept holy unto him:[1] which, from the beginning of the world to the resurrection of Christ, was the last day of the week; and, from the resurrection of Christ, was changed into the first day of the week,[2] which in Scripture, is called the Lord's Day,[3] and is to be continued to the end of the world, as the Christian Sabbath.[4]

[1]Ex 20:8, 10–11; Isa 56:2, 4, 6–7; [2]Gen 2:2–3; 1 Cor 16:1–2; Acts 20:7; [3]Rev 1:10; [4]Ex 20:8, 10; Mt 5:17–18.

This section teaches us:

- *Firstly*, that the Sabbath is both a creation ordinance ("law of nature") and a moral commandment, and so all men in all ages are obliged to observe it.

  a. *It is a Moral Institution.*

    Since the 4th Commandment is part of the Decalogue which summarises the Moral Law of God, the Sabbath must be a moral institution. Therefore, all men, at all times are as obligated to observe the Sabbath as they are to observe the sanctity of life. The Sabbath is still applicable to Christians. The Sabbath is also applicable to non-Christians. It would hardly do to say that it is wrong to murder but it is alright to break the Sabbath. The 4th Commandment, like all the other nine commandments, was engraven by the finger of God. God gave 10 commandments, not 9 commandments.

  b. *It is a Creation Ordinance.*

    God could have created the world in a twinkling of the eye. Or He could have created it in 6 seconds, or 6 minutes or 6 hours. Why did He create it in 6 days? Why are we told that He rested the 7th day? But God need not rest! Yet in the creation account, we read: "And on the seventh day God ended his work which he had made; and he rested on the seventh day from all his work which he had made. And God blessed the seventh day, and sanctified it: because that in it he had rested from all his work which God created and made" (Gen 2:2–3). God rested to set an example for us to follow. Thus, when He spoke the 4th Commandment, He said: "For in six days the LORD made heaven and earth, the sea, and all that in them is, and rested the seventh day: wherefore the LORD blessed the sabbath day, and hallowed it" (Ex 20:11).

- *Secondly*, we are taught that the day we should observe this sabbath is now the 1st day of the week. The Scripture supports this change:

  a. The Fourth Commandment (Ex 20: 8–11; Dt 5:12–15) does not indicate that the Sabbath is to be on Saturday, but on the seventh day. It does not say that Saturday is the sabbath of the Lord, but the seventh day. Thus, according to the command, the Sabbath could morally and technically be on any day of the week—so long as it occurs every 7th day.

  b. The second giving of the 4th Commandment cites deliverance from Egypt as a reason for observing the Sabbath (Dt 5:15); and the New Testament teaches us that Israel's deliverance from Egypt typifies our deliverance from the bondage of sin (Lk 1:71–74), which means that the Sabbath is also to commemorate the work of redemption by Christ. Psalm 118 anticipates a change of day based on the completion of the redemptive work of Christ: "The stone which the builders refused is become the head stone of the corner. This is the LORD's doing; it is marvellous in our eyes. This is the day which the LORD hath made; we will rejoice and be glad in it" (Ps 118:22–24).

  c. Though the commandment does not dictate which day of the week the Sabbath is to be observed, the Lord does indicate by other means. Thus, when the Jews forgot which day they should observe the Sabbath after their stint in Egypt—where they had a 10 days week, —the Lord indicated the day by a double portion of manna on the day before the Sabbath day (Ex 16:22–23). Similarly, in the New Testament, the Lord indicates to us a new day to observe the Sabbath by the post-resurrection appearance of the heavenly manna (Jn 6:31-33). He rose on the first day of the week, which is also the day the stone which the builders reject became the head stone of the corner (Ps 118:22).

d. The practice of the Apostles and the early church confirms that the Sabbath should be observed on the first day of the week (Acts 20:7; 1 Cor 16:2; Rev 1:10)

21.8 This Sabbath is then kept holy unto the Lord, when men, after a due preparing of their hearts, and ordering of their common affairs before-hand, do not only observe an holy rest all the day from their own works, words, and thoughts about their worldly employments and recreations;[1] but also are taken up, the whole time in the public and private exercises of His worship, and in the duties of necessity and mercy.[2]

[1]Ex 20:8; 16:23, 25–26, 29–30; 31:15–17; Isa 58:13; Neh 13:15–22; [2]Isa 58:13; Mt 12:1–13.

This section teaches us how we should properly observe the Sabbath day:

a. We should make ample preparation with regard to our worldly affairs by disposing of our daily work so we would not have to be hindered by them on the Lord's day.

b. We should make heart preparation by prayer and reading of God's Word.

c. We should "*observe an holy rest all the day from their own works, words, and thoughts about their worldly employments and recreations.*" As the Prophet Isaiah puts it: "If thou turn away thy foot from the sabbath, from doing thy pleasure on my holy day; and call the sabbath a delight, the holy of the LORD, honourable; and shalt honour him, not doing thine own ways, nor finding thine own pleasure, nor speaking thine own words" (Isa 58:13).

d. We should spend the day in "public and private exercises of His worship, and in the duties of necessity and mercy." It would be consistent with our *Confession* to say that four kinds of activities are allowed on the Lord's Day: (i) Acts of Necessity (such as eating, sleeping, bathing etc); (ii) Acts of Mercy (cf. Lk 13:14-16); (iii) Acts of emergency (cf. Lk 14:5); and (iv) Acts of Piety (Mt 12:5–6; Mt 12:8).

WCF 22: OF LAWFUL OATHS AND VOWS

During the days of the 16th Century Reformation, the Protestant cause was divided into three camps. The first was the Lutherans, led originally by Martin Luther; the second may be known as the Reformed camp led by Zwingli and Calvin; while the third may be known as the Anabaptists. They are known as Anabaptists because they denied the legitimacy of infant baptism, and so required their converts who were baptised as infants to be re-baptised. But the Anabaptists were also known as 'Radical Reformers' because they felt that the Reformation achieved by the Lutherans and also the Reformed camp did not go deep enough. Amongst some of the things that they felt the Reformers did not go far enough is to denounce the use of oaths and vows. They insisted based on passages such as Matthew 5:37 that it is now sinful to make oaths and vows. The Reformers saw, however, that to take such a view would be to make Scripture contradict Scripture. They saw that the consistent view of Scripture is that while taking of oaths and vows lightly is to be condemned, oaths and vows might be legitimately used when the occasion calls for. This is the view propounded in our *Confession*. It is also the view of all major Reformed and Calvinistic Confessions, including, the *Baptist Confession of Faith* of 1689 (cf. *BCF* 23).

On Lawful Oaths

22.1 A lawful oath is part of religious worship,[1] wherein, upon just occasion, the person swearing solemnly calleth God to witness what he asserteth, or promiseth; and to judge him according to the truth or falsehood of what he sweareth.[2]

[1]Dt 10:20; [2]Ex 20:7; Lev 19:12; 2 Cor 1:23; 2 Chr 6:22–23.

- An oath is an exercise in which a person calls upon God to witness the truth of what he is asserting (assertory oath) or to witness a promise (promissory oath) he is making. The difference between an oath, and a mere a statement or simple promise is that it involves calling upon God to judge, or, in other words, to punish the swearer if he were to fail to tell the truth or fail to keep his promise.

- The making of oaths is clearly legitimate in the Old Covenant since the Jews were taught to swear by God's name: "Thou shalt fear the LORD thy God; him shalt thou serve, and to him shalt thou cleave, and swear by his name" (Dt 10:20). In fact, the 3rd commandment assumes the legitimacy of swearing by the name of God, but warns against false swearing (Ex 20:7, Lev 19:12).

- What about under the New Covenant? It is clearly still permissible and indeed, proper since the Apostle Paul frequently make use of oaths to affirm what he says: "Moreover I call God for a record upon my soul, that to spare you I came not as yet unto Corinth" (2 Cor 1:23; cf. Rom 9:1; Gal 1:20).

- Notice that our *Confession* defines oaths and vows as being legitimate parts of religious worship (here and *WCF* 21.5). The reason for this is found in the nature of oaths and vows, namely that they are to be made in the presence of the God and His people.

22.2 The name of God only is that by which men ought to swear, and therein it is to be used with all holy fear and reverence:[1] therefore to swear vainly or rashly by that glorious and dreadful Name, or to swear at all by any other thing, is sinful, and to be abhorred.[2] Yet, as in matters of weight and moment, an oath is warranted by the Word of God, under the New Testament, as well as under the Old;[3] so a lawful oath being imposed by lawful authority, in such matters, ought to be taken.[4]

[1]Dt 6:13; [2]Ex 20:7; Jer 5:7; Mt 5:34, 37; Jas 5:12; [3]Heb 6:16; 2 Cor 1:23; Isa 65:16; [4]1 Kgs 8:31; Neh 13:25; Ezra 10:5.

- Because God alone is able to see our hearts and has the power to execute judgement, and will always act justly, an oath in the name of God is an appeal to his omniscience, omnipotence and justice. Therefore, an oath may be taken only in the name of God. To swear by any other thing is sinful because: (1) It would be a violation of Deuteronomy 6:13, "Thou shalt ... swear by his name;" (2) It would rob God of the honour due to Him; and (3) It would involve a superstitious idolatry in which the thing swore by is ascribed some power it does not have.

- Also, since God is transcendently holy and sovereign, any oath in His name must be used with all holy fear and reverence and not vainly or rashly. Instead we must swear "in truth, in judgment, and in righteousness" (Jer 4:2).

- It was the Jew's habit of swearing rashly and trivially that the Lord spoke against in Matthew 5:34-37—

  "Again, ye have heard that it hath been said by them of old time, Thou shalt not forswear thyself, but shalt perform unto the Lord thine oaths: But I say unto you, Swear not at all; neither by heaven; for it is God's throne: Nor by the earth; for it is his footstool: neither by Jerusalem; for it is the city of the great King. Neither shalt thou swear by thy head, because thou canst not make one hair white or black. But let your communication be, Yea, yea; Nay, nay: for whatsoever is more than these cometh of evil."

Someone may object that the Lord seems to be declaring a blanket prohibition. But this cannot be the case, since the Lord does not condemn swearing in God's name, but swearing by the furnishings of the temple. Perhaps the Jews had trivialised the making of oaths so much that they knew better than to swear in God's name. It appears that our Lord is really condemning this abuse of the ordinance. And thus the Apostle Paul continued to make use of oaths and vows without giving a hint that he thought it was improper.

- Our *Confession* therefore advises that oaths should be taken only in "matters of weight and moment." This would include testifying in a trial or making important declarations or even in swearing allegiance to a nation—which, of course, would be on condition that it does not compromise your faith and fidelity to the Lord. Moreover, our *Confession* advises that when the law requires an oath to be taken, the Christian who may do so with a clear conscience ought to oblige. This is for the maintenance of peace and order in the land: "An oath for confirmation is to them an end of all strife" (Heb 6:16).

22.3 Whosoever taketh an oath, ought duly to consider the weightiness of so solemn an act, and therein to avouch nothing but what he is fully persuaded is the truth.[1] Neither may any man bind himself by oath to anything but what is good and just, and what he believeth so to be, and what he is able and resolved to perform.[2] Yet it is a sin to refuse an oath touching anything that is good and just, being imposed by lawful authority.[3]

[1]Ex 20:7; Jer 4:2; [2]Gen 24:2–3, 5–6, 8–9; [3]Num 5:19, 21; Neh 5:12; Ex 22:7–11.

Some important conditions must be observed when making oaths:

- Firstly, if it is an oath to assert a truth (such as during a trial), we must be fully persuaded of the truth of the matter before making the oath. We may not, for example, swear that something is true for which we have no little or no knowledge or recollection. To do so would not only be to take God's name in vain, but potentially to bear false witness.

- Secondly, if it involves a promise to do something, we must ensure:
  (1) That we believe that what we are promising to do is just or fair, and good or righteous both from the perspective of the Law God and of a good conscience; and
  (2) That we are able and have enough resolve to do what we promise to do.

  If these two conditions are met, the Christian ought to oblige when required to take an oath by all lawful authority, both civil and ecclesiastical. On the other hand, if these two conditions are not met, we should refrain from taking the vow, or we would be binding ourselves sinfully.

22.4 An oath is to be taken in the plain and common sense of the words, without equivocation or mental reservation.[1] It cannot oblige to sin; but in anything not sinful, being taken, it binds to performance, although to a man's own hurt;[2] nor is it to be violated, although made to heretics or infidels.[3]

[1]Jer 4:2; Ps 24:4; [2]1 Sam 25:22, 32–34; Ps 15:4; [3]Ezk 17:16, 18–19; Josh 9:18–19; 2 Sam 21:1.

1. How an oath should be taken?

    a. It should be taken in the plain and common sense of the words.

    b. It must not be made with equivocation or mental reservation. i.e., there must be "entire correspondence between the sentiments of the mind and the words of the oath, in their common obvious meaning, and as understood by those who administer it" (Shaw, 288). "To allow of mental reservation in swearing, as the Church of Rome in certain cases does, is to defeat the very end of an oath, to destroy all confidence among men, and to involve the swearer in the heinous sin of perjury" (Shaw, 288–9).

2. What are the limits of an oath?

    a. It cannot oblige to sin.

    b. It binds the swearer to performance even if it is to his own hurt, so long as what is required is not sinful: "He honoureth them that fear the LORD. He that sweareth to his own hurt, and changeth not" (Ps 15:4b).

3. What if the oath is made to infidels or heretics?

    Contrary to Romish teaching, it is still to be kept. This is clearly taught in Scripture in the case of the oath that the Israelites made with the Gibeonites who tricked them into the oath (2 Sam 21:1; cf. Jos 9:1-15), and the case of the oath made by Zedekiah to the Nebuchadnezzar (Ezk 17:16–19).

On Vows

22.5 A vow is of the like nature with a promissory oath, and ought to be made with the like religious care, and to be performed with the like faithfulness.[1]

[1] *Isa 19:21; Eccl 5:4–6; Ps 61:8; 66:13–14.*

22.6 It is not to be made to any creature, but to God alone:[1] and that it may be accepted, it is to be made voluntarily, out of faith, and conscience of duty, in way of thankfulness for mercy received, or for the obtaining of what we want; whereby we more strictly bind ourselves to necessary duties, or to other things, so far and so long as they may fitly conduce thereunto.[2]

[1] *Ps 76:11; Jer 44:25–26;* [2] *Dt 23:21–23; Ps 50:14; Gen 28:20–22; 1 Sam 1:11; Ps 66:13–14; 132:2–5.*

22.7 No man may vow to do anything forbidden in the Word of God, or what would hinder any duty therein commanded, or which is not in his own power, and for the performance whereof he hath no promise of ability from God.[1] In which respects, popish monastical vows of perpetual single life, professed poverty, and regular obedience, are so far from being degrees of higher perfection, that they are superstitious and sinful snares, in which no Christian may entangle himself.[2]

[1] *Acts 23:12, 14; Mk 6:26; Num 30:5, 8, 12–13;* [2] *Mt 19:11–12; 1 Cor 7:2, 9; Eph 4:28; 1 Pet 4:2; 1 Cor 7:23.*

- *Definition*: A vow is like a promissory oath except that it is made to God rather than man. Unlike an oath in which God is called as a witness, in the vow, both God and men are called as witness, though the lack of human witness does not diminish the responsibility attached to the vow. It is to be made with the same kind of care:

    "When thou vowest a vow unto God, defer not to pay it; for he hath no pleasure in fools: pay that which thou hast vowed. Better is it that thou shouldest not vow, than that thou shouldest vow and not pay. Suffer not thy mouth to cause thy flesh to sin; neither say thou before the angel, that it was an error: wherefore should God be angry at thy voice, and destroy the work of thine hands?" (Ecc 5:4–6).

- *Purpose*: (a) To acknowledge *"thankfulness for mercy received"*; (b) *"For the obtaining of what we want [i.e., lack]."* It was for such a reason that Hannah vowed to the Lord: "O Lord of hosts, if thou wilt indeed look on the affliction of thine handmaid, and remember me, and not forget thine handmaid, but wilt give unto thine handmaid a man child, then I will give him unto the LORD all the days of his life, and there shall no razor come upon his head" (1 Sam 1:11).

- *Use*: To more strictly bind ourselves to necessary duties. This is a helpful aid which recognises us of the weakness of human flesh and of our forgetfulness. The difference between a vow and the law of God is that in the latter, God binds us by His authoritative command; in the former, we bind ourselves by our voluntary engagements. A vow carries secondary obligations, while the law carries primary obligations and must be given priority if the vow contradicts it. A vow is especially useful in cases where an obligation is morally indifferent or of a positive nature, e.g., in the church membership vow to "give to the Lord's work as He shall prosper me." A marriage vow is similarly of great use.

- *Condition for legality*: (a) *"made voluntarily,"* i.e., not compelled; (b) *"out of faith"*; (c) out of *"conscience of duty."*

- *Restrictions*: (a) Must not be anything forbidden in the Word of God; (b) Must be something the person vowing has ability to fulfil; or (c) Something which God has promised ability to fulfil. As such, monastic vows of celibacy (*contra* 1 Cor 7:2, 9), voluntary poverty (*contra* Eph 4:28) and regular obedience to the Pope (*contra* 1 Pet 4:2; 1 Cor 7:23) are not legitimate and are instead *"superstitious and sinful snares, in which no Christian may entangle himself."*

- *Note*: An illegitimate vow is not binding. A person who had previously vow a vow that is contrary to the Word of God, or will cause him to sin against God (not just causing him to lose wealth or reputation—Ps 15:4), ought to repent and renounce his vow and consider it to be null and void. Herod, as such, ought to have repented and renounced his vow rather than added to his sin by beheading John the Baptist for the sake of his vow (Mk 6:23, 26).

- *Summary:*

	Content	Made to	Witness(es)	Restrictions
Oath	Assertion	Men	God	• Persuaded of its truth.
	Promise			• What is good and just; • What person making the vow believes to be good and just • What he is able and resolving to perform.
Vow	Promise	God alone	God & optionally, Men	• What is not forbidden in the Word of God; • What the person vowing has ability to fulfil; • What God has promised to give ability to fulfil.

- *Additional note*: The preferred mode of taking an oath or vow is the lifting up of the hand. This is the usual mode mentioned in the Scripture: "And Abram said to the king of Sodom, I have lift up mine hand unto the LORD, the most high God, the possessor of heaven and earth" (Gen 14:22). "And the angel which I saw stand upon the sea and upon the earth lifted up his hand to heaven, And sware by him that liveth for ever and ever, who created heaven, and the things that therein are, and the earth, and the things that therein are, and the sea, and the things which are therein, that there should be time no longer" (Rev 10:5–6).

WCF 23: OF THE CIVIL MAGISTRATE

The *Westminster Confession of Faith* as agreed upon by the Westminster Assembly of divines on 4 December 1646 has been adopted as the Confessional Standard of Pilgrim Covenant Church. However, because of some considerations related to chapters 23 and 31, it was deemed necessary to include the revision of the First General Assembly of the American Presbyterian Church in 1789 in the footnotes, together with a preface to explain the reason for doing so. The second paragraph of the preface reads:

> In view of the fact, however, that Singapore continues at present to be a multi-religious society, it is deemed that the modifications, —pertaining to the role of the civil government in chapters 23 and 31, —as adopted by the First General Assembly of the American Presbyterian Church in 1789 would be open to less dispute and abuse. These modifications are included in the footnote and deemed to be applicable until such time the Lord may be pleased to transform Singapore into a Christian nation. The original statements, —which envisaged a national church endowed by the state in line with the provisions of the Solemn League and Covenant subscribed in 1643, is nevertheless retained with an understanding: firstly, that the ideals hoped for by the divines are not impossible, —all things being possible with God (Lk 18:27); secondly, that the power of the civil magistrate, —to take order in the Church and call synods, —referred to in paragraph 23.3 and 31.2 are only applicable where the civil magistrate is constituted on true Christian principles; and thirdly, that kingship and authority of Christ over our nation is no way diminished even if the civil magistrate may be openly antagonistic towards Him (Dan 7:14). Such being the case, the original statements are not, in fact, erroneous, though less rigorous when applied to a multi-religious society such as Singapore.

This exposition, as such, will cover both the original statements and the American revision.

On the Establishment of the Civil Government

23.1 God, the supreme Lord and King of all the world, hath ordained civil magistrates, to be, under Him, over the people, for His own glory, and the public good: and, to this end, hath armed them with the power of the sword, for the defence and encouragement of them that are good, and for the punishment of evil doers.[1]

[1] Rom 13:1–4; 1 Pet 2:13–14.

- *The supreme authority over the world*: God, or more specifically Christ. He is the *"supreme Lord and King of all the world"* says our *Confession*. The prophet Daniel referring to the ascension of Christ after his resurrection, speaks of the dominion of Christ:

  "I saw in the night visions, and, behold, one like the Son of man came with the clouds of heaven, and came to the Ancient of days, and they brought Him near before Him. And there was given Him dominion, and glory, and a kingdom, that all people, nations, and languages, should serve Him: His dominion is an everlasting dominion, which shall not pass away, and His kingdom that which shall not be destroyed" (Dan 7:13-14).

  The apostle John, similarly, acknowledges Christ as the "Lord of lords, and King of kings" (Rev 17:14).

  The Kingship and Lordship of Christ is in no way diminished though the world and the civil governments of the world are not submitted to Him. Christ is on the throne of David. God has highly exalted Christ and given Him a name that is above every name that: "That at the name of Jesus every knee should bow, of things in heaven, and things in earth, and things under the earth; And that every tongue should confess that Jesus Christ is Lord, to the glory of God the Father" (Phil 2:10-11). The inspired language of Paul allows for no exception. All will one day acknowledge Him as King of kings and Lord of Lord—some with joy while others with fear and dread.

- *The warrant of Civil Government*: civil magistrates or the civil government is established by divine ordination to be *"under him, over the people"* and therefore derives its authority from God. This is clearly a Scriptural doctrine. The Apostle Paul says:

"Let every soul be subject unto the higher powers. For there is no power but of God: the powers that be are ordained of God. [2] Whosoever therefore resisteth the power, resisteth the ordinance of God: and they that resist shall receive to themselves damnation" (Rom 13:1-2).

The Apostle Peter, who was probably writing under the shadow of Nerodian persecution teaches the same thing:

"Submit yourselves to every ordinance of man for the Lord's sake: whether it be to the king, as supreme; [14] Or unto governors, as unto them that are sent by him for the punishment of evildoers, and for the praise of them that do well" (1 Pet 2:13-14).

- *The goal of Civil Government*: *"For God's own glory, and the public good."* Paul explains:

"For rulers are not a terror to good works, but to the evil. Wilt thou then not be afraid of the power? do that which is good, and thou shalt have praise of the same: [4] For he is the minister of God to thee for good" (Rom 13:3-4a).

- *The means of Civil Government*: They are armed *"with the power of the sword."*

"But if thou do that which is evil, be afraid; for he beareth not the sword in vain: for he is the minister of God, a revenger to execute wrath upon him that doeth evil" (Rom 13:4b).

The sword, of course, represents the authority to inflict temporal punishments upon wrong-doers.

- *The Establishment Principle*: This section provides the basis for what may be known as the Establishment Principle. This principle, teaches that since both the Church and the State are divinely ordained authorities, they ought to support each other, — according to their respective spheres, without interfering with each other's responsibilities, in the promotion of Christ as Lord and

King of all the world.

This principle is sometimes known as the theory of co-ordinating authorities. It may best be understood by looking at three other principles with regard to the relationship between the Church and the State which have been held by Christians of various other positions:

(1) *The Erastian Principle*: This advocates State control over the Church. This was the view promoted by Thomas Erastus (1524-83), who was a student of Zwingli. Erastus taught that the State has the power to intervene in ecclesiastical matters. In fact, according to him, the Church has no power to excommunicate any of its members or to withhold the sacrament from anyone because all punitive powers belong to the State. This is the position of the Church of England, whereby the King or Queen, through parliament appoints the Bishops. Erastianism was defended by some parliamentary representatives at the Westminster Assembly, but was defeated, particularly through the contributions of George Gillespie, the young Scottish Commissioner of note.

(2) *The Papal Principle*: This principle teaches that the Church controls the State. This was and is the position held by the Roman Catholic Church. It asserts that the Pope is the vicar of Christ and therefore has the right to claim allegiance of all civil governments. Apart from the fact that there is no Scriptural grounds for the Pope to claim the vicarage of Christ (the Vicar of Christ is the Holy Spirit), there is also no Scriptural basis for saying that State authorities must submit to Church authorities.

(3) *The Voluntary Principle*: This advocates *total* separation of Church and State. It was held by the anabaptists and by most modern evangelical. In reality, if held as dogma, this principle is a denial of the headship of Christ over the State. However, it must be acknowledged that because of the secularisation of the State in most countries, an implementation of this principle may be the best compromise.

23.2 It is lawful for Christians to accept and execute the office of a magistrate, when called thereunto:[1] in the managing whereof, as they ought especially to maintain piety, justice, and peace, according to the wholesome laws of each commonwealth;[2] so, for that end, they may lawfully, now under the new testament, wage war, upon just and necessary occasion.[3]

[1] Prov 8:15–16; Rom 13:1–4; [2] Ps 2:10–12; 1 Tim 2:2; Ps 82:3–4; 2 Sam 23:3; 1 Pet 2:13; [3] Lk 3:14; Rom 13:4; Mt 8:9–10; Acts 10:1–2; Rev 17:14, 16.

- This section hints at the condition that must be satisfied for the establishment principle to be applicable, namely: that the magistrate or members of the government are Christian. This is, however, stated from another angle, which is that it is "lawful for Christians to accept and execute the office of a magistrate, when called thereunto." This statement was designed to refute the teachings of anabaptist and some English sects at the time of the Westminster Assembly which taught that no Christian may be a magistrate and that magistrate will not be admitted into membership of the Church. The assertion of the *Confession* may be shown to be correct for three reasons:

  (1) There were godly believers in the Old Covenant who were also civil magistrates, such as David, Josiah, Hezekiah and Nehemiah;

  (2) Cornelius the centurion was not asked to renounced his civil appointment when he became a Christian; and

  (3) If it were indeed true that a Christian cannot be a magistrate then it would be chaos whenever a country becomes Christian by choice of vast majority.

- The magistrate, —which in the context are Christians, —"ought especially to maintain piety, justice, and peace, according to the wholesome laws of each commonwealth." In other words, he is responsible to make sure that the laws of the land does not contradict the Word of God and that, rather, they should promote piety, justice and peace (Ps 82:3; 2 Sam 23:3; 1 Tim 2:2). Note also that this section suggests that the Westminster divines were not concerned about the type of government. They were only concerned that the laws be wholesome or Scriptural. Rulers should not only be concerned with crimes such as dishonesty, they ought to be concerned with piety.

- Thirdly, this section teaches that there is such a thing as a just war, which a Christian may legitimately engage in. Though war is a great evil, it is sometimes inevitable because of the present state of the world. As such nations may act justly when fighting a war. Thus, when Cornelius became a Christian, he was not asked to resign from his vocation of war. Neither were the soldiers who came to John the Baptist asked to renounce their profession. Instead, he charged them to "do violence to no man, neither accuse any falsely; and be content with your wages" (Lk 3:14).

What are just wars? Shaw summaries well:

> "...aggressive wars, or such as are undertaken to gratify views of ambition or worldly aggrandizement, cannot be justified; but that defensive wars, or those which, as to the first occasion of them, are defensive, though in their progress they must often be offensive, are lawful."[74]

On the Duties and Limitations of the Civil Government

23.3 The civil magistrate may not assume to himself the administration of the Word and sacraments, or the power of the keys of the kingdom of heaven:[1] yet he hath authority, and it is his duty, to take order that unity and peace be preserved in the Church, that the truth of God be kept pure and entire, that all blasphemies and heresies be suppressed, all corruptions and abuses in worship and discipline prevented or reformed, and all the ordinances of God duly settled, administered, and observed.[2] For the better effecting whereof, he hath power to call synods, to be present at them and to provide that whatsoever is transacted in them be according to the mind of God.[3]

[1] *2 Chr 26:18; Mt 18:17; 16:19; 1 Cor 12:28–29; Eph 4:11–12; 1 Cor 4:1–2; Rom 10:15; Heb 5:4;* [2] *Isa 49:23; Ps 122:9; Ezra 7:23, 25–28; Lev. 24:16; Dt 13:5–6, 12; 2 Kgs 18:4; 1 Chr 13:1–9; 2 Kgs 24:1–16; 2 Chr 34:33; 15:12–13;* [3] *2 Chr 19:8–11; 2 Chr 29; 30; Mt 2:4–5*

---

[74] Shaw, *op. cit.*, 244.

This section contains essentially three points.

- *Firstly*, in opposition to the *Erastian Principle*, it is declared that the civil magistrate *"not assume to himself the administration of the Word and sacraments, or the power of the keys of the kingdom of heaven."* The *"power of keys of the kingdom of heaven"* (cf. Mt 16:19) is the power of admission to and excommunication from church membership, i.e. the power of church discipline. This power clearly belongs to the Church. In describing the final step pertaining to the discipline of an erring brother, the Lord prescribes: "And if he shall neglect to hear them, tell it unto the church: but if he neglects to hear the church, let him be unto thee as an heathen man and a publican" (Mt 18:17). The State has the power of the sword to inflict temporal punishment on evil doers (Rom 13:1-4), but not the power to exercise church discipline. Indeed, it is possible for a person who cannot be a member of the Church to be a reasonable citizen in the State.

- *Secondly*, in opposition to the English Sectarians who held to the opposite extreme that the Civil Magistrate has no responsibility over the affairs of the Church, our *Confession* teaches that the Civil Magistrate *"hath authority, and it is his duty, to take order that unity and peace be preserved in the Church, that the truth of God be kept pure and entire, that all blasphemies and heresies be suppressed, all corruptions and abuses in worship and discipline prevented or reformed, and all the ordinances of God duly settled, administered, and observed."* This duty is deduced from the Scripture, which teaches (1) that "kings shall be thy nursing fathers" (Isa 49:23); (2) that certain transgressions of the law of God in the Old Testament required the death penalty, which is a civil prerogative; and (3) that God approved of the civil intervention in the religious affairs of the land by such as Hezekiah, Josiah, Nehemiah etc.

Shaw explains this seeming encroachment on the responsibility of the Church well:

> "Although the proper and immediate end of civil government, in subordination to God's glory, is the temporal good of men, yet

the advancement of religion is an end which civil rulers, in the exercise of their civil authority, are bound to aim at; for even this direct end of their office cannot be gained without the aids of religion. And although magistracy has its foundation in natural principles, and Christianity invests civil rulers with no new powers, yet it greatly enlarges the sphere of the operation of that power which they possess, as civil rulers, from the law of nature. That law binds the subjects of God's moral government, jointly and severally, to embrace and reduce to practice whatsoever God is pleased to reveal as the rule of their faith and duty."[75]

It must be remembered that the duty here described, though belonging to both believing and unbelieving magistrates, cannot be fulfilled by an unbelieving magistrate—just as the moral law is binding on believers and unbelievers but only the believers are given the power to obey them. This is partly the reason for the American revision which we shall see below. But once a government is organised under Christian principles, it should begin to exercise these responsibilities. Again Shaw has well remarked:

"And therefore nations and their rulers, when favoured with divine revelation, should give their public countenance to the true religion; remove everything out of their civil constitution inconsistent with it, or tending to retard its progress; support and protect its functionaries in the discharge of their duty; and provide, in every way competent to them, that its salutary influence have free course and be diffused through all orders and department of society."[76]

- *Thirdly*, we are taught that for the better effecting of the above, the magistrate *"hath power to call synods, to be present at them and to provide that whatsoever is transacted in them be according to the mind of God."* In the *Adopting Act* of the General Assembly of the Church of Scotland on Aug 27, 1647, it was qualified that this power

---

[75] Ibid., 247

[76] Ibid.

of the magistrate to call synods pertains "only of kirks not settled, or constituted in point of government" (*Confession of Faith*, xxvii). In other words, where the Church has a settled government, the power to call synods rests with the Church itself, the civil magistrate may not intervene to call any synod or assembly. However, the power "to be present" at the synods and "*to provide that whatsoever is transacted in them be according to the mind of God*" is a power that the magistrate will always have; after all, (1) the magistrate ought to have the right to attend any public meeting within his dominion; (2) even ordinary Christian have a right "*to provide that whatever is transacted … be according to the mind of God*." This does not imply that the magistrate may interfere with the decisions made by the synod, but that he like any other ordinary member of the church may observe and raise queries. Moreover, in a Christian nation, the magistrate would want to be present in a synod meeting so as to know what decisions are made and how he may assist in the implementation of it if necessary.

The revision of the First General Assembly of the American Presbyterian Church in 1789 reads:

23.3 Civil magistrates may not assume to themselves the administration of the Word and sacraments;[1] or the power of the keys of the kingdom of heaven;[2] or, in the least, interfere in matters of faith.[3] Yet, as nursing fathers, it is the duty of civil magistrates to protect the Church of our common Lord, without giving the preference to any denomination of Christians above the rest, in such a manner that all ecclesiastical persons whatever shall enjoy the full, free, and unquestioned liberty of discharging every part of their sacred functions, without violence or danger.[4] And, as Jesus Christ hath appointed a regular government and discipline in his Church, no law of any commonwealth should interfere with, let, or hinder, the due exercise thereof, among the voluntary members of any denomination of Christians, according to their own profession and belief.[5] It is the duty of civil magistrates to protect the person and good name of all their people, in such an effectual manner as that no person be suffered, either upon pretence of religion or of infidelity, to offer any indignity, violence, abuse, or injury to any other person whatsoever: and to take order, that all religious and ecclesiastical assemblies be held without molestation or disturbance.[6]

[1] *2 Chr 26:18;* [2] *Mt 18:17; 16:19; 1 Cor 12:28–29; Eph 4:11–12; 1 Cor 4:1-2; Rom 10:15; Heb 5:4;* [3] *Jn 18:36; Mal 2:7; Acts 5:29;* [4] *Isa 49:23;* [5] *Ps 105:15; Acts 18:14–15;* [6] *2 Sam 23:3; 1 Tim 2:1–2; Rom 13:4.*

- This statement, it should be understood, is a compromise between the Establishment Principle and the Voluntary Principle. There is an indication that clear segregation of responsibilities is to be desired. The magistrate, is therefore, not "in the least, interfere in matters of faith." The proof given is the Lord's words to Pilate: "My kingdom is not of this world: if my kingdom were of this world, then would my servants fight, that I should not be delivered to the Jews: but now is my kingdom not from hence" (Jn 18:36). Nevertheless, the civil magistrates are recognised "as nursing fathers" (Isa 49:23) and so has the duty "to protect the Church of our common Lord." Three things may be said about this phrase and the explication following. *First*, it does not require the magistrate to recognise or sanction non-Christian religions. *Secondly*, it does not require the magistrate to show preference to any denomination of Christianity. *Thirdly*, the duty of the magistrate involves only the maintenance of justice, peace, order and freedom that Church and Christians may practice their religion without prejudice, molestation and disturbance.

- As mentioned earlier, this statement would be open to less dispute and abuse, and can immediately be applied by any Christian person who may be called to serve in the office of the magistrate in a multi-religious society.

On the Duties of the Citizens with Respect to the Government

23.4 It is the duty of people to pray for magistrates,[1] to honour their persons,[2] to pay them tribute or other dues,[3] to obey their lawful commands, and to be subject to their authority, for conscience' sake.[4] Infidelity, or difference in religion, doth not make void the magistrates' just and legal authority, nor free the people from their due obedience to them:[5] *from which ecclesiastical persons are not exempted,*[6] *much less hath the Pope any power and jurisdiction over them in their dominions, or over any of their people; and, least of all, to deprive them of their dominions, or lives, if he shall judge them to be heretics, or upon any other pretence whatsoever.*[7]

[1] 1 Tim 2:1–2; [2] 1 Pet 2:17; [3] Rom 13:6–7; [4] Rom 13:5; Tit. 3:1; [5] 1 Pet 2:13–14, 16; [6] Rom 13:1; 1 Kgs 2:35; Acts 25:9–11; 2 Pet 2:1, 10–11; Jude 8–11; [7] 2 Th 2:4; Rev 13:15–17.

a. The Papal Principle of Church's dominion over the State is denounced. *"Ecclesiastical persons are not exempted"* from obedience to the civil magistrate in matters not contrary to the Word of God. The Pope has no right to demand civil obedience of anyone except his citizens in Vatican City. He has no right to depose any civil magistrate. Even if the civil magistrates are of a different religion, Christians must subject themselves to them as long as obedience does not cause them to compromise their faith. That this is the will of God is clear from the fact that Peter urged his readers to submit to the king though they were at that time being oppressed by the Roman government (cf. 1 Pet 2:13-20).

b. The duty of the citizen as such involves:

(1) Praying for the magistrates:

"I exhort therefore, that, first of all, supplications, prayers, intercessions, and giving of thanks, be made for all men; For kings, and for all that are in authority; that we may lead a quiet and peaceable life in all godliness and honesty" (1 Tim 2:1-2).

(2) Honouring their persons:

"Honour the king" (1 Pet 2:17).

(3) Paying the required taxes:

"For for this cause pay ye tribute also: for they are God's ministers, attending continually upon this very thing. Render therefore to all their dues: tribute to whom tribute is due; custom to whom custom; fear to whom fear; honour to whom honour" (Rom 13:6-7).

(4) Obeying the laws of the land and the commands of the

magistrates:

"Put them in mind to be subject to principalities and powers, to obey magistrates, to be ready to every good work" (Tit 3:1).

"Submit yourselves to every ordinance of man for the Lord's sake: whether it be to the king, as supreme; Or unto governors, as unto them that are sent by him for the punishment of evildoers, and for the praise of them that do well" (1 Pet 2:13-14).

WCF 24: OF MARRIAGE AND DIVORCE

Marriage is not a sacrament as taught by the Roman Catholic Church. However, it is an important creation ordinance instituted by the Lord, for which a proper understanding and use is essential for the spiritual well-being of believers and of the Church of Christ. For this reason, although Presbyterian and Reformed churches generally accept that the administration of marriage (i.e. the contractualisation and dissolution of marriage) is a civil rather than ecclesiastical prerogative, the church has the warrant to affirm or deny, —based on biblical reasons, —the moral legitimacy of every marriage and divorce, as well as to teach what God's will is for every married couple. For this reason also, most Protestant churches would gladly accept the responsibly of administering the marriage covenants (but not divorce) of their members when the authority is vested upon them by the State.

This chapter is not about the administration of marriage covenant, which for many churches is conducted either as part of a special wedding service or a ceremony before family and friends. Neither is this chapter about the biblical roles and responsibilities of husbands and wives.

This chapter pertains, rather, to the design and purpose of marriage, as well as the biblical criteria for legitimate marriage and divorce.

On the Monogamous Design of Marriage

24.1 Marriage is to be between one man and one woman: neither is it lawful for any man to have more than one wife, nor for any woman to have more than one husband, at the same time.[1]

[1] *Gen 2:24; Mt 19:5–6; Prov 2:17.*

That God has ordained that marriage should be monogamous is clear from:

a. The statement of the institution of marriage:

   "Therefore shall a man leave his father and his mother, and shall cleave unto his wife: and they shall be one flesh" (Gen 2:24).

b. The commentary on this statement by Malachi:

"And did not he make one? Yet had he the residue of the spirit. And wherefore one? That he might seek a godly seed. Therefore take heed to your spirit, and let none deal treacherously against the wife of his youth" (Mal 2:15).

We may paraphrase what Malachi is saying with: "Did not God make only one wife for Adam? Why did He make only one? Was it that He did not have any more spirit to constitute more wives for him? Of course not! It is by God's design that Adam should only have one wife by which he may have godly descendants. Therefore take heed to your spirit that you do not deal treacherously with the wife that God has given you by marrying another."

c. The theological design of marriage, namely to reflect the union between Christ and His Church:

"For this cause shall a man leave his father and mother, and shall be joined unto his wife, and they two shall be one flesh. This is a great mystery: but I speak concerning Christ and the church" (Eph 5:31–32).

On the Purposes of Marriage

24.2 Marriage was ordained for the mutual help of husband and wife;[1] for the increase of mankind with a legitimate issue, and of the Church with an holy seed;[2] and for preventing of uncleanness.[3]

[1]Gen 2:18; [2]Mal 2:15; 31 Cor 7:2, 9.

Apart from the theological purpose of marriage, there are three other purposes as they relate to man:

a. For the mutual help of husband and wife. This purpose was given as the reason for God's creation of Eve:

"And the LORD God said, It is not good that the man should be alone; I will make him an help meet for him" (Gen 2:18).

b. For the increase of mankind with a legitimate issue, and of the Church with an holy seed. The first part speaks about the purpose of marriage as a creation ordinance. God commanded Adam and Eve: "Be fruitful, and multiply" (Gen 1:28). The second part speaks particularly to Christian couples. The "holy seed" refers to covenant children (1 Cor 7:14) or more particularly children of the promise (Rom 9:8). This is again given in Malachi 2:15: "And wherefore one? That he might seek a godly seed." Thus, it may be said that the Reformed church propagates in two ways: evangelical and biological.[77] We are, of course, not speaking about the church invisible, which comprises the elect of God. We are referring rather to the church visible. Children born to believing parents are covenant children or members of the church visible, and for this reason are to be baptised to ratify their membership (see comments on *WCF* 28.4). We have good reasons to believe that such children, when brought up in the nurture and admonition of the Lord under the covenant, are rarely lost.

c. For the prevention of uncleanness:

"Nevertheless, to avoid fornication, let every man have his own wife, and let every woman have her own husband.... But if they cannot contain, let them marry: for it is better to marry than to burn" (1 Cor 7:2, 9).

For this reason, a healthy conjugal relationship in marriage is imperative (1 Cor 7:3–5).

On the Criteria for Marriages

24.3 It is lawful for all sorts of people to marry who are able with judgment to give their consent:[1] yet is it the duty of Christians to marry only in the Lord.[2] And therefore such as profess the true reformed

---

[77] It is also for this reason that the Reformed Church in the beginning did not approve of contraception. Calvin, in his commentary on Genesis 38:10, suggests that by the use of contraception, "one quenches the hope of his family, and kills the son, which could be expected, before he is born... [and by doing so] destroy a part of the human race." Other Protestant theologians such as Martin Luther, Ulrich Zwingli, John Wesley, A.W. Pink, Martyn Lloyd-Jones also condemned contraception. Indeed the Protestant Church before 1930 did not approve of the use of contraception. The Anglican Lambeth Conference of 1930 approved of the use of contraception in some circumstances, and soon almost all branches of Protestantism began to regard it as a matter of indifference.

religion should not marry with infidels, papists, or other idolaters: neither should such as are godly be unequally yoked, by marrying with such as are notoriously wicked in their life, or maintain damnable heresies.[3]

[1]*Heb 13:4; 1 Tim 4:3; 1 Cor 7:36–38; Gen 24:57–58;* [2]*1 Cor 7:39;* [3]*Gen 34:14; Ex 34:16; Dt 7:3–4; 1 Kgs 11:4; Neh 13:25–27; Mal 2:11–12; 2 Cor 6:14.*

a. It is "*lawful for all sorts of people to marry who are able with judgment to give their consent.*" This means:

   (1) Marriage is not to be forbidden to any class of persons—rich, poor, laypersons, clergymen, young, old, Christian and non-Christian.

   (2) The persons marrying must be "*able with judgment to give their consent.*" In other words, they must be mature and of sound mind, enough to make a rational decision to marry someone.

b. Christians must only marry "in the Lord" (1 Cor 7:39). This is taught in many passages of Scripture, for examples:

   • "Neither shalt thou make marriages with them; thy daughter thou shalt not give unto his son, nor his daughter shalt thou take unto thy son. For they will turn away thy son from following me, that they may serve other gods: so will the anger of the LORD be kindled against you, and destroy thee suddenly" (Dt 7:3–4).

   • "Judah hath dealt treacherously, and an abomination is committed in Israel and in Jerusalem; for Judah hath profaned the holiness of the LORD which he loved, and hath married the daughter of a strange god. The LORD will cut off the man that doeth this, the master and the scholar, out of the tabernacles of Jacob, and him that offereth an offering unto the LORD of hosts" (Mal 2:11–12).

   • "Be ye not unequally yoked together with unbelievers: for what fellowship hath righteousness with unrighteousness? and what communion hath light with darkness?" (2 Cor 6:14).

Practically, this means:

(a) Christians may not marry non-Christians;

(b) Christians of Reformed persuasion should not marry *infidels* (i.e., unbelievers), *papists* (i.e., Roman Catholics), or *other idolaters* (e.g., Eastern Orthodox adherents and perhaps even Lutherans);

(c) Godly Christians should not marry anyone who is notoriously wicked in their life or who "*maintain damnable heresies*" (i.e., belongs to a cult group, is a liberal, or a Pelagian, etc.).

24.4 Marriage ought not to be within the degrees of consanguinity or affinity forbidden by the Word;[1] nor can such incestuous marriages ever be made lawful by any law of man or consent of parties, so as those persons may live together as man and wife.[2] The man may not marry any of his wife's kindred, nearer in blood than he may of his own, nor the woman of her husband's kindred, nearer in blood than of her own.[3]

[1]*Lev 18; 1 Cor 5:1; Amos 2:7;* [2]*Mk 6:18; Lev 18:24–28;* [3] *Lev 20:19–21.*

a. The Word of God forbids marriage between persons of near relation. Such marriage is considered incestuous and always unlawful in our *Confession*. How near is a near relative before the marriage is considered unlawful? Leviticus 18 gives us the guideline. Basically there are three groups:

(a) First degree blood relatives, e.g., brother and sister, father and daughter; including half-brothers, half-sisters, step-mothers or step-fathers.

(b) Second degree blood relatives, e.g., father and granddaughter, nephew and aunt.

(c) In-law relation of the first and second degrees, e.g., brother and sister-in-law, father and daughter-in-law, father and grand-daughter-in-law, nephew and father's sister-in-law, etc.

b. The third category, which is reflected in the last sentence of this *WCF* paragraph is particularly difficult to prove, and as such has been deleted from most American editions of the *Confession*.

It can, however, be proven by a careful study of Leviticus 18. For at first sight it appears that Leviticus 18:18—"Neither shalt thou take a wife to her sister, to vex *her*, to uncover her nakedness, beside the other in her life *time*" contradicts the prohibition in our *Confession*. But a careful study of the chapter will indicate that verse 18 has to do with polygamous union, which was winked at in Old Testament times. The actual statement of prohibition is in verse 16—"Thou shalt not uncover the nakedness of thy brother's wife: it is thy brother's nakedness." We know that this verse cannot be about adultery because all adultery is forbidden. Neither can it be about polyandry for it was simply unheard of in Ancient Near Eastern Cultures. So it has to be that the prohibition is against marrying the sibling of a decease spouse. A sister-in-law must be treated as a sister when the wife is alive and even when the wife has passed away. The in-law relationship is not erased by death. A man may not marry his daughter-in-law even if he son dies before him (Lev 18:15). So likewise, a man must not marry his sister-in-law just as he must not marry his sister.

This interpretation is supported by Leviticus 20:21:

"And if a man shall take his brother's wife, it is an unclean thing: he hath uncovered his brother's nakedness; they shall be childless."

But the Levirate marriage law appears to require the brother of a deceased man to marry his brother's wife if she has no child:

"If brethren dwell together, and one of them die, and have no child, the wife of the dead shall not marry without unto a stranger: her husband's brother shall go in unto her, and take her to him to wife, and perform the duty of an husband's brother unto her" (Dt 25:5).

This seeming inconsistency may perhaps be understood as an exceptional provision to preserve the family inheritance and to perpetuate the family line (cf. Num 27:1–11). We may say that it is, as a rule, forbidden but nevertheless divinely tolerated for a special circumstance even as polygamy was tolerated in Old Testament days. Thus, John the Baptist charged King Herod: "It is not lawful for thee to have thy brother's wife" (Mk 6:18).

On the Dissolution of Marriage

24.5   Adultery or fornication committed after a contract, being detected before marriage, giveth just occasion to the innocent party to dissolve that contract.[1] In the case of adultery after marriage, it is lawful for the innocent party to sue out a divorce,[2] and, after the divorce, to marry another, as if the offending party were dead.[3]

[1]Mt 1:18–20; [2]Mt 5:31–32; [3]Mt 19:9; Rom 7:2–3.

a. Marriage ought to be permanent: "Wherefore they are no more twain, but one flesh. What therefore God hath joined together, let not man put asunder" (Mt 19:6). However, the corruption of nature and sin sometimes make divorce necessary. This section lays down the *only* two lawful grounds for divorce, namely,

   (1) Adultery, since the Lord clearly gave this reason as a lawful ground for divorce: "He saith unto them, Moses because of the hardness of your hearts suffered you to put away your wives: but from the beginning it was not so. And I say unto you, Whosoever shall put away his wife, except it be for fornication, and shall marry another, committeth adultery: and whoso marrieth her which is put away doth commit adultery" (Mt 19:8–9; cf. Mt 5:32).

   (2) Wilful and irreconcilable desertion, since the Apostle Paul instructs: "But if the unbelieving depart, let him depart. A brother or a sister is not under bondage in such cases: but God hath called us to peace" (1 Cor 7:15). Notice that our *Confession* makes no mention of the fact that the deserting party must be an unbeliever, unlike Paul. This is because a party who deserts his or her spouse wilfully and refuses to heed the call of the church to return will come under Church

discipline, and if unrepentant will be excommunicated and considered an unbeliever (cf. Mt 18:17).

b. According to our *Confession*, when either of these conditions happens, the aggrieved party may sue for a divorce. Note carefully that neither adultery nor wilful desertion automatically dissolves the marriage, —indeed the marriage bond will still be in force, and reconciliation should be sought, —but it does give the aggrieved party a right to sue for a divorce. Our *Confession* also teaches that the innocent party, after he/she is lawfully divorced may treat his/her former spouse as if she/he were dead and so remarry legally.

This is the position of Calvin, and has been the majority view of the Reformed church historically. It appears to be supported by 1 Corinthians 7:27–28a:

> "Art thou bound unto a wife? seek not to be loosed. Art thou loosed from a wife? seek not a wife. But and if thou marry, thou hast not sinned...."

But note that *"innocent party,"* does *not* include one who is divorced by his/her spouse unjustly. Matthew 5:32 and 19:9 suggest that innocent party in an illegitimate divorce would commit adultery if he/she remarries.

c. Some Reformed theologians, however, believe that only death dissolves the marriage bond, and that although the Scripture allows for divorce in the sense of rightful or legal separation, it does not follow that the bond is therefore broken and so, even the innocent party may not remarry without committing adultery.

The reasons given are:

(1) Marriage between man and woman symbolises the union between Christ and His Church which cannot be broken.

(2) If the marriage bond can be broken by divorce, then the guilty party would also be free to remarry. What is there to stop a guilty party from expressing repentance, and then seeking re-

admittance to church membership and then marrying the person he or she was having an adulterous affair with?

(3) The warrant for divorce does not imply a warrant for remarriage.

(4) Matthew 5:32b and 19:9 do not say, "Whosoever shall marry her that is divorced *unlawfully* committeth adultery." Indeed Mark 10:11–12 suggests that remarriage in any circumstance will involve adultery: "And he saith unto them, Whosoever shall put away his wife, and marry another, committeth adultery against her. And if a woman shall put away her husband, and be married to another, she committeth adultery." Neither is there any indication in these verses that an aggrieved or innocent wife may remarry.

(5) Paul says: "And unto the married I command, yet not I, but the Lord, Let not the wife depart from her husband: But and if she depart, *let her remain unmarried, or be reconciled to her husband*: and let not the husband put away his wife" (1 Cor 7:10–11). This verse seems to be an interpretation of the Lord's statement in Matthew 5:32 and 19:9, and would include the case of a wife suing for divorce on account of her husband's unfaithfulness.

(6) 1 Corinthians 7:27–28 has to do with a marriage bond being broken by death (v. 39; cf. Rom 7:1-3).

(7) 1 Corinthians 7:15 does not say that the marriage bond is broken by wilful desertion of the unbelieving party. 'Bondage' here translates the Greek δουλόω (*douloô*), meaning slavish-bondage whereas 'bound' in verse 27 is δέω (*deô*), meaning union or matrimonial commitment.

c. These arguments are very compelling and seem to be a clean-cut solution to the problem of remarriage of guilty parties in today's churches. However:

(1) Matthew 5:32 and 19:9 do suggest that a husband who divorces his wife, for any reason other than marital

unfaithfulness, causes her to commit adultery if she should marry again, seeing that the marriage bond is still in force; which also implies that a divorce on account of marital unfaithfulness breaks the marriage bond; which then would allow at least the innocent party to pursue remarriage if he or she so desire. Unless this is the case, then divorce would essentially mean for both parties: "You may no longer sleep with your spouse, who will remain your spouse for life, though you no longer need to fulfil your spousal obligations, nor does your spouse need to fulfil it! You will have to suppress your bodily desires for the rest of your life or until your spouse dies, otherwise you will sin by way of adultery!" Calvin agrees with this observation, in his comments on the phrase *"And whosoever shall marry her that is divorced."* He says:

> "This clause has been very ill explained by many commentators; for they have thought that generally, and without exception, celibacy is enjoined in all cases when a divorce has taken place; and, therefore, if a husband should put away an adulteress, both would be laid under the necessity of remaining unmarried. As if this liberty of divorce meant only not to lie with his wife; and as if Christ did not evidently grant permission in this case to do what the Jews were wont indiscriminately to do at their pleasure. It was therefore a gross error; for, though Christ condemns as an adulterer the man *who shall marry a wife that has been divorced*, this is undoubtedly restricted to unlawful and frivolous divorces."[78]

(2)   1 Corinthians 7:10–11 must be read in a cultural context in which in general only husbands 'put away' their wives (Mt 5:31, 32; 19:3, 8, 9; Mk 10:2, 11; Lk 16:18). Wives did put away their husbands (see Mk 10:12), but only very rarely done. So when Paul speaks about the wife departing from her husband, it is unlikely that he is speaking about divorcing, but simply leaving

---

[78] Calvin's *comm.* on Mt 19:9.

the husband. To 'remain unmarried' in this context is not to seek marriage to another because she is still married to her husband.

(3) Mark 10:11-12 must be read together with Matthew 19:9 as they were said on the same occasion (cf. Mt 19:3-12; Mk 10:2-12).

(4) The bill of divorcement which Moses commanded the husband to give to his wife if he should divorce her allows her to be remarried: "And when she is departed out of his house, she may go and be another man's wife" (Dt 24:2).

d. The difficulties attending to using Deuteronomy 24:2 are:

(a) In the case that the man divorces his wife for reasons other than marital unfaithfulness, the divorce according to the Lord is not legal;

(b) in the case that the man divorces his wife because he found her to be unfaithful, then she is the guilty party and no provision is given in our *Confession* for her to remarry; and

(c) the KJV translation of Deuteronomy 24:1-2 which puts the writing a bill of divorcement as imperative, and remarriage of the divorced woman as permissive is not universally accepted.

We are unable to deal with the third difficulty in this brief study except to say that if the alternate indicative (rather than imperative and permissive) translation is adopted, the WCF position would be weakened, but not at all refuted. As for the other two difficulties, the solution lies in the fact that even in the Old Covenant, the only acceptable ground of divorce was adultery, thus Moses said: "[if] she find no favour in his eyes, *because he hath found some uncleanness in her*: then let him write her a bill of divorcement..." (Dt 24:1). In other words, the Lord was not teaching anything new in Matthew 5 and 19. It is true that the Civil Law of Israel required stoning for adultery (Lev 20:10); but Deuteronomy 24:1 and the Lord's treatment of the woman caught in adultery, suggest that it is not mandatory to bring the sin of adultery to the civil court for civil punishment. Now, what Deuteronomy 24:2 suggests is that it is possible for (legitimate) divorce to dissolve the marriage bond, which would imply that both parties in a legitimately divorced couple may remarry without committing adultery.

But note carefully that our *Confession* sanctions the remarriage of the innocent party. This is because the guilty party should be excommunicated from the church if he remains unrepentant, and we may add that, for the sake of peace, he/she should not be restored into the particular communion, —even if he/she expresses repentance, —if the marriage bond is not restored. But in the case of the innocent party, our *Confession* is surely right not to penalise him/her any further by disallowing from remarriage. Paul asserts: "Art thou loosed from a wife? … if thou marry, thou hast not sinned…" (1 Cor 7:27–28a). This verse cannot refer to being loosed from marriage by death because Paul says "seek not to be loosed" (v. 27b).

24.6   Although the corruption of man be such as is apt to study arguments, unduly to put asunder those whom God hath joined together in marriage; yet nothing but adultery, or such willful desertion as can no way be remedied by the Church or civil magistrate, is cause sufficient of dissolving the bond of marriage:[1] wherein, a public and orderly course of proceeding is to be observed, and the persons concerned in it not left to their own wills and discretion, in their own case.[2]

[1]Mt 19:8–9; 1 Cor 7:15; Mt 19:6; [2]Dt 24:1–4.

a.   This paragraph is added in the recognition that when a married couple want to part company, they will be tempted to put up many persuasive arguments such as irreconcilable differences, physical or emotion abuse, inability to consummate the marriage, loss of affection, etc. Some of these are accepted as legitimate reasons for divorce in many modern societies. But the Word of God is clear. God will only recognise a divorce on grounds of adultery or irremediable wilful desertion. The church, the civil magistrate or anyone else who recognises divorce on any other grounds, acts in sin. Therefore, even if the civil magistrate recognises a divorce, though it is unlawful in

God's eyes, the church and every believer should continue to recognise that couple as being still husband and wife.

b. May the Lord deliver our church from ever having to deal with the crime of adultery and the complicity of divorce suits. But should any member in the church be faced with such a trial, the member must not presume to solve the problem himself or herself. It is a matter for the church to assist, to counsel and to ensure that *"a public and orderly course of proceeding… be observed; and the persons concerned in it not [be] left to their own wills and discretion, in their own case."*

WCF 25: OF THE CHURCH

The Greek word translated 'church' is ἐκκλησία (*ekklêsia*), which means "call-out ones." The call of God is twofold—the external call or preaching for all, and the internal effectual call of the Holy Spirit for the elect. Therefore, the church may be viewed from two angles: visible and invisible. The invisible church comprises all the elect. The visible church, on the other hand, comprises genuine believers and false professors, just like a field with wheat and tares.

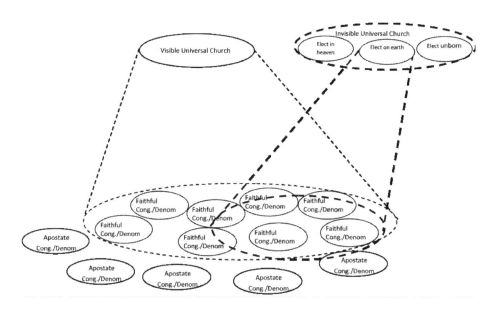

On the Church Invisible

25.1 The catholic or universal Church, which is invisible, consists of the whole number of the elect that have been, are, or shall be gathered into one, under Christ the Head thereof; and is the spouse, the body, the fullness of Him that filleth all in all.[1]

[1]*Eph 1:10, 22–23; 5:23, 27, 32; Col 1:18.*

- The head of the *Church Universal Invisible* is Christ: "For the husband is the head of the wife, even as Christ is the head of the church: and he is the saviour of the body" (Eph 5:23).

- The body of Christ is the Church: "And hath put all things under his feet, and gave him to be the head over all things to the church, *which is his body*, the fullness of him that filleth all in all" (Eph 1:22–23; cf. Col 1:18). The "all things" in this verse probably include angels and all intelligent beings capable of submission. These two verses may be paraphrased: "He hath put all things under His feet and gave Him to be head over all things for the sake of the Church, which is His body...."

- The members of this body are the elect throughout the ages: "That in the dispensation of the fullness of times he might gather together in one [head] all things in Christ, both which are in heaven, and which are on earth; even in him" (Eph 1:10). Since this verse has to do with redemption in Christ, "all things" would refer to all the elect throughout the ages (v. 4; see Charles Hodges' commentary). Since it is impossible to tell if a person is elect or not, the Church comprising the elect is said to be *Invisible*.

On the Church Visible

25.2 The visible Church, which is also catholic or universal under the Gospel, (not confined to one nation, as before under the law), consists of all those throughout the world that profess the true religion,[1] and of their children;[2] and is the kingdom of the Lord Jesus Christ,[3] the house and family of God,[4] out of which there is no ordinary possibility of salvation.[5]

[1] 1 Cor 1:2; 12:12–13; Ps 2:8; Rev 7:9; Rom 15:9–12; [2] 1 Cor 7:14; Acts 2:39; Ezk 16:20–21; Rom 11:16; Gen 3:15; 17:7; [3] Mt 13:47; Isa 9:7; [4] Eph 2:19; 3:15; [5] Acts 2:47.

- Most of us tend to think of the visible Church as being synonymous with 'local Church,' but we notice that our *Confession* is not here referring to the local church (which is addressed in 25.4). It is rather, speaking about the visible Church as a whole, or the sum total of all the genuine local churches. So defined, the visible Church consists of:

a. "*All those throughout the world that profess the true religion.*" Notice that the members are no more the elect but those who profess true religion. Notice also the "proof-text":

"For as the body is one, and hath many members, and all the members of that one body, being many, are one body: so also is Christ. For by one Spirit are we all baptised into one body, whether we be Jews or Gentiles, whether we be bond or free; and have been all made to drink into one Spirit" (1 Cor 12:12–13).

This verse suggests that membership in the Church is by spirit-baptism (which is regeneration). This means that a *true* member of the Church is regenerate and indwelt by the Holy Spirit. However, it is impossible for us to know with certainty the spiritual condition of fellow men, though we may be persuaded by their credible profession of faith that they are genuine believers (Heb 6:9–10). Thus, spirit-baptism cannot be used to affirm one's membership in the visible church. Spirit-baptism makes one a member of the Church *militant*—the congregation of the righteous or the elect of God *on earth*.

Why then is this verse used here? The answer lies in the fact that water-baptism points to spirit-baptism (cf. Mk 1:8); and water-baptism is to visible church membership as Spirit-baptism is to invisible church membership. An elect person is a member of the invisible Church, but his membership is ratified only by spirit-baptism. So, similarly, one who professes faith becomes a member of the visible church, but his membership is ratified only upon water-baptism (see table below).

It is for this reason that the church cannot accord the privileges of a church member to a person who professes faith until he or she is baptised. Conversely, the church must treat every legitimately baptised person as a Christian. Members of the church who sin scandalously and refuse to repent should be excommunicated from the church, by which the church declares that they were baptised in error. Otherwise, all baptised members in the church are to be treated as believers, only that covenant infants should not be admitted to the Lord's Table until they publicly confess their faith in the Lord.

	Membership Criteria	Ratification of Membership		
		Theol. terms	OT terms	NT terms
Church Invisible	Election	Regeneration	Heart-Circumcision	Spirit Baptism
Church Visible	Profession of Faith, Covenant Birth	Sacrament of membership	Fleshly-Circumcision	Water Baptism

b. The children of those who profess true religion. The apostle Peter had in mind the Abrahamic Covenant when he said:

"For the promise is unto you, and to your children, and to all that are afar off, even as many as the Lord our God shall call" (Acts 2:39).

This becomes very clear when we compare what he says with what the apostle Paul says in Galatians 3:14—

"That the blessing of Abraham might come on the Gentiles through Jesus Christ; that we might receive the promise of the Spirit through faith" (Gal 3:14).

The Abrahamic Covenant required children of the members of the Old Covenant Church to be circumcised so as to be included into the covenant community:

"And I will establish my covenant between me and thee and thy seed after thee in their generations for an everlasting covenant, to be a God unto thee, and to thy seed after thee.… This is my covenant, which ye shall keep, between me and you and thy seed after thee; Every man child among you shall be circumcised.… And the uncircumcised man child whose flesh of his foreskin is not circumcised, that soul shall be cut off from his people; he hath broken my covenant" (Gen 17:7, 10, 14).

Why should children be included in the covenant community? Because God does not only view the church organically, but the family organically as well. That is why the children in a Christian family, or a family with one Christian parent, are considered covenantally holy (1 Cor 7:14). That is why God considers the children born to covenant families as having been born unto him (Ezk 16:20–21). This is what Paul means when he says: "If the root be holy, so are the branches" (Rom 11:16).

Note that according to our *Confession*, the children of a professor of faith may be said to be the members of the visible church. Indeed, it should be carefully noted that we baptise infants of believers because they are covenant children. We do not make them covenant children by baptism. But again, the ratification of membership and the privileges of church membership (e.g., church discipline, etc.) are accorded only upon baptism.

- The visible church is also known in the Scriptures as "the kingdom of heaven" or "the kingdom of God" or, in other words, "the kingdom of the Lord Jesus Christ": "Again, the kingdom of heaven is like unto a net, that was cast into the sea, and gathered of every kind" (Mt 13:47; cf. Isa 9:7). In this kingdom, there are also bad fishes which are cast away at the Last Day (Mt 13:48). The existence of false professors in the visible church, however, does not therefore make the visible church unholy or any less important than the church invisible. Paul obviously believes that there are false professors in the Church of Corinth, for he wrote:

"Examine yourselves, whether ye be in the faith; prove your own selves. Know ye not your own selves, how that Jesus Christ is in you, except ye be reprobates?" (2 Cor 13:5).

Yet, his letter is addressed "unto the church of God which is at Corinth" (2 Cor 1:1) and he greets them with: "Grace be to you and peace from God our Father, and from the Lord Jesus Christ" (2 Cor 1:2). In other words, he wrote to them as an assembly of Christians, though it is almost certain that there are false believers in the church.

To put it in another way, a local congregation must be regarded organically as a Christian church if it exhibits the marks of a true church—even though it is possible that majority of the members may be unregenerate. Indeed, even the unregenerate members are considered covenantally holy, just as an unbelieving member of a family, in which either the father or mother is a believer, is considered covenantally holy (1 Cor 7:14). The only difference is that in the case of a family, membership is automatic, whereas in the case of a church, membership is by baptism (or circumcision in the old covenant).

The reality of covenantal concept explains why in the Parable of the Vine and Branches, one who is considered a branch can be cast out and burned if he is unfruitful (Jn 15:6). Such a person is a branch of Christ covenantally.

- The visible church may also be known as "the house and family of God": "Now therefore ye are no more strangers and foreigners, but fellowcitizens with the saints, and of the household of God" (Eph 2:19).

- Notice the last phrase in our *Confession*: "*out of which there is no ordinary possibility of salvation.*" The Roman Catholic Church claims that salvation may only be found in the Roman Catholic Church. The *WCF* denies this claim but makes it clear that ordinarily, a person may not expect to be saved unless he is joined to the visible Church universal by way of a local branch, which of course, must profess true religion.

- Notice that the parenthetical remark, "*not confined to one nation, as before under the law.*" This clearly suggests that the *WCF* sees the nation of Israel as the Church (or Church under-age) in the Old Covenant. It is not as nation, *qua* nation, that Israel was beloved of the Lord, but as the church or a covenant body. Thus, the Jews wandering in the desert was called "the church in the wilderness" (Acts 7:38).

25.3 Unto this catholic visible Church Christ hath given the ministry, oracles, and ordinances of God, for the gathering and perfecting of the saints in this life, to the end of the world; and doth by His own presence and Spirit, according to His promise, make them effectual thereunto.[1]

[1] *1 Cor 12:28; Eph 4:11–13; Mt 28:19–20; Isa 59:21.*

The reason why there is ordinarily no salvation outside the visible Church is that the catholic visible Church has been entrusted "the ministry, oracles, and ordinances of God, for the gathering and perfecting of the saints in this life, to the end of the world." This is achieved by way of spiritual gifts as well as by the power and authority of Christ, which makes the exercise of the gifts and duties of the church effectual:

> "And Jesus came and spake unto them, saying, All power is given unto me in heaven and in earth. Go ye therefore, and teach all nations, baptising them in the name of the Father, and of the Son, and of the Holy Ghost" (Mt 28:18–19; cf. 1 Cor 12:28; Eph 4:11–13).

On the True Member-Churches of the Visible Catholic Church

25.4 This catholic Church hath been sometimes more, sometimes less visible.[1] And particular churches, which are members thereof, are more or less pure, according as the doctrine of the Gospel is taught and embraced, ordinances administered, and public worship performed more or less purely in them.[2]

[1]*Rom 11:3–4; Rev 12:6, 14;* [2]*Rev 2; 3; 1 Cor 5:6–7.*

• The catholic (i.e. universal) Church has existed since the beginning, though sometimes it is not very visible. Elijah thought that he was the only one left of the true Church in Israel, but the Lord rebuked him and told him that He had reserved for Himself 7,000 men who had not bowed their knees to Baal (1 Kgs 19:10, 18; cf. Rom 11:3–4).

The same may be said of the true Church during the Medieval Ages, for only a remnant had remained faithful to Christ and professed true religion. As a body, the Waldenses would have been part of the visible catholic Church.

The visible catholic Church was at times driven into hiding just as the woman in Revelation 12:

> "And the woman fled into the wilderness, where she hath a place prepared of God, that they should feed her there a thousand two hundred and threescore days.... And to the woman were given

two wings of a great eagle, that she might fly into the wilderness, into her place, where she is nourished for a time, and times, and half a time, from the face of the serpent" (Rev 12:6, 14).

- The current paragraph of our *Confession* speaks not only of the visibility of the catholic Church, but also of the purity of the Church. The purity of the Church may be measured according to the marks of the particular or local churches which are part of it. Reformed theologians are not all agreed on the number and nature of these marks. Calvin and his immediate successors held that there are only two such marks:

  (a) that "the Word of God [be] purely preached and heard"; and

  (b) that "the sacraments [be] administered according to Christ's institution."[79]

  The *Belgic Confession of Faith* (1561), on the other hand, includes a third mark: "if church discipline is exercised in punishing of sin" (*BCF* 29).

  Interestingly, though Calvin affirmed the importance of discipline (*ICR* 4.12.1), he had denied, albeit rather weakly, that a failure to enact discipline is sufficient ground to classify a church as being false and so requires separation by faithful members (see *ICR* 4.1.15). Nevertheless, in 1539, in his reply to Cardinal Sadoleto Calvin wrote: "Since there are three things on which the safety of the Church is founded, viz., doctrine, discipline, and the sacraments, and to these a fourth is added, viz., ceremonies [in worship]..."[80]

- Remarkably, our *Confession*, as if taking the cue from Calvin, speaks of the purity of public worship as a mark of the true church. Moreover, if you examine the "proof-texts" carefully, you will notice that 1 Corinthians 5:6–7 has to do with Church discipline and not just about administration of the sacraments. The Apostle

---

[79] *ICR* 4.1.9; c.f. the *Genevan Confession* (1536), art. 18; Turretin, *Institutes*, 18.12).

[80] John Calvin, *A Reformation Debate: John Calvin and Jacopo Sadoleto*, ed, John C. Olin [Baker Book House, 1966], 63.

Paul was rebuking the Corinthian church for condoning the sin of incest in the church:

"Your glorying is not good. Know ye not that a little leaven leaveneth the whole lump? Purge out therefore the old leaven, that ye may be a new lump, as ye are unleavened. For even Christ our passover is sacrificed for us" (1 Cor 5:6–7).

Indeed, very few Reformed theologians today will deny that the proper administration of church discipline is a mark of a true church, while only some churches, —that are still holding firmly on the Regulative Principle according to the *WCF*, —will emphasise biblical worship as an essential mark of a true church. But perhaps the best way for us to look at doctrine, sacrament and discipline as defining the being of the church, whereas worship as defining the well-being of the church.

- That said, it is important for us to note carefully, how our *Confession*, unlike the *Belgic Confession* (Article 29) does not give the impression that it is always easy to distinguish a true church from a false church. Instead, it speaks of how we may subjectively assess the degree of purity of a church depending on how closely it fulfils the criteria set down. Our *Confession* does affirm (in the next paragraph) that it is possible for a church to become so degenerated that it ceases to be a true church of Christ. From such churches all faithful believers should flee, though from churches which adhere to the marks, "no man has a right to separate himself" (*BCF* 29). However, it must be admitted that in so far as there is an element of subjectivity, true believers should not be prevented or discouraged if they desire to leave a church (for a purer church), where the legitimacy or the being of the church of their membership is in question because of false doctrine, flippant administration of the sacraments or neglect of church discipline, or even where biblical worship is not observed.

- Furthermore, in regard to preaching, note how our *Confession* is careful to state that the doctrine of the Gospel must be both taught and embraced. This means that a church in which the doctrine is taught, but in which none of the members embrace the doctrine may be regarded as a false church. The Church of Sardis was regarded as "dead" (Rev 3:1), but it remained a true branch because there remained a few who had "not defiled their garments" (Rev 3:4). But if these are removed and the church would not repent, the Lord would soon visit in judgement (Rev 3:3).

25.5 The purest churches under heaven are subject both to mixture and error;[1] and some have so degenerated as to become no churches of Christ, but synagogues of Satan.[2] Nevertheless, there shall be always a Church on earth to worship God according to His will.[3]

[1] 1 Cor 13:12; Rev 2; 3; Mt 13:24–30, 47; [2] Rev 18:2; Rom 11:18–22; [3] Mt 16:18; Ps 72:17; 102:28; Mt 28:19–20.

- Because of the corruption of sin, it is necessary that even the purest churches on earth be subject to both mixture and error. As long as truth prevails and there are genuine believers in it, we can be quite sure that these mixture and error do not destroy the essence of a church. But a church can so degenerate that it becomes no more a Church of Christ but synagogues of Satan. This was what happened to the Church of the Old Covenant, namely Israel (cf. Rom 11:18–22). This is also what happened to the Roman Catholic church:

  "And he cried mightily with a strong voice, saying, Babylon the great is fallen, is fallen, and is become the habitation of devils, and the hold of every foul spirit, and a cage of every unclean and hateful bird. For all nations have drunk of the wine of the wrath of her fornication, and the kings of the earth have committed fornication with her, and the merchants of the earth are waxed rich through the abundance of her delicacies" (Rev 18:2–3).

  This has also happened to some of the large denominations in the United States and United Kingdom such as the Presbyterian Church of USA (in the assessment of the late Dr John H. Gerstner).

- Nevertheless, there will always be a Church on earth to worship God according to His will. This is the promise of Christ: "And I say also unto thee, That thou art Peter, and upon this rock I will build my church; and the gates of hell shall not prevail against it" (Mt 16:18; cf. Mt 28:19–20). Like the burning bush, she is subjected to trials and persecutions, but is not consumed.

On the Pope of the Roman Catholic Church

25.6 There is no other head of the Church but the Lord Jesus Christ:[1] *nor can the Pope of Rome in any sense be head thereof; but is that antichrist, that man of sin, and son of perdition, that exalteth himself in the Church against Christ, and all that is called God.*[2]

[1]Col 1:18; Eph 1:22; 2Mt 23:8–10; [2] Th 2:3–4, 8–9; Rev 13:6.

- This paragraph explicates what the "proof-text" in the previous paragraph hinted, namely, that the Church of Rome is now a synagogue of Satan. As such, the Pope cannot be the head of the church as claimed by the Roman Catholic church. The head of the Church, rather, is Christ and Christ alone: "And he is the head of the body, the church: who is the beginning, the firstborn from the dead; that in all things he might have the pre-eminence" (Col 1:18; cf. Eph 1:22). Indeed, it is precisely for the reason that the Pope has claimed supremacy that our *Confession* firmly identifies the Pope as the Antichrist. For the Greek ἀντί as in ἀντίχριστος (*antichristos*, cf. 1 Jn 2:18) does not only signify opposition, but standing in place of. Who, but the Pope stands in place of Christ to oppose Christ?

This identification is typically Reformed and was and is held by the best Reformed theologians—especially, those who have worked on historical theology. An excellent article by Maurice Roberts on this subject, entitled "Francis Turretin on the Antichrist," was published in the Aug/Sep 1991 issue of *The Banner of Truth Magazine*. We may summarise the salient arguments with the follow extract:

a. *2 Thessalonians 2:3–12*

The Antichrist or 'Man of Sin' cannot be a term referring to one single person but must refer to an office or succession of persons in office in the visible church. Paul expressly declares that Antichrist's beginning, or first manifestations, were in his own day (2 Th 2:7: "doth already work") whereas his eventual destruction would not occur till the second coming of Christ (2 Th 2:8: "whom the Lord shall destroy with the brightness of His coming").

[1 Jn 2:18 teaches us] that Antichrist was to emerge in "the last time," or New Testament times, but not that his coming was to be postponed to the very *end* of those times. The entire gospel age is meant by "the last time."

[Accordingly, there is in 2 Th 2:3–12] a revelation made of an arch-enemy of Christ who would emerge in the course of history. The full revelation of this mysterious man of lawlessness was in Paul's day held by the presence and power of the Roman empire [2 Th 2:7— "he who now letteth will let, until he be taken out of the way"] But the mystery was "already at work" and, once Imperial Rome fell in the fifth century AD, the antichristian force at work in the church would mature and grow. So the Antichrist (the term is used synonymously with the "man of sin") is not a figure to be looked for at the end of the Christian dispensation but rather a mysterious process of spiritual evil concentrated in the church-office which we know as the Papacy.

This unscriptural office would attach to itself blasphemously arrogant powers and, under the guise of love to Christ, would act as His enemy and substitute. The term "Antichrist" bears the twofold sense of one who is against Christ and one who is His ape or vicar.

In the light of the evidence given by Paul in this passage of Scripture, the way to identify this Antichrist is to search in the annals of church history to see what, if any, figure has ever emerged in the Christian church who might correspond with this description. As a matter of fact, the one ecclesiastical institution which appears exactly to fit the evidence is that of the Papacy.

This phenomenon is the key which fits every lock in the passage. The Papacy arose just when the Roman Empire collapsed. The mystery of its pretentions to power and authority grew and developed after AD 410 till, by the later Middle Ages and the time of Hilderbrand, Popes were claiming to be God's sole vice-regents on earth with power to open and shut heaven itself, to make and unmake laws, to demand worship of mankind and to perform 'miracles.' All these claims were made by the Papacy in the name of Christ and on the assertion of His express authority. The corruption of the lives of many Popes is well known and their violent persecutions of God's people is a thing very fully documented in the annals of the past.

It therefore follows that we must make the identification to which Paul's epistle leads us. The Antichrist of this passage is the Papacy. Nor can we expect the Papacy to be entirely abolished till the second coming of Christ at the end of time.

We might add to the comment, from the point of view of this twentieth century, that the Popes who have arisen since Turretin's time have not withdrawn their extravagant claims one iota but have in various ways added to them, notably by the dogma of papal infallibility brought in by Pius IX in 1870.

b. *Revelation 17*

This chapter adds in various ways to the identification of the Antichrist given by Paul in the above-discussed passage. It refers to a "mystery Babylon" full of filthiness and spiritual fornication whose influence would infect the whole earth. Though gorgeously arrayed in gold and scarlet with precious stones and pearls, its whole inward character is one of blasphemy, of abominations before God, and wicked cruelty. An extraordinary mark of identification of this mystery is given in that she is said to have her seat at a place where there are "seven mountains" (v. 9). It is notorious that the only city on earth to fit that description is Rome, where the Papacy has always had its seat and from which their church takes its very name. This mysterious agency describes here by John in Revelation 17 has the power to intoxicate the nations. This well accords with the fascination which Catholicism exerts over mankind and is exerting at the present time. For as alcoholic drink robs men of their reason, so does ecumenical propaganda rob church leaders of their ability to see the errors of Catholic doctrine or to remember Rome's cruel treatment in the past.

c. *1 Timothy 4:1–3*

This apostolic prophecy describes certain forms which the antichristian apostasy would take on. These include a departure from the original faith of Christ and the introduction into the church of unscriptural and therefore devilish doctrines, such as forbidding to marry and the command not to eat meats. Every one of these marks can be found in the Papacy.

d. *Revelation 13:11ff*

This apocalyptic beast is said to look like a lamb but to speak like a dragon. He supersedes the first beast but is like him in tyranny and is more subtle in that he appears harmless, while all the time he deceives and enslaves men's soul to error. He has power to put to death all who refuse to receive his mark in their hands and heads and he bears the mystery number of 666. The first beast mentioned in the chapter is evidently intended to represent the persecuting power of the Roman Empire. The second beast is taken by many writers to be Rome ecclesiastical. It exercises the persecuting power of pagan Rome but has the outward appearance of innocence.

e. To the Catholic objection to the fact that Antichrist will deny Christ (a thing, they say, not done by the Papacy), we answer that the Antichrist referred to by the Scriptures would not deny Christ openly, as a professed enemy, but would deny Him nonetheless as a professed friend of Christ. To this effect is the telling comment of Augustine of Hippo: "Antichrist is the more deceitful in that he professes Jesus Christ with the mouth but denies Him by his actions." This the Popes do because they arrogate to themselves the three offices of Christ, bury the gospel under their own traditions, and destroy Christ's redemptive work by their own masses, merits, purgatory and indulgences. Furthermore, the Papacy has substituted idolatrous worship for the pure worship and ordinances of the New Testament, as Daniel 11:31 prophesied that he would; for Antiochus Epiphanes in Old Testament times was a type and figure of the Antichrist who was to come.[81]

---

[81] By Maurice Roberts, originally entitled "Francis Turretine on the Antichrist" reproduced, with author's permission, from the August/September 1991 issue of *The Banner of Truth Magazine*.

WCF 26: OF THE COMMUNION OF SAINTS

The word κοινωνία (*koinônia*) occurs 20 times in the New Testament. It is translated as 'fellowship,' 12 times; 'communion,' 4 times; and once each as 'communication,' 'distribution,' 'contribution,' and 'to communicate.' The basic idea of the term, is best captured with the word 'participation' which is probably less vague for modern ears than the words 'fellowship' or 'communion.' When two parties have *koinônia*, they participate in each other's experiences, works and offices.

Examining the usage of the word, we find the Scripture teaching us that believers have *koinônia* (1) with the Persons of the Triune God, especially with Christ, and (2) with one another: e.gs.

- 1 John 1:3— "That which we have seen and heard declare we unto you, that ye also may have *fellowship* with us: and truly our *fellowship* is with the Father, and with his Son Jesus Christ";

- 1 Corinthians 10:16-17— "The cup of blessing which we bless, is it not the *communion* of the blood of Christ? The bread which we break, is it not the *communion* of the body of Christ? For we being many are one bread, and one body: for we are all partakers of that one bread" (1 Cor 10:17);

- 2 Corinthians 13:14— "The grace of the Lord Jesus Christ, and the love of God, and the *communion* of the Holy Ghost, be with you all."

Notice that these verses express both a vertical and a horizontal dimension of communion. "Communion of the Saints" refer to the horizontal dimension, but it is based on our union and communion with Christ.

But 'communion of saints' is seldom emphasised today, I believe, for two reasons: *Firstly*, individualism has so seriously infected the church that the for many modern Christians, being in a church means no more than gathering for worship once a week. The concept of communion in a covenant body has been eroded. *Secondly*, the term 'fellowship' has taken a weak modern connotation which clouds the original meaning of *koinônia*. Today when a Christian talks about 'fellowship,' he would probably be referring to a fraternal or camaraderie gathering. And so we talk about "fellowship groups" as groups that are gathered based on common interest or for the purpose of supporting one another in the faith. But the original meaning of *koinônia* is much richer, and it is the subject of this chapter of our *Confession*.

On the Union and Communion of the Body of Christ

26.1 All saints, that are united to Jesus Christ their Head, by His Spirit, and by faith, have fellowship with Him in His grace, sufferings, death, resurrection, and glory:[1] and, being united to one another in love, they have communion in each other's gifts and graces,[2] and are obliged to the performance of such duties, public and private, as do conduce to their mutual good, both in the inward and outward man.[3]

[1] 1 Jn 1:3; Eph 3:16–19; Jn 1:16; Eph 2:5–6; Phil. 3:10; Rom 6:5–6; 2 Tim 2:12; [2] Eph 4:15–16; 1 Cor 12:7; 3:21–23; Col. 2:19; [3] 1 Th 5:11, 14; Rom 1:11–12, 14; 1 Jn 3:16–18; Gal 6:10.

26.2   Saints by profession are bound to maintain an holy fellowship and communion in the worship of God, and in performing such other spiritual services as tend to their mutual edification;[1] as also in relieving each other in outward things, according to their several abilities and necessities. Which communion, as God offereth opportunity, is to be extended unto all those who, in every place, call upon the name of the Lord Jesus.[2]

[1] Heb 10:24-25; Acts 2:42, 46; Isa 2:3; 1 Cor 11:20; [2] Acts 2:44-45; 2Cor 8; 9; 1Jn 3:17; Acts 11:29-30.

These two paragraphs teach us three things, namely: (a) The basis of communion between saints, namely their union with Christ; (b) the benefits of union with Christ; and (c) the obligations arising from our union with Christ and with one another.

a. Christians are covenantally and mystically united to Christ and so share in His suffering, death, resurrection, and glory.

  i. We are *covenantally* united with Him as He is our Covenant Representative, and so we are "chosen... in him before the foundation of the world" (Eph 1:4; cf. Jn 17:2, 6); and so Christ lived on our behalf that His righteousness may be imputed on us so that by His active obedience we are made righteous in the sight of God (Rom 5:19); and Christ died on our behalf as a propitiation for our sins (Eph 5:2; 1 Jn 2:2, 4:10).

ii. We are *mystically* united with Christ in that His Spirit indwells and works in us: "For as the body is one, and hath many members, and all the members of that one body, being many, are one body: so also is Christ. For by one Spirit are we all baptised into one body, whether we be Jews or Gentiles, whether we be bond or free; and have been all made to drink into one Spirit" (1 Cor 12:12–13; cf. Rom 8:9; 1 Cor 6:11). This union is mystical only in the sense that it may be not be understood by the natural mind, but must be explained by the Scriptures. Scriptures moreover illustrate this union with the vine and the branches (Jn 15:5); the body and the head (Eph 4:15–16; 1 Cor 12:12); and husband and wife (Eph 5:31–32).

b. The benefits of our union with Christ is that we have communion with Christ in that:

i. We receive all the benefits of His passive and active obedience, as our Covenant Head. We are "complete in him" (Col 2:10); we share His offices of prophet, priest and king (1 Jn 2:27; 1 Pet 2:5, 9 and Rev 3:21).

ii. We receive the sanctifying benefits of the indwelling of His Spirit: we have the "mind of Christ" (1 Cor 2:16; cf. Phil 2:5); and the likeness of Christ (1 Jn 3:2).

iii. All our experiences, sufferings and victories are reckoned to be those of Christ. Not only were our sins and guilt imputed on Christ on the Cross (Is 53:5–6; Col 2:14); but our sufferings are reckoned His sufferings, so we are called "partakers of Christ's sufferings" (1 Pet 4:13); and when we suffer bodily for Christ's sake, we bear "the marks of the Lord Jesus Christ" (Gal 6:17), and our afflictions may be called "the afflictions of Christ" (Col 1:24). Moreover, "we are more than conquerors through him that loved us" (Rom 8:37).

c. Since believers are intimately united with Christ, it follows that they themselves are intimately united to one another. Note that we are not saying as Rome does, that individuals are united to the Church through the sacraments, and through the Church to Christ. Rather, individuals are united to Christ by the Holy Spirit, through effectual calling, and are therefore automatically members of the Body of Christ: "For as the body is one, and hath many members, and all the members of that one body, being many, are one body: so also is Christ. For by one Spirit are we all baptised into one body, whether we be Jews or Gentiles, whether we be bond or free; and have been all made to drink into one Spirit…" (1 Cor 12:12–27).

This unity is the basis of the communion of the saints one with another. Our *Confession* rightly notes that this unity is realised "in love." We see this over and over again in the Scriptures (cf. 1 Jn 5:2; 1 Pet 1:22). It is most instructive, however, that the Apostle Paul writes:

> "And he gave some, apostles; and some, prophets; and some, evangelists; and some, pastors and teachers; For the perfecting of the saints, for the work of the ministry, for the edifying of the body of Christ: Till we all come in the unity of the faith, and of the knowledge of the Son of God, unto a perfect man, unto the measure of the stature of the fullness of Christ: … [And] speaking the truth in love, may grow up into him in all things, which is the head, even Christ: From whom the whole body fitly joined together and compacted by that which every joint supplieth, according to the effectual working in the measure of every part, maketh increase of the body unto the edifying of itself in love" (Eph 4:11–16).

What Paul is saying is that it is by divine appointment that the members in the church may be able to show love one to another beyond a superficial, mundane level because each have been given spiritual gifts to edify one another (cf. 1 Cor 3:21). In other words, the members in the body are dependent on one another; or our *Confession* puts it: "have communion in each other's gifts and graces." So intimate is this communion, that no member can suffer without others suffering with him and no member can rejoice, but that others should rejoice with him (1 Cor 12:26).

Such being the case, every member of the church have obligations towards other members in the church. For examples:

- We have the obligation to love one another (1 Jn 3:11, 23);
- to speak the truth to one another in love (Eph 4:15);
- to edify one another (1 Th 5:11);
- to receive one another (Rom 15:7); to admonish one another (Rom 15:14; Col 3:16);
- to lay down our lives for the brethren (1 Jn 3:16);
- to help one having material needs (1 Jn 3:17);
- to consider one another, to provoke one another unto love and to good works (Heb 10:24);
- to exhort one another daily, while it is called To day; lest anyone be hardened through the deceitfulness of sin (Heb 3:13);
- to exhort one another pertaining to attendance at worship (Heb 10:25);
- to confess our faults one to another, and pray one for another (Jas 5:16);
- to prefer one another in honour (Rom 12:10);
- to forebear judging one another (Rom 14:13);
- to serve one another (Gal 5:13); to bear one another's burden (Gal 6:2);
- to forebear one another in love (Eph 4:2; Col 3:13);
- to be kind one to another, tender-hearted, forgiving one another (Eph 4:32), etc

Note that these obligations are extended to all members of the Visible Universal Church, i.e., to all credible professing believers. So our *Confession* asserts: *"Which communion, as God offereth opportunity, is to be extended unto all those who in every place call upon the name of the Lord Jesus."* However, for pragmatic reasons, the exercise of these obligations would mostly be confined within the local assembly simply because that is where the opportunities are most frequently recognised. The Lord does not require us to do the impossible by attempting to do good to every man at all times. Rather, as Paul puts it: "As we have therefore opportunity, let us do good unto all men, especially unto them who are of the household of faith" (Gal 6:10). In other words, good must be done whenever we have the opportunity or become aware of a need.

On the Errors Pertaining to the Doctrine of Communion

26.3 This communion which the saints have with Christ, doth not make them in any wise partakers of the substance of His Godhead; or to be equal with Christ in any respect: either of which to affirm is impious and blasphemous.[1] Nor doth their communion one with another, as saints, take away, or infringe the title or propriety which each man hath in his goods and possessions.[2]

[1] Col. 1:18–19; 1 Cor 8:6; Isa 42:8; 1 Tim 6:15–16; Ps 45:7; Heb 1:8–9; [2] Ex 20:15; Eph 4:28; Acts 5:4

There are basically two errors pertaining to this doctrine.

- *Firstly*, the Eastern Orthodox Church teaches that the union between Christ and believers involves an inter-penetration of Christ's being and ours. This concept, known as *theosis*, involves the deification of man. This whole idea is a heresy with no scriptural basis. In our union with Christ, we remain distinct from Christ and do not in any wise partake of His divinity. God alone "is the blessed and only Potentate, the King of kings, and Lord of lords; Who only hath immortality, dwelling in the light which no man can approach unto; whom no man hath seen, nor can see: to whom be honour and power everlasting. Amen." (1 Tim 6:15–16).

- *Secondly*, the German Anabaptists in the 16th century taught that Christians do not have individual rights or possession of their property. This communistic idea, again, has no basis in Scripture.

The *"communion one with another, as saints, [do not] take away, or infringe the title or propriety which each man hath in his goods and possessions."* The 8th commandment: "Thou shalt not steal" teaches us that respect for individual property rights is a perpetual, universal obligation.

It is true that in the early church, "all that believed were together, and had all things common; And sold their possessions and goods, and parted them to all men, as every man had need" (Acts 2:44–45). However, to say that this implies that Christians must share their possession with one another in a kind of communistic ownership scheme is reading too much into the passage. Not only must it be noted that the sharing is only with the poor and not with everyone, but that this sharing was entirely voluntary. For, we find in the judgement of Ananias and Sapphira that they were not in fact required to sell their property, nor to distribute to the members of the church. Peter said: "Whiles it remained, was it not thine own? and after it was sold, was it not in thine own power? why hast thou conceived this thing in thine heart? thou hast not lied unto men, but unto God" (Acts 5:4). Peter was telling Ananias that the property belonged to him and when he sold it, the money belonged to him. He had a right to keep the whole sum or to keep what he needed, and give a part of it to the church if he so desired. However, to lie that he had sold the possession and that he was giving the whole amount to the church when, in fact, he had held back a part of the sum shows his hypocrisy and wickedness.

WCF 27: OF THE SACRAMENTS

It is sometimes objected that the term 'sacrament' is not found in the Scripture and carries with it a vestige of Romish sacerdotalism, and therefore should not be used in the Christian Church, much less in a Confession of Faith. This is one of the reasons, it is supposed, why the *Baptist Confession of Faith* of 1689 dropped the term, preferring to call baptism and the Lord's Supper simply as ordinances.

But in so far as the sacraments (Circumcision and the Passover in the Old Testament; and Baptism and the Lord's Supper in the New Testament) are distinguishable from the other ordinances of God (e.g., Lk 1:6; Rom 13:2; 1 Cor 11:2; Eph 2:15; Col 2:14, etc.), there is a good reason for us to retain a special term for them, and to treat them separately.

Why do we use the term sacrament? Calvin suggests that the "the ancients [Church Fathers] had no other intention than to signify that they are [sacred] signs of holy and spiritual things."[82] In other words, they could have used other words, but the word sacrament (or the Latin *sacramentum*) was chosen for the purpose because it was deemed suitable enough.

Others have tried to explain why the term is retained. It is suggested that the word *sacrament* is derived from the Latin word *sacramentum* which was employed by the early Christian writers as synonymous with the scriptural term *mystery* (Greek: μυστήριον, *mustērion*). It is thought that this synonymous meaning of *sacramentum* was the basis for the Latin Christians to call the ordinances of the Lord's Supper and Baptism sacraments. They did so partly because, under the external symbols and rituals, the spiritual blessings and significance of the ordinances are veiled, and partly also because of the secrecy with which Christians under persecution were obliged to observe them.

---

[82] *ICR* 4.14.13.

Yet others have pointed to the classical and dictionary meaning of the word *sacramentum*, i.e., an "oath taken by newly enlisted soldiers."[83] When a soldier makes a *sacramentum*, he pledges himself to be faithful to his general and not to desert his standard. In the same way, when we who are enlisted in the service of Christ participate in the sacrament, we solemnly pledge to be faithful to the Captain of our salvation and to follow Him whithersoever He leads us (cf. 1 Pet 3:21 where "answer" [ἐπερώτημα, *eperōtēma*] can be translated "pledge"). But as Calvin noted, we must understand that the sacrament is not so much the soldier's pledge, but "the commander's act of receiving soldiers into the ranks. For by the sacraments the Lord promises that "he will be our God and we shall be his people" [2 Cor 6:16; Ezk 37:27]."[84]

On the Nature of Sacraments

27.1 Sacraments are holy signs and seals of the covenant of grace,[1] immediately instituted by God,[2] to represent Christ and His benefits, and to confirm our interest in Him;[3] as also to put a visible difference between those that belong unto the Church and the rest of the world;[4] and solemnly to engage them to the service of God in Christ, according to His Word.[5]

[1]Rom 4:11; Gen 17:7, 10; [2]Mt 28:19; 1 Cor 11:23; [3]1 Cor 10:16; 11:25–26; Gal 3:27; 17; [4]Rom 15:8; Ex 12:48; Gen 34:14; [5]Rom 6:3–4; 1 Cor 10:16, 21.

- Sacraments are immediately instituted by God, or more specifically, as both the *Larger Catechism* (Q. 162) and the *Shorter Catechism* (Q. 92) state: "A sacrament is an holy ordinance instituted by Christ" (Mt 28:19; 1 Cor 11:23–26).

- Sacraments serve three purposes:

  a. They serve as *"holy signs and seals of the covenant of grace… to represent Christ and His benefits; and to confirm our interest in Him."* A *sign* is something that visibly represents or makes known that which it points to. A *seal* is something that

---

[83] *Oxford Latin minidictionary* (1997), sv. "sacramentum"; cf. *ICR* 4.14.13.

[84] Ibid.

authenticates or confirms that to which it is attached. As a sign a sacrament represents the benefits of Christ in the Covenant of Grace pictorially, just as preaching presents them audibly. As a seal, it confirms our interest in Christ. The terms "sign" and "seal" were used by Paul to describe circumcision: "And he received the sign of circumcision, a seal of the righteousness of the faith which he had yet being uncircumcised" (Rom 4:11a; cf. Gen 17:7, 10). But it is not difficult to see how it can be applied also to the Lord's Supper and baptism.

The Lord's Supper was clearly instituted in the context of the Covenant of Grace for when the Lord instituted the Lord's Supper, He said: "This is my body which is given for you: this do in remembrance of me.... This cup is the new testament in my blood, which is shed for you" (Lk 22:19–20). The word translated 'testament' (διαθήκη, diathēkē) may be translated 'covenant.' The Lord was referring to the New Covenant (cf. Jer 31:31–34; Heb 8:8–12, 10:16–17). As a *sign* the Lord's Supper points to the death of Christ and the benefits that come with it. Thus, Paul declares that when we partake of the Lord's Supper, we "do shew the Lord's death till he come" (1 Cor 11:26). It is as a *seal* that the Lord's Supper is denoted a communion of the blood and body of Christ (1 Cor 10:16); i.e., it points to our spiritual union and communion with Christ. It ratifies our interest in Christ.

That baptism is instituted in the context of the Covenant of Grace is not only seen in its identification with circumcision (Col 2:11–12), but also in Acts 2:38–39 where Peter ties baptism with the promise of the Abrahamic Covenant (cf. Gal 3:14–16). In Acts 2, Peter preached: "Repent, and be baptised every one of you in the name of Jesus Christ for the remission of sins, and ye shall receive the gift of the Holy Ghost. For the promise is unto you, and to your children, and to all that are afar off, even as many as the Lord our God shall call." This promise is the Abrahamic promise, according to Galatians 3:14–16: "That the blessing of Abraham might come on the Gentiles through Jesus

Christ; that we might receive the promise of the Spirit through faith.... Now to Abraham and his seed were the promises made. He saith not, And to seeds, as of many; but as of one, And to thy seed, which is Christ." Thus, Paul speaks about our being baptised into Christ and made partakers of the Abrahamic promise: "For as many of you as have been baptised into Christ have put on Christ. There is neither Jew nor Greek, there is neither bond nor free, there is neither male nor female: for ye are all one in Christ Jesus. And if ye be Christ's, then are ye Abraham's seed, and heirs according to the promise" (Gal 3:27–29). As a *sign*, baptism points to our being baptised by the Holy Spirit into Christ (1 Cor 12:13). As a *seal*, it ratifies our membership in the Church visible which serves to reflect membership in the Church invisible.

b. They *"put a visible difference between those that belong unto the Church and the rest of the world."* This is clearly the case for baptism: "Then they that gladly received his word were baptised: and the same day there were added unto them about three thousand souls" (Acts 2:41). Baptism then is the divinely appointed badge to mark out a person as a member of the visible Church. That this is not the case for the Lord's Supper can be seen in the fact that the Lord's Supper, like the Passover, is not open to any but believers. In the Old Covenant, the LORD declared to Moses: "And when a stranger shall sojourn with thee, and will keep the passover to the LORD, let all his males be circumcised, and then let him come near and keep it; and he shall be as one that is born in the land: for no uncircumcised person shall eat thereof" (Ex 12:48). In the New Covenant Paul declared: "Wherefore whosoever shall eat this bread, and drink this cup of the Lord, unworthily, shall be guilty of the body and blood of the Lord. But let a man examine himself, and so let him eat of that bread, and drink of that cup. For he that eateth and drinketh unworthily, eateth and drinketh damnation to himself, not discerning the Lord's body" (1 Cor 11:27–29).

c. They serve *"solemnly to engage [believers] to the service of God in Christ, according to His Word."* Paul, for example, tells us that those who are baptised "should walk in newness of life" (Rom 6:3, 4) and that those who participate in the Lord's Table ought not to be partakers of "the table of the devils" (1 Cor 10:16, 21). Moreover, we are to partake of the Lord's Supper in remembrance of Christ (1 Cor 11:25), which surely means much more than a mere bringing to mind what Christ has done. It surely involves a solemn resolution to love Him, serve Him and obey Him.

27.2 There is in every sacrament a spiritual relation, or sacramental union, between the sign and the thing signified; whence it comes to pass, that the names and effects of the one are attributed to the other.[1]

[1]*Gen 17:10; Mt 26:27–28; Tit 3:5.*

- A sacrament has two parts: the sign and the thing signified. In baptism, the sign is water, which can be felt and seen. The water signifies the Holy Spirit and application of the water signifies regeneration or Spirit-Baptism: Thus, John the Baptist declared: "I indeed have baptised you with water: but he shall baptise you with the Holy Ghost" (Mk 1:8; cf. Mt 3:11). Similarly, in the Lord's Supper, the signs are the bread and wine which may be seen, handled and tasted. The bread and wine signify the body and blood of Christ respectively.

- The spiritual relationship between the sign and thing signified, i.e., the sacramental union, is so close that Scripture frequently uses expressions in which the names of the signs and the things signified are exchanged. Thus, in the Old Testament, the Lord said: "This is my covenant, which ye shall keep, between me and you and thy seed after thee; Every man child among you shall be circumcised" (Gen 17:10). Obviously circumcision is not the covenant but signifies the benefit of the covenant. Similarly, Christ giving the bread to His disciples said: "this is my body, which is broken for you" (1 Cor 11:24); and when He passed the wine, He said, "this is my blood of the new testament, which is shed for many for the remission of sins" (Mt 26:28). Obviously, Christ does not mean as Rome and the Lutherans teach that the bread was literally His flesh or contains His flesh, nor the wine literally His blood or contains His blood. In the case of Baptism, it is the same, for Paul says: "Not by works of righteousness which we have done, but according to his mercy he saved us, by the washing of regeneration, and renewing of the Holy Ghost" (Tit 3:5). Clearly, Paul is referring primarily to the spiritual reality of regeneration, but he alludes to the sign of baptism to remind his readers that baptism as a work does not save, rather, it signifies and seals regeneration. Indeed, sometimes, the name of the sacrament is used, at the same time, to refer both to the sign, —in one sense, — and the thing signified, —in another sense. This is probably how we should understand Colossians 2:11–12—"In whom also ye are circumcised with the circumcision made without hands, in putting off the body of the sins of the flesh by the circumcision of Christ: Buried with him in baptism, wherein also ye are risen with him through the faith of the operation of God, who hath raised him from the dead." Here Paul is clearly referring to water baptism (cf. Rom 6:3), yet he says that baptism is "circumcision made without hands" alluding to inward grace. The difficulty is resolved when we realise that Paul is comparing physical circumcision with water baptism by pointing to the same inward reality they both represent. The modern significance to understanding this union becomes clear in the next section.

On the Efficacy of Sacraments

27.3 The grace which is exhibited in or by the sacraments rightly used, is not conferred by any power in them; neither doth the efficacy of a sacrament depend upon the piety or intention of him that doth administer it,[1] but upon the work of the Spirit,[2] and the word of institution; which contains, together with a precept authorising the use thereof, a promise of benefit to worthy receivers.[3]

[1]Rom 2:28–29; 1 Pet 3:21; [2]Mt 3:11; 1 Cor 12:13; [3]Mt 26:27–28; 28:19–20.

- This paragraph is levelled against two errors, namely, (1) that the sacrament has power in themselves to confer grace *ex opere operato* upon every recipient who does not positively resist; and (2) that the efficacy of the sacrament is dependent on the piety or intent of the person administering it. Rome admits that the efficacy of the sacrament is not dependant on the piety of the person, but they insists that it depends: (a) Upon the fact that the administrator is canonically authorised; and (b) Upon the fact that the administrator exercises at the moment of administration the secret 'intention' of doing what the Church intends in the definition of the sacrament.[85] Against these erroneous views, our *Confession* asserts that "*the efficacy of a sacrament depend... upon the work of the Spirit, and the word of institution; which contains, together with a precept authorising the use thereof, a promise of benefit to worthy receivers.*" The fact that sacraments do not have intrinsic power can be seen in that many who partake of the sacraments are not partakers of the grace of God. Simon Magus is a classic example (Acts 8:13, 23). The efficacy of the sacrament is, rather, dependent on two things primarily: (1) the work of the Holy Spirit and (2) the word of institution—which contains both a command and promise. On the second, Calvin asserts: "the right administering of the Sacrament cannot stand apart from the Word."[86] It is also secondarily dependant on the faith of the partakers.

- It should also be carefully noted that a sacrament does not only signify and seal, but is also a means to apply Christ and the benefit of the Covenant of Grace. The *WSC* 92 makes it clear: "A sacrament is an holy ordinance instituted by Christ; wherein, by sensible signs, Christ, and the benefits of the new covenant, are represented, sealed, and *applied* to believers." The word 'applied' as used here may surprise some of us because most of us have a tendency to overreact to the Romish doctrine in which the efficacy of the sacrament are derived *ex opere operato*, i.e., grace is conferred by

---

[85] See AA Hodge, *Confession*, 333.

[86] *ICR* 4.17.39.

the actions of the priest; so that we swing to the other end of a clean dichotomy between the sacrament and the things signified, so that the meaning of the sacraments are changed. Thus, the Lord's Supper is seen only as a commemorative rite and baptism is seen as testimony of faith to the public. This is partly the reason why many prefer not to call sacraments as sacraments. But the Scripture with its frequent interchange of terms applying to the sacramental signs and the things signified; and the *Westminster Confession* teaches otherwise. Thus, *WCF* 28.6 speaks of the efficacy of the baptism on this wise: "*The efficacy of Baptism is not tied to that moment of time wherein it is administered; yet, notwithstanding, by the right use of this ordinance, the grace promised is not only offered, but really exhibited and <u>conferred</u> by the Holy Ghost, to such (whether of age or infants) as that grace belongeth unto, according to the counsel of God's own will, in His appointed time.*" In other words, baptism is a means by which the benefit of the covenant, namely regeneration is applied, though the actual application is not dependant on the time of the baptism, i.e., it may be before or after. Thomas Boston remarks:

> "[Baptism] is not of absolute necessity to salvation, as if the simple want thereof could hinder salvation; for God has not made baptism and faith equally necessary, Mark 16:16.... It is necessary by divine precept, as an instituted means of salvation. So that the contempt of it is a sin, and a great one, that will damn men, unless it be pardoned through the blood of Christ, Luke 7:30..."[87]

This position must be distinguished from that of those who hold to baptismal regeneration, —that regeneration is dependent upon baptism so that those who are not baptised remain unregenerate until they are.

On the Number and Administration of the Sacraments

---

[87] Thomas Boston, *Commentary on the Shorter Catechism* (Edmonton: Still Waters Revival Books, 1993 [1853]), 2.479.

27.4 There be only two sacraments ordained by Christ our Lord in the Gospel, that is to say, Baptism, and the Supper of the Lord; neither of which may be dispensed by any but by a minister of the Word, lawfully ordained.[1]

[1]*Mt 28:19; 1 Cor 11:20, 23; 4:1; Heb 5:4.*

This paragraph is again levelled against two errors of Rome.

- Firstly, she has added five spurious sacraments, namely ordination, marriage, confirmation, penance, and extreme unction. None of these can be considered a sacrament solely by Scripture alone.

- Secondly, Rome also permits laymen and midwives to administer the sacrament of baptism in cases of necessity. This is due to the Romish doctrine that unless a person or infant is baptised, he is doomed. Our *Confession* asserts, rather, that none but a minister of the Word, lawfully ordained, has any warrant to dispense the sacrament. This is because, firstly, "the sacraments have the same office as the Word of God: to offer [i.e., apply] and set forth Christ to us, and in Him the treasures of heavenly grace" (*ICR* 4.14.17); and secondly, on 1 Corinthians 4:1—"Let a man so account of us, as of the ministers of Christ, and stewards of the mysteries of God." The "mysteries of God" appears to refer to the sacraments.

27.5 The sacraments of the Old Testament, in regard of the spiritual things thereby signified and exhibited, were, for substance, the same with those of the New.[1]

[1]*1 Cor 10:1–4.*

- The sacraments of the Old Testament were circumcision and the Passover. The sacraments of the Old Testament pointed to Christ to come, while the sacraments of the New Testament point to Christ who has already completed His work pertaining to His incarnation. Baptism has taken the place of circumcision. Both are rites of initiation (cf. Gen 17:14; Acts 2:41). Both signify spiritual regeneration (cf. Dt 10:16, 30:6; Mt 3:11). Thus, circumcision was to a Jew what baptism is to the New Testament Christian (Gal 3:27, 29; Col 2:10–12). In the same way, the Lord's Supper supersedes the Passover when the Lord took the elements of the Passover and gave them new meaning (Mt 26:26–29). Thus, Paul speaks of Christ as our passover: "Christ our passover is sacrificed for us" (1 Cor 5:7); and John refers to Christ as being the passover Lamb of God (Jn 1:29, 36; 19:33, cf. Ex 12:46).

- The Covenant of Grace is called the everlasting covenant (Gen 17:7 and Heb 13:20). This means that there is only one plan of salvation running throughout all history. The outward form has changed, but the covenant has not changed. The way in which the covenant has been administered has changed, but not the covenant itself. This is illustrated as follows:

ONE EVERLASTING COVENANT Gen 17:7; Heb 13:20	
The Old Testament Form	**The New Testament Form**
Circumcision - Gen 17:7 (1-14) Administered once to believers and their children picturing cleansing from sin and covenant union in a bloody sign.	*Baptism* - Acts 2:39 (Gal 3:29, etc.) Administered once to believers and their children picturing cleansing from sin and covenant union in a bloodless sign.
Passover - Ex 12:43 (12:3-17) Administered often to believers picturing nurture in a bloody sign.	*Lord's Supper* - 1 Cor 5:7 (11:23-34) Administered often to believers picturing nurture in faith in a bloodless sign.

WCF 28: OF BAPTISM

Baptism is one of the most visible and well-known ordinances of the Christian Church to the 'outside world'. Many religious non-Christians will not regard someone as truly Christian unless he or she is baptised. Yet, baptism is poorly understood by many professing Christian and differing understanding of what it entails have created sharp denominational lines within conservative Protestantism. Many professing Christian assume that baptism is a ritual usually involving immersion in water for a new convert to Christianity to testify of his faith, or perhaps to 'wash away' his sin. But is this what baptism is according to the Scriptures? The present chapter of our *Confession* presents what may be known as the covenantal-paedobaptist view of baptism, which we believe is the correct biblical understanding of baptism.

On the Purpose of Baptism

28.1 Baptism is a sacrament of the New Testament, ordained by Jesus Christ,[1] not only for the solemn admission of the party baptised into the visible church,[2] but also to be unto him a sign and seal of the covenant of grace,[3] of his ingrafting into Christ,[4] of regeneration,[5] of remission of sins,[6] and of his giving up unto God through Jesus Christ, to walk in the newness of life:[7] which sacrament is, by Christ's own appointment, to be continued in His Church until the end of the world.[8]

[1]Mt 28:19; [2]1 Cor 12:13; [3]Rom 4:11; Col 2:11–12; [4]Gal 3:27; Rom 6:5; [5]Tit 3:5; [6]Mk 1:4; [7]Rom 6:3–4; [8]Mt 28:19–20.

In the previous chapter, we have already seen why it is appropriate to call baptism a sacrament of the New Testament Church. This paragraph asserts that it was personally ordained by Christ: "Go ye therefore, and teach all nations, baptising them in the name of the Father, and of the Son, and of the Holy Ghost" (Mt 28:19). It is also an ordinance that will be continued in the Church until the end of the world: "Teaching them to observe all things whatsoever I have commanded you: and, lo, I am with you alway, even unto the end of the world. Amen" (Mt 28:20). Note that "unto the end of the world" does not mean "to every corner of the world" as commonly understood. The Greek of the phrase (ἕως τῆς συντελείας τοῦ αἰῶνος, heōs tēs sunteleias tou aiōnos) may be literally translated "until the consummation of the age."

More importantly, this paragraph teaches us that baptism serves six purposes, namely:

a. It serves as *a sign and seal of the Covenant of Grace*. This can be shown from two angles, firstly, from the relationship between baptism and circumcision; and secondly, from the fact that Peter's command to the believers at Pentecost to be baptised was made in the context of the Covenant of Grace.

   i. The relationship between baptism and circumcision can be seen from the clear parallel between the two ordinances. Contrary to popular belief, circumcision in the Old Testament was not to mark out the nation of Israel. "For he is not a Jew, which is one outwardly; neither is that circumcision, which is outward in the flesh" (Rom 2:28). Circumcision was a spiritual exercise, it signifies the change wrought by God in the heart of God's covenant people. This is why the OT frequently speaks of the circumcision of the heart (Lev 26:40–41; Dt 10:16, 30:6; Jer 4:4). In other words, *physical* circumcision points to the *real* circumcision, which is of the heart. Baptism has the same spiritual significance. Paul makes this clear. In his letter to the Philippians, he intimates that Christians are "the [true] circumcision, which worship God in the spirit, and rejoice in Christ Jesus" (Phil 3:3). In his letter to the Colossians, Paul is correcting the errors of those who emphasise externalism, including circumcision. And so he assures the Colossian Christians that they do not need to be circumcised physically, because they have been circumcised spiritually. But when did that happen? Paul says "[being] buried with him in baptism, wherein also ye are risen with him through the faith of the operation of God, who hath raised him from the dead" (Col 2:12). To paraphrase, Paul is saying, "Don't you see: physical circumcision does not save, it is a sign of the circumcision of the heart, and when you were baptised with water to signify your union with Christ, it was a sign of your heart circumcision." Paul, in effect, is saying that baptism has replaced circumcision.

Since circumcision was a sign and seal of the Covenant of Grace (Rom 4:11), it follows that baptism is a sign and seal of the Covenant of Grace.

ii. In Acts 2:38–39, the Apostle Peter preached: "Repent, and be baptised every one of you in the name of Jesus Christ for the remission of sins, and ye shall receive the gift of the Holy Ghost. For the promise is unto you, and to your children, and to all that are afar off, even as many as the Lord our God shall call." The promise mentioned by Peter is frequently seen as merely the promise of the Holy Spirit. But the promise of the Holy Spirit is not a promise that stands by itself, which is why Peter does not say "*this* promise," but "*the* promise." Peter is referring to the promise of the Abrahamic Covenant, which, of course, is an administration of the Covenant of Grace. The words of Paul in Galatians 3:14–16 confirms: "That the blessing of Abraham might come on the Gentiles through Jesus Christ; that we might receive the promise of the Spirit through faith.… Now to Abraham and his seed were the promises made. He saith not, And to seeds, as of many; but as of one, And to thy seed, which is Christ." Thus, Paul speaks about our being baptised into Christ and made partakers of the Abrahamic promise: "For as many of you as have been baptised into Christ have put on Christ. There is neither Jew nor Greek, there is neither bond nor free, there is neither male nor female: for ye are all one in Christ Jesus. And if ye be Christ's, then are ye Abraham's seed, and heirs according to the promise" (Gal 3:27–29). It is, therefore, undeniable that baptism is a sign and seal of the Covenant of Grace.

b. It serves as *a sign and seal of…* the individual's *ingrafting into Christ*. In other words, baptism points to and ratifies our identification and union with Christ. Paul is alluding to this aspect of baptism when he says that the Jews who passed through the Red Sea "were all baptised unto Moses" (1 Cor 10:2). By this, he is saying that they were identified with Moses. In the same way when a believer is baptised, he is identified with Christ. But unlike the Jews' identification with Moses which is representative and external, the believer's identification with Christ in baptism is a vital, mystical, spiritual union. This is hinted by John the Baptiser when he said, "I indeed have baptised you with water: but he shall baptise you with the Holy Spirit" (Mk 1:8). Since our baptism with the Spirit unites us to Christ (cf. 1 Cor 12:13), our sacramental baptism points to that union. Thus, Paul says, "For as many of you as have been baptised into Christ have put on Christ" (Gal 3:27). It is on the account of this union that Paul says that believers are baptised into Christ's death (Rom 6:3). Christ represented us covenantally and spiritually in His death.[88] Indeed, the Westminster divines, moreover, astutely observe that it is also because of this union with Christ, that believers may participate in resurrection and everlasting life (see *WLC* 165; *WSC* 37; 1 Cor 15:29; Rom 6:5).

c. It serves as *a sign and seal... of regeneration*. In other words, it points to and ratifies the Word of God in the individual's heart. Note that the ratification of a seal speaks only of how the inward reality is *perceived*, and this perception is not necessarily in accord with what is actual. Simon Magus was said to believe (Act 8:13) and was baptised by Philip, but later when Peter arrived, Simon sought to purchase the power of the Holy Spirit and so proved himself to be yet in unbelief (Acts 8:18–23). Though ministers of the Word have the responsibility to screen baptismal candidates, there is no guarantee that all who are baptised are genuine. Indeed, it should be carefully noted that baptism is not a sign and seal of faith, but of inward grace or, in the words of Paul, "the righteousness of faith" (Rom 4:11). This is why ministers may

---

[88] Note that Paul is not saying that baptism symbolises Christ's death, as Baptists who insist on immersion would insist. Christ's death is symbolised by another sacrament, namely the Lord's Supper. Baptism represents our union with Christ, and immersion is no better than sprinkling or pouring, as a symbol for it.

baptise anyone base on credible profession, —since it is impossible for ministers to know for certain if inward grace has begun.

This is also one of the reasons why infants of believing parents may be baptised though they are incapable of believing. Infants in covenant families are covenantally holy (1 Cor 7:14). While we must not presume that they are all regenerate before they are able to understand the Gospel, we must also not swing to the other extreme to say that God must regenerate them only after they come to rational faith. In fact, the Scripture suggests that John the Baptiser was regenerated while he was in his mother's womb (Lk 1:15, 44). In fact, as baptism is the seal of the righteousness of faith, the church, without presuming regeneration, ought to treat baptised children as Christians and accord them the privileges of church membership.

d. It serves as *a sign and seal... of remission of sins*, i.e., cleansing or washing from sin. This is clearly seen in Ananias' instruction to Paul: "Arise, and be baptised, and wash away thy sins, calling on the name of the Lord" (Acts 22:16). Ananias, of course, must not be understood as telling Paul a theological fact that his sins are washed away when he is baptised, but that he should be baptised to symbolise the forgiveness of his sins, which had already occurred while he was on the road to Damascus. Washing from sin, or justification, is after all entirely by grace through faith (Rom 3:24).

e. It seals and ratifies one's *"giving up unto God through Jesus Christ, to walk in the newness of life."* Since the symbolism of washing in baptism lends itself to the idea of renewing what is old, Paul speaks also of "washing of regeneration" (Tit 3:5) and that we who are baptised "should walk in newness of life" even as "Christ was raised up from the dead" (Rom 6:4). In a sense every adult baptism carries with it an implicit vow that the candidate will seek to walk in newness of life. When baptised member of the church is tempted to stray away or to have doubts concerning his salvation, he should look back to his baptism and through the baptism, to Christ who called him. Every infant baptism also carries a vow on the part of the parents, especially the father: to "command his children ... [to] ... keep the way of the LORD, to do justice and judgement" (Gen 18:19); and to "bring them up in the nurture and admonition of the Lord" (Eph 6:4). So, when a father brings his child to be baptised, he is covenanting with the Lord not to allow the child to grow up like an unbeliever but as a covenant child.

f.   It is necessary *"for the solemn admission of the party baptised into the visible church."* In other words, it serves as a badge to ratify the membership of a professing believer in the visible Church. It is the divinely instituted rite to admit a credible professor of faith into the visible covenant community, namely the church (Acts 2:41; 1 Cor 12:13). But it may be asked: What if the person who is baptised is not born-again? Would he still be a member of the church? My answer is: Yes, unless and until his unregeneracy becomes so obvious that the church excommunicates him. But how can a church be called "the people of God" (Heb 4:9; see also 2 Cor 6:16) or "the body of Christ" (see 1 Cor 12) if there are unregenerate people within? The answer is to be found in the fact that God views His people covenantally and organically. This is why Israel of old was called God's people though a great majority of the people were unbelievers and unregenerate. This is why the whole nation of Israel could be represented by an olive tree in Romans 11, and why the unbelieving parts could be cut off. It is a tree covenantally and organically, which was pruned when the unbelieving parts excommunicated themselves by saying: "His blood be on us, and on our children" (Mt 27:25). And this is why Christ said: "I am the vine, ye are the branches: He that abideth in me, and I in him, the same bringeth forth much fruit: for without me ye can do nothing. If a man abide not in me, he is cast forth as a branch, and is withered; and men gather them, and cast them into the fire, and they are burned" (Jn 15:5–6). How can a branch that is in Christ (v. 2) ever be cast away when Christ said: "they shall never perish, neither shall any man pluck them out of my hand" (Jn 10:28)? The answer lies in the fact that Christ is referring to His external covenant people rather the redeemed or those who are mystically united to Him. This final function of baptism is to incorporate a person into the covenant community in this sense. Once he is baptised into the body, he is seen as being part of the external covenant community by God, and he is to be viewed by the rest in the church as a believer, unless his testimony testifies against him, in which case the church must excommunicate him before regarding him as an unbeliever. The situation is the same in the case of infants who are baptised into the church. For all intents and purposes, they are to be treated as believers, apart from participation in the ordinance that requires self-examination, namely the Lord's Supper. Thus, young covenant children, being treated as believers, are taught the catechism, how to pray and allowed to sing the songs of Zion. This does not mean that covenant infants must be presumed to be regenerate. No, they must still be exhorted to repent and believe and warned that if they disbelieve and live in sin that they will perish in their sin.

On the Manner of Baptism

28.2 The outward element to be used in this sacrament is water, wherewith the party is to be baptised, in the name of the Father, and of the Son, and of the Holy Ghost, by a minister of the Gospel, lawfully called thereunto.[1]

[1]*Mt 3:11; Jn 1:33; Mt 28:19–20.*

Three things are asserted in this paragraph:

a. The outward element to be used in baptism is to be water, not oil or red flag or anything else. In the Scripture, water is used to represent two things: (1) the Spirit of Christ: "Not by works of righteousness which we have done, but according to his mercy he saved us, by the washing of regeneration, and renewing of the Holy Ghost" (Tit 3:5; see also Jn 7:38); and (2) the blood of Christ: "And from Jesus Christ, who is the faithful witness, and the first begotten of the dead, and the prince of the kings of the earth. Unto him that loved us, and washed us from our sins in his own blood" (Rev 1:5).

As water washes the body of dirt, so the blood of Christ removes the guilt of sin and cleanses the defile conscience, while the Spirit of Christ purifies the soul from the pollution of sin.

b. Christian baptism is to be administered in the name of the Father, and of the Son and of the Holy Ghost (Mt 28:19). This means that we are baptised under the authority of the persons of the Triune Godhead, and that we are therefore identified with the worship and service of the blessed Trinity.

c. Baptism is to be administered by "*a minister of the Gospel, lawfully called thereunto.*" Just as the command to preach the Gospel was given to the disciples of Christ, they were also given the commission to baptise (Mt 28:19). No one else is given the command to baptise. This is why we do not find any case in the New Testament in which baptism is carried by anyone other than those called to preach. The reason behind this restriction, as we have mentioned, is that the sacraments are inextricably tied to the preaching of the Word. Without preaching, the rites of the sacrament become mere superstition (see also comments on *WCF* 27.4). Apart from this reason, it is the "the ministers of Christ" lawfully ordained who are the "stewards of the mysteries of God" (1 Cor 4:1; 1 Tim 4:14).

On the Mode of Baptism

28.3 Dipping of the person into the water is not necessary; but Baptism is rightly administered by pouring or sprinkling water upon the person.[1]

[1]Heb 9:10, 19–22; Acts 2:41; 16:33; Mk 7:4.

Note how carefully our *Confession* is worded so as not to deny that baptism may be lawfully performed by immersion, and yet suggesting that the proper mode is pouring or sprinkling water upon the person. Despite the insistence of our Baptist brethren, the word Greek word βαπτίζω (*baptizō*) does not actually mean "dip, immerse or plunge."

- *Firstly*, that while there are instances where βαπτίζω could *possibly* mean immersion. For example, the Septuagint translation of 2 Kings 5:14 uses βαπτίζω to translate the Hebrew טָבַל (*ṭâbal*) which usually mean 'dip' or 'plunge.' We say 'possibly' because βαπτίζω could be used to mean 'wash' here, especially when Elisha's instruction in verse 10 was to "wash in Jordon seven times."

- *Secondly*, there are instances where immersion is *unlikely* or *impossible*. Such is the case of the Septuagint of the apocrypha Judith 12:7, which suggests that Judith βαπτίζω herself in a fountain or spring.

- *Thirdly*, there are places in the inspired Scripture where βαπτίζω clearly *cannot* mean immersion. For example, in Luke 11:38— "And when the Pharisee saw it, he marvelled that he had not first washed [βαπτίζω] before dinner," surely the Pharisees did not expect Jesus to immerse Himself before dinner? Again Mark 7:4 speaks of 'baptisms' of tables or couches (Greek κλίνη, klinē). Surely these washings refer to ceremonial purifications, which are probably *done by* pouring or sprinkling.

- *Fourthly*, there are places where βαπτίζω carries no suggestion of mode, e.g., Matthew 20:22–23— "… Are ye able to drink of the cup that I shall drink of, and to be baptised with the baptism that I am baptised with?" Also, no one would translate Galatians 3:27 with "immersed into Christ."

- *Fifthly*, there are instances where βαπτίζω is auto-suggestive of pouring. For example, John the Baptiser compares water baptism with the Baptism of the Holy Spirit (Lk 3:16), and indeed, our water baptism points to our Spirit baptism. But according to Acts 2:4; 17–18, the Holy Spirit is poured out; we are not immersed in the Holy Spirit.

- *Sixthly*, in Hebrews 6:2, βαπτισμός (baptismos), literally 'baptism,' probably refers to the OT rites of sprinkling (cf. Heb 9:13 and Num 19:17–18: Heb 9:19 and Ex 24:6–8; Heb 9:21 and Lev 8:19).

- *Seventhly*, the verb βάπτω (baptō) which is commonly seen as the root word of βαπτίζω and almost consistently meaning 'dip' (e.g., Jn 13:26; Lk 16:24) is never used interchangeably with βαπτίζω in the Bible. Βαπτίζω always imply cleansing or purification, whereas βάπτω, never.

- *Eighthly*, whenever the object (e.g., liquid) involved in βαπτίζω is specified, it is always applied to the subject, not vice versa, as would be implied in immersion. This is seen in Matthew 3:11; Luke 3:16; Mark 1:8; John 1:26 and Acts 1:5. I believe the KJV translators, together with almost all modern translators, have correctly rendered the Greek preposition ἐν (*en*) in these verses as 'with' (instrumental) rather than 'in.'

The weight of evidence up to this point suggests very strongly that βαπτίζω and βαπτισμός do not imply immersion at all. Indeed, although the words themselves signify purification and cleansing more than anything else, the mode that they suggest is pouring or sprinkling. This is confirmed in the instances of baptism recorded in the New Testament, such as:

(1) The baptism of John. It is a common misconception that John Baptist baptised by immersion. This is not likely. John stood in the Jordan simply because it was the most convenient place to baptise the thousands who came to him (see Mt 3:5-6). John was a priest by descent as Zacharias was a priest (Lk 1:5). Surely the Jews coming for John's baptism of repentance would not have been expecting an innovative ritual. More likely, John was sprinkling water on those who came with a sweep of a sprig of hyssop as suggested by the OT: "Purge me with hyssop, and I shall be clean: wash me, and I shall be whiter than snow" (Ps 51:7) and "Then will I sprinkle clean water upon you, and ye shall be clean" (Ezk 36:25a). This must also have been the way in which the 3,000 could have been baptised in a day (Acts 2:41), in an event which, incidentally, took place in Jerusalem (Acts 2:5), more than 20 miles from any river which may be used for immersion for such a large crowd of people!

(2) The baptism of our Lord. There is also no evidence that Christ was baptised by immersion. Did He not come "up out of the water"? Yes, but that is no suggestion of immersion: (a) The phrase simply means stepping out of the river. Otherwise, Acts 8:39— "And when they [Philip and the Eunuch] were come up out of the water," would mean that Philip was himself

immersed when he baptised the Eunuch. (b) Christ, in fulfilling "all righteousness" (Mt 3:15), was probably referring to His priestly ordination which involves sprinkling (cf. Num 8:6–7). After all, it would be meaningless and fulfilling no righteousness for Him to have a "baptism of repentance for the remission of sins" (Mk 1:4, Lk 3:3) since He knew no sin. This also explains why He waited till He was 30 years old to begin His ministry (Lk 3:23), since the Old Testament priests were taken into the number and ordained only when they reach 30 (cf. Num 4:3, 23, 30, 35, 39, etc.).

(3) The baptism of the Ethiopian Eunuch. Again there is no evidence that he was baptised by immersion. They were in a desert. Philip must have explained to him about John baptising in the river so that when he saw some water (Acts 8:36), he asked to be baptised. Not only would a pool of water in the desert be unlikely to be sufficient for immersion, it is likely that Philip explained to him that baptism is by sprinkling. The Eunuch was reading Isaiah 53:7–8 (Acts 8:32–33). Surely he would have read Isa 52:15 — "So shall he sprinkle many nations; the kings shall shut their mouths at him: for that which had not been told them shall they see; and that which they had not heard shall they consider." These words are just a few verses up! And remember that there were no chapter divisions then.

(4) All other instances of baptism. When we examine all the other instances of baptism recorded, again we find that in most instances immersion is *impossible* or *improbable*. Saul "arose, and was baptised" (Acts 9:18) or, literally in the Greek: "and arising he was baptised." He did not go out to the river, nor do I think he "received meat" (v. 19) while dripping wet from immersion. The Philippian Jailer and his household were baptised in the middle of the night (Acts 16:33) in the outer prison (cf. vv. 24, 30). It is unlikely there was a tub of water sufficient for immersion there, nor is it likely that they went to a river in the dead of the night. There were no street lamps nor heated rivers! How much probable that Paul and Silas had

baptised them with the same basin used to wash their wounds, for we read: "And he took them the same hour of the night, and washed their stripes; and was baptised, he and all his, *straightway*" (Acts 16:33; italics added).

Our Baptist brethren may protest that these are circumstantial: Surely, Paul was pointing to immersion when he speaks of our being buried with Christ in baptism (Col 2:12)? We respond: Besides the fact that Christ was entombed in a rock cavity rather than buried in the ground (which immersion may picture), this text is not directly speaking about the act of water baptism, but about what baptism symbolises. Besides that, if we want to press the case, we find Paul speaking about the Jews being "baptised unto Moses" as they passed through the sea (1 Cor 10:1–2). The Jews were being sprinkled by the sprays of droplets from the wall of water to their left and to their right (Ex 14:22). The Jews were not immersed. The Egyptians were (v. 28).

On the Subject of Baptism

28.4 Not only those that do actually profess faith in and obedience unto Christ,[1] but also the infants of one or both believing parents are to be baptised.[2]

[1]Mk 16:15–16; Acts 8:37–38; [2]Gen 17:7, 9; Gal 3:9, 14; Col 2:11–12; Acts 2:38–39; Rom 4:11–12; 1 Cor 7:14; Mt 28:19; Mk 10:13–16; Lk 18:15.

It is clear that *"those that do actually profess faith in and obedience unto Christ"* should be baptised: "And he said unto them, Go ye into all the world, and preach the gospel to every creature. He that believeth and is baptised shall be saved; but he that believeth not shall be damned" (Mk 16:15–16); "And Philip said, If thou believest with all thine heart, thou mayest. And he answered and said, I believe that Jesus Christ is the Son of God. And he commanded the chariot to stand still: and they went down both into the water, both Philip and the eunuch; and he baptised him" (Acts 8:37–38).

Baptism of *"infants of one, or both, believing parents"* is however not as explicitly commanded in the Scripture, for which reason our Baptist brethren, in particular, object to the practice. The practice is, however, firmly biblical.

- *Firstly*, we have already seen that baptism is the New Testament is equivalent of circumcision in the Old Testament as the sign and seal of the Covenant of Grace. As infants were applied the sign and seal of the Covenant of Grace by circumcision though they understood not the significance of it, so in the New Testament, it is right that children may also be given the sign and seal of the Covenant of Grace by baptism. Thus, Peter proclaimed: "Repent, and be baptised every one of you in the name of Jesus Christ for the remission of sins, and ye shall receive the gift of the Holy Ghost. For the promise is unto you, and to your children, and to all that are afar off, even as many as the Lord our God shall call" (Acts 2:38–39).

  What about the fact that only baby boys were circumcised? Well, the New Testament not only give us the warrant to baptise girls and women as in the case Lydia's baptism, but Paul says: "For as many of you as have been baptised into Christ have put on Christ. There is neither Jew nor Greek, there is neither bond nor free, there is neither male nor female: for ye are all one in Christ Jesus. And if ye be Christ's, then are ye Abraham's seed, and heirs according to the promise" (Gal 3:27–29). Note that Paul was contrasting circumcision with baptism. What about the fact that babies were circumcised at 8 days old (Gen 17:12)? Well, apart from possible physiological reasons, the number 8, which is 7 + 1 is probably a symbolic number pointing to completion of the Old Covenant and beginning of the New Covenant when all bloody ordinances would be abrogated or replaced with bloodless ordinances.

- *Secondly*, infant baptism is founded on the fact that God views Christian families organically, so that when the head of household is a believer, then the whole family is regarded as being covenantally holy. This has always been the way that God views families. We see for example how God saved Noah and his family although only Noah is said to have found grace with the Lord (Gen 6:8–9). We see it in God's dealing with Abraham (Gen 17:7). An infant born into a covenant family under the Old Covenant was automatically part of the visible covenant community and was to be circumcised to ratify his membership and to signify to the rest of the community that he is a covenant child. The circumcision is not efficacious until the Lord circumcises the child's heart. But until then, he is considered part of the covenant community, externally, and he is to receive the benefits of being part of the community. Thus, he is instructed and taught the way of the Lord and called to worship with the covenant assembly.

In the New Testament, God continues to view the families organically and covenantally. Thus, we read of the Lord Jesus raising Jairus' daughter on account of her father's faith; raising the widow's dead son out of compassion for her; healing the epileptic boy because of his father's faith; and healing the son of an official of the city of Capernaum on account of his faith. This is why when the Lord came to stay with Zacchaeus, he said: "This day is salvation come to this house, forsomuch as he also is a son of Abraham" (Lk 19:9).

Peter in his Pentecostal sermon also suggests that when believers are engrafted into Christ, their children are subject to God's covenantal promises (Acts 2:38–39; cf. Gal 3:14–16, 29).

This principle is also confirmed in 1 Corinthians 7:14, where Paul argues that even the children of a family which has only one believing parent are relationally and covenantally holy, i.e., set apart to God together with the believing parent. But there is a problem: 1 Corinthians 7:14 indicates that the unbelieving spouse is also covenantally holy is it not? To be fair in our interpretation, should we not also baptise the unbelieving spouse? Well, I believe that if the spouse did not consciously object to the faith, he / she would also be baptised. In other words, the norm in those days would be household baptisms rather than individual baptisms, though an unbelieving and consciously objecting spouse certainly would not be forced to be baptised.

This fact is confirmed in the records of baptism in the books of Acts and 1 Corinthians. Several households (not just husband and wife) baptisms were recorded in these books: (1) the household of Lydia (Acts 16:15); (2) the household of the Philippian jailer (Acts 16:33); (3) the household of Stephanas (1 Cor 1:16); (4) almost certainly the household of Cornelius (Acts 10:24, 46, 48); and (5) the household of Crispus (Acts 18:8). The evidence suggests that it was the common practice in those days for whole families to be baptised. In the first century, where the head of the household had a very important place in the family and the society, it would have been an exception rather than the rule for anyone in a household to disagree with the head of the house. True, every adult would be responsible to repent and believe individually, but the family solidarity would be so strong in those days that if you read Acts alone, you will get the impression that whole households were baptised solely on account of the faith of the head of the household. Thus, no mention is made of the faith of the members in Lydia's household. And the Greek of Acts 16:34 tells us that it was the Philippian Jailer who believe. Note that the phrase "with all his house" is one word, πανοικί (panoiki) in the Greek, which suggests that they were represented by the Jailer. These records suggests that Luke had in mind that it is normal and correct for the whole family to be baptised on account of the faith of the head of household. Indeed, if Luke, had not intended to convey that idea, then he would be an ambiguous and misleading historian.

I believe, Luke, writing under inspiration, was accurately reflecting what was being practised in the church. And the basis of this practice is simply the unchanging doctrine of the covenant and organic family. This being the case, it would have been odd if whole families were baptised and included into the covenant community, but the young children were forbidden. It is no wonder that the church father Origen believed that the doctrine of Infant Baptism was passed down from the Apostles. Origen himself was baptised as an infant in A.D. 185.

The first century Christians probably did not have the same problem of understanding that we may have. Having their infants baptised was probably understood as a natural extension to the

Abrahamic covenant (especially for the Jews), or simply practised without question in view of the strong family solidarity of the age. In fact, to deny baptism for the children would probably have been more awkward for the first century believer than to include them. If infant baptism is forbidden, or unbiblical, the Apostles would probably have written against it. Thus, their relative silence speaks more loudly for the doctrine than against the doctrine.

On the Efficacy of Baptism

28.5 Although it be a great sin to contemn or neglect this ordinance,[1] yet grace and salvation are not so inseparably annexed unto it, as that no person can be regenerated or saved without it,[2] or that all that are baptised are undoubtedly regenerated.[3]

[1]Lk 7:30; Ex 4:24–26; [2]Rom 4:11; Acts 10:2, 4, 22, 31, 45, 47; [3]Acts 8:13, 23.

This section teaches us two important points of doctrine pertaining to baptism:

1. *"Grace and salvation are not so inseparably annexed unto it, as that no person can be regenerated or saved without it."* Although the sacramental union between ritual-baptism and real-baptism is taught and assumed in the Scriptures, so that there is not a clean dichotomy between the sign and the things signified, yet it is clear that they are not inextricably tied together so that no one can be regenerate without being baptised, as Rome teaches. This distinction between the ritual-baptism and real-baptism is clearly indicated in the Scripture:

   a. The Lord told Nicodemus: "Except a man be born again, he cannot see the kingdom of God" (Jn 3:3) and the Apostle Paul says: "For by grace are ye saved through faith; and that not of yourselves: it is the gift of God" (Eph 2:8). Even faith is a gift of God through regeneration, it is not the condition for salvation, how then can baptism be a condition?

   b. Abraham had righteousness of faith before he was circumcised (Rom 4:11).

c. Paul, writing to the Corinthians, says: "I thank God that I baptised none of you, but Crispus and Gaius" (1 Cor 1:14). If Paul believed in baptismal regeneration, it would be a very strange thing to say, for he would be thanking God that he was not instrumental in the salvation of any.

d. The penitent thief on cross did not have opportunity for baptism, and yet he was certainly saved, for the Lord said: "And Jesus said unto him, Verily I say unto thee, Today shalt thou be with me in paradise" (Lk 23:43).

e. On the other hand, Simon Magus was baptised, but he remained "in the gall of bitterness, and in the bond of iniquity" (Acts 8:13, 23).

2. However, it is "*a great sin to contemn or neglect this ordinance*." Notice that the way in which the Westminster divines phrase the paragraph shows that the contempt of the ordinance was not such a great problem in the 17th century as it is today.

The sentiments expressed in our *Confession* is well expressed by Robert Shaw: "Baptism is an instituted means of salvation, and the contempt of it must be a great sin on the part of the parents, though the neglect cannot be ascribed to the child before he arrives at maturity, and cannot, therefore, involve him in the guilt" (*Exposition of WCF*, 346). Shaw rightly emphasises the neglect of baptism for infants because few adult believers will neglect the ordinance, but is there a basis for his and our Confessional assertion that it is a "great sin to contemn or neglect this ordinance"? Yes, the basis is found in the 'proof-text' given in our *Confession*:

"And it came to pass by the way in the inn, that the LORD met him [Moses], and sought to kill him. Then Zipporah took a sharp stone, and cut off the foreskin of her son, and cast it at his feet, and said, Surely a bloody husband art thou to me. So he let him go: then she said, A bloody husband thou art, because of the circumcision" (Ex 4:24–26).

Moses, as a leader of the covenant people of God, had neglected the sign and seal of the covenant for his own children. It was a neglect so grievous the Lord sought to kill him. We live today in a dispensation of greater light and communication of the Holy Spirit; would not our neglect of duty be equally grievous?

What about our Baptist brethren and those who are yet to be persuaded of infant baptism? I believe that God is no respecter of persons (Acts 10:34), the importance of a sacrament is not diminished by personal inability to understand or accept the doctrine. However, recognising that we are all sinners saved by grace, we do not condemn our brethren, but urge them to study the issue with a mind open to the Scripture and we admonish them that they should consider that they will be guilty of neglect and contempt of God's ordinance if indeed the Scripture does require infants to be baptised, as we believe it does.

28.6 The efficacy of Baptism is not tied to that moment of time wherein it is administered;[1] yet, notwithstanding, by the right use of this ordinance, the grace promised is not only offered, but really exhibited and conferred by the Holy Ghost, to such (whether of age or infants) as that grace belongeth unto, according to the counsel of God's own will, in His appointed time.[2]

[1]Jn 3:5, 8; [2]Gal 3:27; Tit 3:5; Eph 5:25–26; Acts 2:38, 41.

We have already touch on this paragraph in our exposition of *WCF* 27.3, where we noted that baptism is a means by which the benefit of the covenant, namely regeneration is applied. We saw that the actual application is not dependant on the time of the baptism, i.e., it may be before or after. We reiterate again that this is not the same as the doctrine of baptismal regeneration, which teaches that salvation and grace is inextricably annexed to water baptism. But there is enough evidence in Scripture for us to confess that "the grace promised is not only offered, but really exhibited and *conferred* by the Holy Ghost" in baptism:

- Mark 16:16— "He that believeth and is baptised shall be saved; but he that believeth not shall be damned."

This verse not only show the greater priority of faith, but also baptism as the ordinary means of salvation.

- 1 Peter 3:21— "The like figure whereunto even baptism doth also now save us (not the putting away of the filth of the flesh, but the answer of a good conscience toward God,) by the resurrection of Jesus Christ."

This verse shows that salvation is dependent on inward grace, but nevertheless shows us that the ordinary means is baptism.

- Galatians 3:27— "For as many of you as have been baptised into Christ have put on Christ."

It is clear that Paul is talking about water baptism and what it symbolises. There is no evidence at all that Paul ever speak about baptism without a reference to water baptism.

- John 3:5— "Jesus answered, Verily, verily, I say unto thee, Except a man be born of water and of the Spirit, he cannot enter into the kingdom of God."

The meaning of the phrase "born of water" is greatly disputed, but it is taken by numerous theologians who believe in sovereign grace in salvation as referring to baptism.

Commenting on the phrase, the *Westminster Annotated Commentary of the Whole Bible*, purportedly written by some of the Westminster divines or their associates states:

> "Of baptism the sacrament of regeneration, which is the ordinary way into the Church and kingdom of God, though his grace be not tied to external means: and it is the contempt, not the privation of the sacrament which condemneth."[89]

John Owen, commenting on the verse remarks:

> "[Our Saviour] tells [Nicodemus] it [i.e. our regeneration] is wrought by 'water and the Spirit;' —by the Spirit, as the principal

---

[89] *See The Second Volume of Annotations Upon all the Books of the Old and New Testament &c*, reprinted as vol. 6 of 6 of the *Westminster Annotations & Commentary of the Whole Bible* (Edmunton: Still Water Revival Books, nd [1657]), np.

efficient cause; and by water, as the pledge, sign, and token of it, in the initial seal of the covenant..."[90]

Matthew Henry comments most judiciously:

"It is probable that Christ had an eye to the ordinance of baptism, which John had used and he himself had begun to use, 'You must be born again of the Spirit,' which regeneration by the Spirit should be signified by washing with water, as the visible sign of that spiritual grace: not that all they, and they only, that are baptised, are saved; but without that new birth which is wrought by the Spirit, and signified by baptism, none shall be looked upon as the *protected privileged* subjects of the *kingdom of heaven*."[91]

The doctrine taught in this paragraph may best be understood if we remember the statement in *WCF* 25.2 that out of the visible Church, "*there is no ordinary possibility of salvation.*" A person may be saved who is outside the visible church, but only in extraordinary circumstances. So we may say that a person may be saved without baptism, but only in extraordinary circumstances. We remember that a person is in the visible church by profession of faith, and a person born to believing parents is also a member of the visible church by extension of the Covenant of Grace. But a wilful neglect of baptism is equivalent to cutting a person off from the visible covenant community or the visible church, albeit passively.

On the Frequency of Baptism

28.7 The sacrament of Baptism is but once to be administered unto any person.[1]

[1]*Tit 3:5.*

Baptism may not be administered more than once to any person without holding the sacrament in contempt seeing that: (1) baptism

---

[90] John Owen, *The Works of John Owen*, edited by William H. Goold (Edingburgh: The Banner of Truth Trust, 1981 [1950-3]), 3.208.

[91] Matthew Henry, *Matthew Henry's Commentary on the Whole Bible: New Modern Edition* (Peabody: Hendrickson Publishers, 1991), 5.713b.

symbolises inward grace that once bestowed is not retracted; (2) baptism is not a necessary work unto salvation: "Not by works of righteousness which we have done, but according to his mercy he saved us, by the washing of regeneration, and renewing of the Holy Ghost" (Tit 3:5); and (3) the efficacy of baptism is "not tied to that moment of time wherein it is administered."

What about the case of a person baptised as an infant or adult in a Mormon church or a church that does not believe that God is Triune? I believe that his baptism would not be a valid baptism and he should seek to baptised in the name of the Triune God in a Christian Church.

What about in the case of the Roman Catholic church? Though we do not regard the Roman Catholic church as a true Church of God, yet, baptism in the Roman Catholic church is in the name of the Holy Trinity. Thus, Calvin spoke against the need for those who have been baptised in the Roman Catholic church to be baptised again:

"A sacrament must not be judged by the hand of the one by whom it is ministered, but as if it were from the very hand of God, from whom it doubtless has come. From this we may infer that nothing is added to it or taken from it by the worth of him by whose hand it is administered. Among men, if a letter is sent, provided the handwriting and seal are sufficiently recognised, it makes no difference who or of what sort the carrier is. In like manner, it ought to be enough for us to recognise the hand and seal of our Lord in His sacraments, whatever carrier may bring them. … when we teach what ought to be done in order that baptism may be pure and free from defilement, we do not abolish God's ordinance, however idolaters may corrupt it. For when in ancient times circumcision was corrupted by many superstitions, it did not cease nevertheless to be regarded as a symbol of grace" (*ICR* 4.15.16).

WCF 29: OF THE LORD'S SUPPER

The Lord's Supper is recognised in all mainstream Christian denominations as one of the most important ordinances of Christ, together with Baptism. And like baptism, it ought to be a symbol of unity in Christianity, "For we being many are one bread, and one body: for we are all partakers of that one bread" says the apostle Paul (1Cor 10:17). But sadly, sharply differing views of the Lord's Supper have made it one of the most divisive issues in visible Christendom. And the difference is not only between Rome and Protestantism!

Sometime after the Reformation begun, Luther and the Swiss Reformer Ulrich Zwingli decided to meet to discuss their rediscovered evangelical understanding. The meeting was convened at Marburg in 1529. When the two Reformed groups met, they soon discovered that they agreed on every point of doctrine except one—the Lord's Supper. Luther insisted that the bread of the sacrament was the body of Christ, and kept repeating the phrase *Hoc est corpus meum*, which is Latin for "This is my body." It is said that he wrote the words, using his gavel, so forcefully that it could be seen on the velvet cloth that covered the rostrum for a long time: *Hoc est corpus meum*! The result was that the Protestant movement failed to unite. Luther refused even to shake the hand of Zwingli, declaring him to be of a different spirit.

Today, most Lutherans continue to hold to Luther's view, while most others (including many who are professedly Calvinistic) tend to adopt the view which was supposedly held by Zwingli.

Our *Confession*, however, presents what may be known as the *Calvinistic View*, also known as the *Spiritual Presence View*, or as the Reformed theologian Keith Mathison puts it, the *Suprasubstantiation View*.

While acknowledging the doctrine surrounding the Lord's Supper is not easy to grasp or to prove from the Scripture, we would commend what is taught in this chapter of our *Confession* as the most biblically accurate, balanced and heart-warming of all creedal statements on the Supper.

On the Design of the Lord's Supper

29.1 Our Lord Jesus, in the night wherein He was betrayed, instituted the sacrament of His body and blood, called the Lord's Supper, to be observed in His Church, unto the end of the world, for [1] the perpetual remembrance of the sacrifice of Himself in His death; [2] the sealing all benefits thereof unto true believers, their spiritual nourishment and growth in Him, their further engagement in and to all duties which they owe unto Him; [3] and, to be a bond and pledge of their communion with Him, and with each other, as members of His mystical body.[1]

[1] *1 Cor 11:23–26; 10:16–17, 21; 12:13.*

a. When was it instituted?

"The same night in which He was betrayed" (1Cor 11:23).

b. How long should it be practised in the Church?

"Till He come" (1Cor 11:26).

c. Purpose of the Sacrament:

i. "*For the perpetual remembrance of the sacrifice of Himself in His death*" I.e. as a *sign* pointing to the Lord's death ("shew the Lord's death"—1Cor 11:26). A sign is a visible representation that points to something we cannot see. The words of the institution "broken for you" (1Cor 11:24) and "shed for many" (Mt 26:28) point to the fact that the death of Christ was a sacrificial one. Christ died for and in place of His people. It also symbolises the believer's participation in the crucified Christ.

ii. For "*the sealing of all benefits thereof unto true believers, their spiritual nourishment and growth in Him, their further engagement in and to all duties which they owe unto Him.*" A seal is something to attest, confirm or certify the genuiness of the benefits that believers receive from Christ. As a seal, the Lord's Supper not only points to, but affirms the genuiness of the application of the benefits of redemption to the participants. This is partly the reason why a person eats and drinks judgement at the Lord's Table if he does not believe. In such a case he uses an official seal when he has no right to use it. And conversely he who partakes of the Supper with faith, "eats the flesh of the Son of Man, and drink His blood" (Jn 6:53); that is, he sacramentally appropriates the benefits secured by the sacrificial death of Christ.

iii. *"To be a bond and pledge of their communion with Him, and with each other, as members of His mystical body."* A *bond* is the friendship shared by two or more parties. In sharing a meal at the Lord's Table, believers signify their union with Christ and with one another. As members of the same mystical body of Jesus Christ, we eat of the same bread and drink of the same wine: "The cup of blessing which we bless, is it not the communion of the blood of Christ? The bread which we break, is it not the communion of the body of Christ? For we being many are one bread, and one body: for we are all partakers of that one bread" (1 Cor 10:16-17; cf.12:13). Receiving the elements, the one from the other, we exercise intimate communion with one another.

A pledge is a token which points to a promise. As such it gives the believing partakers the personal assurance that all the promises of the covenant and all the riches of Christ are in their actual possession. Reciprocally, it serves as a badge of profession on the part of those who partake the sacrament. Whenever they eat the bread or drink the wine, they: (1) Profess their faith in Christ as their Saviour; (2) Confess their allegiance to Him as their King; (3) Solemnly pledge a life of obedience to His divine commandments; and (4) Testify of their desire to participate in each other's life in the communion of saints.

On What the Lord's Supper is Not:

29.2 In this sacrament, Christ is not offered up to His Father; nor any real sacrifice made at all, for remission of sins of the quick or dead;[1] but only a commemoration of that one offering up of Himself, by Himself, upon the cross, once for all: and a spiritual oblation of all possible praise unto God, for the same:[2] so that the popish sacrifice of the mass (as they call it) is most abominably injurious to Christ's one, only sacrifice, the alone propitiation for all the sins of His elect.[3]

[1] Heb 9:22, 25–26, 28; [2] 1 Cor 11:24–26; Mt 26:26–27; [3] Heb 7:23–24, 27; 10:11–12, 14, 18.

This paragraph is designed to refute the Romish doctrine that the Lord Supper, which they call Mass involves a sacrifice of Christ again. According to them, each time the Mass is celebrated, Christ is sacrificed again. This cannot be true since that author of Hebrews is emphatic that "Christ was once offered to bear the sins of many" (Heb 9:28); and that Christ "needeth not daily, as those high priests, to offer up sacrifice, first for His own sins, and then for the people's: for this He did once, when He offered up Himself… For by one offering He hath perfected for ever them that are sanctified." (Heb 7:27, 10:14). The Romish Mass, which is an imitation of the Old Covenant shadows, is therefore "*most abominably injurious to Christ's one, only sacrifice, the alone propitiation for all the sins of His elect.*"

On the Conduct of the Lord's Supper:

29.3 The Lord Jesus hath, in this ordinance, appointed His ministers to declare His word of institution to the people; to pray, and bless the elements of bread and wine, and thereby to set them apart from a common to an holy use; and to take and break the bread, to take the cup, and (they communicating also themselves) to give both to the communicants;[1] *but to none who are not then present in the congregation.*[2]

[1] Mt 26:26–28; Mk 14:22–24; Lk 22:19–20; 1 Cor 11:23–26; [2] Acts 20:7; 1 Cor 11:20.

The Lord's Supper must be conducted in an orderly manner (1Cor 14:40—"Let all things be done decently and in order"). This paragraph teaches us that it must have the following steps:

a. Word of institution, Prayer & Blessing.

    In all four accounts of the institution of the Lord's Supper, the Lord Jesus is said to have blessed (Mt 26:26; Mk 14:22) or given thanks for (Lk 22:17, 19; 1Cor 11:24) the bread and wine before breaking the bread and handling out the wine.

We believe therefore that the minister administering the Lord's Supper should set apart the bread and wine from common use by the word of institution, thanksgiving and prayer (cf. *WLC* 169). The bread and wine in themselves, or as found in common use are not symbols of the body and blood of Christ until they are 'blessed' or set-aside.

b. Breaking of Bread.

"And when He had given thanks, He brake it, and said, Take, eat; this is my body which is broken for you: this do in remembrance of Me" (1 Cor 11:24; cf. Mk 13:22; Mt 26:26).

All the accounts of the institution of the Lord's Supper makes mention of the breaking of the bread, and the Lord Jesus clearly indicates that this was intended to symbolise the breaking of His body for the redemption of sinners. Also, as the Lord broke the bread in the presence of His disciples it should be insisted that the bread be broken in the sight of the congregation. This is also in accordance with the Lord's command recorded in 1 Corinthians 11:24: "this *do* in remembrance of me." This action of breaking the bread is so essential and integral to the sacrament that in Acts 2:42, the Lord's Supper is known as "breaking of bread." The Roman Catholic practice of using the wafer, which is placed unbroken in the mouth of the communicant is therefore unscriptural. The minister should, rather, break the bread before the congregation to symbolise that His body is broken for them.

c. Handing out of the Cup.

"And He took the cup, and gave thanks, and gave it to them, saying, Drink ye all of it; For this is my blood of the new testament, which is shed for many for the remission of sins" (Mt 26:27-28).

None of the four accounts of the institution speaks about the Lord pouring out the wine. Therefore, we infer that pouring of the wine is not part of the ordinance.

Note that it is clear from the accounts that the Lord intended both elements to be used in the sacrament: "For as often as ye eat this bread AND drink this cup, ye do show the Lord's death till He comes" (1 Cor 11:26).

Note also that the reference to the "cup" is really a metonymy for the wine contained. To see how this is the case we need only to note how we do not really drink the cup. For this reason, having multiple cups or even individual disposable "cuplets" instead of a single cup is neither biblically nor confessionally unacceptable.

29.4   Private masses, or receiving this sacrament by a priest, or any other, alone;[1] as likewise, the denial of the cup to the people,[2] worshipping the elements, the lifting them up, or carrying them about, for adoration, and the reserving them for any pretended religious use; are all contrary to the nature of this sacrament, and to the institution of Christ.[3]

[1] 1 Cor 10:16; [2] Mk 14:23; 1 Cor 11:25–29; [3] Mt 15:9.

This paragraph is essentially targeted against the superstitions of the Roman Catholic Church.

- *Firstly*, since the Lord's Supper is a corporate communion of the body and blood of Christ (cf. 1 Cor 10:16), private masses in which, for example, a minister goes to a hospital to dispense the element to a sick man privately is an act superstition. This, nevertheless, does not rule out having worship which includes the Lord's Supper in the home of a person who is indisposed to come for public worship. Such a service should only be conducted if at least a part of the congregation is present.

- *Secondly*, private receiving of the sacraments, such as by a priest in the Roman Catholic Church is meaningless and superstitious.

- *Thirdly*, the Roman Catholic practice of withholding the wine from the communicants is unscriptural.

- *Fourthly*, all adoration and worship of the elements is idolatrous since the Scripture allows no room for any degree of venerating the elements.

- *Fifthly,* the bread and wine that are left over from a Lord's Supper do not retain any magical or spiritual properties.

On the Four Views Pertaining to the Lord's Supper

29.5 The outward elements in this sacrament, duly set apart to the uses ordained by Christ, have such relation to Him crucified, as that, truly, yet sacramentally only, they are sometimes called by the name of the things they represent, to wit, the body and blood of Christ;[1] albeit, in substance and nature, they still remain truly and only bread and wine, as they were before.[2]

[1] Mt 26:26–28; [2] 1 Cor 11:26–28; Mt 26:29.

29.6 That doctrine which maintains a change of the substance of bread and wine, into the substance of Christ's body and blood (commonly called transubstantiation) by consecration of a priest, or by any other way, is repugnant, not to Scripture alone, but even to common sense, and reason; overthroweth the nature of the sacrament, and hath been, and is, the cause of manifold superstitions; yea, of gross idolatries.[1]

[1] Acts 3:21; 1 Cor 11:24–26; Lk 24:6, 39.

When Christ instituted the Lord's Supper, He referred to the elements as His body and blood although by nature, they remained bread and wine. This is so because there is an intimate sacramental union between the signs and the things signified.

The Roman Catholic Church fails to see that this as the reason, and so invented the repugnant idea of transubstantiation in which bread is miraculously transformed into the real flesh of Christ, and the wine is miraculously transformed into His blood. It is repugnant to morality since the eating of the wafer in the mass would be cannibalism if the doctrine were true. It is contrary to reason since the physical body of Christ cannot be in heaven and on earth at the same time. It is repugnant to our senses because the bread and wine still look and taste like wine without any alteration at all after the blessing.

We note that in the Bible, there is actually a case of transubstantiation: when the Lord Jesus changed the water into wine (Jn 2:1-11). But in that case the wine tasted like wine. The guests who drank it even thought that it was the best wine they had tasted all evening. Not so in the alleged transubstantiation in the Roman Mass.

29.7 Worthy receivers, outwardly partaking of the visible elements, in this sacrament,[1] do then also, inwardly by faith, really and indeed, yet not carnally and corporally but spiritually, receive and feed upon, Christ crucified, and all benefits of His death: the body and blood of Christ being then, not corporally or carnally, in, with, or under the bread and wine; yet, as really, but spiritually, present to the faith of believers in that ordinance, as the elements themselves are to their outward senses.[2]

[1] 1 Cor 11:28; [2] 1 Cor 10:16.

- This paragraph, while mainly speaking about the efficacy of the Lord's Supper, also speaks against the Lutheran view of consubstantiation. This is seen in the phrase: "the body and blood of Christ being then, not corporally or carnally, *in, with, or under the bread and wine.*" At the time of the Reformation, Martin Luther rejected the Romish doctrine of transubstantiation, and taught that instead of replacing the bread and the wine, Christ's presence is *added* to the bread and wine. He maintained that the body and blood of Christ are somehow present in, under, and through the elements of bread and wine. This view may be known as *consubstantiation*. This view, while more logical than the Romish view, is nevertheless problematic. For one, how could the flesh and blood of Christ be in and under the elements when his human nature remains in heaven.

- On the opposite extreme, there is yet another view of the Lord's Supper, which appears to have been held by Zwingli and the Anabaptists. In this view, the Lord's Supper is seen to be purely *commemorative* and symbolic. Any benefits derived from partaking it arise only through outward moral suasion.

- The view taught in our *Confession* may be known as the *Spiritual Presence* View or John Calvin's View.

Calvin denied the "substantial" presence of Christ at the Lord's Supper when he debated with Rome or the Lutherans. Yet when he debated with the Anabaptists, who, like Zwingli reduced the Lord's Supper to a mere memorial, he insisted on the "substantial" presence of Christ.

On the surface it seems that Calvin was caught in a blatant contradiction. However, upon closer scrutiny we see that Calvin used the term *substantial* in two different ways. When he addressed Catholics and Lutherans, he used the term *substantial* to mean "physical." He denied the physical presence of Christ in the Lord's Supper. When he addressed the Anabaptists, however, he used the term *substantial* in the sense of "real." Calvin thus argued that Christ was *really* or *truly* present in the Lord's Supper, though not in a physical sense. The human nature of Jesus is presently localised in heaven. It remains in perfect union with His divine nature. Though the human nature is contained in one place, the *person* of Christ is not so contained because His divine nature (which is hypostatically united to His human nature) is omnipresence. This is why the Lord could say, "I am with you always, even to the end of the age" (Mt 28:20).

Calvin taught that though Christ's body and blood remain in heaven, they are spiritually "made present" to us by the power of the Holy Spirit. When the Lord's Supper is participated in faith, the Holy Spirit presents to us and feeds us with the flesh and blood of the ascended Christ. This is how we are to understand 1Corinthians 10:16. The Lord's Supper is a mystical communion with Christ in which "from the substance of His flesh, Christ breathes life into our souls— indeed, pours forth His very life unto us—even though Christ's flesh itself does not enter into us."[92] Herein is the difference between the Calvinistic view of the Lord's Supper which the Reformed Church has accepted and the Zwinglian memorial view. And it is in this way that the believer "*spiritually receive and feed upon, Christ crucified, and all benefits of His death: the body and blood of Christ being ...*

---

[92] *ICR* 4.17.32.

spiritually, present to the faith of believers in that ordinance, as the elements themselves are to their outward senses."

It is difficult to find a good analogy for the Spiritual Presence View. But Mathison has suggested that certain elements of the View may be roughly illustrated using the concept of electricity. He says:

"Calvin himself speaks of the human nature of Christ and the Holy Spirit as 'conduits' of divine life, so the analogy may not be too far afield.

If we approach Calvin's thought using this analogy, we may say that the body of Christ, which is locally present in heaven, is analogous to the power plant or electrical generator. God is analogous to the source that powers the generator. The divine life of God is analogous to the electricity. The Holy Spirit is analogous to the power lines that transmit the electricity and connect the power plant to millions of individual homes, while the sacramental signs are analogous to the individual light switches in those homes. The individual communicants in the church are analogous to the millions of light bulbs that receive the electricity from the plant, the individual communicant's faith (or lack thereof) is analogous to the filament in the light bulb (either broken or whole).

Obviously, the illustration is not perfect because all analogies breakdown, and it should not be pushed, but it does communicate a few of the main ideas of Calvin's doctrine in a way that is more easily grasped. God is the ultimate source of divine life. The Incarnation makes it possible for that divine life to be communicated to the human nature of Christ. Christ's human body is now in heaven and physically separated from us, but by the power of the Holy Spirit we have been united to Christ. By virtue of this union, we are able to partake of the divine life of Christ that is found in his body. We participate in ongoing union with Christ particularly in the sacrament of the Lord's Supper. However, unless we partake of the sacrament in faith, we receive nothing but the visible sign and judgement from God. Our faith or lack thereof does not change or affect the objective nature of the sacrament in any way."[93]

On the Fencing of the Table

29.8 Although ignorant and wicked men receive the outward elements in this sacrament; yet, they receive not the thing signified thereby; but, by their unworthy coming thereunto, are guilty of the body and blood of the Lord, to their own damnation. Wherefore, all ignorant and ungodly persons, as they are unfit to enjoy communion with Him, so are they unworthy of the Lord's table; and cannot, without great sin against Christ, while they remain such, partake of these holy mysteries,[1] or be admitted thereunto.[2]

[1] *1 Cor 11:27–29; 2 Cor 6:14–16;* [2] *1 Cor 5:6–7, 13; 2 Th 3:6, 14–15; Mt 7:6.*

a. Because believers "*receive and feed upon, Christ crucified, and all benefits of His death*" (*WCF* 29.7) by faith, it is clear that "all ignorant and ungodly persons" receives no spiritual blessing when they partake of the elements of the Supper. And not only that, but the Scripture and our *Confession* teach us that such a person will be "guilty of the body and blood of the Lord, to their own damnation" (cf. 1 Cor 11:29). Calvin explains that the Lord's Supper, which is spiritual food for those who partake it by faith, "[turns] into a deadly poison for all those whose faith it does not nourish and strengthen, and whom it does not arouse to thanksgiving and to love."[94]

b. Nevertheless, doesn't 1 Corinthians 11:27-29 teach us that the responsibility of examination is only on the individual partakers themselves? Why does our *Confession* teach us that ignorant and ungodly persons must not be admitted to the Lord's Table?

The answer is multi-fold.

---

[93] Keith A. Mathison, *Given For You: Reclaiming Calvin's Doctrine of the Lord's Supper* (Phillipsburg: Presbyterian & Reformed Publishing, 2002), 285-6.

[94] *ICR* 4.17.40.

- *Firstly*, allowing such a person to partake of the Supper would be to allow him to incur great damnation on himself knowingly.

- *Secondly*, the apostle Paul teaches us a church, though having many members is, in the eyes of the Lord, one body (1 Cor 12:12). As such, the actions of an individual in a church has corporate implications for the church as a whole. This is particularly so in the Lord's Supper. Referring to the Lord's Supper, the Apostle Paul insists, "The cup of blessing which we bless, is it not the communion of the blood of Christ? The bread which we break, is it not the communion of the body of Christ? For we being many are one bread, and one body: for we are all partakers of that one bread" (1 Cor 10:16-17). Clearly then, the Lord's Supper is not to understood as an individual exercise but a corporate exercise of the body of Christ.

- *Thirdly*, Paul teaches us that "if any man that is called a brother be a fornicator, or covetous, or an idolater, or a railer, or a drunkard, or an extortioner; with such an one no not to eat" (1 Cor 5:11). It is possible that Paul is saying that we must not even share a meal in private with such as person. But if that be the case, then, shouldn't this injunction be taken even more seriously with regards to participation in the Lord's Supper which is a corporate exercise?

- *Fourthly*, Christ preached the gospel to all without distinction, but He did not administer the sacraments to all. When he instituted and administered the Lord Supper, it was only to His disciples.

- *Fifthly*, as the Lord's Supper is same in substance with the Old Testament Passover, it would appears that the same restrictions that applied to the Passover would also apply to the Lord's Supper (see Ex 12:42-44 and Ezr 6:21). As the Passover were only to be eaten by those who have been circumcised, the Lord's Supper is only to be partaken by those who have been baptised. It is possible that a baptised person may not be true believer. Therefore, it becomes the solemn responsibility of the church to baptise only credible professors of faith (in the case of adults). It also becomes the church's responsibility to bar anyone who does not have a credible profession of faith (including covenant children) from the Lord's Table.

For these reasons, it is the practice of most confessional Reformed denominations, that if someone from another church wishes to participate in their communion service, then the person would be examined to see if he gives evidence of walking in obedience to the Word of God as a credible professor of faith.

WCF 30: OF CHURCH CENSURES

The exercise of church discipline is perhaps the most painful of all the duties that elders in the church are called to perform. And to add to the woes of faithful elders, most modern churches simply do not practice church discipline. Churches that do are branded as authoritarian or cultish; and those who are disciplined would often simply leave the church for others, which would gladly receive them. This sad situation flies in the face the fact that faithful church discipline is one the three marks of a true church as given in the *Belgic Confession of Faith* (*BCF* 29); hinted in our own *Confession* (*WCF* 25.3) and agreed by most conservative Reformed churches. In other words, churches that fail to exercise church discipline have either ceased to be true churches of Christ, or are apostatising. This is so, for local congregations are manifestations of the body of Christ. As such, churches that fail to exercise faithful church discipline are destroying the testimony of Christ and blaspheming His name by allowing scandals to be attributed to His name.

Our present study is therefore an extremely important one.

On the Divine Right of Church Government

30.1   The Lord Jesus, as King and Head of His Church, hath therein appointed a government, in the hand of Church officers, distinct from the civil magistrate.[1]

[1] *Isa 9:6–7; 1 Tim 5:17; 1 Th 5:12; Acts 20:17–18; Heb 13:7, 17, 24; 1 Cor 12:28; Mt 28:18–20.*

- There are two public structures of authority revealed in the New Testament: Civil government and Church government. We saw the institution of the Civil government in chapter 23. In the present paragraph, we see that Christ, as the King and Head of the Church (Isa 9:6–7), has appointed a church government with church officers, as distinct from the civil magistrate, *contra* Erastianism. The Scripture refers to these officers as 'elders': "Let the elders that rule well be counted worthy of double honour, especially they who labour in the word and doctrine" (1 Tim 5:17; cf. 1 Th 5:12; Acts 20:17, 28; etc.).

- The form of Church government must be in accordance to what is taught in the Scriptures, for the Lord told His disciples to teach those they evangelised "to observe all things whatsoever I have commanded you" (Mt 28:20). There are essentially four forms of Church government in practice today:

  a. *Papacy,* which teaches that the Pope is the successor of Peter, the vice-regent of Christ, and is the visible head of the whole church. Under the Pope are bishops who derive their authority from him.

  b. *Episcopacy*, which does not have a Pope, but nevertheless sees a distinction in rank among the ministers in the church. Authority is vested on bishops, archbishops, etc.

  c. *Independency* or *congregationalism*, which asserts that every congregation forms a complete church and has an independent power of jurisdiction within itself, and therefore lodges the authority of church government with the congregation.

  d. *Presbyterianism*, which unlike episcopacy maintains that every minister of the Gospel is on a level in respect of office and authority. Presbyterianism also teaches that a particular congregation may be ruled by a Session comprising all teaching and ruling elders in the church. But this church and Session are only part of a larger body of believers; and representative elders from the church may sit in a higher court known as Presbytery which has jurisdiction over all the churches represented. Again, members of the Presbytery may sit in the synod, which has authority over the Presbyteries represented. Thus, Presbyterianism teaches that there is a subordination of courts and that the higher courts may review, affirm or reverse the decisions of the lower courts.

- Though our *Confession* does not explicitly name the system that is favoured, it is clear that the Assembly had in mind Presbyterianism. This can be seen not only in the next chapter, but in the document entitled, *The Form of Presbyterial Church-*

Government and of Ordination of Minister, which was written as an annex to the *Confession*.

30.2   To these officers the keys of the kingdom of heaven are committed; by virtue whereof, they have power, respectively, to retain, and remit sins; to shut that kingdom against the impenitent, both by the Word, and censures; and to open it unto penitent sinners, by the ministry of the Gospel; and by absolution from censures, as occasion shall require.[1]

[1] *Mt 16:19; 18:17–18; Jn 20:21–23; 2 Cor 2:6–8.*

• The Lord told Peter on one occasion:

> "And I will give unto thee the keys of the kingdom of heaven: and whatsoever thou shalt bind on earth shall be bound in heaven: and whatsoever thou shalt loose on earth shall be loosed in heaven" (Mt 16:19).

That He was referring to the power of church discipline is clear from the fact that the same idea is repeated in another context which is clearly about how to deal with an erring yet unrepentant brother:

> "And if he shall neglect to hear them, tell it unto the church: but if he neglects to hear the church, let him be unto thee as an heathen man and a publican. Verily I say unto you, Whatsoever ye shall bind on earth shall be bound in heaven: and whatsoever ye shall loose on earth shall be loosed in heaven" (Mt 18:17–18).

This authority is restated in another way after the resurrection of the Lord:

> "Whose soever sins ye remit, they are remitted unto them; and whose soever sins ye retain, they are retained" (Jn 20:23).

• From the latter two passages, it is clear that the authority is not just vested on Peter, but on the other Apostles, and on the permanent officers of the church, namely the elders who represent particular congregations.

- But what does 'binding' and 'loosing' (of persons) or 'retaining' and 'remitting' sin as reflected in our *Confession* mean?

  a. It must be noted that the phrase "kingdom of heaven" or "kingdom of God" is used in three senses in the Scripture, namely:

     (i) Christ's mediatorial authority, or its administration, and the power and glory which belong to it, as when we ascribe to Him the "kingdom, and the power, and the glory" (Mt 6:13), or affirm that of "his kingdom there shall be no end" (Lk 1:33)

     (ii) The blessings and advantages of all kinds, inward and outward, which are characteristic of this administration, as when we say the "kingdom... is... righteousness, and peace, and joy in the Holy Ghost" (Rom 14:17)

     (iii) The subjects of the kingdom collectively, as when we are said to "enter... the kingdom," and speak of "the keys of the kingdom," which admit to or exclude from this community. In this latter sense the phrase "kingdom of God," or "of heaven," is synonymous with the word 'Church'.[95]

     It is in the third sense that Matthew 16:19 and our *Confession* speaks of the "kingdom of heaven." Moreover, the phrase "whatsoever thou shalt bind *on earth*" suggests that the power to bind and loose or to receive or expel from membership has to do with the visible church, which is the kingdom of God on earth.

  b. Thus, it is clear that the power to "retain, and remit sins" is *declarative* rather than *absolute*. This is consistent with the fact that only God can forgive sin absolutely (Lk 5:21). Thus, our *Confession* tells us that the officers of the church have power "*to shut that kingdom against the impenitent, both by the Word, and censures; and to open it unto penitent sinners, by*

---

[95] See A.A. Hodge, *Outline of Bible Topics*, chap. 27.

the ministry of the Gospel; and by absolution [i.e., exoneration or vindication] from censures, as occasion shall require."

In other words, the officers of the church (i.e., elders), are responsible to ensure discipline and purity in the church, and when Church discipline is carefully carried out, then, no manifestly unregenerate, unjustified person would be found in the kingdom of God on earth, which explains why out of the visible Church of Christ, "*there is no ordinary possibility of salvation*" (*WCF* 25.2). But since the members of the visible church are not confirmed in righteousness or sin, there is possibility of repentance on the part of those who are censured, and indeed repentance should be the aim of every church censure. And when a person repents, then the officers of the church have the power and duty to absolve the censure and to receive the erring brother back into fellowship (cf. 2 Cor 2:6–8).

On the Necessity of Church Discipline

30.3   Church censures are necessary, for the reclaiming and gaining of offending brethren, for deterring of others from the like offenses, for purging out of that leaven which might infect the whole lump, for vindicating the honour of Christ, and the holy profession of the Gospel, and for preventing the wrath of God, which might justly fall upon the Church, if they should suffer His covenant, and the seals thereof, to be profaned by notorious and obstinate offenders.[1]

[1] *1 Cor 5; 1 Tim 5:20; Mt 7:6; 1 Tim 1:20; 1 Cor 11:27–34; Jude 23.*

This paragraph outlines the purposes and importance of Church Discipline, namely:

a. "*For the reclaiming and gaining of offending brethren*"—"Of whom is Hymenæus and Alexander; whom I have delivered unto Satan, *that they may learn not to blaspheme*" (1 Tim 1:20); "To deliver such an one unto Satan for the destruction of the flesh, *that the spirit may be saved in the day of the Lord Jesus*" (1 Cor 5:5).

b. *"For deterring of others from the like offences"*—"Them that sin rebuke before all, *that others also may fear*" (1 Tim 5:20).

c. *"For purging out of that leaven which might infect the whole lump"*—"Purge out therefore the old leaven, *that ye may be a new lump, as ye are unleavened*. For even Christ our passover is sacrificed for us" (1 Cor 5:7).

d. *"For vindicating the honour of Christ, and the holy profession of the Gospel."* Sin when allowed in the church greatly dishonours and blasphemes the name of Christ. Thus, Paul indicts the Jews (members of the church under the old covenant) for their bad testimonies, "For the name of God is blasphemed among the Gentiles through you" (Rom 2:24). Thus, Hymenæus and Alexander were "delivered unto Satan, *that they may learn not to blaspheme*" (1 Tim 1:20).

e. *"For preventing the wrath of God, which might justly fall on the Church."* This is with specific reference to the use of the Sacrament: *"if they should suffer His covenant, and the seals thereof, to be profaned by notorious and obstinate offenders."* The apostle Paul, in particular, speaks about how the Lord visits a church in wrath when sin is tolerated:

> "For he that eateth and drinketh unworthily, eateth and drinketh damnation to himself, not discerning the Lord's body. For this cause many are weak and sickly among you, and many sleep. For if we would judge ourselves, we should not be judged. But when we are judged, we are chastened of the Lord, that we should not be condemned with the world" (1 Cor 11:29–32).

On the Steps for Church Discipline

30.4   For the better attaining of these ends, the officers of the Church are to proceed by admonition, suspension from the sacrament of the Lord's Supper for a season; and by excommunication from the Church, according to the nature of the crime, and demerit of the person.[1]

[1] *1 Th 5:12; 2 Th 3:6, 14–15; 1 Cor 5:4–5, 13; Mt 18:17; Tit. 3:10.*

- When our Lord teaches about church discipline, He begins right from the inception of an offence, and proceeds in four steps to the point of excommunication:

"Moreover if thy brother shall trespass against thee,

[1] go and tell him his fault between thee and him alone: if he shall hear thee, thou hast gained thy brother.

[2] But if he will not hear thee, then take with thee one or two more, that in the mouth of two or three witnesses every word may be established.

[3] And if he shall neglect to hear them, tell it unto the church:

[4] but if he neglects to hear the church, let him be unto thee as an heathen man and a publican"

(Mt 18:15–17).

Notice that it is only in the third step, that what might have been a private dispute or a private observation of sin becomes an ecclesiastical matter to be dealt with by the church.

- Our *Confession* begins with this third step and suggests three possible actions, —"*according to the nature of the crime, and demerit of the person*,"—to take in censuring an erring brother:

  a. *Admonition*—"Now we command you, brethren, in the name of our Lord Jesus Christ, that ye withdraw yourselves from every brother that walketh disorderly, and not after the tradition which he received of us.... And if any man obey not our word by this epistle, note that man, and have no company with him, that he may be ashamed. *Yet count him not as an enemy, but admonish him as a brother*" (2 Th 3:6, 14–15).

  b. *Suspension* from the Lord's Supper for a season. This is often known as lesser excommunication, or if you like, the "second admonition" (Tit 3:10). If the brother demonstrates genuine repentance after the period of suspension, he may be restored to the full privileges of church membership.

c. *Excommunication*—this is known as greater excommunication and involves declaring the offending party to be an unbeliever ("let him be unto thee as a heathen man and a publican") and delivering "unto Satan for the destruction of the flesh, that the spirit may be saved in the day of the Lord Jesus" (1 Cor 5:5). This does not consist, as Rome erroneously teaches, in literally handling over the soul unto the devil, but in casting him out of the Church into Satan's kingdom, i.e., the world, by revoking his membership.

WCF 31: OF SYNODS AND COUNCILS

As mentioned in our comments on the previous chapter, our *Confession* does not clearly state what form of Government is to be considered legitimate. The Westminster Assembly, however, also produced a document known as *The Form of Presbyterial Church Government*. In this document, it is declared:

> It is lawful and agreeable to the Word of God, that the Church be governed by several sorts of assemblies, which are congregational, classical and synodical (s.v., "Of Church-Government, and the several sort of Assemblies for the Same").

The relationship between the three levels of governing assemblies may be pictured as follows:

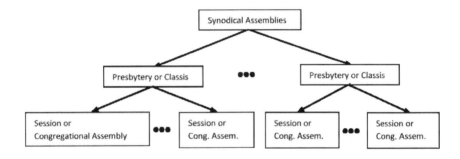

It is the conviction that individual church Sessions should come under the oversight of Presbyteries or classes (comprising of representative ministers and elders from the Sessions) that distinguishes Presbyterian churches from a Congregational or Independent churches.

The biblical basis for this conviction is laid down in *The Form of Presbyterial Church Government* (s.v. "Of Classical Assemblies"), viz.:

> THE scripture doth hold out a Presbytery in a church.

> A Presbytery consisteth of ministers of the word, and such other publick officers as are agreeable to and warranted by the word of God to be church-governors, to join with the ministers in the government of the church.

The scripture doth hold forth, that many particular congregations may be under one Presbyterial government.

This proposition is proved by instances:

I. **First**, Of the church of Jerusalem, which consisted of more congregations than one, and all these congregations were under one Presbyterial government.

   This appeareth thus:

   a. *First*, The church of Jerusalem consisted of more congregations than one, as is manifest:

      • 1st, By the multitude of believers mentioned, in divers [places], both before the dispersion of the believers there, by means of the persecution, and also after the dispersion.

      • 2dly, By the many apostles and other preachers in the church of Jerusalem. And if there were but one congregation there, then each apostle preached but seldom; which will not consist with Acts vi. 2.

      • 3dly, The diversity of languages among the believers, mentioned both in the second and sixth chapters of the Acts, doth argue more congregations than one in that church.

   b. *Secondly*, All those congregations were under one Presbyterial government; because,

      • 1st, They were one church.

      • 2dly, The elders of the church are mentioned.

      • 3dly, The apostles did the ordinary acts of presbyters, as presbyters in that kirk; which proveth a presbyterial church before the dispersion, Acts vi.

      • 4thly, The several congregations in Jerusalem being one church, the elders of that church are mentioned as meeting together for acts of government; which proves that those several congregations were under one presbyterial government.

And whether these congregations were fixed or not fixed, in regard of officers or members, it is all one as to the truth of the proposition.

Nor doth there appear any material difference betwixt the several congregations in Jerusalem, and the many congregations now in the ordinary condition of the church, as to the point of fixedness required of officers or members.

    c. *Thirdly*, therefore, the scripture doth hold forth, that many congregations may be under one presbyterial government.

II. **Secondly**, By the instance of the church of Ephesus; for,

    a. *First*, That there were more congregations than one in the church of Ephesus, appears by Acts xx. 31, where is mention of Paul's continuance at Ephesus in preaching for the space of three years; and Acts xix. 18, 19, 20, where the special effect of the word is mentioned; and ver. 10. and 17. of the same chapter, where is a distinction of Jews and Greeks; and 1 Cor. xvi. 8, 9, where is a reason of Paul's stay at Ephesus until Pentecost; and ver. 19, where is mention of a particular church in the house of Aquila and Priscilla, then at Ephesus, as appears, Acts xviii. 19, 24, 26. All which laid together, doth prove that the multitude of believers did make more congregations than one in the church of Ephesus.

    b. *Secondly*, That there were many elders over these many congregations, as one flock, appeareth.

    c. *Thirdly*, That these many congregations were one church, and that they were under one presbyterial government, appeareth.

Our present study is, however, not so much on classical assemblies as it is on synodical assemblies. Indeed, the astute student of our *Confession* will realise that nothing is said about Presbyteries or Classes in it. This is so because not all the members of the

Westminster Assembly were Presbyterian. The Assembly was in that sense ecumenical, and therefore the *Confession* produced by it allowed for differences in church polity, though the fact that a whole chapter is reserved to discuss synodical assemblies, does indicate a leaning towards Presbyterianism.

On the Convening of Synodical Assemblies

31.1 For the better government, and further edification of the Church, there ought to be such assemblies as are commonly called Synods or Councils.[1]

[1] Acts 15:2, 4, 6

The Form of Presbyterial Church Government (s.v. "Of Synodical Assemblies"), in agreement with this assertion, states:

> THE scripture doth hold out another sort of assemblies for the government of the church, beside classical and congregational, all which we call Synodical.
>
> Pastors and teachers, and other church-governors, (as also other fit persons, when it shall be deemed expedient,) are members of those assemblies which we call Synodical, where they have a lawful calling thereunto.
>
> Synodical assemblies may lawfully be of several sorts, as provincial, national, and oecumenical.
>
> It is lawful, and agreeable to the word of God, that there be a subordination of congregational, classical, provincial, and national assemblies, for the government of the church.

- Notice how according to the Assembly, synodical assemblies, unlike congregational and classical assemblies, need not consist only of elders and ministers in the same denomination. It can be œcumenical and national, which was precisely what the Westminster Assembly itself was.

- The basis for this assertion is found largely in Acts 15, which describes the meeting of the Jerusalem council or as the case appears to be, the first synodical assembly of the early church. The record is telling:

> [1]And certain men which came down from Judæa taught the brethren, and said, Except ye be circumcised after the manner of Moses, ye cannot be saved. [2]When therefore Paul and Barnabas had no small dissension and disputation with them, they determined that Paul and Barnabas, and certain other of them, should go up to Jerusalem unto the apostles and elders about this question.... [4]And when they were come to Jerusalem, they were received *of the church, and of the apostles and elders*, and they declared all things that God had done with them.... [6]And *the apostles and elders came together for to consider of this matter*.... [22]Then pleased it *the apostles and elders, with the whole church*, to send chosen men of their own company to Antioch with Paul and Barnabas; namely, Judas surnamed Barsabas, and Silas, chief men among the brethren: [23]And they wrote letters by them after this manner; *The apostles and elders and brethren* send greeting unto the brethren which are of the Gentiles in Antioch and Syria and Cilicia (Acts 15:1, 2, 4, 6, 22–23).

- Notice that it was the apostles and elders who met to consider the matter at hand. It is likely that these elders and apostles were regularly serving in different congregations seeing that number of believers at Jerusalem was quite large, and seeing that the apostles preached so frequently that there was a necessity to free them from administrative work (Acts 6:2). If it were one large congregation, they would hardly be so busy since there are so many of them. And since there are more than one congregation and yet one church, it must have been, as shown earlier, that they were ruled not only by Sessions (for each congregation) and by a Presbytery (for, perhaps, the whole of Jerusalem). If there were a Presbytery in Jerusalem, it is not difficult to see that the members of Presbytery (whether in whole or in part) must have made up the synodical assembly together with members from the Presbyteries of Antioch, Syria, Cilicia, etc.

- Such synodical assemblies, when they are convened, will certainly, as in the case of the Jerusalem Assembly, serve the purpose of "better government, and further edification of the Church," for "in the multitude of counsellors there is safety" (Prov 11:14).

- But notice the less than dogmatic language of the *Confession*. Why is this the case? Does it not reflect the fact that it is not also easy or expedient to convene synodical assemblies? Some of these difficulties are suggested in the next paragraph of our *Confession*.

31.2   As magistrates may lawfully call a synod of ministers, and other fit persons, to consult and advise with about matters of religion;[1] so if magistrates be open enemies to the Church, the ministers of Christ, of themselves, by virtue of their office, or they, with other fit persons upon delegation from their churches, may meet together in such assemblies.[2]

[1] Isa 49:23; 1 Tim 2:1–2; 2 Chr 19:8–11; 29; 30; Mt 2:4–5; Prov 11:14; [2] Acts 15:2, 4, 22–23, 25.

- In the Adopting Act of the Church of Scotland in 1647, it was noted that it is only in the case of churches "not settled, or constituted in point of government," that the civil ruler may call for synodical assemblies of ministers. Indeed, in such a case, the ministers may meet synodically without commission from their churches. But in the case of churches that are settled or constituted, then the ministers and elders may meet together in such assemblies as often as necessary whether they have the approval of the magistrate or not.[96]

---

[96] "It is further declared, That the Assembly understands some parts of the second article of the thirty-one chapter only of kirks not settled, or constituted in point of government: And that although, in such kirks, a synod of ministers, and other fit persons, may be called by the magistrate's authority and nomination, without any other call, to consult and advise with about matters of religion; and although, likewise, the ministers of Christ, without delegation from their churches, may of themselves, and by virtue of their office, meet together synodically in such kirks not yet constituted, yet neither of these ought to be done in kirks constituted and settled; it being always free to the magistrate to advise with synods of ministers and ruling elders, meeting upon delegation from their churches, either ordinarily, or, being indicted by his authority, occasionally, and *pro re nata*; it being also free to assemble together synodically, as well *pro re nata* as at the ordinary times, upon delegation from the churches, by the intrinsical power received from Christ, as often as it is necessary for the good of the church so to assemble, in case the magistrate, to the detriment of the Church, withhold

- The keys to understanding why the civil magistrate is allowed to call synodical assemblies are twofold: firstly, Isaiah 49:23 refers to kings as nursing father; secondly, the kings of Judah did, with God's approval, intervene to set the Church in the Old Testament on the right path again (e.g., 2 Chr 19:8–11; 2 Chr 29, 30); and thirdly, Proverbs 11:14 teaches: "Where no counsel is, the people fall: but in the multitude of counsellors there is safety." This surely demands that a Christian civil magistrate should seek the counsel of the officers of the church.

- In the case of a nation that is constitutionally and societally multi-religious, the revision of the First General Assembly of the American Presbyterian Church in 1789 may be more applicable and less open to dispute until such a time as the nation should in the providence of God become Christian:

For the better government, and further edification of the Church, there ought to be such assemblies as are commonly called Synods or Councils:[a] and it belongeth to the overseers and other rulers of the particular churches, by virtue of their office, and the power which Christ hath given them for edification and not for destruction, to appoint such assemblies;[b] and to convene together in them, as often as they shall judge it expedient for the good of the Church.[c]

[a] Acts 15:2, 4, 6; [b] Acts 15; [c] Acts 15:22–23, 25.

On the Purpose of Synods and Councils

31.3 It belongeth to synods and councils ministerially to determine controversies of faith, and cases of conscience; to set down rules and directions for better ordering of the public worship of God, and government of His Church; to receive complaints in cases of mal-administration, and authoritatively to determine the same: which decrees and determinations, if consonant to the Word of God, are to be received with reverence and submission, not only for their agreement

---

or deny his consent; the necessity of occasional assemblies being first remonstrate unto him by humble supplication."

with the Word, but also for the power whereby they are made, as being an ordinance of God, appointed thereunto in His Word.[1]

[1]Acts 15:15, 19, 24, 27–31; 16:4; Mt 18:17–20.

- When the council of Jerusalem met, it is clear that the decision arrived were not merely advisory but authoritative. This is why, in the synodical letter, it could be said: "For it seemed good to the Holy Ghost, and to us, to lay upon you no greater burden than these necessary things" (Acts 15:28). If it was advisory, this language would be out of place. Luke understood the same when he referred to what was decided on by the council as "decrees for to keep, that were ordained of the apostles and elders which were at Jerusalem" (Acts 16:4).

- Based on Acts 15 and Matthew 18:17–20, our *Confession* infers that the following may be ministerially (i.e., not absolutely since Christ alone is the law-giver) determined by the council:

    a. Controversies of faith—such as when there is a dispute concerning doctrine or interpretation of Scripture.

    b. Cases of conscience—i.e., pertaining to Christian liberty or conduct relative to matters of indifference.

    c. Manner and rules for worship and government of the Church as far as left to be determined by the light of nature, i.e., in circumstances or if you like, secondary issues.

    d. Complaints—such as in the case of mal-administration. These are to be received, investigated and a verdict given.

- The "decrees and determinations" of the councils, when handled down to the congregations "are to be received with reverence and submission," "if consonant to the Word of God." But the basis for their reception must not just be because they are in agreement with the Word of God, but because of the "power whereby they are made, as being an ordinance of God, appointed thereunto in His Word."

The implication of this statement is that if the synod should make a decision which it regards as being consonant with the Word of God, but a particular congregation believes that it is a matter of indifference (not contrary to the Word), then, it must still submit to it as authoritative. For example, a synod may decree that the ministers under her purview may not administer the Lord's Supper in any congregation other than in the same denomination. All ministers of the denomination must then submit to the decision even if they do not agree with the ruling.

On the Limitations of Synods and Councils

31.4 All synods or councils since the Apostles' times, whether general or particular, may err, and many have erred; therefore they are not to be made the rule of faith or practice, but to be used as a help in both.[1]

[1]*Eph 2:20; Acts 17:11; 1 Cor 2:5; 2 Cor 1:24.*

- This statement refutes the Romish claim that councils and Popes are infallible. The only rule infallible of faith for the church is the Holy Scripture and it is the duty of members and officers of the church to test everything that is decreed against the Scripture as the Bereans did (Acts 17:11). History has also shown that councils do err, as Shaw neatly illustrates:

"In the Arian controversy, several councils decreed in opposition to that of Nice. The Eutychian heresy was approved in the second council of Ephesus, and soon after condemned in the Council of Chalcedon. The worship of images was condemned in the Council of Constantinople, and was approved in the second Nicene Council, and again condemned at Francfort. Finally, the authority of councils was declared, at Counstance and Basil, to be superior to that of the Pope; but this decision was reversed in the Lateran."[97]

31.5 Synods and councils are to handle or conclude nothing but that which is ecclesiastical; and are not to intermeddle with civil affairs, which concern the commonwealth, unless by way of humble petition, in

---

[97] Shaw, *op. cit.*, 369.

cases extraordinary; or by way of advice for satisfaction of conscience, if they be thereunto required by the civil magistrate.[1]

[1]*Lk 12:13–14; Jn 18:36.*

As our *Confession* denounces any Erastian interference of the civil government on any matter purely ecclesiastical or spiritual, so it also denounced any interference of the church or her councils on the civil affairs of the land, *contra* Papalism.

The church and her synod should only interact with the civil magistrate on matters pertaining to the civil affairs of the commonwealth, when she is required by the civil magistrate, or when, —in extraordinary circumstances, —the satisfaction of conscience requires her to submit a humble petition or advice.

WCF 32 OF THE STATE OF MEN AFTER DEATH, AND OF THE RESURRECTION OF THE DEAD

The last two chapters of our *Confession* are dedicated to eschatology, which is the study of last things. This locus of theology usually covers what happens to man at the point of death (personal eschatology) as well as what happens when Christ returns again (general eschatology). It is sometimes thought that the doctrine of last things is only found in the last book of the Bible. This is a fallacy. The reality is that the doctrine of last things is actually taught throughout the Scriptures, and indeed it is by comparing Scripture with Scripture and systematising the biblical data that the student of eschatology can get a biblically balanced doctrine. This is the approach of the writers of our *Confession*.

Although these two chapter present a biblical doctrine of eschatology in a positive rather than polemical or negative way, it is clear that in so far as personal eschatology is concerned, such aberrant doctrines as soul sleep (of the Seventh Day Adventism) or Purgatory (of Roman Catholicism) cannot be reconciled with the doctrine herein propounded. Likewise, as far as General Eschatology is concerned, it is clear that Premillennialism, especially Dispensational Premillennialism cannot be reconciled with the Confessional doctrine presented here and in the accompanying Catechisms.

On the State of Man after Death

32.1 The bodies of men, after death, return to dust, and see corruption:[1] but their souls, which neither die nor sleep, having an immortal subsistence, immediately return to God who gave them:[2] the souls of the righteous, being then made perfect in holiness, are received into the highest heavens, where they behold the face of God, in light and glory, waiting for the full redemption of their bodies.[3] And the souls of the wicked are cast into hell, where they remain in torments and utter darkness, reserved to the judgment of the great day.[4] Beside these two places, for souls separated from their bodies, the Scripture acknowledgeth none.

[1] *Gen 3:19; Acts 13:36;* [2] *Lk 23:43; Eccl 12:7;* [3] *Heb 12:23; 2 Cor 5:1, 6, 8; Phil. 1:23; Acts 3:21; Eph 4:10;* [4] *Lk 16:23–24; Acts 1:25; Jude 6–7; 1 Pet 3:19.*

a. Death entered into the world and passed upon all men because of the fall of Adam (Gen 3:19; Rom 5:12). Since then, death is the universal experience of all men (with the extraordinary exception of two: Enoch and Elijah). The psalmist declares: "What man is he that liveth, and shall not see death? shall he deliver his soul from the hand of the grave?" (Ps 89:48). The author of Hebrews refers to death as an immutable appointment: "And as it is appointed unto men once to die" (Heb 9:27a).

But man is a two-part being with an immortal soul. Therefore, death cannot be the end of man's existence. Death must, rather, refer to the separation of the body and soul of the person. The body being constituted of corruptible material, will decompose and return unto the ground. The soul, on the other hand, returns "unto God who gave it" (Ecc 12:7).

b. What happens when the soul meets with God? It immediately faces a preliminary judgement of God. "And as it is appointed unto men once to die, *but after this the judgment*" (Heb 9:27; cf. 12:23). Then those who die in Christ are confirmed in righteousness and "received into highest heavens, where they behold the face of God in light and glory." This is often known as the beatific vision.

That this is the case, is the clear teaching of Scripture. The Lord told the penitent thief on the cross: "Verily I say unto thee, Today shalt thou be with me in paradise" (Lk 23:43). The apostle Paul speaks about his desire to be in the presence of the Lord and suggests that the moment he leaves the mortal body, he will behold the face of God:

- "For we know that if our earthly house of this tabernacle were dissolved, we have a building of God, an house not made with hands, eternal in the heavens.... Therefore we are always confident, knowing that, whilst we are at home in the body, we are absent from the Lord:... We are confident, I say, and willing rather to be absent from the body, and to be present with the Lord" (2 Cor 5:1, 6, 8).

- "For I am in a strait betwixt two, having a desire to depart, and to be with Christ; which is far better" (Phil 1:23).

In addition, the author of Hebrews speaks of the saints in heaven as "the spirits of just men made perfect" (Heb 12:23).

c. The souls of the wicked, i.e., those who die in unbelief, on the other hand, are confirmed in unrighteousness and "cast into hell, where they remain in torments and utter darkness, reserved to the judgment of the great day." This again is a biblical doctrine. In the parable of Lazarus and the rich man, the rich man, being an unbeliever, was incarcerated in hell, where we are told he suffers the torment of the flame (Lk 16:23–24). In Jude 7, we are told that the wicked men of Sodom and Gomorrah are "suffering the vengeance of eternal fire." And the Apostle Peter calls those who died in the deluge "the spirits in prison" (1 Pet 3:19). There is a vast difference between the death of the righteous and the death of the wicked. For the righteous, death translates him to glory, for the wicked death confirms him in unrighteousness. For the righteous, death is great gain; for the wicked, death is ultimate loss.

d. Although the doctrine stated in this paragraph appears so straight forward, there have been in the church numerous different erroneous teachings on the subject. Thus, our *Confession* concludes the paragraph with the statement: "*Beside these two places for souls separated from their bodies, the Scripture acknowledgeth none.*" Briefly, some of the errors with regards to the state of men after death are:

i. *Purgatory*. This error of Rome stems from an erroneous understanding of justification and teaches that those who are not completely cleansed of the guilt of venial sins must undergo a process of purification in purgatory where they have to suffer for their sins. This period can be shortened by prayers, sacrifice of the Mass, indulgences, etc. This gross error is largely based on the apocryphal 2 Maccabees 12:41–45[98], but has no support in Scripture.

ii. *Limbus Patrum.* This is another Romish error which teaches that the Old Testament saints were detained in the state of expectation (limbo) in a part of hades until the Lord at His death went down to release them and carried them to heaven. This again has no scriptural support. The Lord did not descend into hades. He said: "*Today* shalt thou be with me in paradise" (Lk 23:43).

iii. *Limbus Infantum.* Another error of Romish invention. Since salvation is by faith and works, it is impossible for infants who were not baptised to enter heaven. But yet they are not accounted guilty, so they are held in a state of eternal limbo.

iv. *Soul Sleep.* This is held by Russellites (Jehovah's Witnesses). Basing their theory on the passages that represent death as a sleep (e.g., Mt 9:24; Acts 7:60, etc), they teach that the soul goes into an unconscious existence after death until the resurrection. But the Scripture teaches that believers enjoy a conscious life in communion with God and Christ immediately after death (e.g., Lk 16:19–31; Phil 1:23, etc).

v. *Intermediate Place*: Sheol and Hades. This doctrine, popular among some dispensationalists, is that the souls of both believers and unbelievers go into an intermediate place of weakened consciousness until the resurrection and judgement. This is based on a misinterpretation of the words *sheol* (Hebrew, שְׁאוֹל) and *hades* (Greek, ᾅδης). These two words

---

[98] "[41]All men therefore praising the Lord, the righteous Judge, who had opened the things that were hid, [42]Betook themselves unto prayer, and besought him that the sin committed might wholly be put out of remembrance. Besides, that noble Judas exhorted the people to keep themselves from sin, forsomuch as they saw before their eyes the things that came to pass for the sins of those that were slain. [43]And when he had made a gathering throughout the company to the sum of two thousand drachms of silver, he sent it to Jerusalem to offer a sin offering, doing therein very well and honestly, in that he was mindful of the resurrection: [44]For if he had not hoped that they that were slain should have risen again, it had been superfluous and vain to pray for the dead. [45]And also in that he perceived that there was great favour laid up for those that died godly, it was an holy and good thought. Whereupon he made a reconciliation for the dead, that they might be delivered from sin" (2 Maccabees 12:41–45).

frequently refer to the state of death (e.g., Job 14:13; Acts 2:27; 1 Cor 15:55); and sometimes to the grave (e.g., Gen 42:38). But there is strong evidence that the two words often refer to hell as translated in the KJV (e.g., Job 21:13; Ps 9:17; Lk 16:23). The meaning of these two words must be derived from the context. Assuming a lexicographical meaning of a word and then imposing it on the text can lead to serious errors.

vi. *Annihilation and Conditional Immortality*. This is the doctrine of Jehovah Witnesses and Seventh Day Adventists and is popular among some modern 'evangelicals,' such as Clark Pinnock and John Stott. The idea in this view is that the soul of the wicked does not experience eternal torment, but will either be positively annihilated or will simply cease to exist. But the Bible teaches that the soul of sinners as well as saints will continue to exist forever: "And these shall go away into everlasting punishment: but the righteous into life eternal" (Mt 25:46; Rev 14:11, 20:10). Also the Scripture speaks of degrees of punishment for the wicked (Lk 12:47–48; Mt 11:20–24). Annihilation not only makes these passages meaningless, but makes punishment for sin altogether meaningless: Why worry if you will ultimately cease existence altogether?

On the Resurrection of the Dead

32.2   At the last day, such as are found alive shall not die, but be changed:[1] and all the dead shall be raised up, with the self-same bodies, and none other (although with different qualities), which shall be united again to their souls forever.[2]

[1] 1 Th 4:17; 1 Cor 15:51–52; [2] Job 19:26–27; 1 Cor 15:42–44.

32.3   The bodies of the unjust shall, by the power of Christ, be raised to dishonour: the bodies of the just, by His Spirit, unto honour; and be made conformable to His own glorious body.[1]

[1] Acts 24:15; Jn 5:28–29; 1 Cor 15:43; Phil. 3:21.

a. The "last days" in the history of redemption begun with the incarnation of the Lord Jesus Christ. We are in the "last days" (Acts

2:17; 2 Tim 3:1; Heb 1:2; 2 Pet 3:3), or the final *period* in redemptive history (1 Cor 10:11). But the "Last Day" refers the final *event* in redemptive history. The rest of our *Confession* relates to this Last Day.

b. In §32.1, we note that though believers *"are received into the highest heavens, where they behold the face of God in light and glory,"* there is a sense in which they are still not complete, as they await *"the full redemption of their bodies."* Men, unlike angels, are created with a soul and a body. Though a Christian has perfect joy suited to a spiritual existence when he leaves his mortal body, he is not complete until his body is reunited to his soul. Thus, the Scripture speaks about a future resurrection when all the dead shall be raised up, i.e., their bodies will be resurrected and reunited with their souls. This resurrection involves the same body that was laid in the grave, though it is reconstituted with different qualities; and it involves not just the believers, but unbelievers as well:

- "And many of them that sleep in the dust of the earth shall awake, some to everlasting life, and some to shame and everlasting contempt" (Dan 12:2).

- "Marvel not at this: for the hour is coming, in the which all that are in the graves shall hear his voice, And shall come forth; they that have done good, unto the resurrection of life; and they that have done evil, unto the resurrection of damnation" (Jn 5:28–29).

c. The bodies of the unjust shall, by the power of Christ, be raised to dishonour or "to shame and everlasting contempt" (Dan 12:2). They are said to be raised by the power or authority of Christ because Christ said that "all that are in the graves shall hear his voice."

- On the other hand, the bodies of the just will be raised by His Spirit, unto honour; and be made conformable to His own glorious body:

    "… the Lord Jesus Christ… shall change our vile body, that it may be fashioned like unto his glorious body, according to the working whereby he is able even to subdue all things unto himself" (Phil 3:20–21).

- It was with this confidence that Job exclaimed:

"Though after my skin worms destroy this body, yet in my flesh shall I see God: Whom I shall see for myself, and mine eyes shall behold, and not another; though my reins be consumed within me" (Job 19:26–27).

- The resurrected body of the believer will have similar, if not the same, qualities as the resurrected body of Christ. It shall be incorruptible and will never face death again:

"For this corruptible must put on incorruption, and this mortal must put on immortality. So when this corruptible shall have put on incorruption, and this mortal shall have put on immortality, then shall be brought to pass the saying that is written, Death is swallowed up in victory" (1 Cor 15:53–54).

d. What about those who are found alive on that last day? Our *Confession* makes no explicit mention about the reprobate in that day. Though they appear to be included in §32.2, the Scripture references cited suggest that the divines had believers in mind. The Scripture is not explicit about what will happen to the living reprobate, but the sight of the coming King of glory and the knowledge of His wrath against sin would surely kill them (cf. Rev 6:15–17). If so, they will, with the rest of the dead, face the resurrection of damnation with a body adapted to judgement and corruption. Those who are in Christ, on the other hand, will clearly not die, but be changed in a moment:

"Behold, I shew you a mystery; We shall not all sleep, but we shall all be changed, In a moment, in the twinkling of an eye, at the last trump: for the trumpet shall sound, and the dead shall be raised incorruptible, and we shall be changed" (1 Cor 15:51–52).

e. The order of event is given by the Apostle Paul:

"For the Lord himself shall descend from heaven with a shout, with the voice of the archangel, and with the trump of God: and the dead in Christ shall rise first: Then we which are alive and remain shall be caught up together with them in the clouds, to meet the Lord in the air: and so shall we ever be with the Lord" (1 Th 4:16–17).

Though Paul's emphasis is on the fact that the saints will from thence forever be with the Lord, he uses a very interesting word to describe the meeting of the saints with the Lord. This word, translated 'meet,' is the Greek ἀπάντησις (apantēsis). It is used only four times in the New Testament. Apart from 1 Thessalonians 4:17, it is the word that the Lord used in His Parable of the Ten Virgins to describe the virgins' going out to meet the bridegroom (Mt 25:1, 6). It is also used by Luke to describe how the brethren at Rome came up as far as Appii forum to meet Paul to accompany him in the rest of his journey to Rome (Acts 28:15–16). In secular Greek literature, this word is used to describe the citizens of a city going out to meet a visiting dignitary and then returning with him. It is also used to describe the practice of Roman citizens going out to meet a victorious army and marching back with them. Thus, the living saints at the Second Coming are transformed and glorified suddenly (1 Cor 15:51–52) and, together with believers raised from the dead, are caught up to meet the Lord in the air (1 Th 4:17), and then usher Him together with His mighty angels to earth in His return as the glorious and triumphant Judge (Rev 19:14; Jude 14). This spectacle will be witnessed by the whole world at the same time (cf. Rev 6:15–17).

WCF 33: OF THE LAST JUDGMENT

What happens after the Resurrection? Our Standards does not leave us to speculate:

> *WLC* 88 What shall *immediately* follow after the resurrection?
>
> A. Immediately after the resurrection shall follow the general and final judgement of angels and men; the day and hour whereof no man knoweth, that all may watch and pray, and be ever ready for the coming of the Lord"

This General Judgement is the subject of the final chapter in our *Confession*.

On the General and Comprehensive Scope of Judgement

33.1 God hath appointed a day, wherein He will judge the world, in righteousness, by Jesus Christ,[1] to whom all power and judgment is given of the Father.[2] In which day, not only the apostate angels shall be judged,[3] but likewise all persons that have lived upon earth shall appear before the tribunal of Christ, to give an account of their thoughts, words, and deeds; and to receive according to what they have done in the body, whether good or evil.[4]

[1] Acts 17:31; [2] Jn 5:22, 27; [3] 1 Cor 6:3; Jude 6; 2 Pet 2:4; [4] 2 Cor 5:10; Eccl 12:14; Rom 2:16; 14:10, 12; Mt 12:36–37.

a. The appointed Judge will be the Lord Jesus Christ: "For the Father judgeth no man, but hath committed all judgment unto the Son:… [the Father] hath given him authority to execute judgment also, because he is the Son of man" (Jn 5:22, 27).

b. That judgment will be in a day, i.e., with no events intervening: "He hath appointed a day, in the which he will judge the world in righteousness by that man whom he hath ordained; whereof he hath given assurance unto all men, in that he hath raised him from the dead" (Acts 17:31).

c. This Day of Judgement will involve the world, or more precisely, all the elect and reprobates who ever lived. This is clear from the Parable of the Sheep and Goats:

"³¹When the Son of man shall come in his glory, and all the holy angels with him, then shall he sit upon the throne of his glory: ³²And before him shall be gathered all nations: and he shall separate them one from another, as a shepherd divideth his sheep from the goats: ³³And he shall set the sheep on his right hand, but the goats on the left. ³⁴Then shall the King say unto them on his right hand, Come, ye blessed of my Father, inherit the kingdom prepared for you from the foundation of the world: ³⁵For I was an hungred, and ye gave me meat: I was thirsty, and ye gave me drink: I was a stranger, and ye took me in: ³⁶Naked, and ye clothed me: I was sick, and ye visited me: I was in prison, and ye came unto me.... ⁴¹Then shall he say also unto them on the left hand, Depart from me, ye cursed, into everlasting fire, prepared for the devil and his angels: ⁴²For I was an hungred, and ye gave me no meat: I was thirsty, and ye gave me no drink: ⁴³I was a stranger, and ye took me not in: naked, and ye clothed me not: sick, and in prison, and ye visited me not.... ⁴⁶And these shall go away into everlasting punishment: but the righteous into life eternal" (Mt 25:31–46).

d. This judgement will involve everything that is ever done in this life by every individual. We shall then have *"to give an account of their thoughts, words, and deeds, and to receive according to what they have done in the body, whether good or evil."* This is the emphatic teaching in many passages of Scriptures such as:

"For we must all appear before the judgment seat of Christ; that every one may receive the things done in his body, according to that he hath done, whether it be good or bad" (2 Cor 5:10).

"But I say unto you, That every idle word that men shall speak, they shall give account thereof in the day of judgment. For by thy words thou shalt be justified, and by thy words thou shalt be condemned" (Mt 12:36–37).

"For God shall bring every work into judgment, with every secret thing, whether it be good, or whether it be evil" (Ecc 12:14).

"There is a place that is better than heaven and worst than hell: this present life for our lot in eternity will be determined in this life" (John H. Gerstner).

e. Apostate angels will also be judged on that day as they are now "reserved in everlasting chains under darkness unto the judgment of the great day" (Jude 6; cf. 2 Pet 2:4).

On the Purpose of the General Judgement

33.2   The end of God's appointing this day is for the manifestation of the glory of His mercy, in the eternal salvation of the elect; and of His justice, in the damnation of the reprobate, who are wicked and disobedient. For then shall the righteous go into everlasting life, and receive that fullness of joy and refreshing, which shall come from the presence of the Lord: but the wicked who know not God, and obey not the Gospel of Jesus Christ, shall be cast into eternal torments, and be punished with everlasting destruction from the presence of the Lord, and from the glory of His power.[1]

[1] *Mt 25:31–46; Rom 2:5–6; Rom 9:22–23; Mt 25:21; Acts 3:19; 2 Th 1:7–10.*

a. The purpose of this judgement will be the display (i) "of the glory of His *mercy* in the eternal salvation of the elect"; (ii) "of His *justice* in the damnation of the reprobate, who are wicked and disobedient." As Paul surmises:

"What if God, willing to shew his wrath, and to make his power known, endured with much longsuffering the vessels of wrath fitted to destruction: And that he might make known the riches of his glory on the vessels of mercy, which he had afore prepared unto glory" (Rom 9:22–23).

b. Those who are clothed with the righteousness of Christ are deemed righteous and will enter into everlasting life, and "*receive that fullness of joy and refreshing which shall come from the presence of the Lord.*" "His lord said unto him, Well done, thou good and faithful servant: thou hast been faithful over a few things, I will make thee ruler over many things: enter thou into the joy of thy lord" (Mt 25:21). Edwards, who is fondly known as the theologian of heaven and hell, puts it beautifully:

"The souls of departed saints with Christ in heaven, shall have Christ as it were unbosomed unto them, manifesting those infinite riches of love towards them, that have been there from eternity: and they shall be enabled to express their love to him, in an incomparably better manner than ever they could while in the body. Thus, they shall eat and drink abundantly, and swim in the ocean of love, and be eternally swallowed up [in] the infinitely bright, and infinitely mild and sweet, beams of divine love; eternally receiving that light, eternally full of it, and eternally compassed round with it, and everlastingly reflecting it back again to its fountain" (Jonathan Edwards, *Works* 2.29a).

c. All unbelievers are accounted wicked for their sin and their refusal to obey the Gospel of Jesus Christ. They "shall be cast into eternal torments, and be punished with everlasting destruction from the presence of the Lord, and from the glory of His power" (cf. 2 Th 1:7–9). Note that this does not mean that hell is where God is not as if the wicked will no more have anything to do with God. On the contrary, it is the wrath of God that makes hell so terrible. Though hell will have a form of literal fire which will torment the bodies of the wicked, it is the presence of an angry God that makes the suffering intolerable. Thus, Edwards preached:

"Tis the infinite almighty God himself that shall become the fire [of] the furnace exerting his infinite perfections that way.... The appearance of the presence of an angry God in them and everywhere round about them, can be represented by nothing better than by their being in the midst of an exceedingly hot and furious fires..." (*Unpublished sermon* on Job 41:9–10).

On our Response to Eschatology

33.3   As Christ would have us to be certainly persuaded that there shall be a day of judgment, both to deter all men from sin; and for the greater consolation of the godly in their adversity:[1] so will He have that day unknown to men, that they may shake off all carnal security, and be always watchful, because they know not at what hour the Lord will come; and may be ever prepared to say, Come Lord Jesus, come quickly. Amen.[2]

[1] 2 Pet 3:11, 14; 2 Cor 5:10–11; 2 Th 1:5–7; Lk 21:7, 28; Rom 8:23–25; [2] Mt 24:36, 42–44; Mk 13:35–37; Lk 12:35–36; Rev 22:20.

a. Eschatology has always been a subject of great interest to Christians throughout the ages. This is not wrong since a good proportion of the Scripture deals with the subject. Unfortunately, it has also become a subject of great differences and contention among believers. And it has also become the chief preoccupation of many a Christian and church so much so that other important doctrines revealed in the Word of God are neglected or not given due proportion of attention.

b. What is the purpose of eschatology? Our *Confession* offers two pastoral appraisals: *Firstly*, the knowledge that there will certainly be a day of judgement ought to deter men from sin (2 Pet 3:11–12). *Secondly*, believers who are suffering adversity may have greater consolation knowing that the Lord not only knows their sufferings, but will bring all things to justice and will vindicate the righteous:

    "[The endurance of persecution and tribulation] is a manifest token of the righteous judgment of God, that ye may be counted worthy of the kingdom of God, for which ye also suffer: Seeing it is a righteous thing with God to recompense tribulation to them that trouble you" (2 Th 1:5–6).

c. For these reasons, God does not reveal to us the exact timing of Christ's return (and the resurrection and judgement): "But of that day and hour knoweth no man, no, not the angels of heaven, but my Father only" (Mt 24:36). For if men know when Christ will return, then they will become complacent.

d. In view of the knowledge of the soon return of Christ:

   (i)   We should live in constant watchfulness (Mt 25:1–13; Mk 13:33; Rev 16:15), to be ready to receive Christ and to be received of Him at His return. This requires us to endeavour to live holy lives according to His Word.

   (ii) We must be mindful to live as pilgrims in this world (1 Pet 2:11), not amassing wealth or storing up treasures upon the earth at the expense of treasures in heaven that have eternal values.

   (iii) We should serve the Lord and invest our time in what would last (cf. 1 Cor 3:13–15). We should be more fervent in evangelism and preaching since there would be no more opportunity of repentance when the wrath of God is poured out in judgement (cf. Mt 25:14–30).

   (iv) We should not neglect worship and fellowship; but constantly exhort one another in the things of God as we see the day approaching (Heb 10:25), knowing that apostasy will be rampant in these last days (2 Tim 3:1–5).

   (v)   We should continue to walk worthy of our vocations (Eph 4:1), to glorify God with our lives. We are not called to sell all we have and to wait in inactivity, rather we are to occupy till He comes (Lk 19:13).

   (vi) We should redouble our efforts to study the Scriptures and theology to prepare for our future reign with Christ.

   (vii) We should work out our salvation with fear and trembling and examine ourselves honestly to make sure that we are indeed in the faith (Phil 2:12; 2 Cor 13:5).

   (viii) We should not quarrel over who is right (2 Tim 2:24–25).

   (ix) We should be ever prepared to say, "Come, Lord Jesus, come quickly. Amen" (cf. 1 Cor 16:22; Rev 22:20).

—FINIS—

WORKSHEETS

1. On Revelation:
    a. Name the 2 ways in which God reveals himself.
    b. Cite a chapter or passage in the Scripture that refers to these two modes of revelations.
    c. What are revealed in each of these two ways?

2. On the Canon the Scripture:

    a. What does the word 'canon' mean?
        i.   A list of books.
        ii.   A measuring standard.
        iii. A metal ball used to sink ships.
        iv.   A bishop.
        v.   An imprimatur on a book.

    b. Is the Canon of Scripture closed? . Cite a verse to show that this is so. How many books are there in the canon?

    c. How should we view the apocrypha?
        i.   As secondarily inspired Scripture
        ii.   As uninspired Scripture.
        iii. As authoritative history.
        iv.   As any other Christian literature.
        v.   As any other human writings.

    d. On what authority is the Bible to be believed?
        i.   On the testimony of thousands of ancient manuscripts.
        ii.   On the corroboration of archeology and science.
        iii. On the authority of Church through the ages.
        iv.   On the authority of God, who is truth itself.
        v.   On the inward testimony of the Holy Spirit.

    e. List 2 external and 3 internal evidences supporting the fact that the Bible is the Word of God.

    f. From where does our full persuasion and assurance of the infallibility and authority of the Word of God come from?

3. On the characteristics of the Word of God:

    a. Match the following terms with their corresponding description:

i.	Authoritative	Every word and sentence inspired
ii.	Perspicuity	Complete in itself, not needing additional material
iii.	Verbally Inspired	Without error in any detail
iv.	Plenarily Inspired	Having the absolute right to govern our lives
v.	Inerrancy	Faultless in all it teaches
vi.	Infallability	All essential doctrines can be clearly understood
vii.	Sufficiency	Wholly, not partially inspired

b. Quote from memory a verse that teaches the authority, sufficiency and plenary inspiration of the word of God.

4. On translation:
   a. In which of the following languages was the Bible originally written in?

i.	English	vi.	Akkadian
ii.	French.	vii.	Arabic
iii.	Latin.	viii.	Hebrew
iv.	Aramaic.	ix.	Syraic
v.	Greek.	x.	Coptic.

   b. Why is there a need for translations?
   c. Are translations inerrant and infallible?
   d. Which version or translation does the Westminster Divines urge the church to finally appeal to in all controversies of religion? Why?

5. On interpretation:
   a. What is the infallible rule of interpretation of Scripture?
   b. Why is the *Westminster Confession of Faith* known as a subordinate standard of our church?
   c. How many times must God say something for it to be true?
   d. Must every doctrine that church hold to be supported by at least one clear and direct proof-text from the Bible? Explain.
   e. Critique this axiom: "When the plain sense make sense seek no other sense."
   f. Explain what the divines mean in WCF 1.10, "The supreme Judge, by which all controversies of religion are determined ... can be no other but the Holy Spirit speaking in the Scripture."

WCF 02: OF GOD, AND OF THE HOLY TRINITY

1. On God's Uniqueness:
   a. Quote from memory, the first 9 words of *WCF* 2.1.
   b. What are some errors refuted by this statement.
   c. Memorise and quote from memory WSC Q. 4.

2. On the Communicable and Incommunicable Attributes of God:
   a. What are incommunicable attributes?
   b. List 3 incommunicable attributes of God: [Hint: Not Omnipresence, Omniscience and Omnipotence]
   c. What are communicable attribute?
   d. List 5 communicable attributes:

3. On God's infinity of Being:
   a. What do the divines mean by saying that God "is infinite in being"? [Hint: What does 'infinite' mean? Give a couple of synonyms for 'being']
   b. List 3 adjectives to further describe God's infinity of being. Explain the 3 terms you listed.
   c. Comment on this statement: "It is impossible for man to comprehend God."

4. God is a most pure, invisible, without body, parts, or passions:
   a. How do you explain verses such as Psalm 91:4 and Exodus 31:18?
   b. How do you explain Genesis 6:6?
   d. Is it right to say that God desires to save the reprobate? Explain.
   e. If God is without passions, why do we read that "Jesus wept" (Jn 11:35)?

5. On the immutability of God:
   a. What does immutability mean?
   b. Cite at least 2 verses to show that God is immutable.
   c. Critique the statement, "Prayer changes things."
   d. What does *WSC* 1 mean by saying that the chief end of man is to *glorify God* and to enjoy Him forever? Can God increase in glory?

6. On the goodness of God:
   a. What are the two ways in which the goodness of God may be reckoned?
   b. Someone ask: "If God is good, why is there evil in the world, and why does He punish sin?" You agree that God is good. How then would you explain the apparent contradiction?
   c. What is the difference between the goodness of God that is displayed to His elect and to all others?

7. God's knowledge and sovereignty.
   a. Which statement best explain why the Divines say that "nothing is to [God] contingent, or uncertain"?
      i. God is without passions, therefore, nothing surprises Him.
      ii. God knows all things, including what will happen in future, therefore He is not surprised by anything that comes to pass.
      iii. God has from eternity sovereignly ordained all things that comes to pass, therefore nothing happens by chance or accident.
      iv. God is in providential control over the affairs of the world, so that whenever there is an occasion for things to turn out one way or another, God is the one who decides which way it should turn out (Prov 16:33), so there is nothing contingent or uncertain to Him.
      v. God can sovereignly intervene to make things happen according to His will, therefore nothing is out of His control or uncertain.
   b. How would you explain the Lord's words: "But of that day and that hour knoweth no man, no, not the angels which are in heaven, neither the Son, but the Father" (Mk 13:32).

8. Of the Holy Trinity.
   a. Draw a diagram which depicts (not illustrates) the doctrine of the Trinity.
   b. Which of the following perfectly illustrate the doctrine of the Trinity:
      i. The trifoliate clover leaf ♣.
      ii. I am a father, a son and an uncle at the same time.
      iii. H_2O is only one substance, but it can exist as liquid, gas or solid.
      iv. The sun is known by its light, its heat and its rays.
      v. An equilateral triangle.
      vi. None of the above.

c. Which of the above best illustrate the doctrine? Why? What aspect is not captured in the illustration?

d. List the 6 propositions that must be shown from Scripture to prove the doctrine of the Trinity [Hint: think of the objections to the doctrine, by say a Jehovah's Witness]

e. Without looking at your notes, show (briefly) from Scripture that Jesus Christ is God.

f. Prove that the Holy Spirit is a personal God.

g. Cite one verse that shows that there is unity in essence in the Trinity.

h. Is there anything wrong with the statement: "The Son was begotten of the Father, and the Holy Spirit proceeded from the Father and the Son"?

WCF 03: OF GOD'S ETERNAL DECREE

1. On God's Decree in General:
   a. Which of the following best represents God's sovereignty in His decree according to the WCF?
      i. God is said to ordain all things that will come to pass because He foreknew all things from eternity past, and also because all things can happen only by His sovereign permission.
      ii. God has ordained the outcome of all events that will happen in the world so that although independent decisions are made by rational beings and circumstances occur randomly, the outcome that God has ordained will always prevail so that all things work together for good to them that love God.
      iii. God foreknew from eternity past all the supposed conditions that will occur in the world, and He decrees the outcome of them either by special intervention or by directing secondary causes so that rational creatures will make decisions in conformity to His secret will.
      iv. God has from eternity ordained all things and events of every kind; and all things will come to pass as God has ordained because He will bring them to pass.
      v. God has from eternity ordained all things and events of every kind; and all things will come to pass as God has ordained because the script of fate has already been written and cannot be altered.
   b. Cite a few verses which may serve to support your answer above.
   c. Memorise and quote from memory WSC Q. 7, "What are the decrees of God?"
   d. Based on WCF 3.1, that God does not do violence to the will of His creatures, how would you interpret Proverbs 21:1?
   e. In view of what you understand of the sovereignty and decree of God, surmise on the statement, "God answers prayers."
   e. If God has decreed all things, is He not the author of sin? Is He not responsible for the sins of His creatures? Explain as best as you can._____

2. God's Decree in Relation to the Eternal Destinies of His Rational Creatures:
   a. Which of the following best explains the difference between the terms 'foreordained' and 'predestinated' as used by the divines:
      i. Predestination is a stronger term than foreordination.
      ii. Predestination speaks about a final destination, foreordination speaks about a final state.

      iii.   Predestination includes extraordinary and supernatural acts to bring the object to his final destiny, foreordination refers to the decree to leave the object to its own liberty and to ordinary means to reach his final destination.

      iv.   Predestination includes extraordinary and supernatural acts to bring the object to his final destiny, foreordination refers only to foreknowledge of the destiny of those passed by.

      v.   They are synonymous terms used in order to show that the final destiny of the elect and the reprobate are not based upon the same grounds.

   b.   Read Berkhof's *Systematic Theology*, pp. 118–125 on Supralapsarianism and Infralapsarianism. Record your impression.

   c.   T / F — The Westminster Confession of Faith is explicitly infralapsarian.

   d.   The difference between infralapsarianism and supralapsarianism is best explained as follows:

      i.   Infralapsarianism is the order of decree adopted by Arminians, while supralapsarianism is the order of decree adopted by Calvinists.

      ii.   Infralapsarianism is the order of decree adopted by Calvinist, while supralapsarianism is the order of decree adopted only by hyper-Calvinists.

      iii.   Infralapsarianism is the view that God's decree of election was made only after the Fall, while supralapsarianism believes that God's decree of election and reprobation were made before the Fall.

      iv.   Infralapsarianism is the view that God's decree of election logically follows His decree to permit the Fall, while supralapsarianism believes that God's decree of election and reprobation precedes His decree to create and to permit the Fall.

      v.   There is no difference between infralapsarianism and supralapsarianism, they are different terminology to describe the same thing: that God has decreed before time.

3.   On God's Decree with Reference to His Elect:
   a.   How do Arminians understand predestination?
   b.   Give at least three arguments to show that the Arminian position is not valid.
   c.   How would you respond to the Arminian's charge that your concept of God makes God unfair and unjust since everyone does not have a fair chance to be saved.
   d.   Write the words in *WCF* 3.6 that show that the Westminster divines believed in particular atonement.

4.   On God's Decree with Reference to the Reprobate:
   a.   Show from Scripture that there is such a thing as reprobation.
   b.   According to the Confession, what is the difference between the ground and goal of election and reprobation?

5.   Counsel and Caveat Regarding this Doctrine:
   a.   Memorise and quote Deuteronomy 29:29.
   b.   Since election lies in the foundation of grace, why do we not address only the elect in the preaching of the Gospel? How should the unsaved be addressed and exhorted in the preaching of the Gospel?

WCF 04: OF CREATION

1.   On the Creation of the World.
   a.   Memorise and quote from memory *WSC* Q. 9, "What is the work of creation?"

b. T / F — The Scripture attributes the work Creation to the Father alone, though sometimes this work is said to be through the Son and sometime through the Spirit.

c. Proof that God created *ex nihilo* (out of nothing) from Scripture and logic:

d. To teach children that God is the Creator, the Children's Catechism, question 1 asks: "Who made you?" and answers "God." A child learning the catechism was obviously not made when God created the world in 6 days. How then is the catechism still correct with? Is there a sense in which the child was created during the creation week?

e. Explain the phrase "very good" as it applies to God's initial creation.

2. On Creation of Man:

a. T / F — Adam was created *ex nihilo*, Eve was formed out of Adam's rib.

b. What does the Scripture and our Confession mean when it teaches that man is created in the image of God? In what sense does natural man still retain the image of God, and in what sense does he not?

c. Does 1 Thessalonians 5:23 teach that man has a body, a soul and a spirit? Discuss.

d. You warned your unbelieving friend that he will face the judgement of God one day if he does not repent of his transgression of God's Laws. Your friend replied that it would be unfair for God to judge the world seeing that only Christians know the Law of God. How would you respond?

WCF 05: OF PROVIDENCE

1. On God's Providence Over the World:

a. Memorise and quote from memory *WSC* Q. 11, "What are God's works of Providence?"

b. Identify the following four views pertaining to Providence, and indicate which view is the view adopted in the Westminster Confession of Faith:
   i. God created the world, set it in motion, and left it to run on its own: _
   ii. The world is the manifestation of God's mode of existence:
   iii. God sustains the world by creating it over and over again every fraction of duration:
   iv. God has given all He created real and sustained existence as entities exterior to Himself, but He continues to govern all their action according to their nature and modes of existence: _____

c. Which of the following is *not* under God's absolute providential control?
   i. The natural world, including such motion as a leave dropping to the ground.
   ii. Chance events, such as accidents.
   iii. The circumstances and affairs of man, such as promotion at work.
   iv. The good actions of men, including believing in Christ.
   v. The sinful actions of men, including rejecting Christ.
   vi. All the above.
   vii. None of the above.

2. On Second Causes in Providence:

a. T / F — God is the First Cause in that He was the first to set everything in motion after He created the world. Everything else happen as a reaction or consequence to the first motion.

b. Give an example each of necessary, free and contingent second cause.

c. Does God still work without, above or against means today? If so, give an example.

3. On God's Providence in Relation to Sinful Actions:

a. What are the two propositions laid out in *WCF* 5.4 in relation to sinful acts?

b. T / F — The apparent paradox that exists between the two propositions is most ably resolved in the Confession.

c. Give three reasons why God some time permits His children to fall into temptation or sin.

d. Which of the following are ways by which God hardens the reprobate?

   i. By positively and directly influencing or affecting their hearts.

   ii. By withholding grace that is necessary to enlighten their understanding or to soften their hearts.

   iii. By withdrawing opportunities of hearing the Gospel and opportunities of repentance, etc.

   iv. By causing them to sin more so that they are dulled to the accusation of their conscience.

   v. By exposing them to situations and objects which their own sin nature will make occasion of to sin.

   vi. By giving them over to their own lusts, the temptations of the world, and the power of Satan.

e. Distinguish between God's purpose in allowing sin in His children and in the reprobate:

4. On General and Special Providence:

a. Explain the difference between general and special providence.

b. Give an example of God's special providence:

WCF 06: OF THE FALL OF MAN, OF SIN, AND OF THE PUNISHMENT THEREOF

1. On the Fall.

a. T / F — The Westminster Confession of Faith adequately explain the question of the origin of sin, i.e. If God is good, why is there evil in the world.

b. T / F — Adam and Eve were created with *neither* an inclination to evil or an inclination to good.

c. T / F — Babies which are born today have *neither* an inclination to evil or an inclination to good.

d. Which of the following is the best response to the question: If God is good, why does He allow evil to enter into the world:

   i. That greater good may come out of it.

   ii. God is *ex Lex* (above the Law).

   iii. Since goodness is the absence of evil, without evil, goodness is meaningless.

   iv. God had to allow evil to enter the world because He had created independent beings whose constitution requires them to make independent decisions.

   v. For the glory of God.

2. On the Consequence of the Fall:

a. In how many ways did Adam and Eve die as a consequence of the Fall? Name and explain them. In what sense did Adam and Eve experience the these ways of death *immediately* after they fell.

b. Explain the statement "became dead in sin, and wholly defiled in all the parts and faculties of soul and body" (*WCF* 6.2).

c. Critique this statement: "Total depravity does not mean that man is not able to do good towards his fellow men. It does mean however that man's nature is wholly sinful, corrupt, and perverse to the extent that sin has affected all his parts rendering him absolutely incapable of saving himself from the judgement to come … Even when man performs good works, his motives for doing so are often not pure."

d. What does Jonathan Edwards mean when he says that man has "natural ability" but no "moral ability" to seek after God?

e. Which of the following best describe Original Sin?
   a. The sin of eating the forbidden fruit.
   b. The sin of pride by which Lucifer fell.
   c. The sin of Eve when she succumb to the temptation of Satan.
   d. The consequence of Adam's Fall upon his posterity.
   e. The first sin that a fallen man commits at the point when he is capable of sinning.

f. Give at least two reasons why Original Sin is so called.

g. What are the two elements of Original Sin.

h. Memorise and quote from memory WSC 18, "Wherein consists the sinfulness of that estate whereinto man fell?"

i. Why are we considered guilty on account of Adam's sin? Explain.

3. On the Effect of Regeneration:
   a. What is the difference between the Romish idea of the effect of regeneration upon Original Sin and the Reformed doctrine?
   b. Critique the following stanza of the hymn "Love Divine" by Charles Wesley:
   Finish then Thy new creation, pure and spotless let us be;
   Let us see Thy great salvation perfectly restored in Thee:
   Changed from glory into glory, Till in heaven we take our place,
   Till we cast our crowns before Thee, Lost in wonder, love and praise.

4. On the Wages of Sin:
   a. T / F — Sin involves only the outward transgression of the Law of God.
   b. Memorise and quote WSC 14: What is sin?
   c. What does the Confession mean by the "curse of the law"? How is it effected in this world and the world to come?

WCF 07: OF GOD'S COVENANT WITH MAN

1. On Reason for Covenant.
   a. According to the Westminster divines, why does God deal with man by way of covenant?
   b. Which of the following definition best describe a divine covenant?
      i. An agreement between God and man.
      ii. A contract jointly framed between God as creator and man as creature.
      iii. A treaty between God and man in which a third party is called as a witness.

      iv.   A bond between God and man, committing both to loyalty on pain of death, in which God stipulate the term.

      v.   A sovereignly entered bond between God and man, —which is sealed with blood.

  c.   What are the five elements of a covenant in the Ancient Near Eastern Culture that is also found in a divine covenant?

2.   On the Covenant of Works:

  a.   Briefly explain why we believe that God did enter into a covenant with Adam though the word 'covenant' does not appear until Genesis 6?

  b.   Identify the essential elements (of a covenant) of the Covenant of Works.

  c.   Why do some covenantal theologians (e.g. Hoeksema), while believing that God has made a covenant with Adam object to its being called a Covenant of *Works*?

  d.   Some theologians (Buswell) have come up with a neat scheme in which Adam and Eve would die if they eat of the Tree of Knowledge of Good and Evil, whereas if they ate of the Tree of Life, they would have been granted eternal life. Comment on this scheme.

  e.   Memorise and quote from memory *WSC* 12, "What special act of providence did God exercise toward man in the estate wherein he was created?"

  f.   Memorise and quote from memory *WSC* 16, "Did all mankind fall in Adam's first transgression?"

3.   On the Covenant of Grace:

  a.   T / F — The *WCF* distinguish between the Covenant of Grace and the Covenant of Redemption.

  b.   T / F — The *WCF* teaches that the Covenant of Grace is a covenant between God and man.

  c.   T / F — The parties of the Covenant of Grace is the Truine God on the one hand, and all mankind on the other hand.

  d.   T / F — The WCF teaches that the Covenant of Grace is a bond-in-blood between God the Father representing the entire Godhead, and God the Son representing the elect.

  e.   T / F — The Covenant of Grace was made after the Covenant of Works was violated.

  f.   T / F— The Covenant of Grace is the basis of God's common grace towards all mankind.

  g.   T / F — The Covenant of Grace according to the *WCF* does not have any conditions or requirements.

  h.   T / F — The Covenant of Grace according to the *WCF* is a unilateral, unconditional as it relates to man.

  i.   T / F — As the condition of the Covenant of Works is perfect, personal obedience on the part of man, so the condition of the Covenant of Grace is faith in the Lord Jesus Christ.

  j.   Identify the five elements (of a covenant) of the Covenant of Grace, describing each very briefly (one sentence):

  k.   In what sense is the Covenant of Grace a continuation of the Covenant of Work? In what sense is the Covenant of Works still valid today?

  l.   Memorise and quote from memory *WSC* 20, "Did God leave all mankind to perish in the estate of sin and misery?"

m.   Cite the *classical locus* (the central and most important text pertaining to) of covenant theology which refers to both the Covenant of Works and the Covenant of Grace.

4.   On Covenant Versus Testament:
a.   Read O. Palmer Robertson, *The Christ in the Covenants*, p. 3-15. Explain briefly the difference a testament and a covenant.
b.   How should we understand the word 'testament' whenever it occurs in the confession?

5.   On The Covenant of Grace in the Old and New Testament
a.   T / F —   The Old Covenant is the Covenant of Works, the New Covenant is the Covenant of Grace.
b.   T / F —   Believers under the Old Covenant were saved by obedience to the Law, whereas believers under the New Covenant are saved by faith in Christ.
c.   T / F —   Old Testament saints were saved by grace through faith in Christ.
d.   T / F —   Old Testament saints were regenerated in the same way as New Testament believers.
e.   T / F —   The Holy Spirit indwelt Old Testament believers just as they do New Testament believers.
f.   T / F —   The gift of regeneration, indwelling of the Holy Spirit *properly* belong to the New Covenant dispensation.
g.   T / F —   God has two programmes in His salvation plan: one for Israel, and another for the Church.
h.   T / F —   Old Testament promises are made to the nation of Israel, therefore they cannot be fulfilled in the Church.
i.   Name 5 subordinate covenants of the Old Testament, together with the passage that describe the covenant:
j.   In what two ways are the subordinate covenants united? Explain briefly.
k.   In what ways is the New Covenant superior to the Old Covenant?
l.   Critique as best as you can the following statement: "When God made a covenant with Abraham, He promised that his seed will inherit the land of Canaan. That covenant is unilateral and therefore Israel will certainly inherit the land of Canaan permanently. Since this has not been completely fulfilled, it will be fulfilled in the millennium. As such a Covenant theologian must necessarily be a Premillennialist."

WCF 08: OF CHRIST THE MEDIATOR

1.   On the Mediatorial offices of Christ
a.   Define the office of a mediator
b.   T / F —   Adam was the mediator of all mankind before the Fall.
c.   In what 3 ways does Christ function as the mediator of the elect?
d.   Write down *WSC* 23-26, stating question and answer. If possible, write from memory.
e.   Which of the three offices is particularly in focus in these titles or names of Christ? (i) Chief Shepherd; (ii) Angel of the LORD; (iii) Bread of life; (iv) Saviour; (v) Shiloh;(vi) Wisdom; (vii) Second Adam; (viii) Branch; (ix) Lamb of God; (x)Christ; (xi) Comforter; (xii) Lord; (xiii) Potentate; (xiv) Almighty; (xv) Word.

2.   On the Person of the Lord Jesus Christ:

a. *FITB*. Jesus Christ is _____ man and _____ God.

b. T / F — Christ is one person with 2 wills, one human and one divine.

c. T / F — Every action of Christ recorded in the New Testament can clear be attributed to Christ as God or Christ as man.

d. T / F — Christ has a human body and a soul. Since He is also God, His soul is the Spirit of God (or His divinity).

e. T / F — Christ became the Son of God only at the incarnation.

f. T / F — Christ is still fully human today.

g. T / F — When Christ was a baby in the arms of Mary, He was not omniscient as he has to grow in wisdom (Lk 2:52).

h. T / F — The *earliest* error pertaining to the Person of Christ which the Church had to deal with has to do with a denial of the deity of Christ.

i. T / F — The unity between Christ's divine nature and human nature is perfectly illustrated by the unity between the human soul and the human body.

j. State in English the four adjectival phrases (or adjectives) which were used to describe the relationship between the two natures of Christ in Chalcedonian Creed of AD 451:

k. Why was it that Christ was not imputed with Adam's guilt nor inherit his sinful nature?

3. On Christ's Qualification for the Mediatorial Office:
   a. T / F — The Westminster divines believed that Christ was not equipped for His mediatorial office until the Holy Spirit descended upon Him during his baptism.
   b. Was Christ able to sin during His incarnation?

4. On the Humiliation and Exaltation of Christ:
   a. Why is it important that Christ willingly took up the office of a Mediator as appointed by the Father?
   b. Memorise and quote from memory *WSC* 27: "Wherein did Christ's humiliation consist?"
   c. Memorise and quote from memory *WSC* 28: "Wherein did Christ's exaltation consist?"

5. On the Work of Redemption
   a. Distinguish between the nature and purpose of Christ Active Obedience and Passive Obedience:
   b. T / F— The sufficiency of the death of Christ means that Christ has accomplished all that is necessary to make salvation possible for everyone without exception.
   c. T / F— The sufficiency of the death of Christ means that sinner should always be encouraged to come to Christ by telling them that Christ died for them.
   d. Why is Christ's death perfectly sufficient to accomplish what it is designed to accomplish?
   e. T / F — Although Old Testament saints were saved by grace through faith in Christ Jesus, they were kept in an intermediate state until Christ's work of redemption is accomplished.

WCF 09: OF FREE WILL

1. On the Liberty of Free Agents
   a. T / F — According to the *WCF* , all the actions of man, including his sinful actions are foreordained of God and ordered by His providence.
   b. Does not the doctrine of predestination make men robots? Explain:

2. On Free Will in the Fourfold State of Man
   a. Name the four states of man and describe the will's relation to sin in that state.
   b. Which of the following statements (more than one) are TRUE about the will of a fallen and unregenerate person?
      i. He has a free will in the sense that he has the power and ability to do what right and good in the sight of God.
      ii. He has a free will in the sense that he has the power and ability to do all that he wants to do.
      iii. He has a free will in the sense that he has the liberty to act according to his heart's desire.
      iv. He does not have free will at all since he cannot do what he may consider to be right.
      v. He does not have free will in the sense that his will is held bondage to the inclinations of his heart.
   c. Which of the following illustration best describe the relationship between an unregenerate sinner and the Kingdom of God.
      i. The door of the Kingdom is locked, so the sinner cannot enter.
      ii. The Kingdom is hidden, so the sinner cannot see it.
      iii. The door of the Kingdom is open, the sinner can see within clearly, but he prefers the outside.
      iv. The door of the Kingdom is open, but the sinner cannot see what is within clearly. He does not enter because he sees the world, and loves it.
      v. All the above will do.
      vi. None of the above because:
   d. Which of the following illustration best describe the entrance of a sinner into the Kingdom of God (i.e. regeneration or effectual call).
      i. The door of the Kingdom is suddenly unlocked, the sinner who is leaning against the door falls within.
      ii. The door of the Kingdom appears out of nowhere, someone stood at the door to persuade the sinner. The sinner decides to take a step of faith into the Kingdom.
      iii. The door of the Kingdom is open and has been open. The sinner who had hitherto love the world and hated the King, suddenly and supernaturally finds the Kingdom and the King attractive and feels compelled to enter into the door and he does so most willingly.
      iv. The door of the Kingdom is open and has been open, the sinner is standing outside the door. He does not enter because he sees the world, and loves it. Suddenly a hand reaches out of the door and dragged him in kicking and screaming unwillingly.
      v. The door of the Kingdom is open and has been open, the sinner who has hitherto stayed outside decides to step in to see what he may find since he was told that there are treasures to be found beyond the door.
      vi. All the above will do.
      vii. None of the above because:

e. Which of the following best describe the relationship between a sinner and the Gospel?
   i. The sinner is like a sick man, the Gospel is like a bitter pill that will cure him. All he needs to do is to reach out to take hold of the pill and he will be saved.
   ii. The sinner is like drowning man, the Gospel is like a life buoy that has been thrown beside him, all he needs to do is to reach out for the life buoy and he will be saved.
   iii. The sinner is like one among many in a large pit, a few ropes have been lowered into the pit, those who are elect have the robe lowered directly over them and all they need to do is to grab the rope and they shall be saved.
   iv. The sinner is like a beggar. He does not need to do anything but to reach out his hand to receive the life saving packages that are handed out to him.
   v. The sinner is like Lazarus, dead and rotting, the Gospel comes to him as Christ's call to Lazarus to come out of the grave. He is resurrected and comes out to Christ.
   vi. All the above.
   vii. None of the above.

f. T / F — An unregenerate person can prepare to receive grace by living a righteous life, listening to sermons and reading the Bible. These activities assure that God will be graciously disposed to convert.

g. T / F — An unregenerate person can listen to sermons and read the Bible. However, these activities are not considered righteous in the eye of God seeing they are tainted with sin.

h. T / F — After the Fall the ability of the will to do good was destroyed, but the liberty of the will remains the same.

i. T / F — When a believer is glorified, he is unable to sin because the liberty of his will is clipped.

WCF 10: OF EFFECTUAL CALLING

1. On the Nature of the Effectual Call:
   a. Which of the following best define the *ordo salutis*?
      i. The steps that a sinner must take in his salvation.
      ii. The time sequence of event that must take place in the salvation of a soul
      iii. The steps in time that God takes in the salvation of a soul.
      iv. The logical steps in God's work of salvation in and upon the soul of His elect.
      v. An order to salute each other with a holy kiss.
   b. Distinguish between the effectual call and the external call? Cite a couple of passages in Scripture to demonstrate that the Scripture supports such a distinction:
   c. T / F — The external call is automatically in operation when the Word of God is faithfully preached.
   d. T / F— The internal call is automatically in operation whenever the word of God is faithfully preached.
   e. T / F— The external call involves hearing with the physical ear, effectual call involves hearing with spiritual ears that are implanted by the Holy Spirit.
   f. T / F— The Holy Spirit is God's instrument of effectual call whereas the Word acts as the Agency.

g.　T / F—　The effectual call involves the Holy Spirit wooing the sinner unto salvation. The sinner must respond to the Spirit's overture for conversion to begin.

h.　What are the common operations of the Holy Spirit upon the heart of the sinner? What is the difference between the effectual call and such operations?

i.　Why do the divines say that in the effectual call, the soul is "altogether passive" when the sinner obviously could and should read the Word and attend sermons?

2.　On the Effectual Call of those Incapable of being Outwardly Called

a.　T / F—　The Westminster divines believe that all infant of believing parents are elect and therefore if they die in infancy they will be regenerated and saved by Christ.

b.　What's wrong with the view that all infants dying in infancy will be regenerated and saved by Christ.

3.　On those who have not been Effectually Called.

a.　What do you think will happen to the innocent pagans who die without having the opportunity to hear the Gospel?

b.　Why do you think theologians such as Gerstner believe that the deepest part of hell is reserved for professing believers who never truly believe?

WCF 11: OF JUSTIFICATION

1.　On the Nature of Justification

a.　T / F —　Justification involves God ignoring the sins of His elect so that their sins need not be paid for.

b.　Memorise and quote *WSC* 33, "What is justification?"

c.　Distinguish between justification and effectual calling (or regeneration).

d.　Which of the following *best* illustrate justification. Remember that it need not describe justification in exact details.

　　i.　A delinquent child was in court standing trial. His father who happened to be the judge lovingly admonished him. He was so moved that he turned over a new leave and from then on lived a just and moral life.

　　ii.　A delinquent child was in court standing trial. His father who happened to be the judge admonished him and said: "Because you are my child, I forgive you for the wrong you have done. Do not repeat the same sin."

　　iii.　A murderer was in court standing trial, the judge found him to be not guilty, and pronounced him righteous.

　　iv.　A murderer was in court standing trial, the judge found him guilty, but out of compassion gave a 'not guilty' verdict.

　　v.　A boy was in court standing trial, the judge found him guilty, but the boy's father paid a ransom sum, and so the judge set him free.

　　vi.　A man was in court standing trial for murder, the judge found him guilty, but the boy's best friend offered to be punished on his behalf. The judge accepted his offer and freed the boy.

　　vii.　A man was in court standing trial for defrauding a sum of money committed to his trust. The person whom this man owed happened to be the judge. The judge tried him and found him guilty, but then forgave him his debt and freed him.

      viii. A man was in court standing trial for murder, the judge happens to be the man's father. The judge sentenced him to death, but that night he went to the death row, and exchanged place with his son. The judge was executed the next day, and the son went free.

    e.   Explain briefly why you chose the particular answer in (d) and why you did not chose the others:

    f.   T / F — The Roman Catholic doctrine of justification is the same as that of the Protestant. The only problem is that when Rome speaks of justification, she includes sanctification into the term, but when the Reformers spoke about justification, they do not include sanctification.

    g.   T / F— The Protestant doctrine of justification teaches that a person becomes righteous in the eye of God though he remains a sinner.

    h.   T / F — The Protestant doctrine of justification teaches that a person who is justified remains actually a sinner.

    i.   T / F — The Protestant doctrine of justification teaches that a person who is justified may continue to live in sin consciously.

    j.   T / F — Sola Fides or "the just shall live by faith" means that faith is the ground of our justification, or we are justified on account of faith.

    k.   Write from memory the three formulae of justification, representing the Roman Catholic view, the antinomian view and the Reformed view.

    l.   What are the two benefits of justification? How are they made possible?

    m. In September 1992, a group of Roman Catholics and Protestant theologians got together and framed what is known as the *Evangelical & Catholic Together* (ECT) paper. In the paper, the following statement was made: "We affirm together that we are justified by grace through faith because of Christ....All who accept Christ as Lord and Saviour are brothers and sisters in Christ." Comment or critique on this statement.

2.   On the Timing of Justification
    a.   T / F — All who believes in eternal justification are hyper-Calvinists.
    b.   Explain the difference between eternally justified, historically justified and actually justified.
    c.   T / F— The *WCF* speaks of justification only in the third sense.
    d.   Why is it important to distinguish the three aspects of justification?

3.   On Justification and Forgiveness:
    a.   T / F— When God justifies a sinner, He forgives him his sins in the same way that a Christian ought to forgive a person who asks our forgiveness for a sin committed against us.
    b.   If God had forgiven the sins of those He justifies, why does the Lord teach us to pray "forgive us our debts as we forgive our debtors"?

WCF 12: OF ADOPTION

1.   On Adoption
    a.   Memorise and quote *WSC* 34, "What is adoption?"
    b.   What is the difference between justification and adoption?
    c.   Compare and contrast God's adoption of us as His children and civil adoption of a child by a childless couple:

WCF 13: OF SANCTIFICATION

1. On the Nature of Sanctification.
   a. What does the word 'sanctification' or 'sanctify' literally mean?
   b. Memorise and quote *WSC* 35, "What is sanctification?"
   c. Compare and Contrast Justification and Sanctification.

2. On the Extent, Degree and Triumph of Sanctification
   a. 1 Cor 1:2, 6:11; Heb 10:10, 14 and Jude 1 speak of 'sanctification' as happening at a point in time rather than as a process. Some theologians call this form of sanctification "positional sanctification," "definite sanctification," or "initial sanctification." Without spending time to check these terms up in the Systematic Theologies, what do you think this kind of 'sanctification' involve? [Hint: consider Q1(a) above; consider also the phrase "further sanctified" in *WCF* 13.1].
   b. i. T / F — Regeneration is monergistic (God working alone), Sanctification is synergistic (God and man co-operating).
      ii. Explain your answer:
   c. T / F — The believer must participate in God's work of sanctification by the use of the Means of Grace.
   d. T / F— The believer ultimately determines how much he will be sanctified in this life.
   e. What does the Confession mean by "sanctification is throughout, in the whole man" (*WCF* 13.2)?
   f. T / F — It is possible to be free from wilful sin in this life.
   g. What are some of the means of grace, or of sanctification?
   h. What is wrong with the view of sanctification that teaches that normal Christians should have victory over all known sin?
   i. Is there such a thing as a Carnal Christian? Why, why not?
   j. T / F — A regenerate man has two natures: a sinful nature and new nature—just as Christ has two natures.
   k. When the Confession speaks about the "continual and irreconcilable war" (*WCF* 13.2), what are the parties at war, how is this war fought?
   l. T / F — The Confession teaches that the Christian will have no victory over sin in this life.

WCF 14: OF SAVING FAITH

1. On the Nature of Faith
   a. What may we learn about faith from Heb 10:39-1:3, 6?
   b. Memorise and quote *WSC* 86, "What is Faith in Jesus Christ?"
   c. Prove from Scripture that there is such a thing as non-saving or hypocritical faith.
   d. T / F— Faith is initially wrought in the heart of a sinner by an act of regeneration by the Holy Spirit.
   e. T / F— Faith is wrought ordinarily through the instrumentality of the Word.
   f. T / F— When ever the Word of God is preach, faith comes as a consequence.

2. On the Objects and Acts of Saving Faith:
   a. T / F— It is sufficient for salvation for sinner to believe that Christ died for him.

b. T / F— It is not possible for a person who does not apprehend the doctrine of the Trinity to be saved.

c. Identify the three elements of Saving Faith. Which two aspects are emphasised in the Confession. Which two aspects may be present in an unregenerate person?

3. On the Degrees of Faith
   a. Prove from Scripture that weak faith may still be genuine faith.
   b. T / F — A person who has strong faith is a person who does not doubt the truth of the Word of God.
   c. What is the difference between assurance of faith and assurance of sense?
   d. T / F — A Christian must have assurance of faith because a true Christian cannot possibly doubt his own salvation.
   e. T / F — A Christian must have assurance of faith because faith without assurance of the truth of what is believed is not faith.

WCF 15: OF REPENTANCE UNTO LIFE

1. On the Nature of Repentance:
   a. What does the word 'repentance' (*metanoia*) or 'repent' literally mean? _____
   b. Memorise and quote *WSC* 87, "What is Repentance unto Life?"
   c. Quote a Scripture reference to show that repentance is a gift of God: _____
   d. What is the difference between evangelical repentance and legal repentance?
   e. T / F — A unregenerate person may only repent legally while the repentance of a regenerate person will always be evangelical.
   f. T / F — Only the elect will be enabled to truly obey the call to repentance. Therefore, legal repentance may be said to be false repentance.
   g. T / F— Legal repentance may involve the sinner knowing the grave danger that his soul is in. In evangelical repentance, the sinner not only see the danger that his soul is in, but sense the odiousness and filthiness of his sin in the sight of God.
   h. Why is it necessary to know the difference between evangelical repentance and legal repentance?
   i. What are the two grounds of evangelical repentance and how would the regenerate sinner respond in each of the two grounds?
   j. Contrast between the way that the Gospel was preached by the Puritans and by the modern evangelists?

2. On the Necessity and Efficacy of Repentance:
   a. What is the difference between the Romish doctrine of repentance and the Protestant doctrine of repentance?
   b. T / F — The Protestant doctrine of repentance teaches that pardon for sin is granted independently of repentance so that a person may be pardoned and clothed with the righteousness of Christ when he embrace Him as Saviour even though he had no conviction of sin.
   c. An evangelist quotes Matthew 11:28, "Come unto me, all ye that labour and are heavy laden, and I will give you rest." He invites all who are tired of their pursuit of worldly pleasures and wealth; all who are burdened by the marital problems that they have; and all who have laboured unsuccessfully to kick their bad habits like

drinking and smoking to come to Christ. Is there anything wrong with this invitation? Why, why not?

    d.   T / F —   Every sin is equally sinful in the eye of God.

    e.   T / F —   Every sin deserves eternal damnation.

    f.   T / F —   There is no sin that cannot be pardoned.

    g.   T / F —   Every sinner that genuinely repents can expect pardon.

    h.   T / F —   Only a person who has repented of all his particular sins in particular may expect to enter heaven since it is man's duty to repent of his particular sins, particularly and none can expect pardon without repentance.

3.   On the Duty of Repentance:

    a.   T / F —   Repentance will only be genuine if it includes a confession to the parties offended or injured.

    b.   T / F —   True repentance should manifest itself in confession.

    c.   T / F —   We should only forgive a person if we can be sure that he has genuinely repented of his deed.

    d.   T / F —   We must forgive a person, and tell him so, whether or not he repents of his sins against us.

    e.   T / F —   We must have a forgiving spirit, bearing no grudge and willing to forgive at any time even when a person who did us wrong does not come up to confess his faults to us.

WCF 16: OF GOOD WORKS

1.   On the Nature of Good Works

    a.   What exactly is the will of God mentioned in Romans 12:2 and Hebrews 13:21?

    b.   T / F —   According to the *WCF*, a deed when considered by itself is good so long as it is not forbidden by Scripture.

    c.   T / F —   Whether a deed is good is only dependent on the intention of the doer.

    d.   T / F —   There is such a thing as a matter of indifference in which an action may be considered to be neither good nor bad.

    e.   T / F —   Swimming can be regarded as "good work" as it is good for the body, and Christians have a duty to maintain the health of our bodies.

    f.   T / F —   Reading of the Scriptures and prayer may always be regarded as "good work."

    g.   T / F —   Helping the poor may always be regarded as "good work."

    h.   T / F —   Making a vow to remain celibate so as to serve the Lord with undivided attention may be regarded as good work.

    i.   Which of the following are legitimate uses of good works:

        i.   As a means to have a better standing before God.

        ii.   As a manifestation of our faith.

        iii.   As expression of gratitude to God.

        iv.   As a means to obtain reward and happiness in heaven.

        v.   As a means to stop the mouth of adversaries.

        vi.   As a means to edify the saints.

        vii.   As a means to quieten guilty conscience.

        viii. As a means to invoke material and spiritual blessings.

2.   On the Ability to do Good Works; the Value of Good Works and the Works of the

Unregenerate:
a. T / F—   Although man is totally depraved, and unable to do anything pertaining to his salvation, his work in the civil and cultural realm may be considered as good.
b. What is the Romish doctrine of supererogation? Show that this doctrine is false.
c. T / F—   The *WCF* does teach that good works done in sincerity by Christians, although accompanied with many weaknesses and imperfection may be rewarded by God.
d. What are the three criteria to determine whether a good work (when considered abstractly) may actually be good?

WCF 17: OF THE PERSEVERANCE OF THE SAINTS

1. On the Certainty of Perseverance:
   a. What does the word 'perseverance' emphasise in relation to this doctrine?
   b. What does the word 'preservation' emphasise?
   c. Why do Arminians not believe in the perseverance of the saints?

2. On the Basis of Perseverance:
   a. Does the doctrine of perseverance encourage believers to live in sin and carelessness? Why, or why not?
   b. T / F —   Only those who persevere to the end will be saved.
   c. T / F —   Believers persevere to the end because they choose to do so.
   d. T / F —   Some of the elect may be lost because God ceases to preserve them.
   e. T / F —   Old Testament saints, unlike us, did not have the Holy Spirit abiding in them and, as a result, they had to persevere in their faith by their own free will.
   f. Prove from John 3:16 the perseverance of the saints [Hint: focus on the word "everlasting."]

3. On the Possibility of Backsliding
   a. T / F —   True believers will never fall into any grievous sins and if they do, they prove that they were never truly saved.
   b. T / F—   Therefore, ultimately whether we be eternally saved will be dependant on both God's preservation of us and our perseverance by working out our salvation with fear and trembling.
   c. T / F—   Christians who backslide can expect God to chastise with temporal as well as eternal judgements.
   d. How should the church and the individual view a professing Christian who has severely backslidden from the faith?

WCF 18: OF THE ASSURANCE OF GRACE AND SALVATION

1. On True and False Assurance
   a. List 3 reasons for our assertion that infallible assurance of grace is possible.
   b. List 3 errors related to the handling of the doctrine of assurance.
   c. List 3 ways in which true assurance may be distinguished from false assurance.

2. On the Grounds of True Assurance
   a. Explain briefly the 3 grounds of "infallible assurance of faith" given in *WCF* 18.2.

b. T / F — A person who says "I do not believe that Jesus Christ died to save sinners" can nevertheless be a true Christian.

c. T / F — A person who says "I am not sure if Jesus Christ died to save me" can nevertheless be a true Christian.

3. On the Growth and Renewal of Assurance
   a. Explain briefly what is meant by the "being" and "well-being" of faith.
   b. T / F — Infallible assurance belong to the essence of faith. A person who doubts his salvation cannot possibly be saved.
   c. T / F — It is the duty of every Christian to seek assurance of faith.
   d. What are some ways in which a Christian may cultivate faith.

WCF 19: OF THE LAW OF GOD

1. On the Moral Law as a Perpetual Rule of Life:
   a. Quote a Scripture reference to show that the Moral Law is written in the heart of man and explain how experience affirms this truth:
   b. Memorise and quote the answers to WSC 39-42:
      i. WCF 39 What is the duty which God requireth of man? _____
      ii. WCF 40 What did God at first reveal to man for the rule of His obedience?
      iii. WCF 41 Where is the Moral Law summarily comprehended?
      ii. WCF 42 What is the sum of the Ten Commandments?
   c. I am able / unable* to quote Exodus 20:1-17 [If you are unable, do make an attempt to memorise this *very* important passage in the Bible]
   d. List the Ten Commandments (from memory) in its abbreviated form such as given in the notes.
   e. What is the difference between the way in which the Reformed Church divides the Ten Commandments and the way in which the Lutherans and the Roman Catholic Church divide it? What is the practical implication of the difference?

2. On the Threefold division of the Law of God:
   a. What are the three categories of laws that can be found in the Word of God?
   b. What is the primary purpose of the Ceremonial Law? Show from Scripture that it has been abrogated:
   c. What is a secondary purpose of the Ceremonial Law highlighted in our Confession?
   d. What was the purpose of the Judicial Law. Why is it no longer directly applicable?
   e. Prove from Scripture that the Moral is still authoritative:
   f. What does Paul mean when he says, "For sin shall not have dominion over you: *for ye are not under the law, but under grace*" (Rom 6:14)?

3. On the Uses of the Moral Law:
   a. T / F— The Moral Law is useful for both believers and unbelievers, but only unbelievers are obliged to keep it since only unbelievers are under it as a covenant of works.
   b. T / F— According to the WCF, one of the functions of the Moral Law as it pertains to the regenerate (true believer) is that it drives him to conviction, humiliation and hatred for sin.
   c. What are 3 uses of the Law according to Calvin? Explain each use briefly.

4. On the Law's Relation to Grace:

a. T / F — The difference between a true Christian and an unregenerate man is that a Christian will obey the Law only out of gratitude and love for the Lord, whereas an unregenerate person obeys the law because of its threats.
b. T / F — The Gospel is meaningless without the Law.
c. Explain your answer to (b):

WCF 20: OF CHRISTIAN LIBERTY, AND LIBERTY OF CONSCIENCE

1. On the Aspects of Christian Liberty:
   a. The Lord Jesus said: "If the Son therefore shall make you free, ye shall be free indeed" (Jn 8:36). Enumerate the 5 aspects of this freedom given in *WCF* 20.1.
   b. T / F — These privileges are only available to New Testament believers.
   c. What does the Confession mean when it teaches us that believers are delivered from the "bondage to Satan, and dominion of sin"?

2. On the Advantage of N.T Saints over O.T. Saints:
   a. Which of the following are the privileges that the New Testament believer has over the Old Testament believer ?
      i. They are freed from the stipulations of the Moral Laws
      ii. They are freed from the Ceremonial Laws.
      iii. The Holy Spirit indwells them.
      iv. They have access to the throne of grace.
      v. They have greater boldness of access to the throne of grace.
      vi. They have a fuller communication of the free Spirit of God.

   b. Explain what the Confession mean by "fuller communications of the free Spirit of God."

3. On the Liberty of Conscience:
   a. Define 'Conscience':
   b. T / F— The conscience is infallible (cannot be wrong).
   c. T / F— The conscience should always be obeyed when it objects to a particular deed.
   d. T / F— When the conscience approves of a particular deed, the Christian need not necessary engage in the deed.
   e. T / F— The *WCF* distinguishes between doctrine and commandments of *men* and the doctrine and commandments of *God*.
   f. T / F— The *WCF* distinguishes between doctrine and commandments found in the Word of God pertaining to faith & worship, and those pertaining to conversation or the Christian Life.
   g. What two classes of doctrines and commandments of men are distinguished in *WCF* 20.2 and 20.4. How should our conscience relate to them?

4. On Licentiousness:
   a. T / F — The Christian are freed from the Law of Moses, but not freed from the Law of Christ.
   b. James was probably referring to the Moral Law of God in Jas 1:25. Explain why he calls it the "perfect law of liberty":

5. On the Duty of a Church Member or a Citizen

a. Quote two biblical references to show that church member or a citizen of a nation ought to submit to the constitution of the church or the nation: ___

b. Quote a reference to show that such submission is to be subject to demands of the Word of God so that a person must obey only what is not contrary to the word of God: ___

c. T / F— It is the duty of the Church and the State to punish all acts of sin.

d. T / F— The church may impose doctrines and practices which it believes (constitutionally) to be in accordance to the Word of God, even if some members do not think the doctrine and practices are scriptural.

e. T / F— The civil magistrate may punish a Christian who breaks the law of the land because he believes that the law is contrary to the Word of God. The Christian should submit to such punishment with the understanding that God will be his vindicator.

f. T / F— Every member of the church must obey and subscribe to all that is taught in the church constitution or confession.

g. T / F— A church never has a right to censure a member who opposes the constitutional doctrine and practices of the church because he believes it to be anti-Scriptural.

h. T / F— A church never has a right to censure a member who upholds the constitutional doctrine and practices of the church, and therefore opposes the doctrine and practices of the church because they have deviated from the church constitution.

i. Optional Question: Is there any warrant for an opposition party to exist in a church (such as the Free Church Defence Association) or in a nation? What is the basis of their existence and how should it function?

WCF 21: OF RELIGIOUS WORSHIP AND THE SABBATH DAY

1. On the Object and Manner of Worship:
   a. What does the Confession mean by "light of nature." What does the light of nature reveal concerning God and what does it not reveal?
   b. State the *Reformed* Regulative Principle of Worship.
   c. State the *Romish* or *Lutheran* formula.
   d. T / F — The second commandment is not so much about worshipping idols as it is about worshipping God with images.
   e. T / F — The Westminster divines understood the 2nd Commandment to prohibit all forms of worship of God not instituted by God Himself.
   f. Show briefly that the Regulative Principle of Worship is a valid scriptural principle:
   g. Show that worshipping of saints and angels, or the directing of prayers to them is forbidden in the Scriptures:

2. On the Elements of Worship:
   a. What are the five *regular* elements of worship highlighted in the *WCF* ?
   b. Your friend from another church suggests to you that the Lord Supper should be held every week since the Lord said "As often as you meet, this do in remembrance of me..." How would you respond?
   c. Which of the following would *not* be allowed in a public worship of God according to the Regulative Principle of Worship taught in our Confession?
      i. Lighting a candle to represent the illumination of the Holy Spirit.

  ii. Reading from the Apocrypha.

  iii. Reading from sermon notes.

  iv. Using a video tape of a pre-recorded sermon.

  v. Singing of uninspired hymns.

  vi. Use of an overhead projector.

  vii. Using a microphone and loudspeakers

  viii. Reading from the Westminster Confession of Faith (not during sermon).

  ix. Making the sign of a cross at prayer.

  x. Congregation reading the Bible silently to follow sermon.

  xi. Congregational responsive reading.

  xii. Congregation saying 'Amen' aloud after prayer.

  xiii. Choir presentation.

  xiv. Puppet show.

  xv. Piano / Organ recital.

 c. How would you class the 'call to worship' and the 'benediction'?

 d. [Optional] Is collection of offerings permissible during worship?

 e. [Optional] Calvin and all the Puritans including the Westminster divines did not allow the use of musical accompaniment for the singing of Psalms because musical instruments were considered to be part of shadows and types in Old Testament Worship. Can a church that holds to the regulative principle legitimately use an instrument? Explain. (If your answer is yes, explain any restriction you may place).

3. On the Place of Worship:

 a. T / F — The sanctuary that is used for the public worship of God is a holy place. It must never be used for anything other than religious gatherings.

 b. T / F — Prayer made in a worship sanctuary is more efficacious than one made in the supermarket.

 c. When we sing the psalms which refer to the temple of God, e.g. "One thing have I desired of the LORD, that will I seek after; that I may dwell in the house of the LORD all the days of my life, to behold the beauty of the LORD, and to enquire in his temple" (Ps 27:4) or "Enter into his gates with thanksgiving, and into his courts with praise: be thankful unto him, and bless his name" (Ps 100:4). How should we understand the temple to refer to?

 d. T / F— The *WCF* does allow for private personal and family worship be carried out more informally than public worship.

4. On the Time of Worship (the Christian Sabbath):

 a. Explain why the 4th Commandment is a perpetual (always applicable until the end of the world) and universal (applicable to Jews and Gentiles, believers and unbelievers).

 b. Does the change in the day in which the Sabbath is to be observed violate and annul the 4th Commandment? Explain.

 c. What are the Scriptural warrants for Christians to observe the Sabbath on the 1st Day of the week rather than the 7th Day?

 d. How would you respond to a Christian who says that he finds playing golf very restful, and so he likes to play golf after worship service?

 e. Briefly explain (in your own words) how you should sanctify the Sabbath day.

 f. Would you consider doing your marketing on the Lord's Day morning permissible? Why, why not?

g.   [Optional] Would you consider taking public transport permissible on the Lord's Day? Why, why not?

WCF 22: OF LAWFUL OATHS AND VOWS

1.   On Lawful Oaths:
   a.   Distinguish between an oath and a vow. What are the two kinds of oaths?
   b.   In view of Matthew 5:34-37, explain why oaths and vows are still legitimate under the New Covenant.
   c.   Why must an oath only be taken in the name of God?
   d.   Explain in your own words the usefulness of an oath and on what occasions an oath would be legitimately used.
   e.   What are the two conditions that must attend our making an oath?
   f.   Explain the terms "mental reservation" and "equivocation." Why does the *WCF* forbid the use of them in the making of oaths and vows?

2.   On Vows:
   a.   T / F —   A vow must always be made in the presence of others just like an oath.
   b.   T / F —   A vow may be disregarded if the execution of it would result in financial hardship for the person making the vow.
   c.   T / F —   A vow may be regarded as null and void if it was made in ignorance as to the gravity of making such a vow.
   d.   T / F —   A vow made by a believer when he was still an unbeliever would still be binding to him.
   e.   Consider the case of Joe and Mary. They were eighteen years of age, —both believers, —when they vowed to marry one after they complete their studies, Joe in U.S., Mary in Australia. This vow was taken in a simple engagement ceremony attended by their pastor and close friends. Two years past and Mary met another young man in Australia, and is planning to marry him. Joe heard about the intention and comes to you for advice. How would you advise him?
   f.   T / F —   The *WCF* teaches that it is legitimate to make a vow in connection with a prayer to obtain something that we are desirous of having.
   g.   Explain your answer in (f)
   h.   In your own words, explain how a vow can be useful for your Christian walk.
   i.   Explain how taking vows rashly can be 'dangerous' for Christians?

WCF 23: OF THE CIVIL MAGISTRATE

1.   On the Establishment of the Civil Government:
   a.   Show from Scripture that Christ is to be regarded as the supreme authority over the world today.
   b.   How do you know that Daniel 7:13-14 is not about an earthly political millennium after Christ returns to judge the world?
   c.   Cite two Scripture references to show that the civil government of the land is instituted by God.
   d.   Distinguish between (1) the Establishment Principle; (2) the Erastian Principle; (3) the Papal Principle and (4) the Voluntary Principle.
   e.   What condition must be fulfilled before the Establishment Principle can be applied? In what sense may it be applied when that condition is not yet fully realised?

f.   T / F —War is a great evil therefore Christians ought never to participate in any war

2.   On the Duties and Limitations of the Civil Government:
   a.   According to the original statement of our Confession, what may and what may not the civil magistrate take upon itself with respect to the Church and to Christianity in the land?
   b.   What further limitation does the American Revision place on the role of the civil magistrate? Why?

3.   On the Duties of the Citizen with Respect to the Government:
   a.   Why does the Pope claim that he has the right to be obeyed by everyone in every nation? How do you know that this pernicious claim has no basis?
   b.   According to our Confession, what are the four duties required of citizen with respect to the civil magistrate?

WCF 24: OF MARRIAGE AND DIVORCE

1.   On the Monogamous Design of Marriage:
   a.   Show from Scripture that monogamy is God's design for marriage.
   b.   How would you explain the many instance of polygamy by godly men in the Old Testament such as Abraham, Jacob, David and Solomon?

2.   On the Purpose of Marriage:
   a.   What is the theological design of marriage and what are the other three purposes of marriage?
   b.   What would you say to a couple who decides to get married but do not wish to have children at all?

3.   On the Criteria for Marriage:
   a.   The *WCF* insists that Christians must "marry only in the Lord." Show that this is a Scriptural doctrine.
   b.   T / F —   When the *WCF* speaks of marrying in the Lord, it does not forbid a Reformed person from marrying another person in any Christian denomination.
   c.   T / F —   *WCF* 24.4 and the corresponding Scripture texts given forbids marriage between first cousins (i.e. between the children of two siblings).

4.   On the Dissolution of Marriage
   a.   What are the two lawful grounds for divorce given in our Confession? Give relevant Scripture texts to support your answer.
   b.   Explain why the Confession seems to be more lax than Paul in allowing divorce in the case of wilful desertion?
   c.   T / F —   According to the *WCF*, adultery breaks the marriage bond.
   d.   T / F —   According to the *WCF*, a wife whose husband committed adultery should sue for divorce.
   e.   T / F —   According to the *WCF*, after a legitimate divorce, the "innocent party" may remarry.
   f.   T / F—   The *WCF* condemns remarriage by the guilty party in the case of divorce on account of adultery.

g. T / F— The *WCF* does not countenance the remarriage of the guilty party because the marriage bond remains in force for him.

h. Consider the case of a Christian husband who manages to divorces his wife for reason of incompatibility despite the wife's plea and legal challenges to stall the divorce. Under what circumstance, if any, would the wife be allowed to remarry?

i. [Optional] Summarise the argument for and against allowing marriage after legitimate divorce.

WCF 25: OF THE CHURCH

1. Introduction

   Draw from memory (without looking at the notes) a diagram to depict the (a) Visible Universal Church; (b) the Invisible Universal Church; (c) true particular or local churches; and (d) false local churches. Remember to reflect the fact that not all in the visible church are in the invisible church, and also the fact that in extraordinary circumstances, some members of false churches could be in the universal church by the grace of God.

2. On the Church Invisible:
   a. T / F — The universal Church is the catholic Church.
   b. T / F — The catholic Church is a false Church.
   c. T / F — The invisible Church alone is universal.
   d. T / F— The invisible Church may be known as the Church triumphant.
   e. T / F— Membership in the invisible Church is entered into by regeneration and profession of faith.
   f. T / F— Membership in the invisible Church is entered into by birth.

3. On the Church Visible:
   a. T / F— The visible Church refers to the local Church.
   b. T / F— According to our Confession, a person becomes a member in the visible Church only after baptism.
   c. Fill in the blanks to indicate the relationship between membership in the church visible and church invisible.

	Membership Criterion	Ratification of Membership		
		Theol. terms	OT terms	NT terms
Church Invisible				
Church Visible				

   d. What is the role of infant baptism in a local Church?
   e. James and Robert are communicant members in Reformed Church. One day they had a serious quarrel, and it led James to suspect that Robert was not a genuine believer because of his behaviour. After some time, James approached Robert for reconciliation. But Robert was not only abusive but refused to reconcile with him even after mediation by a mutual friend. This appears to confirm James' suspicion that Robert was an unregenerate man. He decided to write a letter to Robert to inform him that he is bringing up their case to the Session. His letter to Robert begins with the word "My dear brother-in-Christ Robert,..." In his letter to the

Session, he also refers to Robert as his "beloved brother-in-Christ." Is there something wrong with the way James addresses Robert in his two letters? Explain.

   f.   T / F—   The *WCF* teaches that no one who is a member in the Roman Catholic Church or the Mormon Church may be saved.

4.   On the True Member-Churches of the Visible Catholic Church:
   a.   What are the four marks of true branch of the visible Church suggested in the *WCF* ?
   b.   T / F —   The *WCF* teaches that there will always be a perfectly pure church on earth for His saints to worship in.
   c.   What does the *WCF* call a particular church that has degenerated in error until it can no more be regarded as a Christian Church? Why do you think this designation is very apt?

5.   On the Pope and the Roman Catholic Church:
   a.   T / F —   According to the *WCF*, the head of a particular church is the pastor.
   b.   What does the word 'antichrist'   mean when it is used in Scripture?
   c.   T / F —   The Antichrist will only appear shortly before Christ's second coming.
   d.   T / F —   The *WCF* can be reconciled with the view that the Antichrist will be "a great Dictator, full of charisma and devilish cunning [who] will arise out of [the] European Union or rather the Nato nations."
   e.   Who is the Antichrist according to the *WCF*? Why?

WCF 26: OF THE COMMUNION OF SAINTS

1.   On the Union and Communion of the Body of Christ:
   a.   What are the two ways in which Christians are united to Christ? Briefly explain.
   b.   What does the Apostle Paul mean by say that his sufferings for the sake of the Colossians: "fill up that which is behind [i.e. lacking] of the afflictions of Christ in my flesh for His body's sake, which is the church"? Has Christ not suffered sufficiently? Explain.
   c.   The union and communion of saints is based on (select the correct answers):
      i.   The common assent to the truth of the Gospel.
      ii.   Union with the Church through the application of the Sacraments.
      iii. Union with Christ as the head of the Church by regeneration.
      iv.   Union with the Pope as the Vicar of Christ.
      v.   Admission into the visible Church by baptism.
      vi.   Participation in the Lord's Supper or Holy Communion.
      vii. Election in Christ and therefore membership in the invisible Church.
   d   T / F —   The Communion of Saints extends only to the boundary of a particular communion, i.e. local church or denomination.
   e.   List at least 7 obligations that a Christian has toward other members in the Church.
   f.   T / F—   These obligations should be extended only to those who are known as genuine born again Christians.
   g.   According to the Scriptures, what is the purpose of spiritual gifts in a Church? Cite appropriate verses to support your answer.

2.   On the Errors Pertaining to the Doctrine of Communion:
   a.   What is the error of the Eastern Orthodox Church pertaining to the doctrine of the mystical union between Christ and His Church?

b.   In the early church, "all that believed were together, and had all things common; And sold their possessions and goods, and parted them to all men, as every man had need" (Acts 2:44-45). How should we apply this example today?

WCF 27: OF THE SACRAMENTS

1.   On the Word 'Sacrament':
     a.   Explain briefly why the word "sacrament" is retained in our Confession and all the major Reformed Creeds though it is not a biblical term?
     b.   Why do you think we do not practice feet-washing in the Church today when the Lord said: "Ye call me Master and Lord: and ye say well; for so I am. If I then, your Lord and Master, have washed your feet; ye also ought to wash one another's feet. For I have given you an example, that ye should do as I have done to you" (Jn 13:13-15)?

2.   On the Nature of Sacraments:
     a.   Memorise and Quote WSC 92: "What is a sacrament?"
     b.   According to WCF 27.1, what are the three purposes of a sacrament?
     c.   How is Baptism a sign and seal of the Covenant of Grace?
     d.   How is the Lord's Supper a sign and seal of the Covenant of Grace?

3.   On the Efficacy of Sacraments:
     a.   A friend of yours who believes in baptismal regeneration cites 1 Pet 3:21— "...baptism doth also now save us..."; and Gal 3:27— "For as many of you as have been baptized into Christ have put on Christ" to show to you that regeneration is tied to baptism and so only a baptised person is saved. You know that it is highly improbable that Peter and Paul were referring to Holy Spirit-baptism. How would you respond to your friend?
     b.   T / F—   The Lord's Supper merely commemorates the Lord's death till He comes.
     c.   T / F —   The primary purpose of baptism is to show unbelievers that a person is now a Christian.
     d.   T / F —   Baptism and the Lord's Supper always confer grace.
     e.   T / F —   The efficacy of a sacrament is dependant largely on the faith of the recipient.
     f.   Someone from another church refused to partake the Lord's Supper, saying "I will not take bread and wine tainted by [morally] dirty hands." How would you advise this person?
     e.   T / F—   A person who refuses to be baptised cannot possibly be a Christian.

4.   On the Number and Administration of the Sacraments
     a.   What are the seven sacraments of Rome?
     b.   Reformed and Presbyterian Churches usually practise "confession", "confirmation" or "affirmation of faith" for persons who were baptised as infants. What is the difference between the Reformed understanding and practice, and that of Rome?
     c.   Why do Reformed Churches generally restrict the administration of sacraments to those who are lawfully ordained to the ministry of the Gospel?
     d.   In the table below, compare Circumcision & Baptism; and Passover & the Lord's Supper, citing scriptural support.

The Old Testament Form	The New Testament Form
Circumcision	Baptism
Passover	Lord's Supper

WCF 28: OF BAPTISM

1. On the Purpose of Baptism:
   a. Memorise and Quote WSC 94: What is baptism?
   b. Prove from Scripture that baptism is the New Testament equivalence of circumcision.
   c. How do you know that the apostle Peter is referring to the Covenant of Grace in Acts 2:38-39?
   d. T / F — A minister should only baptise a person if he is absolutely sure that he is regenerated.
   e. Since it is possible that an unregenerate person may be baptised and admitted into the membership of the Visible Church, explain how the visible church or local congregation can be denoted "the people of God" or "the body of Christ."
   f. T / F— The main purpose of baptism given in the Scriptures is the public confession of faith of the person being baptised.

2. On the Mode of Baptism:
   a. T / F — The WCF condemns baptism by immersion.
   b. T / F — The word baptizô always mean "immerse, plunge or dip."
   c. T / F — It is an indisputable fact that John the Baptist baptised by immersion and that Christ himself was baptised by immersion.
   d. Explain your answer to (c), above.
   e. T / F — The three thousand converts on the day of Pentecost were baptised in the river Jordan by immersion.

3. On the Subject of Baptism:
   a. T / F — According to our Confession, as long as a person professes faith, he should be baptised.
   b. Memorise and Quote WSC 95, "To whom is baptism to be administered?"
   c. Briefly explain the two grounds on which infant baptism is founded.
   d. T / F— Luke's accounts of baptism in the early church, particularly in Acts 16, gives the impression that whole household were baptised on account of the faith of the head of households.

4. On the Efficacy of Baptism:
   a. T / F — The WCF teaches that no one who is not baptised may be saved.
   b. T / F— The WCF teaches that it a great sin to neglect baptism or to view it with contempt.
   c. T / F — The WCF teaches that the grace promised in baptism is not only offered, but really exhibited and conferred by the Holy Ghost in baptism.

d. T / F— The *WCF* teaches that when the water is applied on the baptismal candidate, grace is imparted.
e. You have a friend who believes in baptismal regeneration. In his attempt to win you over to his position, he says "When we say that only if you are baptised, you will be saved, we are not saying anything different from what the evangelical church teaches, namely, that you will be saved only of you believe in the Gospel and confess Christ. Baptism is faith works. Confession is also faith works. Salvation is by grace through faith and baptism." How would you respond?

WCF 29: OF THE LORD'S SUPPER

1. On the Design of the Lord's Supper.
   a. Memorise and Quote *WSC* 96: What is the Lord's Supper?
   b. T / F— According to our Confession, the Lord's Supper is both a sign and seal of the Covenant of Grace, as well as a bond and pledge of the communion of believers with Him.

2. On the Conduct of the Lord's Supper:
   a. Name the three steps involved in the administration of the Lord's Supper.
   b. T / F — It is not necessary to break the bread in front of the congregation.
   c. T / F — It is not necessary to pour out the wine in front of the congregation.
   d. T / F — Our Confession teaches us that the wine should be drunk from one common cup.
   e. If a member of the church is suffering from a prolonged illness that prevents him from coming to church to participate in the Lord's Supper, can the minister conduct the Lord's Supper in the hospital for him? Why, why not?

3. On the Four Views Pertaining to the Lord's Supper:
   a. List the 4 common views pertaining to the Lord's Supper and give a one line description for each view. Which view is taught in the *WCF* ?
   b. Explain how it is possible (according to Calvin) for believers to "receive and feed upon Christ crucified" when Christ is now physically in heaven?

4. On the Fencing of the Table:
   a. Why do you think most Reformed Churches would not allow unbaptised persons to partake of the Lord's Supper?
   b. List 3 reasons why the Lord's Table should be fenced from ignorant and ungodly persons.
   c. [Optional] Should small children of believing parents be allowed to partake of the Lord's Supper?
   d. Memorise and Quote *WSC* "What is required in the worthy receiving of the Lord's Supper?"

WCF 30: OF CHURCH CENSURES

1. On the Divine Right of Church Government:
   a. Name the four forms of Church Government common practised today and give a one-sentence description of each form that will distinguish it from the rest.
   b. T / F— Any church that is governed by two or more elders has a Presbyterian polity.

c.   T / F—   The *WCF* does not favour any particular form of government.

d.   Explain the phrase "keys of the kingdom of heaven" (*WCF* 30.2; Mt 16:19).

e.   I have / I have not read the *Presbyterial Form of Church Government* in the annex to the *Westminster Confession of Faith*.

2.   On the Necessity of Church Discipline:

a.   Identify the purpose of church censure in the following list:

  i.   For effecting punitive justice upon offenders.

  ii.   For the reclaiming and gaining of offending brethren

  iii. For deterring of others from the like offences

  iv.   For purging out erroneous ideas that may infect the whole church

  v.   For purging out offending brethren who may otherwise influence other members in the church

  vi.   For vindicating the honour of Christ, and the holy profession of the Gospel

  vii. For vindicating the honour of the pastors and elders, and their holy calling.

  viii. For preventing the wrath of God which might justly fall upon the Church

b.   T / F —   The Westminster divines understood 1 Corinthians 11:29-32 as referring to visitation of God's wrath only upon the individuals who profane the Lord's Supper.

3.   On the Steps for Church Discipline:

a.   List the 3 steps of Church censure recommended in the *WCF* .

b.   T / F—   To deliver a person "unto Satan for the destruction of the flesh" (1 Cor 5:5) is to commit the erring brother's body and soul to Satan.

WCF 31: OF SYNODS AND COUNCILS

1.   On the Convening of Synodical Assemblies:

a.   Which of the following best describe a synodical assembly?

  i.   An august assembly of the highest ranking officers in a denomination

  ii.   The assembly of all the Session members in the churches represented.

  iii. An assembly of teaching and ruling elders representing a number of churches which has a common or similar polity and forming a higher court than the Presbyteries or Sessions.

  iv.   A conference attended by pastors and elders.

  v.   A court comprising of pastors of the churches represented in order to effect church censure.

b.   Explain briefly why the Westminster Assembly considered that it biblical to have synodical assemblies:

c.   Which of the following best describe the Westminster Assembly's attitude towards Presbyterianism which includes synodical assemblies?

  i.   It is biblically the ideal system.

  ii.   Churches which are organised any other way cannot legitimately exist.

  iii. It is one of the acceptable systems supportable by Scripture.

  iv.   It is the preferred though not compulsory system.

  v.   None of the above.

d.   T / F —   *WCF* 31.2 in its original formulation vests the power to call synodical assemblies entirely on the civil magistrate if he be not an enemy of the Church.

2.   On the Purpose of Synods and Councils:

a. T / F— The decisions reached by synods and councils are to be regarded by the churches that are under their jurisdiction to be purely advisory.
b. T / F— The decisions made by synods and councils are always binding upon the churches which are under their jurisdiction.
c. T / F— A synodical assembly may legislate on what constitute biblical elements of worship and its legislation is binding on the churches under its purview.
d. T / F— A synodical assembly may legislate on the order of worship, and its legislation is binding on the churches under its purview.

3. On the Limitations of Synods and Councils.
   a. T / F— The decisions of synods and councils are always right.
   b. T / F— The *WCF* recommends that the church or synodical assemblies should try to influence the way in which the civil magistrate govern the land so that Gospel may be better propagated.
   c. T / F— Synods and Councils must never interact with the civil magistrate on matters pertaining to the governance of the land.

WCF 32 OF THE STATE OF MEN AFTER DEATH, AND OF THE RESURRECTION OF THE DEAD

1. On the State of Men after Death:
   a. Memorise and quote *WSC* 37 "What benefits do believers receive from Christ at death?
   b. T / F— It is appointed unto all men, believers and unbelievers, once to die.
   c. T / F— Apart from Enoch and Elijah, the Scripture suggests that *all* men has or will face death.
   d. T / F— Death is a punishment for sin for both believers and unbelievers.
   e. Prove from Scripture that the moment a believer dies, he will be in the presence of the Lord in heaven.
   f. T / F— The doctrine of purgatory of the Roman Catholic Church can be proven from the inspired Scriptures though we may disagree with their interpretation.
   g. Name two theologians who believe in conditional immortality or annihilation. Show that a plain and rational reading of the Scripture show that the doctrine is heretical.

2. On the Resurrection of the Dead:
   a. T / F — "Last days" and "Last Day" is synonymous in the Scripture.
   b. T / F — In the study of last things, the "last day" may represent or include a long period of time.
   c. Memorise and quote *WSC* 38 'What benefits do believers receive from Christ at the resurrection?"
   d. T / F— Both the elect and the reprobate will be raised bodily.
   d. T / F — The *WCF* can be reconciled with the view that says that the resurrection of the just and the resurrection of the reprobate are two separate events.
   e. List two verses that will support view reflected in the Confession (as indicated in your answer above).
   f. T / F— The Westminster divines allowed for the view that after the resurrection of the just there will follow a long period of time before the final judgement.

g. T / F— 1 Thessalonians 4:16-17 teaches us that the saints will be secretly raptured, while sinners will be left on the earth to suffer a period of intense tribulation.

h. T / F— The *WCF* teaches us that believers will go through the great tribulation.

i. T / F— The *WCF* is insistent that we will be raised with the same body that we die with.

j. T / F— Resurrected bodies will have very different qualities from mortal bodies.

WCF 33: OF THE LAST JUDGMENT

1. On the General & Comprehensive Scope of Judgement:
   a. T / F— God the Father will be the Judge on the throne of Judgement.
   b. T / F— According to our Confession, there may be two judgement events, one known as Bema Seat judgement to reward believer, and the other known as Great White Throne to condemn the reprobate.
   c. Do you think there will be two judgements? Prove your answer from the Scriptures.
   d. T / F— The judgement will be for major things done in this life.

2. On the Purpose of the General Judgement:
   a. Distinguish between the purpose of judgement for the elect and the reprobate.
   b. T / F — Our Confession teaches that the wicked will be banished from the presence of the Lord into hell where they will forever feel a sense of emptiness because God will no longer be in their consciousness.

3. On our Response to Eschatology:
   a. T / F — Our Confession teaches us that we should be certainly persuaded of the sequence of events that will take place in the last day.
   b. Write (in your own words) how the study of eschatology and the certainty of the coming events should affect your life?

—The End—

Selected Bibliography

à Brakel, Wilhelmus. *The Christian's Reasonable Service*. 3 Volumes. Translated by Bartel Elshout. Ligonier: Soli Deo Gloria Publication, 1994.

Bannerman, James. *The Church of Christ: A Treatise on the Nature, Powers, Ordinances, Discipline, and Government of the Christian Church*. 2 volumes. New Jersey: Mack Publishing Company, 1960 (1869).

Beeke, Joel R. Assurance of Faith: Calvin, English Puritanism, and the Dutch Second Reformation. New York: Peter Lang Publishing Inc, 1991.

Berkhof, Louis. *Systematic Theology*. Edinburgh: The Banner of Truth Trust, 1988 (1941).

Boston, Thomas. *Commentary on the Shorter Catechism*. 2 volumes. Edmonton: Still Waters Revival Books, 1993 (1853).

Buchanan, James. *The Doctrine of Justification: An Outline of Its History in the Church and of Its Exposition from Scripture*. Grand Rapids: Baker Books, 1970.

Burroughs, Jeremiah. *Gospel Worship*. Pittsburg: Soli Deo Gloria Publications, 1993 (1648).

Bushell, Michael. *The Songs of Zion: A Contemporary Case for Exclusive Psalmody*. Pennsylvania: Crown & Covenant Publications, 1993 (1997).

Calvin, John. *A Reformation Debate: John Calvin and Jacopo Sadoleto*, ed, John C. Olin. Baker Book House, 1966.

Calvin, John. *Calvin: Institutes of the Christian Religion*. 2 volumes. Translated by Ford Lewis Battles. Edited by John T. McNeill. Philadelphia: The Westminster Press, n.d.

Calvin, John. *Calvin's Commentaries*. 22 volumes. Grand Rapids: Baker Book House, reprinted 1989.

Clark, Gordon H. *What Do Presbyterians Believe?* Phillipsburg: Presbyterian and Reformed Publishing Co., 1965.

Confession of Faith and Subordinate Standards of the Free Church of Scotland. Edinburgh: William Blackwood & Sons Ltd, reprinted 1973.

Crenshaw, Curtis I. and Grover E. Gunn, III. *Dispensationalism: Today, Yesterday and Tomorrow*. Memphis, Tennessee: Footstool Publications, 1985.

Dabney, Robert Lewis. *Systematic Theology*. Edinburgh: The Banner of Truth Trust, reprinted 1985.

Dolezal, James E. *God without Parts: Divine Simplicity and the Metaphysics of God's Absoluteness*. Oregon: Pickwick Publications, 2011.

Haldane, Robert. Romans. Edinburgh: Banner of Truth Trust, reprinted 1996 (1874).

Henry, Matthew. *Matthew Henry's Commentary on the Whole Bible: New Modern Edition* (Peabody: Hendrickson Publishers, 1991

Hodge, Archibald Alexander. *The Confession of Faith*. Edinburgh: The Banner of Truth Trust, reprinted 1992.

Hodge, Archibald Alexander. *Outlines of Theology*. Edinburgh: Banner of Truth Trust, reprinted 1991 (1860)

Hodge, Charles. *Systematic Theology*. 3 volumes. Grand Rapids: Wm B. Eerdmans Publishing Co., reprinted 1989.

Hoeksema, Herman. *Reformed Dogmatics*. Grand Rapids: Reformed Free Publishing Association.

Letham, Robert. The Westminster Assembly: Reading Its Theology in Historical Context. Phillipsburg: Presbyterian & Reformed Publishing, 2009.

Mathison, Keith A. *Given For You: Reclaiming Calvin's Doctrine of the Lord's Supper*. Phillipsburg: Presbyterian & Reformed Publishing, 2002.

Mathison, Keith A. *The Shape of Sola Scriptura*. Moscow, Idaho: Canon Press, 2001.

Mitchell, Alexander F. *The Westminster Assembly: Its History and Standards being the Baird Lecture for 1882*. Reprinted by Still Waters Revival Books, 1992.

Mitchell, Alexander F and Struthers, John, editors. Minutes of the Sessions of the Westminster Assembly of Divines. Edmonton: Still Waters Revival Books, 1991 (1874).

Owen, John. *The Works of John Owen*, edited by William H. Goold. Volume 3. Edingburgh: The Banner of Truth Trust, 1981 (1950-3).

Reymond, Robert. *A New Systematic Theology of the Christian Faith*. Nashville: Thomas Nelson Publishing, 1998.

Robertson, O Palmer. *The Christ of the Covenants*. Phillipsburg, New Jersey: Presbyterian and Reformed Publishing, 1980.

Schaff, Philip. *The Creeds of Christendom*. Volume 1 of 3. Grand Rapids: Baker Books, 1983 [1931].

Schenck, Lewis Bevens. *The Presbyterian doctrine of children in the covenant : an historical study of the significance of infant baptism in the Presbyterian Church*. Phillipsburg: Presbyterian & Reformed Publishing, 2002 (1940).

Schwertley, Brian. *Musical Instruments in the Public Worship of God*. Southfield: Reformed Witness, 1999.

Shaw, Robert. *An Exposition of the Westminster Confession of Faith*. Scotland: Christian Focus Publications, 1992.

Smith, Morton H. *Systematic Theology*. 2 volumes. Simpsonville, SC: Christian Classics Foundation, 1997.

Sproul, RC. *Truths We Confess: A Layman's Guide to the Westminster Confession of Faith*. 3 volumes. Phillipsburg, New Jersey: Presbyterian and Reformed Publishing, 2006.

Turretin, Francis. *Institutes of Elenctic Theology*. 3 volumes. Translated by George Musgrave Giger. Edited by James T. Dennison, Jr. Phillipsburg: Presbyterian and Reformed Publishing Co., 1994.

Ursinus, Zacharias. *Commentary on the Heidelberg Catechism*. Phillipsburg: Presbyterian and Reformed Publishing Co., n.d.

Warfield, Benjamin B. *The Westminster Assembly and Its Work*. Edmonton: Still Water Revival Books, 1991 (1959).

Watson, Thomas. *A Body of Divinity*. Edinburgh: The Banner of Truth Trust, 1992 (1692).

Watson, Thomas. *The Lord's Prayer*. Edinburgh: The Banner of Truth Trust, 1982 (1692).

Watson, Thomas. *The Ten Commandments*. Edinburgh: The Banner of Truth Trust, 1990 (1692).

Williamson, G.I. *The Heidelberg Catechism: A Study Guide*. Phillipsburg: Presbyterian and Reformed Publishing Co., 1993.

Williamson, G.I. *The Shorter Catechism for Study Classes*. 2 volumes. Phillipsburg: Presbyterian and Reformed Publishing Co., 1970.

Williamson, G.I. *The Westminster Confession of Faith for Study Classes*. Phillipsburg: Presbyterian and Reformed Publishing Co., 1964.

Woosley, Andrew A. Unity and Continuity in Covenantal Thought: A Study in the Reformed Tradition to the Westminster Assembly. Grand Rapid: Reformation Heritage Book, 2012.

antinomian- a person who believes that under the gospel dispensation of GRACE - the moral law is of no use or obligation because faith alone is necessary to salvation.

Made in the USA
San Bernardino, CA
16 August 2019